Thru-Hiking Will Break Your Heart
An Adventure on the Pacific Crest Trail

Carrot Quinn

Cover design by Alejandra Wilson: rocket-llama.tumblr.com

Some trailnames have been changed to protect the privacy of individuals.

Author's note: In 2013 I walked from Mexico to Canada on the Pacific Crest Trail. It was my first long-distance hike. This is the story of that journey.

For Marie-Claire and Ian

And for Dan

May your trails be crooked, winding, lonesome, dangerous, leading to the most amazing view.

-Edward Abbey

Space and time! Now I see it is true, what I guess'd at
What I guess'd while I loaf'd on the grass
What I guess'd while I lay alone in my bed
And again as I walk'd the beach under the paling stars of the morning

-Walt Whitman

I'm on a ridgetop in the Mojave desert, and I'm trapped in a windstorm. The highway, my portal out of this nightmare, is in just seventeen miles, and I'm trying to hike, but the wind will not let me. I take a step and BAM BAM BAM! The wind hits me like a two-by-four, knocking me to my knees. I plant my legs a certain way and the wind changes direction, knocking me to the ground again. On either side of the trail the ridges fall away, into nothing. The wind, if it wanted, could blow me right off this mountain. The wind smacks my pack straps against my face, pushes my nostrils flat. The wind throws sand and grit at me. It's difficult to breathe. What are these, sixty, seventy mile per hour winds? I have never experienced anything like this in my life. The wind is a furious monster, bent on destroying every living thing. The wind has gone insane.

The trail climbs higher and the wind grows stronger. I stumble forward, one foot at a time. I feel angry at the trail, at myself, at the universe, at everything. I'm dehydrated and hungry, but there's nowhere to stop and rest. The only thing to do is keep moving.

Time disappears, and it is just me and the mountain, and the wind. I have always been in this windstorm, I think, as I fight my way forward. And I will always be in this windstorm. Up ahead, on a ridge, is a single tree. Someday, I think, I am going to be reincarnated as that tree. As punishment for every choice I've ever made.

Or as a reward.

Eight months earlier

I think I'm addicted to the internet. I've noticed a pattern in my life- I get up, look at the internet, make breakfast, look at the internet, work, eat, look at the internet, maybe hang out with friends (*maybe*), look at the internet, go to sleep. I'm only really doing one or two non-internet things a day, working and eating, and the rest of my time, my finite time here on this great green earth, is spent looking at the internet. Even the "sleep" part of my day is kind of an exaggeration. My sleep is terrible. I lie down and I'm awake for a long time, listening to the sounds outside the window of my little trailer, the cats and drunken bicyclists making their way down this dead-end street. And *is* the earth green, anyway? I don't know. The earth outside my window is made of asphalt and noise and people walking around, not looking at each other. Who are these people? Why are they here? Why am *I* here? I wake up too early and get on the internet. There's a static in my brain.

***

We meet at the Cuban restaurant on Broadway. I ride my bike there in the rain and find her in the crowded foyer. She is tall and more beautiful than her photos online- almost impossibly beautiful, with eyes like literal gemstones and pinup model legs. Her name is Elle and she is driving from Austin, Texas, where she works as a dancer, to Washington, where she spends the summers fighting wildfires. She messaged me on okcupid- *I'm passing through Portland on my way north,* she said. *You're cute.*

We order beef tongue, plantains, coconut cake. I tell her about my life in Portland, feeling self-conscious and suddenly poor. After dinner she puts my bike in the bed of her massive pickup truck and drives me home in the rain, to the twenty-foot trailer in my friend's driveway where I am living.

"I come to Portland often," she says. "Maybe I'll see you again?"

***

The party is chaotic, everything too loud beneath the bright overhead lights. There are dogs underfoot, the counter is clustered with sticky mason jars. The table has half-eaten loaves of bread and broken bars of chocolate.

I'm drinking sparkly water with half a lime crushed into it and leaning against the wall, my sobriety almost painful. I am always sober. It's my lot in life. I don't know why, I can't explain it. At least not in any way that makes sense to other people. *Alcohol makes me feel sick.* Or, *I don't like to be intoxicated.* I can feel my clothing pressing into me- the collar of my shirt, the waistband of my pants. I feel as though I'm being smothered. The people standing next to me, who I know, who I've known for years, are passing a phone back and forth, watching a video or looking at a photo, smiling broadly, lipstick bright. I try to smile too, but I can't hear what they're saying.

Outside on the back porch Seamus is chain smoking and talking loudly about grad school, making declarative statements and flicking his ashes in the yard. Others are smoking too, the hoods of their sweatshirts up over their heads, jewelry glinting in the light from the kitchen window. I sit on the back step and look at the old-growth cedar that takes up most of the yard. There once was a giant forest here, the tree seems to be saying, and then they cut it all down. Now there's just a street full of buildings. And inside these buildings, what? Tea kettles, soup pots, drawers full of silverware. Tupperware, coffee mugs, metal ladles. Rubber spatulas and mixing bowls and pasta strainers. I close my eyes and try to catalog all of it.

***

In the morning, I wake to the sound of rain on the aluminum siding of the trailer and pull back the curtains to let in the gloaming. Outside all is gray save for the wet green of the grass and the rhododendrons. Hunger stirs me, and I fire up the avocado-green propane stove in my little kitchenette, cracking two eggs into a cast-iron skillet popping with bacon grease. I eat the eggs with leftover brown rice while looking at my phone. Something makes me laugh, but then the food is gone and I set the phone down and there is no feeling, just a disorienting emptiness. I can't remember what I was thinking about earlier. It's eleven o'clock and I put on my beaten sneakers and rain jacket and step down out of the rocking trailer, shutting the door carefully behind me. The rain is falling hard and I look up at the tarps that cover the roof of the trailer. No leaks, I think. No leaks.

Murphy is a big mutt with a thick pile of fur and he wags his whole body when he sees me, smacking up against my legs. We walk west through the quiet neighborhood streets, past the small school and the house with the classical music that's always playing, then north and east again, making a big loop. He pulls on the leash, stops periodically to take massive dumps, but I don't mind. Back at his house I pocket the pile of dollars on the kitchen counter and then walk around, looking at the things on the walls. Murphy's parents just moved here from San Francisco, a middle school teacher and a designer for Nike. Their house is a remodeled craftsman, huge steel fixtures in the kitchen and uncomfortably chic furniture in the living room. On the walls are framed artworks that I don't understand: crude drawings of peoples' faces and cartoon bears, masks and colorful garlands. A low table has a record player and some ceramic figurines. Back in the kitchen I open the cabinets, letting out the smells of the different foods there- tea, stale pepper, confectioner's sugar. I find a tub of salted caramel gelato in the freezer and eat a few bites, being careful to smooth the gelato with my spoon afterward so the intrusion is not obvious. Then I just stand, looking at the postcards on the fridge, feeling the sugar enter my bloodstream. The house is quiet save for the ticking of a cuckoo clock.

***

When I get home I spend a few hours typing customer service emails and working on the listings in my online bookstore, which is the other half, besides the dog-walking, of what I call my "Portland hustle"- the way I make my living in this strange city where hipsters with masters degrees fight each other for barista jobs. Then I close ebay and start googling, a flush of excitement working its way through my body.

I've found something new on the internet. I've found the trail journals of people who thru-hike the Pacific Crest Trail. This is my new obsession, and I lose whole hours this way- reading about these soft regular people who start out at the Mexican border and walk, somehow, all the way to Canada, via this footpath in the wilderness. The sun in the desert is hot; there are blisters. Many of the hikers quit. I scroll, and scroll, and scroll, wasting the entire afternoon. I look at their photographs, their daily mileages. I read about their injuries and their despair. Twenty miles a day seems impossible, especially with a pack, and yet here it is, happening. I skim the accounts closely, trying to read between the lines, looking for the things the hikers won't say. Is it hard? How hard is it? Could I do it?

Afterward I feel happy in a way I can't define.

***

I'm in Seamus' room, sitting on his bed. He has a wide, expensive bed, some sort of memory foam, lots of nice blankets from Ikea. The room is big, with tall drafty ceilings and thick carpet. There's a long window that looks out at the backyard, the gray sky, and the wind lashing the old-growth cedar there. Seamus is at his desk against the window, looking at shoes online.

"I think I'm going to hike the Pacific Crest Trail," I say. "The whole thing. From Mexico to Canada."

"That's crazy," says Seamus. "Why don't you stay here, and get a job?"

"I do have a job," I say. "I'm a dog walker."

The walls of the room are painted a pale green and hung all over with golden trinkets, drawings done by friends, pictures of Seamus' Russian ancestors. Seamus' parents emigrated from Russia when he was just a baby. In Russia his mother had been a famous chemist.

"How's grad school going?" I say.

"It's crazy," says Seamus. "I'm so busy. What do you think of these shoes?" He turns his computer and shows me a pair of expensive-looking loafers.

"They're nice," I say.

"Liam and I are looking at houses."

"Are you two going to get married?"

"Yeah," says Seamus. "Probably."

***

Elle comes to visit and we go to an art show with a few other friends- a bunch of sculptures in a big empty space, a video about drumming in the desert. Afterward we sit at a little table in a bar nearby and I tear a coaster to shreds while my friends drink cheap whiskey. Elle has a fox tail hanging

10

from her leather bag and I keep looking at it, thinking about what an anachronism it is. There's a soccer game on the big TV behind us. The sound is off and the commercials are terrifying.

I kiss Elle up against the narrow door to the bathroom in my trailer, the only bare spot of wall available. I actually use the bathroom as a closet, and the inside is filled with boxes. Everything I own can fit in there. Elle's lips are soft and her mouth tastes like cinnamon gum, and I can feel the soft down on her upper lip. She's tall, and I have to stand on my tiptoes to reach her. We move to my little twin bed in its alcove and she pulls her shirt over her head, her breasts falling free in the pale light from the windows. She strips off her impossibly tight jeans and unfurls her legs. I run my palms over her body, feeling the electricity in her skin, watching the goosebumps rise. I kiss her, taste the salt of her clavicle, then lie my head on her chest and close my eyes.

"I'm sorry," I say. "I don't know."

"It's ok," says Elle. She's moving her fingers through my hair, making my scalp tingle with her nails. I feel as though I might cry.

***

That night after Elle goes home I try to sleep and can't so finally I get up and open my computer. I sit in the yellow light of my lamps and pull up browser windows indiscriminately, not sure where I'm going. I end up scrolling through backpacking forums and googling hiking gear again, comparing prices and stats, even though I have compared them all before. In a world in which so much is unquantifiable, this, right now, makes sense to me. I think of Elle's breasts as I look at photos of different kinds of alcohol stoves, imagine the curve of her ass as I trawl eBay for a used version of the shelter that I feel I should buy. Sex and hiking gear, hiking gear and sex. It's five in the morning when I finally crawl into my narrow bed and sleep, images and numbers and sensations swirling around in my skull, so full and empty all at once. I am alone and yet, there is a seed of possibility and I cling to this, holding it to my heart as I drift off. Outside the city is just beginning to wake, the darkness paling, the noise of traffic coalescing.

***

The next day I am walking Murphy and I try to imagine it; I try to imagine walking 20 miles. I've never walked twenty miles before. I once walked seventeen miles, on a day hike. That felt far- farther than I had ever conceived of walking before. Today Murphy and I walk three miles, maybe a little less. However far we can go in forty-five minutes. We walk quickly and then I walk the twenty minutes home. Afterward I am tired and I sit on my little bed and eat painfully dark chocolate. It's overcast today, but no rain; just a washed-out color, a lifelessness. I lie down and think about the five backpacking trips that I've been on in my life, each four days long. On those trips I carried an overloaded pack, walked about ten miles a day, and felt completely destroyed. My feet turned to hamburger on each trip and my packstraps bruised my shoulders. I close my eyes and listen to the sounds from the street outside my trailer. Wind chimes, traffic, children playing. Am I really going to do this? Walk across the continent?

Sure, I think. Why not.

***

I order my gear on the internet. A pack made of very lightweight fabric, a sleeping bag with no bottom. It's called a "quilt." A foam sleeping pad the thickness of a yoga mat. I pile everything on the dinette table when it comes and weigh each piece of gear on the little kitchen scale I borrow from my housemate. I am not a strong person; I don't have much in the way of muscles. I am no good at load hauling. I recently discovered "ultralight backpacking" in my online journeying, and I know that this is the only way I'll make it to Canada. I know I can do this, I think. But only if my pack is really, really light. Once I have all the little bits of gear piled up and weighed I masochistically begin to remove things. No sleeping socks. No camp shoes. No book. It feels good to do this; it's satisfying in a way. What I lack in brawn, I decide, I'll make up for in resilience and a willingness to go without. I don't need no stinkin' pillow. I'll lay my head on the goddam ground. When I'm finished subtracting I stuff the remaining gear into my pack and weigh the whole thing; nine and a half pounds. I feel a sort of pride swell up in my chest. I've crossed some sort of threshold.

I have no excuses now.

***

I sell everything I have of value, quit my city life and then it's really happening; I sleep one single excitable hour, lock up my trailer in the pre-dawn, and fly to Los Angeles where I meet my friend Finn, who drives me south, past San Diego, to a little campground near Campo, California. The day is April 20th. Campo sits up against the wall that defines the Mexican border and it is here that you'll find the tall wooden monument, the southern terminus of the Pacific Crest Trail. The afternoon is hot, and we set up our tents in the scratchy grass of the campground, beneath a great oak tree. I'm wearing yellow running shorts, a big ugly sun-hat, and a long-sleeve desert shirt the color of sand. I'm very pale and I feel conscious of this. We make dinner and as I watch the sun drop orange and liquid in the sky I feel suddenly lonely, more lonely than I can bear. As soon as the sun is gone the park grows cold and I dig through my pack, whose contents are still chaotic and unfamiliar, until I find my down jacket. It's an ultralight jacket, seven ounces. A mere wisp of a thing. I pull it on against the cold. It's the only warm layer I have. Will I be warm enough on the trail? I cross my bare legs. Late April in the desert.

"I guess it's time for bed," I say to Finn.

"Yeah," he says.

Part One: The Desert

April 21 to June 5

Mile 0 to mile 698

In any given moment we have two options: to step forward into growth or to step back, into safety.

-Abraham Maslow

April 21st, 2013

The first twenty miles of the Pacific Crest Trail are some of its most brutal. Start early or you won't make it.

I don't start early.

Finn and I have a nice breakfast at the campground, cooking eggs over my little alcohol stove. I'm not in much of a rush to get started. I barely slept the night before; mostly I lay awake, staring at the stars, impossibly bright, through the mesh of the tent. Excitement, wonder, anticipation, fatigue. Anxiety. After breakfast we pack up and I stuff everything awkwardly into my pack, cinching down the straps and hefting it onto my back. I have seven liters of water in there for today's twenty-mile waterless stretch in the desert sun, plus seven days' worth of food. It's a hundred miles to my next resupply, further than I've ever hiked before, and I don't know yet how far I'll be able to walk each day. My pack feels crazy heavy, like a wild animal has jumped down onto my back.

Finn walks me to the border monument and I fumble with my gaiters, my sunglasses, everything that is strange and new. We flip through the trail register, look at the big graffitied wall. The heat is already suffocating.

"Goodbye!" I say, at last, to Finn. Friend! I think. Don't go!

The trail is a dusty ribbon that runs through the hot chaparral hills. I am exhausted from my mad rush of packing, my one-hour sleep on the night before my flight. I already need a day off to rest but instead I am setting out late in the brutal desert to hike the longest stretch I have ever hiked in a single day, and with a super heavy pack.

Will I make it to Lake Morena, the campground at the end of these twenty miles? I wonder. And what will happen if I don't?

In an hour I pass into a shady little grove of oak trees and see a bearded man in a sunhat.

"What are you doing?" I ask him.

"I'm teaching my donkeys to cross the bridge," he says.

There is a little footbridge over a still, tea-colored stream and two giant donkeys stand in the sun on the other side.

"Those donkeys are big," I say. "Good luck!"

"Good luck to you!" Says the man, to me.

I plod along the sandy path, my pack like a giant hand crushing me into the earth. What is even in this thing? Fear, probably. Fear that this or that will happen. My fear is crushing me into the earth.

Around noon, I stop to rest and set my pack down in a nice leafy patch of... poison oak. I look down at the plant, so green and innocuous seeming, where it brushes against my bare legs. I step away in alarm. Well. We'll see what happens with that. I lift my heavy pack back onto my back. Well.

By two p.m. I've gone just eight miles and I am so hot and dizzy that I can barely walk. There is a chunk of shade alongside a giant stone and I spread out my sleeping pad there and sit. I discovered this morning that I should never, ever sit on the bare ground here, as it is a fine mix of clinging sand, thorny plants, and ticks. What do I know about the desert? Nothing! I stare out at the burning hills, and then look down at my legs. The skin below my running shorts is brown with dust that has clung to my thick coating of sunscreen. I pull a log of salami from my pack, unwrap it, and immediately drop it in the dirt. I pick up the meat and scrape the sand off with my knife. I realize that it feels good to be sitting in the dirt, holding something salty in my grubby hands. After eating I lie down on my mat. I decide to nap until it cools down a little.

I pass in and out of sweaty consciousness for an hour and when I wake the shadows have lengthened. The sun is less brutal now and I feel new life running through me, from some reservoir somewhere I didn't know I had. I suck at the warm water in my gatorade bottle and hike on. I pass Hauser Creek, a dry, sandy bed tangled with poison oak. I look up at the bluff next to Hauser Creek and consider the long climb to Lake Morena. The sun is sinking in the cleft between the hills. Should I hike in the dark? Of course, there is only one answer.

I eat a little dinner of pepitas and dried plums partway up the bluff and watch the long red sun set over the chaparral hills. In the east the moon is rising, a big silver dinner plate, bright like a streetlamp. I'll see how long I can hike without my headlamp, I think. That way I won't get so spooked by the dark.

The moonlight shines on the white rock of the bluff as I walk. The light is so bright that I can see everything, all the way to the hills that ripple on the horizon. I can see every rock in the path. Magic, I think. The desert is magic. It's cool now, and I walk quickly, as if powered by the moon.

"If you don't want to hear or see signs of undocumented immigrants in this area," say my maps, "don't hike at night." I practice my Spanish as I walk, and think of what I would do if I ran into anyone. I would give them the last of my water. *Buena suerte*, I would say.

I roll my ankle once, hard, when I am looking out at the hills and not at the trail. A flash of tingling shoots through my foot, and then it is gone. Well, I think, we'll see what happens with that.

I reach the Lake Morena campground at 9:30 p.m. It is like a large city park, and it's eerily deserted. I stumble in the cold past vast empty lots where RVs would go. I can't find the office. There's a meadow where some tiny space-ship tents are pitched. A man is doing calisthenics on a sleeping pad.

"Is this the walk-in camping?" I ask him.

"Walk-in camping?" He says. "What's that? This is the hiker camping, and you look like a hiker, so pick a spot anywhere." I step over the people cowboy camping, like big slumbering larvae, and set my things beneath a tree. I find the bathrooms and tear off my sweaty clothes. There is a shower, a single sputtering fixture in a freezing concrete stall. I stand beneath it, dripping and wringing out my socks. I wipe the caked dirt and sunscreen off my body. My first day on the PCT, my first twenty-mile hike. I have made it to Lake Morena.

***

The screeching desert creatures wake me at dawn. I pick at the sandy crust that has gathered in the corners of my eyes. I'm so stiff I can barely move. And I didn't sleep well. Last night I pitched my frail little tarp shelter, thin as a butterfly's wing and very difficult to set up, bedded down on my rock hard sleeping pad and pulled my deliriously lofty sleeping quilt up over my face to block the moon. Just as I was drifting off, all of the sleeping larvae spread on the grass around me began to snore. I sat up, pulled my earplugs from the depths of my pack and bedded down again, but then I had to pee. I shivered in the cold to the edge of the meadow and peed on the dusty path. It was so cold by the lake! Why was the desert so hot in the day, yet so cold at night? Venus! It was like being on Venus!

Now it's six o'clock and I am peering awkwardly through the mesh of my shelter. Most of the larvae are already gone, having hiked out in the freezing pre-dawn. I extricate myself from my tent, feeling painfully shy, and arrange myself in an upright position on my wooden legs. A dozen hikers remain in the meadow, and they're clustered in tight groups talking loudly about nothing or off by themselves, being solitary. The shade of the campground is beginning to lose its battle with the sun, which is strong enough to vaporize anything in its path. Hikers dash forward to place socks and other damp things in these long yellow trapezoids of fire. I hobble to the bathrooms and smile at another hiker there, brushing her teeth at the sink, although I imagine my smile is more like a grimace and she just looks back at me, confused.

For breakfast I assemble a little pot of food, sitting at the picnic table in the shade. It's a freeze-dried dinner I bought online, curry I think, and it tastes like nothing. I make myself eat all of it and then I clumsily pack away my things. It's eight thirty, and already overwhelmingly hot. I look at my maps. I can barely walk and so I'll only go thirteen miles today. Easy. I wince as I shuffle up the path that runs through the campground. There is a massive blister on the ball of my right foot from yesterday, and each time I take a step it pains me. I bought my trail runners a size and a half too big, on advice from the internet; I usually wear a women's size ten, and I ordered a men's ten. These floppy clown shoes will give my feet lots of room to swell in the heat. But for now, blisters.

An hour into the morning, while walking through the chaparral, the blister pops. "Fuck!" I say, as I stumble in pain. "Fuck!" I say again, a few hours later, when I realized that the popped blister is now full of sand. I've stopped at a little stream to refill my water and I take off my shoes and look in horror at the bottoms of my feet. The skin there is pockmarked with dozens of tiny holes. In each of these holes, way deep down, is one single grain of sand. I grimace as I peel open the soft skin of my blister in order to rinse the sand from it. Arrrrrrrgh! I think, as I wiggle my foot around in the stream, letting the icy water inside.

I follow the sandy path along the exposed face of a mountain of sorts until midday, when I am almost falling over from the heat. There is a little rectangle of shade next to the trail and I spread my sleeping mat there, over some rodent holes. Or are they snake holes? I wake an hour later, and it takes me a minute to remember where I am.

The shadows are growing long again. Late afternoon in the desert. I am tired and so the miles, somehow, grow longer, and it takes me an inexplicable amount of time to reach the dirt road that leads to the campground beneath the oak trees. The campground is nearly empty this early in the season, and there is a little stream there. I sit on a rock next to the stream and soak my feet, cleaning the sand from my blister again. Across the stream there is a picnic table in the woods, hidden from the noisy car campers, and I spread my things across this table and set up my little kitchen, happily filling my pot with water at the spigot. I boil rice noodles and add dried peas and dried spinach. Hallelujah! I eat the pot of food way too fast and burn my tongue.

Beyond the campground is a grassy meadow, and I pitch my shelter there. When dusk falls at eight I am in bed, the quilt pulled up around my face, watching the shadows of the big oak tree move across the tarp. I am so tired I can barely think. When I pulled off my filthy yellow running shorts before bed I found a tick on my thigh, attempting to burrow its little face into my skin. I plucked it off with the tweezers from my tiny Swiss army knife, feeling a sort of distant horror. Then a huge black spider covered all over with shiny black nodules got lost under the mesh floor of my shelter, right where I could see it, and I felt that horror again. What a brutal learning curve this is. The desert, the insects, everything. Was there something I was supposed to do to psychologically prepare for all of this? I fussily arrange my quilt around me to keep out the drafts. Was there some sort of book I was supposed to read? I thought I had read them all and yet, everything just feels so… strange.

***

I wake at dawn in the empty oak meadow and sit in my sleeping bag, eating dried banana. The air is cold and I am wearing my down jacket with the hood up, and my gloves. Nights in the desert are *cold.*

In the campground I find a bar of soap sitting on top of one of the spigots. Soap! I think, picking it up. It smells harsh, like the soap that my grandparents use. Green stuff from Costco. I gleefully push the hunk of soap inside my last ziploc bag, a tiny one that once held the velcro strip for my gaiters. All my plastic bags are disintegrating. And the plastic grocery sack that houses my food is torn all over, and will surely burst at any moment. I also set the mesh stuff-sack for my kitchen on fire when I used it as a potholder. And I am almost out of sunscreen, having only brought a tiny one-ounce bottle. And I don't have any tape or anything for my blisters. But now, at least, I have soap!

And no poison oak yet, I think, as I brush my teeth at the spigot.

At 7:30 a.m. I am walking up the dirt road towards the trail, feeling proud of myself. While I was asleep, the frayed bits of my blister hardened into callus and today the blister doesn't hurt too badly. There is a little bit of pain in my left Achilles tendon, I'm not sure from what. Oh well, I think. The pain will probably go away as my body warms up.

It doesn't. When I reach Mt. Laguna ten miles later I am barely able to walk. But I figure I'm just kind of sore. I imagine I'll feel better tomorrow.

It's noon. There is an outfitter in Mt. Laguna, and I push my way into the dim wooden building. The one single room is crowded with racks, and the racks are piled with gear. I touch a rack of jackets and all of the jackets fall onto the ground.

"Hello," says a man behind the counter. He is wearing a straw hat.

"Hello," I say. "What do you have in the way of stuff sacks?"

The man rises and walks to a corner by the door where he stoops, removes a couple of layers of gear, and produces a fistful of lightweight stuff sacks. I find a beautiful yellow one, thin as a butterfly's wing, big enough to hold all my food. It costs sixteen dollars.

The door jangles and a couple of women walk in. They're wearing socks and limping.

"Our shoes wore our feet completely off," one of them says. "Can you help us?"

"Have you tried insoles?" asks the man, pulling a pair from the wall.

I look at the camp kitchen section. Titanium teapots, miniscule cheese graters. Folding utensils of every kind. I feel like Laura Ingalls Wilder, in town to buy a sack of flour. Where is the wooden barrel of salt pork?

22

"Do you have any duct tape?" I ask the man. He produces a big roll.

"You just want a couple feet?" he says. "Fifty cents." I hand him my tiny bottle of sunscreen and he wraps the duct tape around it. On the counter is an open box of ziploc bags. Good sturdy freezer ones, twenty cents each. I pull out a handful.

After paying for my goods, I shoulder my pack and limp up the road to the general store. A handful of people are sprawled on the wooden deck of the general store, shoes off, feet warming in the sun. I buy an icecream bar.

"Hello," I say, eating my icecream bar. "Can I sit with you?"

"Yes," they say.

A woman with wild eyes and long blonde hair and another woman in a torn silk shirt are complaining about the arduous nature of trail. Their bodies ache, they're tired of junk food already. I sit and listen. It's nice to hear these strangers complain. So far I've been complaining alone, in my head. A young man empties his food bag onto the deck and sorts his snickers bars. He's got a red mustache and wears a little running hat. His name is Rocky, and the women are T-Rex and HairTie.

"My feet hurt so bad," says T-Rex. She's crouched in a bit of shade, wrapping tape around her toes. In a shopping basket next to her are payday bars and gummi worms.

"This icecream bar is really disappointing," I say. "Do you guys want any of it?"

HairTie, the woman in the torn silk shirt, takes a bite and hands it back. "I already had hot doritos," she says. HairTie is sitting up against the wall of the general store, her long sunburnt legs stretched out in front of her. She pulls at the tatters of her shirt.

"I got this shirt for free," she says. "I had a cotton one, but I figured it might give me hypothermia."

Rocky shows me the special way he laces his shoes. He's wearing psychedelic gaiters.

"I run cross country," he says.

The icecream makes me feel speedy and disoriented. I unpack all of my

23

things and spread them on the deck. I pull out my torn grocery sack of food and carefully place everything into my new, bright yellow stuff sack.

HairTie, Rocky and T-Rex have been at the general store since morning. They're about to hike five miles to a Shriners lodge where they've heard that a hiker can maybe take a shower.

"I'll meet you guys there," I say. "We can camp together."

I bought a roll of athletic tape at the outfitter and now I sit on the deck to tape my blisters, happy because I have made some friends. There is sand in the big blister again, and I carefully tip my water bottle to try and get the sand out.

"What are you doing?" asks a woman who has just gotten out of her car.

"There's sand in my blister," I say. "I have to wash it out." The woman makes a face.

Once my feet are taped I slip them happily into my shoes. I fill my water bottles in the general store and then hoist my pack and stand. I take a step, and a bright strong pain shoots through my Achilles tendon. Oh no. I take another step, a small mincing one. Big pain, like stepping on a giant bruise. Oh no.

Well, I think, as I limp across the road, I guess I'll hitchhike to the Shriners lodge. Then I'll rest there for the night, with my new friends, and maybe tomorrow as well, and that will make me better. Right? I have no idea what to expect at the Shriners lodge. I don't even know what a Shriners lodge *is*. Now I stand on the roadside with my thumb out, imagining a carpeted room with lots of electrical outlets, a bare white bathroom with dusty fixtures. I'll plug my phone into the outlet. *Feeeeeed,* I'll whisper into it. *Feeeeed off the griiiiiiiiid.* Its little lights will blink on. *Contact!* I'll hiss.

There is no traffic on the road. I stare at the dappled light that sifts through the cool pine forest. I lean my pack against my legs and eat a little bag of fritos. My foot is tingling in a bad way. I've never had a sports injury before. I've never even played *sports*. I've never done anything like this in my whole life. Is the pain I'm feeling a big deal, or not a big deal? Is my hike doomed now? And what am I supposed to do now? What was it, R.I.C.E? Rest, ice, what else?

A few cars pass but they don't stop. It's getting towards dusk. Nobody picks up hitchhikers after dusk, I know this. There's a campground in the woods across from the general store, a sprawling empty place still closed for the season, all the water and everything shut off. Well, I think. Well.

I commandeer a picnic table in the sprawling deserted campground and cook dinner there, feeling like the lone survivor in some sort of collapse. Beyond me are the darkening woods, and the moon rising in the east. *Woo woo woo,* goes the wind in the trees. I shudder, tingles running up and down my spine. I think of murderers, monsters, meth addicts. If I was off on some remote part of the trail camped where no one could see me, I would be safe. But here, all alone, in this campground out in the open? *But that kind of stuff doesn't happen on the PCT*, I tell myself. I think of the little outfitter, the kindness of the men in the general store. The runners I saw in the woods, loping happily like deer. *It's safe here*, I tell myself. *Safe*.

The campground is creepily, eerily, unnaturally quiet. I lie stiff in my sleeping bag, jaw tight, jumping at the rustling that the fabric makes when I shift, the sound of my sleeping bag moving against my chest with my breath. Any moment I expect to see a monster, silhouetted in the moonlight against the sheer fabric of my tarp. *You're safe*, I kept telling myself. *Safe safe safe safe safe.*

***

In the morning, when I wake, I feel fantastic. Awesome, I think. Time to walk! But when I stand up, the pain in my tendon is so bright-hot I almost fall over. Well fuck, I think, as I sit back in my sleeping quilt. Instead of getting up, I eat handfuls of jerky and dried figs and watch the sun stretch across the pine needles. There were no monsters in the night, although someone with a headlamp did wander through the camp, way over by the bathrooms, a few hours after I went to bed. Something about their gait told me that it was another hiker, carrying a heavy pack, and I wasn't afraid. And after a few minutes the light was gone.

Today I'll hitch to the Shriners, I think. I'll get a ride this morning for sure. I imagine my new friends, T-Rex, Rocky, and HairTie, on the trail, inching further and further north. T-Rex's hair growing progressively more wild and ratted, the tatters of HairTie's silk shirt blowing in the wind. Rocky clutching his small running cap to his head. I'd better hurry, or I might never catch up with them again!

I stand at the road with my thumb out and several cars pass me, slowing just enough to stare at me as though I am a lunatic, and then there are no more cars. My sand-colored desert shirt is filthy and wrinkled, my bright yellow running shorts now edged in brown and spotted with stains. At least I rinsed the dirt-caked sunscreen from my legs, so they are relatively clean.

A glimmer appears in the distance. A van! The van slows and then stops. The man in the passenger seat leans out the open window. He looks kindly, and he's wearing a PCT baseball cap.

"I'm just going a few miles up the road to the Shriners lodge," I say.

"That's fine," says the man. The woman driving waves at me.

The couple introduces themselves as Linda and Bob. They're silver-haired and sparkly-eyed and their cheeks are flushed from the sun. This is my first encounter with what are known as "Trail Angels-" people who help out hikers on the trail, just because. Bob and Linda have just finished dropping a load of hikers off at the Mexican border, and now they're headed on a little day hike before driving home to San Diego. I sink into the comfortable backseat, relieved. After a few minutes we pull into the Shriners, which looks like a weird summer camp. The little brown buildings are all shuttered.

"What is this place?" says Bob. "Looks closed."

"I think you can shower here?" I say. "I've got tendinitis. I was planning on resting here."

"I know all about tendinitis," says Bob, looking over the seat at me. "Had it a few times myself. You'll want to ice it."

"Thanks," I say, reaching for the door handle. But Linda interrupts me.

"Why don't you come with us back to San Diego," she says. "We've got a little RV you can stay in. And on Friday we can bring you back to the trail. That way your tendinitis will have a chance to heal."

"Really?" I say, looking out the window at the sad little brown buildings. "Yes, I would love that. Thank you so much."

Bob and Linda have a small house way up on a hill. The hill overlooks what was once a wetland. There are palm trees in the front yard of the house and the grass is draped in bright clean sun.

In the backyard is a small RV, clean and new. Inside, Linda turns the faucet on and water sluices out. She switches on and off the lights. There is a dinette, a couch, and a cozy bed with real sheets. A big window looks out at the water. I drop my pack gratefully onto the floor.

"The freezer works," says Linda. "So you can put your ice in there."

"This is amazing," I say, overcome with gratitude.

After exploding my gear everywhere and sorting the trash from the edible bits in my food bag I go into the house for dinner and Bob and Linda's towheaded grandchildren are there, crawling all over the furniture. One of them has built a bald eagle out of legos. Another one wraps a snake around his neck.

"That is the coolest scarf ever," I say. I pick up the bald eagle made of legos. "You know bald eagles make really weird noises?"

"It's true," says Bob. "In movies they use the cry of the red tailed hawk for bald eagles, because actually bald eagles make really weird noises."

"Weird noises!" I say, holding the eagle aloft. "Oo oo oo oo oo!"

"Weird noises!" says the towheaded boy. "Oo oo oo oo! Ssssssch chsssss! Oo oo oo oo!"

"I'm faster than the speed of light!" Says the boy's sister, who is four, as she runs across the room.

"No you're not," says the boy, who is seven. "Nothing is faster than the speed of light."

"How do you know that?" asks Linda.

"Because it's true," says the boy.

"Is sound faster than the speed of light?"

"No," says the boy. He's staring at his bald eagle made of legos. "Because when a plane passes over you see it first, and then you hear it. So the speed of light is faster."

"Do you want to play basketball?" Says the boy to me.

"I would, but I have a hurt foot." I say.

After dinner is icecream, and then I retire to the RV. I've been icing my ankle all day and already the pain is much less. Two whole days of this. That's enough time for the tendon to heal completely, right? I am filled with hope, but also with apprehension. I want to hike so badly it's like an ache inside of me. But I also know that, judging from what has happened in the last few days, I greatly underestimated the rigors of the trail. All of this is so new- the desert, the solitude, the extreme physical exertion. The actual experience of this hike is beginning to take shape in my mind, and the vision fills me with both awe and horror.

***

I wake early and lie in bed, googling pictures of snakes on my phone. I've only encountered one snake so far on the trail, a smallish one that had been stretched sleepily across the path.

"Well hello there, baby snake," I said, as I stepped casually around it.

Now I frown as I scroll through *Common Snakes of Southern California.*

That snake had been a rattlesnake.

I'm a fool, I think. A fool, fool, fool.

Why does everything in the desert want to kill me?

Or

Everything in the desert could kill me and yet chooses not to.

"I'll tell you what," says Bob, over breakfast. "I had your exact same injury once. And you know what they told me? They said you hike on it, the endorphins kick in once you get going and the pain goes away. It's not going to get more injured, they told me. You just hike on it."

My ankle is feeling a lot better today- there isn't much pain, although I do feel a sort of grinding when I walk. Vitamin I, I think, as I fish an ibuprofen from my little plastic baggie.

I weigh what's left in my food bag- eight pounds! And that's after hiking for three days!

"That's a lot of weight," says Bob.

"Yeah," I say. "I've probably been carrying too much food."

I remember my brutal first day, my heavy pack, my rolled ankle. Why hadn't I thought to weigh my food? I open the stuff sack and peer inside, at the dusty dried fruit and dirty, melted, half-eaten bags of trail mix. What is this stuff, even? Bits of matter that once were alive. Bits of matter that wanted only to try hard and die an honorable death. Now the once-plants and animals are all sorts of salty shapes and colors, folded up into dusty ziploc bags in my stuff sack. What strange creatures we are, I think. Humans.

In the evening Linda, Bob, and I get fish tacos and take them to the beach. Tan people, looking as if they've never been depressed a day in their lives, rollerblade serenely by.

That night I lie in bed, unable to sleep, and stare at the light pollution on the RV ceiling. In six point five hours, I will wake in the darkened RV and assemble my collection of extremely specific objects in their special order in my "pack," and I will ride with Bob and Linda to the PCT "kickoff," where I will attend a workshop on pooping in the desert and eat burritos. At night I'll lay in the cold grass and the stars will twinkle on the far horizon and the moon will almost burn me with its light. And then I'll walk north until my shoes wear completely off. I close my eyes, listening to the sound of the freeway in the distance. *Turning the wheel of life,* as they say.

***

Annual Day Zero Pacific Crest Trail Kickoff, aka ADZPCTKO, aka kickoff, is in a big campground filled with ultralight spaceship tents, little cottage vendors, and limping, sunburned hikers. I sign in and stumble around in the sun, asking people for advice about my tendinitis. I find T-Rex, Rocky, and HairTie, camped on some dewy grass next to a dry creek bed and laboriously pitch my tent beside them. In the morning I'll get back on the trail and hike just fifteen miles in two days, after which I will have caught up with the three of them- they're nursing injuries too. And we'll all get to hike together!

29

I learn to tape my tendinitis, to stretch it, to scrape the skin with a spoon. I learn to change my walking gait, to "ice" my heel with a wet bandanna, to take ibuprofen before bed to reduce inflammation. I even cut a part off the backs of my shoes, the part that sticks up and hits my heel. I have new socks. And I'll probably never attempt to carry seven liters of water and twelve pounds of food again.

I lie in my tent after dark, quilt pulled up against the icy desert night. I've got so much ahead of me. Tomorrow, the next day, the day after that. The trail, the desert, the universe. Everything.

***

In the morning, a talkative park ranger drives me and a sunburnt German to Mt. Laguna, which is where I got off the trail. The morning is warm and my pack is heavy with plastic soda bottles, fished from the trash, full of water. I set out happily through the dusty pine forest, so glad to be back on the trail I can barely stand it.

An hour later, I have left the pine forest behind. The pine forest was an anomaly in the creosote desert, a little green island on the mountaintop where moisture gathered. Now I've dropped in elevation and there is only the desert again, sweeping away in all directions. To the east, slung between the mountains, is a wide flat valley; currently this valley roasts like a baked potato in the sun.

In a few days I will cross this valley.

There will be no shade.

Three miles into the morning my ankle is just a little sore. This is promising, I think, as I take an ibuprofen, since just a few days ago I could barely walk at all. At kickoff I went to a talk put on by a man who'd healed his brutal shin splints during his thru-hike by changing his gait, and now I try to imitate the gait I saw him do. Short little steps and standing upright as though a string is coming out of the top of my head. *Like ballroom dancing*, I thought, as I watched him mince around the room. Now I hold my arms out in front of me as though I am holding a partner, and imagine that I am two-stepping. Immediately my gait changes. My spine lengthens, my stride shortens, and I can feel the muscles in my legs tense, taking more of the burden. I'm not slapping so hard on my heels with each step.

"You've got 2660 miles," the man said, "to experiment with your gait."

At mile ten, I stop at a strange empty picnic area next to a highway and dip my plastic bottles into a horse trough. I am in the desert; my daily distance and where I rest, cook, and camp are determined by water sources such as this one, scattered sparsely along the trail. The water in the trough is green and murky. I turn the spigot for the trough and am relieved when clear, cold water come rushing out, from a tank somewhere.

I find a picnic table with a little dappled shade and drop my pack there. I do some arbitrary stretches. My ankle feels fucking fantastic. Thank god. Thank god it's healing. Or rather, thank the angels. The trail angels. I spread my things out on the picnic table, elated. I'll cook dinner here, then hike on a few miles to what is, according to my map, "the campsite among the boulders." Then, in the morning, I'll be only two miles from the next horse trough, where I'll meet my friends.

I fire up my little popcan stove and boil water in my pot, adding rice noodles and dried vegetables. I stir in some salt. While I am eating a man appears and sits down opposite me.

The man is from France, and his name is Jean Francois. He is sixty years old. He left Campo two days before, which means that he's already hiking more than twenty miles a day. He removes his hat, a wool beret, and scratches at his sunburnt scalp.

"Made in France," he says, pushing the beret across the table to me. He's knotted a bandanna around the back of the beret, to protect his neck from the sun. He fumbles in his pack and retrieves an orange.

"I have not been hungry," he says. "Maybe just a little bit hungry." He peels the orange slowly, and trims the pith with a pocket knife. He offers me a few wedges.

Jean Francois and I hike together into the afternoon. We come to a dusty road that looks out over the hot desert valley. There are wilted flowers there, and headstones set into the rock.

"Oh," I say. "Ashes!"

Jean Francois frowns.

"Do you understand ashes? When people die, they bring the ashes here and throw them out into the air!" I make a sweeping motion with my arm. Jean Francois frowns harder.

At six o'clock we reach a jumble of rose-colored boulders that overlook everything. Among the boulders are soft flat places in the sand. Jean Francois picks a spot next to the trail.

"Goodnight, Jean Francois," I say. I climb over some boulders to find a hidden spot. The sun is setting in the hills to the west; I feel weary, but not overly so. I am not sore anywhere, and my feet don't even hurt. I only hiked fifteen miles today but still, maybe I am getting strong? I will have to get strong, if I am going to make it all the way to Canada before the snow flies. 2,660 miles by September 30th- that's about eighteen miles a day, if I never take days off. I know I'll want to take days off so on the days I hike, I'll have to do more than eighteen miles. I am no athlete. Can I do it? I don't know. I want to so badly, but can I? And these next few weeks I will have to take it easy, for my tendinitis. Slow and steady wins the race.

I spread my groundsheet over the soft sand and anchor its corners with hunks of quartz. I'm cowboy camping tonight- no tent for me. I feel safe, way up here under the stars, big boulders jumbled all around. I put my hand on my ground sheet.

"This is a no-scorpion zone," I say, to no one in particular.

A warm wind blows as I tuck myself into my sleeping quilt. *Being on the trail is the best thing in the world,* I think, as I watched the stars wink on above me.

***

I wake at dawn and grab my water bottle, but it's empty. I was hungry right before I fell asleep and ate a sugary bar and a bunch of jerky, and then when the moon rose like a flashlight in my face I was both unable to sleep and terribly thirsty. I stared at the moon for two hours, thinking anxious thoughts about life, the future, everything. And I drank all of my water.

I sit in my sleeping bag for a moment, watching the long bands of light stretch over the boulders. Jean Francois passes on the trail below, leaning on his trekking poles, headed out. I yawn and stuff away my quilt.

Three miles is not such a long way unless you are thirsty and you do not have any water. I am overjoyed when I reach the horse trough at the trailhead; it is glorious to pass the gallon jug there through the cool, murky water to the valve that lets out clear water. Last night was my first time dry camping- I am still learning how much water I need to pack.

I stand drinking the good cold water, looking down at the minnows that swim in the horse trough. *How do the minnows get in here?* I wonder.

Back on the trail I find HairTie, T-Rex and Rocky, piling out of the bed of a pickup truck. What serendipity! The four of us set off down the dusty golden path together, single file like we're on an expedition.

In an hour the sun is directly overhead, it's too hot to walk any longer, and there isn't any shade. This makes me feel sort of panicky. Next to the trail is a dirt slope with creosote bushes hanging over it and we wedge ourselves into this as best we can, digging our feet into the slope so we don't slide down. In this way we're a little bit shaded and vaguely uncomfortable. One is never entirely comfortable, I am learning, on a thru-hike. Except at night, in one's sleeping bag, feeling one's spine release into the earth. What glory!

HairTie fires up her stove, which is made from a catfood can, and stirs a pot of instant mashed potatoes. Rocky falls asleep, his water bladder with its in-line filter hanging above him like an IV bag.

HairTie is the first to stir.

"I'm going out into it," she says at three thirty, squinting at the painfully bright desert.

It is now not only just brutally hot- it is windy too. I clutch my hat as I walk carefully along the trail that hugs the edge of the mountain. We are still high up and I gaze with apprehension at the baking valley below. Scissors Crossing is its name. Tomorrow. Tomorrow we cross this valley.

We reach our next water source, a big steel tank, just after six. The spigot, by a stroke of miraculous luck, is working perfectly. While crouched under the creosote bush in the afternoon we formulated a logistical plan for our desert crossing- we'll hike on this evening and into the night, until we cannot hike any longer, and then we'll camp. In the morning, we'll be just a few miles from the highway underpass in Scissors Crossing and the huge water cache stocked by trail angels there.

Night hiking, we've decided. Night hiking is the answer to this heat.

The trail leaving the water tank hugs the folds of the mountain, dipping in and out. Dark falls, but there is no moon; our silver spotlight of a friend won't rise until midnight. I switch on my headlamp as the last of the rosy light fades in the west. I watch as the Big Dipper blinks on above me. I am ten minutes ahead of the others, and I can't see their lights; there is only my small light against the dark backdrop of the creosote mountain and the black valley below. It's a little cooler, now, and I have fresh wind in my sails; I hike quickly, careful of the rocks in the path before me. After a time I look back and see three little lights opposite me, across a stretch of black, empty space. I switch my headlamp to its blinking red setting. *Blink blink blink*, goes my headlamp. *Blink blink blink*, go the little lights across the mountain in the darkness.

We stop to camp in a dusty clearing next to the trail, four miles from Scissors Crossing.

"We can even sleep in if we want to," we agree. "Four miles is not so much."

The moon rises at midnight and shines merrily in our faces. I wake and sleep, wake and sleep.

"It's so moony!" I want to shout, but I don't. I am sweating in my sleeping bag.

It's nighttime and not even cold, I think, as I lie in my sleeping bag, staring at the moon. What does that even mean?

***

In the warm bright morning, we descend off the mountain and towards the blistering valley. We stop after an hour to rest in a dry streambed, where there is shade from a jumble of boulders and the sandy ground is cool. We blearily eat our morning snacks. At six thirty, it is already brutally hot.

At the bottom the trail cuts straight across the valley floor, no fucking around. It crosses sandy dry creekbeds and skirts tall barrel cacti. I keep my eyes on the ground, following the trekking pole drag marks from those that have gone before. After an hour my feet are sore all over, every cell aching in pain from the hot ground. The bright sun reflects off the bright sand, making everything glow painfully white, and I can feel the backs of my legs beginning to burn, in spite of the layer of dirt and sunscreen there. The mountains that ring the valley waver in the heat like a mirage and in the distance I can just make out cars, shimmering on the highway. I plod and plod, feeling as though I am going nowhere. Why won't this end, I think. Why won't this terrible valley ever end.

Cool, dark, piss-smelling highway underpass. A mountain of plastic water jugs. The Scissors Crossing cache. I collapse on the ground and desperately pull off my shoes. Other hikers arrive, filthy and deranged from the heat, and crumple onto the sand around me. It is nine thirty.

"It's hot," I say to no one in particular. "So hot."

An hour later we're at the Stagecoach RV Resort down the road, sitting on the deck of the little store consuming gatorade and icecream sandwiches. The resort is a wild, flat stretch of baking sand, empty save for a couple of RVs hunkered down in the blowing dust. We've paid five bucks each to hang out here all day and hide from the heat.

The icecream sandwiches put me into a stupor and I stumble across the burning sand to the shower house, feeling as though I'll go blind from the sun. The women's shower house is cool and dim and floored in clean white tile. There is a long row of bright sinks. I plug my phone into the wall and stand waiting for a moment, but no-one appears. I strip off my clothes and peel the tape from my feet, grimacing as fluid oozes from the blisters beneath. I crank the shower and scrub at my body with my hanky and my hunk of soap, attempting to remove the thick paste of dirt and sunscreen that has embedded itself into my skin. After patting myself slightly dry with coarse paper towels from the paper towel dispenser I fill the end-most sink with hot water and soap and stand naked, plunging my clothes into it. The next sink becomes the rinse sink and in this way I wash my clothes, churning them up and down in the scalding brown water.

I give up long before the water runs clear and put on my wet shirt and shorts and step gingerly outside in my bare feet, spreading the rest of my clothes on the bright ground to dry.

HairTie is at the pool, skimming the bees from the water with a pool skimmer. Rocky is standing in the shallow end in all his clothes. There is no shade outside so I pull a decomposing pool lounger into the tiny pool bathroom and lie on it to wait out the heat.

By and by a rectangle of shade grows against the concrete wall that borders the pool. Rocky and T-Rex and HairTie wedge themselves into this shade and attempt to cook food on their alcohol stoves in the wind. *Woo woo woo*, goes the wind, blowing dust and grit across the stone patio.

We make up a story of why we are walking to Canada.

"We're in a post-industrial collapse," I say.

"We have to find the others," says HairTie. She has a bar of ganja chocolate, melted from the sun, and she's eating it with a spoon. "We're walking to Canada to find the others."

At five thirty, a Swiss woman who works in the dusty little store gives HairTie and I a ride back to the trail. The woman's dress is a carefully knotted sarong and I imagine her at home, batiking desert landscapes. She's lived in this valley for twenty-nine years.

"This place really grows on you," she says.

The woman drops us at the highway underpass. Rocky and T-Rex are already there, drinking Bud Light they found in a cooler, with ice.

"Very little ice," says T-Rex.

We have a long climb ahead of us, up into the San Felipe hills. But the shadows are long now and the air is a little cooler. The next water cache is in fourteen miles. Our plan is to hike until nine, cowboy camp until the moon rises and then hike the last nine miles in the wee hours. With luck we'll reach the Third Gate cache by dawn.

We've begun to refer to "dawn" as "Don," as in "Don is coming" or "Don will wake us."

At 2 o'clock, the moon rises above the trampled spot in the cacti where we set up camp. The wind has been gusting for hours, whipping over the hills, and we slept restlessly on our groundsheets in the dust. Now we sit up, confused, and rub the sand from our eyes. We stuff our things away, fighting with the wind for our gear.

There are two gates before the Third Gate cache, two gates made of metal pipes stuck in the trail. We stumble forward in the dark, our headlamps trained on the trail. This side of the mountain is in moonshadow and it's difficult to see.

"The first gate!" I shout. We've gone five miles. The miles have stretched out somehow, in this dark no-man's land of the night, and each one seems to take hours. At the second gate we sit in the dust and cook breakfast on our little stoves. The sky is lightening in the east.

"Don is coming!" I exclaim.

We reach the third gate just as the first rays of life-vaporizing light are stretching their way across the land. We open the third gate and step through it. On the other side of this gate we discover a small garden of Eden- fragrant clumps of trees and patches of speckled shade. We stumble down a side trail to the water cache, our feet aching and sore. The cache appears like a mirage, a mound of sparkling bottles in the hot desert. After gathering water we return to the cluster of trees around the third gate and each of us, like a wild animal, finds our own little chunk of shade in which to burrow. I shove myself beneath the thorny branches of a tree whose name I do not know. Inside there is a space just big enough for my body and I unroll my sleeping pad, curl up on my side in my sweaty, dust-covered clothes, and arrange my things around me- water, sunglasses, hat, a hanky to cover my eyes. The crowded limbs of this tree will shelter me from the sun.

Other hikers are just beginning to arrive. It is 6:30 a.m.

***

All day I wake and sleep, wake and sleep beneath the thorny tree. The sun floats above me, the warm dapples shift like constellations across my body. Tiny ants crawl over me, using me as a bridge from one side of the tree to the other. I sleep.

In the afternoon the four of us sit groggily in the dirt, heating pots of water for dinner. By the time we pack up and move out it's six p.m. and we have nine miles to the next water source, Barrel Springs. We'll camp there, and in the morning hike the four miles into Warner Springs, a little cluster of buildings on a narrow rural highway. We all have resupply boxes at the post office in Warner Springs. We've also heard that there will be burgers there and a little store. *Burgers*, we say as we hike. *Burgers burgers*

burgers.

An hour after setting out from our dappled garden of Eden we round a mountainside and meet the cool, damp air from the sea.

"Fuck!" says HairTie. "It's fucking freezing!" It's nearly dark, and big wet clouds race across the sky. The wind is howling.

The landscape begins to change. The shadowy forms of trees and leafy plants now tangle up the mountainside. I shiver as I hike, hungry and exhausted. I am a bit ahead of the others, walking in the dark with the dim light of my headlamp trained on the trail, and I feel a little spooked. There are noises in the forest here, little crunches and shufflings, creatures going about their night-business in the tangled undergrowth. This is no arid expanse of dust and barrel cactus. This is *someplace*- there is moisture here, rain sometimes, plants and fog and springs. It is eerie to feel all this activity around me after the big warm emptiness of the desert.

I hang back and wait for the others.

"It's creepy here," I say. "You think we should all hike together?"

"Yeah," says T-Rex.

A little later we happen upon the number 100 made of stones on the side of the trail.

"Mile 100!" Says T-Rex. "We've reached mile 100!"

"We're not day hikers anymore," I say. We all train our headlamps on the marker for a moment.

"Just one more mile to Barrel Springs," says T-Rex. T-Rex and HairTie are both having intense foot pain.

"Gah," says T-Rex, sitting in the dirt and pulling out one of her insoles. "Fuck fuck fuck fuck fuck." She points to the edge of the insole. "Right there. It feels like knives in my foot."

"At least it's just a mile left," I say.

"Fuck," says T-Rex, as she limps sideways down the trail.

A little while later I round a bend and there, in a sandy wash, is another

100 made of stones.

"What?" says T-Rex. "Which 100 is the real 100?" She's now in so much pain she can barely stand, and she leans on her trekking poles like crutches.

A bit later there is another 100, a small one assembled in the grass.

"The longest mile," says T-Rex. "The mile between the mile."

The dark path curves down a fold in the mountain and suddenly there are oak trees overhead, grass underfoot, and the sound of trickling water. The air smells of lilacs. Barrel Springs! We're in a little clearing, and we swing our headlamps around. There are tents pitched here and beneath the trees there are the downy burritos of cowboy campers.

The spring is water trickling from a pipe into a square stone trough. In the trough float cans of soda. I pluck a few out- diet lemon soda, Big K cola, Mr. Pibb.

"Soda!" I say. "There's soda in these springs!"

We pitch our shelters in a little patch of grass and collapse into them. We haven't slept a full night's sleep in several days, and HairTie hasn't slept at all in the last twenty-four hours; at the last cache she curled up right next to the trail and people woke her again and again throughout the day, saying "Where's the water? Where is the water?"

It's cold here, and there is no wind. I burrow deep into my bag, pulling it up over my face. Then I sleep harder than I can ever remember sleeping.

***

I wake in the morning to a woman bending over my tent. "Good morning!" she says. "Time to get up!" The woman is wearing PCT earrings and holding a case of grapefruit soda.

"Thank you for putting soda in the spring," I say sleepily.

It's after dawn, and all of the other hikers are gone. I walk gingerly across the clearing in my bare feet, reach my arm into the cool water of the trough and fish a diet citrus beverage from the bottom. I know it's silly to drink diet soda, but all the sugar in regular soda will make me feel awful, especially on an empty stomach. I sit cross-legged on the cold ground and drink the soda and eat the last of my dried figs. Now I have no food until Warner Springs, seven miles away.

What is Warner Springs? I wonder.

A couple of hikers arrive while I'm packing up. I met these hikers before, but now I can't recall their names. The hikers are all starting to look the same to me- fit white dudes in safari wear, powering over the passes faster than I will ever be able to. One of these hikers is wearing a sort of sweat-soaked towel around his neck, and presently he stands above the trough and wrings out the towel into the water.

Today the spring is running, and a little water trickles from the pipe into the trough. But the spring is not always running, and hikers after us will have to filter directly from the stone trough.

No bueno, I think.

Another man, dressed nearly identically, appears and dips his sweaty shirt into the trough.

No bueno, I think again.

To reach Warner Springs we must leave our little oasis of soda and croaking frogs and hike a winding dusty path through the windswept yellow hills. The path winds on and on, circling every hill, and the scenery seems to double back on itself like the background of a video game. We are all out of food and crashing hard, and the anticipation of food, wonderful magical food, is growing inside of us like a crazy psychotic monster. My understanding is that this crazy psychotic monster is called "hiker hunger," and that this sensation sets in around day ten.

Today the hiker hunger is strong within me, I think, as I plod despairingly over the dry yellow hills.

We pass some cows and a rock shaped like an eagle. We fan out in a natural way, our little group spreading across the trail as we hike. Each day we go long stretches without seeing each other, and yet we reconvene naturally at water sources and chunks of shade, talking all at once about everything that we have seen.

HairTie and I arrive at the road at the same time. There is a fire station there. We stick out our thumbs. It's a mile or two to the post office, but the last thing we want right now is a two-mile road walk. After walking on a soft sandy path for a long enough time that your feet are screaming in pain, nothing feels more violent than stepping onto hard concrete.

Several cars pass us, and then a half hour has gone by. Rocky and T-Rex took a side trail to the post office and should be there by now. I can feel the panic pounding inside me, the wild hunger. Burgers! Burgers! Burgers! We began to walk past the fire station and then we see a woman, beckoning to us from across the road.

"Over here!" she says. "Over here!"

We follow her across an expanse of concrete to a low wooden building, the Warner Springs Community Center.

Two dozen hikers sprawl languidly on the scratchy grass beneath an oak tree. A man is offering rides to the post office.

"Yes!" I say. "Please!"

The man is Billy Goat. Billy Goat has hiked tens of thousands of miles on the long trails and is a bit of a trail legend. Billy Goat is short and wiry and has a long silver beard. The passenger seat of his little hatchback has been converted into a bed.

"Do you live in this area?" I ask him.

"Don't live anywhere," says Billy Goat. "Live in my car when I'm not on the trail."

At the post office we fill our arms with our packages. T-Rex and Rocky are there, sitting listlessly on the curb. I rip open my box and eat a piece of beef jerky. I wait for my blood sugar to stabilize.

A nice woman gives us a ride back to the community center, and we spread our loot a little ways from the crowd. I wander into the building, feeling crazed.

"No burgers," says a hiker. "No burgers till dinner time."

"What?" I say. "What does that even mean?" The disappointment within me is tangible and bright, like fire.

The store in the community center is stocked with big boxes of little packages of things. I buy a roll of toilet paper, a bottle of ibuprofen, and two icecream sandwiches.

I sit in the grass and eat my icecream sandwiches. My heart pounds with sugar, and time begins to slow. I go back into the community center and dig through the hiker boxes, which is where hikers dump the things that they no longer want. A hundred different kinds of oatmeal, some instant mashed potatoes, one Injinji toe sock. A man is putting his Probars into the hiker box.

"You sick of Probars?" I say.

"Yeah," says the man. "Kind of." I take the Probars, which are smashed from being carried a hundred miles and probably sat on. I also find a little bottle of olive oil.

A woman walks from the back of the community center with a burger.

"Can I order a burger?" I ask her.

"Well of course you can, hon," she says. "Until four o'clock."

I look at my watch- it's three thirty.

"Can I have a burger with a double patty?" I ask the woman with the cash box.

"Sure. What color gatorade you want?"

I enjoy this for a moment, the fact that the woman has asked me what *color* gatorade I want, and not what flavor.

"Orange," I say.

Next to the hiker box is a little table with carafes of coffee and a glass jar of fresh cookies. I return to this jar throughout the afternoon, and at last tally, I've eaten a dozen. I down my burger sitting in the grass beneath our oak tree, squirting the bare, dry patty with mustard and ketchup until it's dripping down my forearms. I can barely fit it into my stomach.

"I feel sick," I say. "I think I feel sick."

"Do you think this is enough food for four days?" asks T-Rex, holding up her tiny food bag. Each of us jettisoned much of our resupply boxes into the hiker box, as our next stop is only a few days away and food, we've decided, is heavy. Sixty-five miles till Idyllwild. We'll hike from the baking desert up into the freezing, wind-blasted peaks of the San Jacinto Mountains. It will be one of the steepest climbs of the entire PCT.

"Yeah, that looks like enough food," I say.

When we first arrived at the center I washed my socks under the spigot behind the building, and now they're dry where I laid them to bake in the sun. I put the socks on, happy that they are warm and now smell of peppermint soap. Foot care is important on the PCT, more important than I ever could have imagined. There are blisters, hot spots, small injuries and at the end of each day the kind of radiating foot pain that keeps a person from sleep. Some days it feels as though I am literally wearing my feet down to nubbins on the jagged surface of the earth. And in a way I am- the desert sand infiltrates my shoes, and if I do not clean this sand off now and then it will abrade my skin until my feet are a bloody, pulpy mess. So every chance I get I wash my feet with my bandanna, dampened with a little water. Eventually, they say, my feet will become strong and callused, and they will no longer blister. I cannot wait for this day to come. I wonder when it ever will?

Suddenly I remember my Achilles tendon. It hasn't hurt for days, and I'd completely forgotten about it. I squeeze my eyes shut. *Thank you,* I whisper.

Now it's almost evening and we are all ill from junk food, nearly comatose beneath our oak tree. The plan is to hike the last few miles to Agua Caliente and to camp next to the creek. A real creek, with real water running over stones! It'll be the first one we've seen since starting the desert.

I am flying high on my burger and I reach the campsite before the others, hiking up into the beautiful hills and then along the burbling little stream. I soak my feet in the water as dusk falls, listening to the small, crunchy noises of the forest. Night comes and at last the others arrive, headlamps swinging in the dark.

***

43

I wake in the cold morning and fill my gatorade bottles in the stream. I didn't sleep well for reasons I don't understand, and I hike slowly into the beautiful mountains. The heat comes on; we heard the day before that there would be a heat wave.

I feel tired, delirious, clumsy; I roll my ankles lightly. I told myself I wouldn't take a break until I'd hiked twelve miles, but the sun is out in full force and I become slower and slower. At last I collapse in the prickly shade of a large rock and drink water and pull the tape off my oozing blisters. I look at my watch- I've been walking so slowly that I may as well have just rested.

Why am I so tired today? I wonder. *Why is every day so different?*

Eventually there is a brightly painted sign stuck in some rocks.

Trail angel Mike! Says the sign. *Water shade shelter!*

I amble down the dusty side trail to a huge steel water tank. *H20* is painted on the side of the tank in big dripping spraypaint letters. Beyond the tank is a house. Behind the house dirty hikers are perched tensely in the shade, picking at their feet. Two leathery men play ultimate frisbee in the dirt yard. On a picnic table is a large carton of potato salad. I scoop a warm mound of this salad onto a styrofoam plate and eat it standing.

The back of the house is shady and quiet and HairTie, T-Rex, Rocky and I convene there, setting up our popcan stoves to cook dinner. T-Rex and HairTie eat fast and fall asleep in the porch swing. I light an Esbit tab, pilfered from the hiker box in Warner Springs, and boil water for my instant refried beans. The air is filled with the smell of burning plastic.

"If you light an Esbit tab in your tent you'll start to hurl," says a big man named Stats, who is next to us on the patio, organizing his pack.

At five thirty we set out for Nance Canyon, where we'll camp. Rocky ate two packets of ramen and downed a Coke at Mike's and is now in considerable pain; otherwise we're feeling pretty good. The campsite in Nance Canyon is a sandy spot next to a dry, weed-choked streambed. It's very cold here- the cold air sinks down at night and settles in low places like this. Tomorrow we'll hike eighteen miles and camp just outside of Paradise Valley Cafe; I have never eaten there but I fall asleep imagining what a place called *Paradise Valley Cafe* might be like, and watching the stars, and feeling happy.

44

***

I have strange dreams, fast asleep in my sleeping quilt in the freezing canyon- a runway designer is critiquing my posture, and I save a boy from drowning. At dawn I wake and assemble my breakfast in a plastic peanut butter jar- oats, chia seeds, dried fruit. I'll put the jar in my pack, and after an hour of hiking it'll be ready to eat. No more cooking breakfast, I've decided. I want to be faster, and this will save me a little time.

The cold makes us slow to rise, and we regret our slow start as soon as the sun reaches us. Another hot day in the desert, stumbling in the dust over rocks. I need some new nouns, I think, as I plod up the hills. Dust dust dust, dirt dirt dirt.

At nine, we reach our first water source- Tule Springs, a little cluster of oak trees next to a ravine. The water comes out of a metal spigot on the edge of a dusty clearing. There's a short length of hose attached to the spigot. I am caked all over with dirt, and my shirt and shorts are stiff with salt. I drop my things in the shade and, as the spigot is a little hidden from the trail, I take a sort of bath there. I also take off my shoes and carefully wash my feet, inspecting my blisters; a few of them are hardening into calluses, thank god, and a few of the blisters have blisters of their own. There is a new one on my heel.

HairTie, Rocky, and T-Rex arrive and we spread our sleeping pads in the shade. A young man appears and sits in the dust next to us, pulls a glass jar of jelly from his pack, and begins to assemble a peanut butter and jelly sandwich. He smiles at us while he eats his sandwich. He has long, shining blonde hair and perfect white teeth. His name is Whistler and he carries a huge pack, stuck all over with patches.

"I hiked the AT," he says. "I got my name there, because I whistled."

"Do you know that there are whistling competitions?" says Rocky, who is stretching his knee. "My hairdresser was in a whistling competition."

T-Rex is eating Runts, those powdery little candies shaped like fruit.

"I'm running low on food," she says. "This is all I have to eat, besides things I have to cook. Do you want some Runts?" T-Rex got the Runts at a candy shop in Portland where they were sorted by fruit, and so she bought only the banana-shaped ones.

Sometime later, after setting out again, I happen upon Whistler and HairTie at an old concrete cistern next to the trail. There is a snake trapped in the cistern, not a rattlesnake but some other kind of snake. The snake is slithering, slither slither slither, but it can't get free of the cistern. Whistler sticks his trekking pole in the cistern to try and save the snake.

"Is that a biting kind of snake?" I ask.

"I don't know," says Whistler. "I guess I'll find out."

Whistler pulls the snake out and it slithers away, into the creosote bushes.

The afternoon is brutally hot and per usual, there is no shade. Our last water source of the day is the Hiker's Oasis cache and I push myself forward in the heat, sweating in my filthy shirt, telling myself that I'll rest in the shade when I get to the cache. I didn't plan my water well and I am out before I reach it. I stumble into the cache thirsty and irritated. Like some sort of cruel joke, there is no shade to be had. I fill up my bottles and sit in the dust, feeling angry and overly hot. The others circle around, looking for bits of shade and laughing deliriously. Whistler passes us and walks on into the baking hills. An hour disappears somehow, with no relief from the sun, and so at last we get up and push on too. I fall behind the others, walking so slowly it is as though I am dragging my own body up the steep trail. The sun, I think. This is what the sun does to me.

The trail climbs up for many hours. I fall further and further behind. At one point I spot two banana shaped Runts, a green one and a yellow one, lying on the dusty path. A half hour later there is another banana Runt- a red one. And then another, garishly blue in the dust of the trail. I round a bend and there are T-Rex and Rocky and HairTie, sprawled in a bit of lumpy shade, looking as though they've died. T-Rex is stretched out on her back in the dirt. Her tiny straw hat, bought at a party store in Portland and made for a small child, is over her face. HairTie is slouched against a tree, her blue silk shirt even more ragged. I lower myself onto the ground next to them, wincing at the pain in my hips.

"Sciatica!" I say. "Goddam sciatica!"

HairTie and T-Rex are having terrible footpain due to their insole situation, and Rocky has his knee problem, which comes and goes. The four of us lie there in the dirt, feeling small and weak and broken. And yet, after a while, there is nothing to do but move on. There is no water here, and night is coming.

At dusk we reach our campsite, a trampled spot in the chaparral three miles from Highway 74 and the Paradise Valley Cafe. I throw down my ground sheet and my sleeping pad and collapse on the warm sand.

"I can barely move," I say, as I attempt to stretch. "All that climbing. I hurt everywhere." I shake my sleeping quilt to loft it and pull it over my body. The thing I read about happening to others has finally happened to me- my exhaustion at the end of each day now overpowers my fear of imaginary desert monsters and so I am cowboy camping each night, too tired to set up my shelter.

"That climb was so steep," I say again, before I drift off. "I can't believe how much climbing we just did. Hours and hours and hours of it."

I have no idea what is to come.

***

In the morning we're up in a flash and at the Paradise Valley Cafe by the time they open at eight. We crowd the deck with our packs and then sit in the chairs there, astonished. Chairs! *Real chairs!* Soon we are surrounded by other chattering humans in their clean cotton separates. There is the noise of cars and music, and our server is bringing us fresh-squeezed orange juice and the hunger monster is so large inside of me that the anticipation is intolerable and I have no choice but the be disappointed.

"My orange juice is sour," I say to Rocky. "Is your orange juice sour?"

"No," says Rocky. "My orange juice is amazing."

I order some wild breakfast that I don't understand, and soon a platter appears in front of me with a huge hamburger patty, three runny eggs, and a hunk of wet hashbrowns. I give my toast away but later take it back and greedily smear it with strawberry jam. I can't eat gluten or dairy without stomach upset, but my hiker hunger overrides any rational thought and so I am doomed to diarrhea for *days* as I set out on my epic quest to Eat All The Things. After finishing the burger, hashbrowns, eggs, toast, and juice, I order decaf coffee and a slice of apple pie with ice cream. The pie is warm and flaky and tastes like pure euphoria and I wish that I could eat it again and again, in an endless loop, for all of eternity. I drink three cups of decaf with cream and sugar.

"Will you be staying for lunch?" asks our server.

"Yes," we say in unison. "We will be staying for lunch."

For lunch, I order a chocolate shake.

Other hikers have arrived and they fill the extra tables on the patio. There is even a motorcycle gang- wealthy retirees in expensive leather. I am eating the whipped cream off the top of my shake when there is a terrific crashing noise. We all turn and catch the last instant of a three-car collision at the intersection in front of the cafe. An SUV slams into a pickup truck and then a Prius slams into the SUV.

"Oh my god," says our server, as she hops the railing and runs out into the intersection. A few men follow her. The door of the pickup flies open and a woman races around the truck, yanking open the passenger door. She pulls out a toddler and clutches it.

"Oh my god," I say.

"Someone call 911!" Our server is screaming, as she darts from vehicle to vehicle. All the people present with any sort of useful experience are now running towards the cars in the intersection. The passengers in the Prius stumble from their vehicle, but the SUV is strangely still. Soon it becomes apparent that the people inside the SUV are trapped by both their airbags and the frame of the car itself, which was crushed during the impact.

A fire truck peals onto the scene, and the firefighters hop out and begin to cut open the SUV. Then there is the pounding of helicopters and dust blowing everywhere. The woman with the baby sits in a plastic patio chair on the deck and holds him while he screams. She is staring forward at nothing. No one on the patio wants to eat any longer.

Rocky appears.

"Where did you go?" says T-Rex.

"The man driving the SUV gave me his phone," says Rocky. "He wanted me to call his sister. So I called her and told her that he'd been in a bad accident but he was alive. She started to cry a little on the phone."

A man with a red beard appears and leans over the woman holding the baby. He cradles her face and strokes her hair. He takes the baby from the woman and the baby screams.

"Daddy's here," says the man. "It's ok, daddy's here."

The woman gets into an ambulance and the ambulance drives away.

"What happens when you're in shock?" I ask HairTie. "Like, what does shock do to your body?" In the regular world HairTie is a nurse.

"Your vitals go all over the place," she says.

It is now noon, and we order our lunches to go. I get a large amount of fries in a styrofoam carton, which I wedge carefully into the top of my pack. We have fourteen miles left to hike this afternoon, and all of it is uphill.

We leave the little valley of the accident and walk towards the looming San Jacintos. I am plodding along by myself and I feel nauseous and ill, as though I might vomit. All that food now aches like hot bricks in my stomach. Each patch of dappled shade I pass calls out to me. *Ressssssst,* says the shade. *Lie down and rest for a little while.*

I walk. The trail begins to climb. Up, and up, and up. I am leapfrogging with some other hikers and we walk and talk together. Then I happen upon Rocky and HairTie and T-Rex, eating their takeout lunches in a bit of shade. I sit down and open my carton of cold french fries.

"Going up, huh?" I say.

"Yeah," they say.

The afternoon cools and a breeze comes up. We climb and climb and climb, our hearts pounding manically, sweat soaking our dirty clothes. HairTie and I walk together and she tells me about her job in the hospital in the city, and about her existential take on life. HairTie has wild eyes, and today her silk shirt is torn almost completely from her body. As we walk she licks the last of a bar of melted ganja chocolate from the wrapper. After eight miles, we stop to stretch in a leafy little area alongside the narrow trail. A woman appears and leans on her trekking poles.

"Are you two going to camp here?" she asks.

"No," I say. "We're just stopping to rest."

"Well then I will," says the woman. "It's the last spot before the wind."

The wind? I think. What does that even mean?

A few moments later the trail curves around to the west side of the mountain and the leafy forest disappears and instead there are only stunted, twisted shrubs. The wind comes booming up out of the valley and begins to beat us so hard we can barely breathe.

"It's freezing!" I shout into this wall of forceful, living air. "It's fucking freezing up here!"

The trail is a narrow rocky path between the steep jagged mountain and the nothingness of the great empty space below. We are way up high and still climbing. How did we get so high? The wind is like a rolled up newspaper, batting us with all its might. I clutch my hat to my head and stagger down the path. The wind is a hand, pushing me off the trail to my death. The wind is icy cold, whipping through my sweat-soaked clothes, smacking my bare legs. I'll stop and put on my down jacket, I think. But there is nowhere to stop.

The rocky path narrows and becomes steeper, the wind increases. We crawl up and over a rocky peak, across a tiny saddle, and over a still higher peak. We repeat this into forever. The rocks in the path are sending bright hot pain into the soles of my feet and I am impossibly cold.

"The rocks are blessing us!" I scream to HairTie. "The rocks are our teachers! They are teaching us about suffering!"

"Thank you, rock teachers!" Shouts HairTie. "Thank you thank you thank you!"

"Everything is fine, forever and ever and ever!" I am laughing. I have some reservoir inside of me, some emergency thing that I didn't know I had, and I am using it now, for this fourteen-mile climb into the freezing wind way on top of the world. My muscles burn and I am dizzy with altitude and fatigue. I lurch down the trail, one small step in front of the other, against the wind. My joints ache and my hands and face and legs are numb with cold. I only have running shorts, no pants! I think. What is this place?

50

We'd planned to camp at the water source in several miles, but then the trail loops around to the east side of the mountain and suddenly the wind is gone. We're in the peaceful leafy forest once again. It's nearly dark now and we swing our headlamps around, looking for a flat place to camp but there is only the mountain, sloping away. We are each in some state of stiff-legged limping, moving forward on just fumes. Below the trail on a little ledge is a cave made of big boulders leaned against each other, and in front of this cave is a small clearing. T-Rex goes to scout it out and returns spooked. There is an old blanket there, she says, and a bowl and fork, and the cave is dark and creepy. But if we keep walking we'll end up back on the west side of the mountain, with the wind.

"I think there's room for us there," I say. "And the ghosts of old hermits will protect us."

Rocky and T-Rex pitch their tent in the little clearing and HairTie and I lie our ground cloths in the cave, over the ashes of many fires. We are all thirsty and cold and have very little water, so we go to bed without dinner. I lie in my sleeping quilt in the cave, feeling the memory of the cold wind move through my body. I toss and turn. My legs and feet ache and I can't get comfortable, and every time I close my eyes I imagine an old hermit ghost, wild and weird and crazy, poking about in the dark, looking for his matted blanket.

***

I wake in the night thirsty but I have no water. I stare at the dark walls of the cave. When dawn comes, I decide, I'm gonna book it that last mile to the spring.

I am up and out of camp before the others. Usually I am slow in the morning- we are all slow. But I am trying to be faster, and I know that this is one of the secrets of doing big miles- getting up fast and on the trail by dawn. But it's hard.

Just past the cave, the wind returns and batters me. I follow a steep side trail downhill, the path turns into a dim grassy road, and there is the spring, trickling from a hose into a huge plastic tub. I stoop to fill my bottles, shivering. It's damp and cold at the spring, and I can't get warm. The cold wind yesterday took all the warmth from me, and I can't seem to get it back. And I used the last of my energy too. I feel as though I have nothing left for today. After filling my bottles I sit on the path and eat my cold oatmeal, then dig through my food bag- all the food I have left until Idyllwild is a salami log and some stale chocolate that has melted and rehardened a dozen times. The day's hike consists of steep climb after steep climb after steep climb, for fourteen more miles, and then a nearly three mile descent to the road. Well, I think. Well.

The path is rocky and narrow, and all day the wind blows. I drag myself forward with infinite slowness, stopping constantly to drink water, to re-tie my shoelaces, to try and suck the warmth from a single rectangle of sunlight. T-Rex passes me, then Rocky, and I don't know where HairTie is. For hours I see no one. I'm the only one on this mountain, I think. I look down the steep, rocky slopes to the convoluted foothills below, feeling as though the wind will blow me off my feet. I'm climbing at eight thousand feet, then ten thousand, then back to eight. I feel nauseous and I don't know why.

I try to eat my salami but then remember that I gave my knife to HairTie in the morning to cut the tape for her blisters. I sit on a rock in the dust and open the salami package with my teeth, tearing at the casing with my fingernails. The meat is oily and salty and I eat half of it in big bites, folding the rest carefully away. The food doesn't help my nausea, but at least I won't be hungry. Altitude sickness, I think. I've got myself some altitude sickness.

There's not enough blood in my blood, I think.

I'm having a low moment, I think an hour later, when I am sitting next to the trail again, unable to move.

As I hike on, exhausted, my anxiety overwhelms me- I think about situations that anger me, ways that everything could go terribly wrong. About things that I have no control over. I am overcome with crashing waves of my own anger- I am suddenly angry at everything, at life itself, angry at the mountains and all humans everywhere. There is no outlet for my anger, nothing for me to rage upon. It's just me, alone on the mountaintop, dizzy and nauseous and fatigued, moving my legs by sheer force of will.

If I can just get down the mountain, I think. My friends, who are more organized than I am, had the foresight to make a reservation for us at the

Idyllwild Inn. A little cabin with space for the whole group. I've never been to Idyllwild. I have no idea what to expect. I imagine a hot bath, a soft bed, a giant pile of food. I feel overwhelmed by my desire for these things. I lose myself in my longing for them, imagine how they will taste and smell and feel, but when I come back into my body I am still on the rocky path, stumbling along alone at eight thousand feet, the wind beating me and the earth dropping away on both sides into nothingness.

Everything is fine, I tell myself. *Forever and ever and ever.*

In the early afternoon I reach the Devil's Slide trail, which switchbacks down through the steep pine forest into Idyllwild. A couple more miles miles, I tell myself. Just a few miles more. My whole body hurts- all my muscles and tendons and joints are crying out, and so I descend slowly so as not to jostle myself too badly. Going down is so hard, I think. So hard when you are sore. Dayhikers from Idyllwild pass me on their way up the switchbacks. I can smell their shampoo and laundry detergent, their hopes and dreams and fears. They stare at me, the dirty windburned person mincing slowly down the trail. I frown back at them. You have no idea how big my desires are, I think.

By the time I reach the trailhead parking lot I am nearly having an anxiety attack. I get this way, I realize, right before I am about to get the thing that I have been anticipating for dozens of miles. What if I don't get it? What if none of it actually comes to be? Oh my god oh my god oh my god.

The parking lot is wide and flat and I can't see the end of it. I choose a direction and begin to walk, looking for the road, but then the lot just ends, and the thought that I have walked for five minutes in the wrong direction fills me with horror. I cut across some brush to the road and stick my thumb out. The day hikers drive past without slowing. Then, after a moment, a sedan appears. A teenage boy is driving.

"You need a ride to town?" he asks.

"Yeah," I say. "How did you know?"

"I hiked the PCT last year," he says. "Me and my brother came up here to go climbing. Today we're just driving around looking for hiker trash."

The boy's name is Minor. I get in the car. My head is buzzing.

"Thank you," I say, overcome.

"You want a Dr. Pepper?" he says.

Minor drops me at the Idyllwild Inn. It has just begun to rain. I limp to cabin 15 and push open the door. The room is dark and quiet. There is a big couch, an easy chair, a fireplace with a stack of wood. A small kitchen with a table and four chairs. In the back is a bedroom. T-Rex and Rocky are in bed, fresh from the shower.

"You made it!" they say.

HairTie appears a moment later. She was just behind me, apparently, but we didn't see each other all day. She is haggard and windburned, scraps of fabric hanging off her pack as though the mountain has shredded her.

"There are no words," she says. "No words for today."

It takes me a long time to wash the dirt from my legs. After showering I stretch, drink a large volume of water, and take a couple of ibuprofen. HairTie has some ginger tea she's been carrying for almost two hundred miles, and she lets me brew a cup.

"I can't believe we have a kitchen," I say, marveling at the little fridge, the range, the drawer of cutlery.

"And a fire!" says HairTie. "We can make a fire!"

T-Rex and Rocky go across the street to get pizza, and HairTie and I limp in the rain to the grocery store. It's a small store, sort of yellowed inside, the food piled haphazardly on the shelves. I buy two bunches of kale, three apples, six eggs, three avocados, a bag of tortilla chips, a jar of cheap salsa, a lime, a tub of chicken salad from the deli, and a container of chocolate pudding. HairTie buys kale, eggs, celery, apples, peanut butter and Ritz Bitz cheese sandwiches. On the way back to the cabin, we pass the pizza place. T-Rex is sitting at a table outside, comatose.

"I ate two pizzas," she says. "I ate two whole pizzas."

I order a gluten-free pepperoni pizza, and HairTie orders one with basil on it. We eat our pizzas back at the cabin with the heat cranked way up and then I sit in the easy chair, a big fleece blanket wrapped a hundred times around me.

"I feel so happy here," I say. "I don't think I ever want to walk again."

Outside the rain falls harder. It's Sunday, and we plan to stay at the cabin until Tuesday, until the storm passes. I shiver, deep in my blanket, as I think of the hikers still up on the mountain. It'll be snowing up there, way up on the rocky passes.

Rocky and T-Rex have the bed in back, so HairTie and I get the foldout sofa. We start a fire and then climb onto the worn mattress, pulling the blankets over us. The cabin is dark, and Rocky is snoring in the other room.

"Do you want to cuddle?" I say to HairTie.

"Yeah," she says. I wrap my arms around her and press my face against back of her neck. She smells like hotel soap and the mountains, like wind and fabric softener. The fire is yellow at our feet, the room dark and warm. I feel as though I've fallen into a soft pit of euphoria. HairTie turns and we kiss. I run my hands under her shirt, over her hot skin. We are alone, the two of us, here in this mountain wilderness. In this strange cabin far from everything. On this journey.

"I'm on a cloud," I say. "I feel like I'm on a cloud. Do you feel it?"

***

I wake at dawn on the sofa bed and get up to crank the heat. I wear a fleece blanket like a cloak as I scramble eggs and kale. I was so cold the day before; I never want to be cold again. HairTie gets up and blearily puts on water for tea. Her hair is wild around her head and her cheeks are windburned; she looks feral, as though she lives in a cave on the mountainside. She looks beautiful. We sit in the light from the window, eating breakfast and quietly running errands on our phones. The rain is coming down hard outside and the world is grey; we were very lucky to make it over the mountains before the storm. Now we have a perfect rainy day for this zero in our warm little cabin in a mountain town.

A zero is a day where you don't hike any miles at all. I am very excited to have my first real zero.

I write a million emails and pay some bills, trying manically to deal with the real-world business that piles up when you're away. I don't want to write emails; I don't want to do internet errands. Everything but this feels so far away; I just want to think about hiking. But what can you do.

The heat pumps merrily from the wall heater. I move to the recliner by the fireplace, blanket still wrapped around me, and put my feet up on the footrest. I can hear the rain outside. I am so happy I can hardly stand it.

Rocky and T-Rex get up and we go on a family field trip to the post office across the street, limping on our sore feet in the cold drizzle. I have my Frogg Toggs rain jacket on. It's the first time that I've unfolded it from its little square. Frogg Toggs are super cheap rain jackets that are lighter than any other rain jacket; they feel as though they're made of paper. Once I unfolded the jacket I discovered that it is huge. It's like a tent on me and I feel ridiculous, walking past all the other hikers sitting at the pizza shop.

Stop feeling ridiculous, I think. Forget about your dignity. Nobody cares.

At the little post office, we pick up the boxes we mailed ourselves from home- "Welcome to Idyllwild!" say the postal clerks- "sign our trail register?" and haul them back to the cabin, where we spread our loot on every available surface. Then we begin the long chore of sorting the goods and objects we'll need for the next hundred-mile stretch of our journey.

I cook a pan of vegetables and eat them. I eat the chicken salad and the apples and the chocolate pudding. T-Rex and Rocky eat more pizza, and bring home a giant cinnamon roll. I eat some of the cinnamon roll, some Reeses Pieces, and a bunch of HairTie's Ritz Bitz sandwiches. I space out for a while, curled up in the recliner in my fleece blanket.

HairTie and I walk in the rain along the highway to the thrift store. HairTie needs a new hiking shirt. Her blue silk shirt now looks, according to Rocky, as though she dug it up from a riverbed.

The thrift store is a ways down the highway, in a little log building called the "help center". Inside locals shuffle about, looking for this or that. Outdated kitten calendars, scuffed tupperware. Lamps missing hardware. We rifle through the racks. We're looking for a cotton-poly blend button-down shirt, because those are cheap and good sun protection for the desert. But the only thing we find is a giant polyester leopard-print blouse. HairTie pulls the blouse over her head and it hangs off her shoulder. You can see light through it.

"It's perfect," says HairTie.

We also find a white dress with bright flowers and a green silk skirt.

"Let's get these too!" I say. "We can wear them at dinner."

For dinner, we make the gluten-free pasta from my resupply box with vegetables and roast chicken from the dusty little grocery store. T-Rex puts on the white dress and Rocky wears the giant leopard-print shirt. After dinner we make a fire in the fireplace and HairTie burns her blue silk shirt in a vaguely symbolic way. Instead of bursting into flames, as we had imagined it would, the shirt melts onto the logs and then disappears.

I take a bath. The water is too hot, but I make myself stay in it. Afterward I am bleary with fatigue and I fall into the sofa bed, blanket wrapped around me. HairTie sits up, smoking a joint.

"You want to hear a story?" she says.

"Yeah," I say.

"One time I had to go get a guy from the morgue," she says, "so they could take out his eyes."

***

The next day is a nero, which is a day where you only hike for a couple of hours. We hang out in Idyllwild until the afternoon, sitting in the pizza shop eating marshmallow cookies and celery and roast chicken and eavesdropping on other people's conversations. At the table next to us is a family having pizza. The mother and father are leathery from the sun and their hair is bleached a stiff blonde. The little boy plays with a plastic billy club.

"Do you know why I'm upset right now?" says the mother to the boy. "I'm upset because my pizza's cold because I had to cut up your food for you." A few minutes later. she turns to the father. "Why are you so stupid?" she says to him.

After they finish eating, the family goes outside and gets into the biggest pickup truck that any of us has ever seen. HairTie notices that the boy left his billy club on the table, and she runs outside to return it to him.

"People in this town are so weird," I say.

"Yeah," says T-Rex.

The health food store is a little shop across the parking lot from the pizza place. A big yellow banner out front says "WELCOME PCT HIKERS." Inside, the shelves are half empty and some limp kale is mounded in a cooler. This morning I bought emergenC, a cherry chia kombucha, and a package of gluten-free graham crackers. Now I eat the graham crackers one by one while we sit in the pizza place, watching the rain. The storm was supposed to blow over the night before, but it's still beating itself out in the mountains. I sit eating my graham crackers, feeling like a spring all wound up inside myself, ready to burst. It's time to hike again, weather be damned.

An hour later we are back on the steep trail up to the PCT, wearing all of our layers, our breath misting in the cold air. I feel incredible after my two days of rest- all I've been doing is eating and sitting and getting strong. Hike hike hike hike hike! I think as I happily bound up the trail and into the pine forest. And all of the pain in my feet is gone!

When we reach the saddle where the side trail rejoins the PCT we find ourselves suddenly in a land of white. Snow! There is a dusting of snow on the ground! The needles on the pine trees are frozen into clusters of icicles, and the icicles sparkle in the long yellow light. We jump up and down, waving our arms in the air. Snow! An enchanted land of winter! We follow the path as it winds up the mountain, looking at the animal tracks on the trail. And then we're on top of everything, looking down at a sea of clouds, little mountain peaks sticking out here and there like islands.

"It's like we're in an airplane," says HairTie.

At dusk we reach our campsite and pitch our tents, shivering in the cold. I sit in the door to my shelter, stirring my dinner in its little pot, watching frost settle over everything.

"You want to share a tent?" says HairTie, to me. Her one-person tent is a little bigger than mine; we can probably both squeeze inside of it.

"Yeah," I say. I drag my bedroll to her tent and crawl in through the vestibule. It's warm and close inside and I scooch into my sleeping bag and wrap my arms around HairTie, pressing my face to the back of her neck. She smells like salt and hotel soap. I don't feel cold anymore.

The next day, I know, we'll come down off the mountains and descend again into the desert valley. These little pine forests are anomalies, high-elevation islands of magic. In the seven hundred miles it will take us to work our way through the desert, we'll go up into the mountains and then down into the valleys, up into the mountains and then down into the valleys, again and again. And as difficult as it was to cross the desert floor that first time, I am looking forward to it now. I am getting better at dealing with the heat, with the lack of water, with the long miles. I am getting better at dealing with everything.

I am getting stronger. I can feel it.

***

It's one of the coldest nights we've had on the trail. Twenty something degrees. In the morning we shiver from our sleeping bags and crouch to eat bits of food with numb fingers, staring out at the frozen world.

We hike in our down jackets, our precious single layer of warmth, our feet crunching on the frozen trail. The sun rises and the light shoots through the ice that clings to the trees. In a few hours we'll begin our long descent, a fourteen-mile waterless stretch that's been so hot at times that hikers have had to be airlifted off the trail. But today the mountain is covered in a dusting of snow and there is meltwater trickling everywhere- it's hard to imagine the heat of the desert.

I stop to fill my bottles at a burbling stream and sit in a patch of sunlight, eating pepitas. I decided, after the first week, that pepitas taste disgusting-sort of like woodchips and then every now and then you get one that tastes like mold. But I sent a pound of them to myself in every resupply box, and they are one of the highest protein foods I have. So I've suffered through them, and then in Idyllwild I discovered something that turned them from a pulpy burden into an exciting trailsnack that I just can't wait to eat- Reeses Pieces. In a couple of weeks I'll go off pepitas entirely, and then, eventually, all other nuts. But for now they still make me happy.

I get a liter of water at the stream. There's another stream in a few miles, in a little meadow next to a dirt parking area, and although the meadow stream is seasonal I figure that today of all days, with the melting snow everywhere, that stream will have water. I'll fill up there for the long descent to the desert floor.

The clusters of pine needles on the trees are each encased in a hunk of ice the size of a stick of butter, and as I walk the sun hits these blocks and they began to fall, all at once and in huge bunches. My hike becomes a bit like a video game, as I dart along the trail attempting to avoid the things that are crashing from the sky. I put on my wide-brimmed hat for protection and laugh out loud.

I get to the dirt parking area and HairTie, T-Rex, and Rocky are there, their things spread out across the picnic tables to dry. All of our stuff is wet from condensation the night before. I take my bottles and walk through the woods to the little meadow where the stream will be, but there is no stream there, just a patch of brittle grass and some tufts of white wildflowers. The next water source is fourteen miles away- a drinking fountain, of all things, at the very bottom of the mountain.

Well, I think. Well.

On the ground beneath the pine trees are the clumps of ice chunks that have fallen from the needles. I break up this ice with my fist, stuffing it into my bottles. This makes me feel happy and resourceful. I woke this morning feeling just great, and now the idea of hiking fourteen miles on not much water seems more like an adventure than anything else.

I fill one plastic gatorade bottle, shaking it to compact the ice. Then I add the last of the liquid water that I have, about a half liter, and it fills in the spaces in the ice until the bottle is full. So that means that a liter of crushed ice makes about a half a liter of water, I think. Maybe less because the ice will lose volume as it melts.

I fill my other gatorade bottle with crushed ice. Now I'll have about a liter and a half of water, once everything is melted and accounted for. A liter and a half for fourteen miles. I feel excited. I usually carry a lot of water, much more than anyone else. I've been wanting to get over my fear of not carrying enough water, and today the odds are in my favor; it's cool and overcast, and the trail is downhill all the way. I can totally do this. No problem.

I don't wait for the others, who filled to capacity at the last stream and so have plenty of water. I have to get to the bottom of the mountain. A few minutes after leaving the dirt parking area the trail turns a corner and suddenly the pine forest is gone- I'm back in the burnt desert, the path strewn with rocks, and I can see the mountain falling away, all the way down to a flat dusty valley. On the other side of the valley are more mountains, partly cloaked in smog. Rows of wind turbines march across the valley floor. As I walk, I imagine that I am leaving the enchanted mountains and descending into the windy valley of a dark lord.

The trail is nicely graded if stuck all over with rocks and I am walking quickly, feeling good. Now and then I take a sip of my water. One bottle has dirt and bits of sand mixed in with the snow, and the other has pine needles and tastes like the forest. Both bottles are gross in their own way and I alternate between them. I race down the switchbacks, thinking about things that make me happy. I thank the universe for the clouds, for the fact that we missed the brunt of the storm and caught the nice cool edge of it. I don't see any other hikers; I haven't seen anyone at all for hours. As I descend the rocks become huge rust-colored boulders, arranged as though frozen in mid-avalanche. Some of the boulders look like faces, or strange animals, or huge clamshells. There are little caves tucked between them, and in the limestone ones are bowl-shaped holes, made by the indigenous people grinding seeds and things over thousands and thousands of years. Magic desert, I think. Magic magic magic.

After several hours, I come upon a Japanese man mincing slowly down the mountain. His name is Toyo, and he is seventy-one years old.

"Only eight more miles to water," I say to him.

"Eight?" he says. "Eight more miles to water?"

"Maybe six," I say.

"Maybe six," I hear him repeat as I pass.

A moment later I reach mile 200. I think about how hard that first hundred miles were, what an epic undertaking it seemed. These second hundred miles, I feel, have flown past by comparison. By god, I think. I am getting better at this.

As I walk my feet began to hurt a little, my knees, even my tendinitis. Long descents, especially on rocky trail, are brutal on my body. I take some ibuprofen. Gotta make it down this mountain, I think. Just gotta make it down the mountain. I am thirsty but I am rationing my water, taking little sips whenever I want them, and I'm not uncomfortable yet.

Five miles before the water fountain, I feel my body slowing down. I'm trying to stay focused on the trail but I keep getting distracted- gazing off at the windmills, looking at the rocks, wondering about the bright beetles on the path. *Stop and rest,* my body is saying. *Take a break for a little while.* Today will be a twenty-two mile day, my longest yet. I'm tired and thirsty and my feet and joints are screaming at me, even through the ibuprofen. I have about an inch of water left in my bottles.

No breaks, I say to myself. *Just walk, Carrot. Walk as fast as you can.*

The last three miles are like pushing through molasses; my body wants to slow down so bad, to stop, to lie in the shade next to a rock. But I need to get to that water fountain, and fast. I begin to have a bit of a spiritual experience.

You're already at the water fountain, I tell myself. *All of this has already happened. Your whole life has already happened. There is no time, and yet isn't it incredible to be here, on this dusty trail, in this body, in May of 2013?*

I feel lonely, and I wish I had someone to talk to. I wonder how far the others are behind me. I stop to pee and just then there is another hiker, rounding the bend behind me. I sling my pack onto my back and then he's right next to me.

"How's it going?" I say.

"Just chillin," he says. "Trying to get down off this mountain." He has trekking poles and the smallest pack I've ever seen. He's wearing a button-down shirt and long desert pants. He passes me and races on down the trail, his poles clack clack clacking. He's so fast! I think. I decide that I will try to keep up with him. I want to talk to him, to ask him if he hiked all the way from Idyllwild today. I want to ask him how he goes so fast, and how he got his pack so small.

I walk as fast as I can, trying to keep him in sight, but each time I round a bend he is a little farther away. No! I think. Come back! And then he is gone, this mysterious person, and it is just me, alone in the desert again.

The wind picks up in the last two miles to the fountain, adding another challenge to my walk. I clutch my hat, terrified to lose it, and stagger forward. Walk, Carrot, I think. Walk walk walk. The valley is close now, the eerily churning windmills, the smog and the hazy mountains in the distance. And then I turn a corner and I can see the fountain below me, and the tiny figures of three hikers clustered around it, their shirts flapping in the wind. One of them, I know, was the speedy hiker. Wait for me! I think. In that moment I feel as though this hiker is some sort of oracle, as though he will have all of the answers I seek. But as I make my way down I see the figures shoulder their packs and walk away.

And then I am at the fountain, and I am holding my bottle up to the little nozzle, and the wind is spraying the arc of water all over the desert, making it hilariously difficult to fill my bottle. And then I am sitting in the dirt, quietly drinking a liter of water, feeling the anxiety and the thirst lift from me like ghosts. Bright ghosts floating away and then I am just me, sitting in the dirt, as though I've always been here. As though I've been here all afternoon. My phone still has battery power and I fumble with it, texting the others. *Will you make it to the fountain? Are you camping down here or on the mountain?*

T-Rex texts me back- they're camping a mile up the trail. They found a cache hidden at the dirt parking area after I left, and they have plenty of water. HairTie, though, will make it. It's dusk, and I sit on my sleeping pad and wash my feet with a little water and my hanky. Then HairTie appears, windblown and practically limping, and we walk a little ways to a flat spot and spread our groundsheets in the sand. It's warm, and the stars come out, and the small red lights of the windmills blink across the valley. It feels special, just the two of us here, eating our little pots of food in the sand. By and by we unfurl our bedrolls and go to sleep, warm in our bags in the endless desert.

***

In the morning, we're filling our bottles at the fountain when Rocky and T-Rex appear. The four of us stretch a little, eat a snack, and emotionally prepare ourselves for the long slog across the windy valley of the dark lord. The sky is bright and hazy, the sand hot beneath our feet, and the wind turbines churn eerily on the hilltops. As we walk we cross beneath powerlines and skirt the edges of strange construction projects; in the distance is a highway.

We reach an underpass in whose deep shade are coolers of soda and beer; we sit in the dirt and drink 7up and then we slog on through the sand.

A few miles later we see a sign stuck in the ground- *Trail angels ahead!* it says. *Ziggy and the Bear's.*

But what does that mean? I think.

We follow a short side trail to a tall white fence and into the backyard of a little house; there are carpets stretched across the ground and big canvas canopies for shade. A tall man with beautiful blonde hair named Cool Ranch pours buckets of hot water into Epsom salt footbaths for us. The footbaths, he says, are mandatory.

I feel alarmed by the mandatory footbaths. *Relax, Carrot*, I say to myself. *It's just a footbath.*

I sit in a lawn chair with my feet in the water, bewildered, and watch as other hikers trickle in. When noone is looking I abandon my foot-bath and take a shower, which finally soothes me. I dig through the hiker box. I eat a snickers bar and two chocolate pudding cups and make a little pot of food. There is a Burger King run, which produces a large order of fries. I wash my laundry in the sink on the side of the house, mashing my socks against each other with plenty of soap. I lie on my stomach on the carpets as my laundry dries instantly in the wind. Overhead the sky curdles into thunderstorms, and a little rain falls. In the afternoon we pack up our things and set out again towards the rolling foothills of the mountains.

We are inching up into a dry and dusty canyon. I can see Rocky up ahead on top of the ridge, backlit with light. What's up there? I think. What's beyond this strange dusty place?

I reach the top of the ridge and see that the cloudy haze is gone; beyond the ridge clear yellow sun shines down on mountains the color of old velvet. We have gone beyond the wind turbines, the dusty valley; we are on the other side of all that, in some sort of enchanted land, some secret place beyond everything. *The San Gorgonio Wilderness!* proclaims a small wooden sign.

We amble over the foothills and down into a wide white riverbed; a twisting stream winds through the valley and its banks are crowded with green plants and the air smells of flowers. The canyon rises up on both sides of us; Rocky points at some bighorn sheep, but I can't see them. The light is doing crazy things with the sun at the end of the canyon.

We reach a row of small buildings that once was a trout hatchery but is now a preservation center of sorts; we camp in a long lawn scattered with picnic tables. There are no people anywhere and the animals are all around us, watching from the edges of things; frogs croak and rabbits dart and Rocky and T-Rex even say they saw a bobcat on the trail.

Dark falls and it starts to rain. I erect my shelter and rest my pack in the dry sand beneath a giant oak tree. HairTie, who was hiking at the back of the group, hasn't yet arrived- Rocky and I go out onto the dark riverbed to look for her. She appears suddenly, panting and disheveled; she missed the turn for the campsite and walked an extra two miles on the trail and had to backtrack in the dark.

"You got here fast!" I say.

"I ran," says HairTie.

"I'm glad you're not lost," I say.

I climb into my tent to sleep and find that it is full of ants. The ants cling to the mesh and the walls; I smush them with my hanky but they are everywhere. I kill two dozen but more appear. The ants smell like floor cleaner when I crush them.

At last I give up. *I am going to go to sleep,* I say, *and I am going to pretend that there are no ants.* I switch off my headlamp and start to drift off; I switch the light back on and the ants are gone. I lift up my shoe, my water bottle, and there they are- clustered together, hiding. Sleeping or being dormant or whatever it is that ants do.

"Goodnight ants," I say.

***

In the morning we hike slowly up the gray riverbed, following the winding stream to its source. The clouds blow apart and the sun bursts through; suddenly we are on top of the hills looking down at the canyon and it is very, very hot. The path is steep and there is no shade. I hike fast because I only have a little water; I stare at the ground and move my legs. I am finding my stride. I am getting faster.

The trail switchbacks down the dusty hillside and then, at the bottom, there is a shallow stream. The stream is clear and cool and it makes a burbling sound. A few oaks bend over the stream, making a chunk of shade.

"Heaven!" I say.

T-Rex and I sit in the stream in our clothes, splashing the cool water over our laps. We lie down in the water. We put our heads in it.

Rocky and HairTie arrive and we make lunch in the patch of dappled shade beneath the oak tree. Another hiker named Brian appears and announces that it is one hundred degrees. He has some dried tilapia that he marinated in tumeric and he gives each of us a chunk to eat. "Tumeric is an anti-imflamatory," he says.

Water is sparse. We are using all sorts of apps and bits of paper to figure out where the water is, and today all our sources are wrong. At dusk we find ourselves looking for a place to camp, almost out of water. There is a stream in the vicinity but we can't seem to reach it, no matter how far we walk. At last we round a corner and there in a gully is a spring that burbles up from the sand. Above the spring is a flat space to camp. There is already a tent there. The flap zips open and a little head pokes out. Toyo! It's Toyo.

We spread out our things and sit on the ground, eating bits of food. We are all running low on food. I squeeze Nutella onto a few graham crackers. Rocky makes instant cheesecake in a plastic bag. Somehow I ate a four-pound bag of trail mix in just two days, and the others seem to be living on bars alone. In two more days we'll be in Big Bear, where we can resupply; we just have to make it until then.

***

Someone's alarm goes off at 5 a.m. and I sit upright in my bag. It's dark and the crickets are doing their thing. I fumble through my pack, eat some dark chocolate and my last piece of jerky and then step carefully across the thorny ground to the trail, where I squat and pee. It's cold.

We are hiking in this cold, bodies stiff, but when the sun breaches the hills and touches us we are instantly hot. I pull off my layers as we climb up, up, up, out of the scrubby sandy desert and into the cool fragrant pine forest. I stop to rest and fill my water at a stream with the others. I eat the last of the almonds in my trail mix.

"Only the prunes remain," I say, displaying what's left in my gallon ziploc bag.

We decide that this is the name of Rocky's metal band- "Only the prunes remain."

T-Rex is sitting in the dirt, mixing instant coffee with stream water in a plastic soda bottle. She and HairTie are talking about the summer they spent working at a camp in rural Maine for the children of the very wealthy. Eddie Murphy's son was there.

"I don't want to watch Shrek," he said. "My dad is the gay-ass donkey." Then they'd gone to the mall and the boy had spent seven thousand dollars on shoes. Another girl had her horse flown in from France so that she didn't have to ride the camp horse.

"What's airport security?" another girl had asked. She'd only flown in her family's private jet.

Steam pipes out from under the piece of folded aluminum foil that serves as my pot lid; my water is boiling. I add the last of my dried vegetables to make a thin soup. I look in my food bag- I have only some dried mango and a few spoonfuls of peanut butter left, and a salami. I figure I'll save the salami for the morning, for the final ten miles into Big Bear.

A hiker arrives at the stream and removes his cap. It's Toyo! Toyo sits carefully on a rock and leans his pack against his legs. I offer him some dried mango, which he accepts with much enthusiasm. After a while he hikes on.

"He looks like he's eighteen," says T-Rex, of the seventy-one year old. "He looks like he's eighteen years old."

We climb and climb. I walk alone for much of the day, feeling a little sick from the altitude. The trail crossed a road and there are some animal cages- rectangular chain-link pens the size of a bedroom, no protection from the sun. A grizzly bear pacing, another grizzly bear standing perfectly still, head hanging in the heat. I set my pack on the ground and look at them. Grizzly bear pacing, grizzly bear hanging his head in the heat. No people anywhere; no caregivers, no stimulation. Two big strong animals, driven insane by sensory deprivation and neglect. These animals have been in movies. Now they are "retired." I can feel their suffering, like a palpable sensation in my own body.

I have to keep hiking, I think.

A little while later I happen upon a cluster of coolers overlooked a big ravine. Inside the coolers are Mountain Dew, Pepsi, and Pabst Blue Ribbon, floating in what once was ice. We're getting close to Big Bear, and all the lodging establishments are competing for the favor of the hikers. The names of the motels, hostels, and trail angels are scrawled in thick black marker on the sides of the coolers. I put a PBR in the mesh pocket of my pack for later.

In a mile is another cache, several cases of soda next to an overstuffed recliner, footrest tipped towards the incredible view. I sit in the recliner for a bit. Someone hauled this onto the mountaintop, I think.

Our plan is to camp at a little campground down the mountain a bit where there is water. Dusk is settling over the land and I walk quickly, running a little on the downhills. I'm imagining the food in Big Bear, thinking of all the things I can eat. A giant salad, I've decided. A giant salad with, like, a roast chicken on it.

I reach the dusty little campsite before the others and sit at the picnic table in the last of the light with my quilt wrapped around me, drinking the PBR. There is nothing more glorious, I decide, when one is thru-hiking, than a picnic table. Except maybe sitting at a picnic table by yourself in the gloaming, drinking a cheap beer after walking twenty-one miles.

Twenty-one miles. I've just walked twenty-one miles. By god, and I don't even hurt.

T-Rex and Rocky and HairTie roll in, looking dusty and bright.

"That wasn't bad," says T-Rex.

"Twenty-one miles," I say. "Bam, no big deal!"

Other hikers trickle in with their loud voices and churning limbs, and HairTie and I wander to the edge of camp and spread our groundsheets in the dirt.

"My feet don't even hurt," I say to HairTie, as we lie next to each other watching the stars come out. "I can't believe it."

***

The pain wakes me in the night; an aching burn radiating from my knees down my calves and into my feet. I lie curled on my sleeping pad on the hard ground, my quilt pulled over my head to keep out the drafts. Why can't I sleep, I think. And when will my joints adjust to all this. When will the aching stop.

Dawn arrives like an icicle so I keep the quilt up over my head. I hear the swish-swish of hikers passing on the trail, headed to Big Bear. By the time I'm up and packed and ready to go, it's seven thirty and the whole campsite is empty. HairTie pokes her head out of her sleeping bag. She looks confused.

"It was so cold last night," she says.

I have half a liter of water left. In my bleary morning state, I read on my map that there was a cache a mile down the trail; of course, after setting out I look at my map and there is no cache until the road in ten miles. Ten miles on half a liter of water, I think, as the sun breaks over the hills and the air becomes stifling hot and there is no shade. Why do I do this to myself.

Because of thirst, I am magically able to hike ten miles in three hours. At the road, someone has dragged a rotted cushion into a patch of shade and left a case of Squirt and a six pack of dark beer. I sit on the cushion, happily drinking squirt and waiting for HairTie, who appears a moment later. We walk out into the road as if to hitchhike but right away a man pulls up and pops the trunk on his rental car. In the trunk is a case of Gatorade and a huge bag of mini Snickers bars.

The man's name is Timmer, and he's feeding hikers candy and shuttling them into Big Bear out of the goodness of his heart.

"You want some Snickers?" he says.

"Really?" I say. "I can eat these Snickers?" All I had for breakfast was four slices of salami, the last of my food. Hours ago.

I sit in the front seat and eat a fistful of mini Snickers. Timmer hands me a bag of a peanut M&M's and I eat some of those too. Food, I think. Everything is food.

The hostel is swarming with hikers and bright light. We drop our packs on the deck. I am overwhelmed and panicky and my blood sugar is doing crazy things.

My phone blerps- T-Rex and Rocky are eating breakfast at a greasy spoon down the road. We set out down the broad boulevard, unsure where the restaurant is or how far. The cars rush past us, our dirty clothes blow in the wind. I can feel the heat of the concrete through the soles of my shoes.

We walk for so long, it becomes inconceivable that we will ever reach the restaurant. At last we see it in the distance, a squat brick building in a sea of asphalt, and the small figures of Rocky and T-Rex, leaving.

"But we just got here," I say when we reach them. I feel heartbroken. Inside the greasy spoon it's insufferably hot and I look sadly at the menu.

"I don't even want breakfast food," I say.

Nothing is right and there aren't any answers. The waitress sets down weeping tumblers of ice water. She has many eyebrow piercings and is wearing blue eyeshadow layered over sparkly purple eyeshadow. I order a massive, greasy plate of eggs and hashbrowns and bacon. HairTie gets eggs and hashbrowns and corned beef hash, which I can't conceptualize. My eggs are like liquid, my bacon tastes like salt, and the hashbrowns are crispy and perfect. Afterward I feel ill, but at least I am no longer hungry.

Back at the hostel we cart our things to the basement room that the four of us will share. It's dim and mercifully cool and lit with a bank of florescent lights. There are two sets of bunkbeds. In the bathroom I peel off my clothes and stare in the mirror, astonished by how dirty I am. When I am in the nature I don't feel dirty, I just feel kind of like everything else around me. Now I see that each exposed pore is stuffed with dirt. And sunburn too.

I plunge my laundry in the tub and rinse it, but the water won't run clear. Above the open window in our room is a curtain rod, and I hang my things there to dry. Outside is the constant dripping noise of a sprinkler, and I can see the feet of people sitting on the patio.

Another trail angel named Aloha gives us a ride to the supermarket in town. The supermarket is massive and strangely arranged, like a labyrinth. We wander around, disoriented, touching things and putting them in baskets. For some reason I buy a bunch of Payday bars. *I like these,* is the thought that goes through my head.

Back at the hostel a raging party is underway. We hide in our basement room. Through the walls we can hear the sounds of drinking and disordered shouting.

"Is the door locked?" says Rocky. "Can you lock the door?"

In the morning, we'll start the next section- one hundred and three miles to Wrightwood. I propose my plan to the others.

"I want to hike twenty-mile days," I say. "Every day. I'm ready."

"Ok," they say.

At the store, HairTie and I bought a roast chicken, and some lettuce, and avocados and cilantro and cucumber and lime, and I am finally able to assemble the fantasy salad of my dreams, sitting cross-legged on the floor of our room. I also eat an entire container of goat yogurt and a small tub of potato salad. And some celery.

After dinner, I spread out my food for the next section. I'm tired of running short on the last day, and so this time I'm bringing extra. As a consequence, my food bag is crazy heavy- will it be too much? It's so hard to know.

Later, laying next to HairTie in the nice soft bunk bed, I can't sleep. It seems that the longer I'm on the trail, the harder it is to come into town. The people, the pavement, the constant noise, the overhead lighting. All of it fills me with anxiety. All of it is too much. Now in the dark room I lie awake, listening to my friends snoring and then not snoring.

Whatever am I going to do with myself, I think.

***

I wake in our basement hostel room before the others and sit in a corner in the dark, looking at the internet on my phone. The sun rises as it tends to do and light seeps through the little window and my friends stir and I remember my tub of yogurt, and the roast chicken, and the cherry chia kombucha, and I am filled with happiness. I sit on the floor in front of the little fridge and eat my breakfast as the others get ready for the day.

71

We reach the trailhead at eleven thirty and immediately take a break to drink water and adjust all of our clothing. My goal is to hike twenty miles today, to a water source on the other side of a bunch of ambiguous contour lines. I set out at last, comfortably uncomfortable, and after a few hours of hiking I sit in some shade and eat one of my Payday bars, which immediately makes me feel sick. Is this food? Why did I buy these? I can't remember.

A few hours later I take another break with T-Rex, Rocky and HairTie, the four of us sprawled out in a little meadow. Two other hikers are there.

"We've passed through three distinct dialects of the mountain chickadee," says one of the hikers.

"What is that bird here that literally says 'Tweet tweet tweet'?" I ask him.

"A black capped chickadee, I think," he says.

A little later I round a bend and the soft pine forest turns to a burn- mountains upon mountains stretching away, stuck all over with the blackened spikes of trees. The undergrowth is a tangle of berry bushes and the light is long, spilling over everything. Suddenly a lizard darts up a tree trunk in front of me, puffs out its bright blue belly, and starts doing pushups.

I have to admit, I am a little intimidated.

This is not my home bioregion, I think. I don't know what sorts of special creatures there are here, and what strange powers they may have.

The sun begins to sink and I walk faster, faster, faster still. The path is soft and gently graded and I don't hurt anywhere. The burnt forest is eerily still in a way that makes me feel as though something is following me. I whip around but of course, there's nothing there. It's just me, alone in the beautiful dusk, my friends a few mountain folds behind me.

The sun quivers like an egg yolk as it sets behind the mountains. I switch on my headlamp for the last half hour of the hike. The trail dips into a little valley and I hear voices and see the lights of other headlamps.

"Hello?" I call, and someone calls back. *Hello!* The camp is an old horse camp- a metal corral in the long grass and a picnic table, glorious thing. I can hear a little brook running nearby.

I sit at the picnic table to assemble my dinner, next to the other hikers, who I can't really see except where their faces are illuminated by their alcohol stoves in the dark. It's eight thirty; I walked twenty miles in nine hours, including a one hour break. And I'm not even in any pain!

I happily stir my pot of food, feeling like a fit little animal who lives in the forest.

I live here, I think. I live here now.

The hikers around me are singing Papa Roach, ironically. *Cut my life into pieces, this is my last resort. Suffocation, no breathing-* but none of us can remember what comes next. Then we're all laughing, our noodles spraying everywhere. I look at the faces, bent over titanium cups of ramen in the dark. Who are these people?

***

Waking to another cold pale dawn, I poke my head from my bag in the freezing dark, sit up and eat a few handfuls of things from my gallon bag of trail mix. My new friends are gone. Beside me, HairTie is still asleep. I drink water, shiver into my hiking clothes. *It'll warm up as soon as the sun hits,* I tell myself. *It'll be so hot I won't be able to stand it.*

The forest is cold then suddenly dry and hot and dusty. Then Deep Creek appears, tumbling gently from a fold in the hills. We walk alongside it, we hop across it on big round stones. The water is clear and bright in the sun and the plants along its edges are soft and green. In some places there are deep tea-colored pools. We haven't seen anything like it yet, this real and persistent body of year-round water- I want to put my whole body into it, I want to lie down beside it on the soft grass and sleep for a hundred years. *The Sierras,* we keep saying. *In the Sierras there will be so much water.* So we keep walking.

Our plan is to stop in the afternoon where a high footbridge crosses the creek and rest through the heat of the day. We don't know what to expect at the bridge- a trickle? A puddle? Will we even be able to reach the water? I walk alone for hours, slowly in the heat.

We reach the tall footbridge above Deep Creek and scramble down the rocks to what is, to our great delight, a beautiful swimming hole and a little

73

sandy beach hung over with cottonwoods. I'm hot, I think, as I drop my pack onto the sand. I've been pushing myself through the heat of the day and I'm flushed and sweaty and covered in dust. I strip off my desert shirt and dunk myself in the cold water. I move my shirt around in the current and wring it out.

Another person appears- it's one of the hikers from the picnic table last night. He's tall and long-limbed, dark facial hair growing in wild. He's got the smallest pack I've ever seen- it looks like he's carrying a daypack.

"How'd you get your pack so small?" I call out to him.

The mysterious hiker just sort of shrugs, and drops his things in the sand.

I stumble dripping onto the riverbank and drape my wet shirt on a hot rock and spread out my foam sleeping pad and sit in the sun. I pour alcohol into my pop-can stove and light it, set on a pot of water to boil.

"Do you have a sleeping pad in there?" I say.

"Yep," he says. He's eating a tiny packet of fruit snacks. When he finishes the packet, he pulls out another. He eats that packet and then produces a third.

"A shelter?"

"Yep."

"Rain jacket?"

"Yep."

"Well, how is your pack so small then," I say.

He shrugs. I look at the fruit snacks.

"What do you eat?" I say.

"Carnation instant breakfast," says the hiker. "Instant coffee. Ramen."

His name is Spark, and he's from Georgia. He's got the most wonderful southern accent. I want to ask him more questions, just to hear him talk. But he seems shy, and I worry that I've already badgered him too much.

"I hiked the Appalachian Trail last year," he says. "Then spent the winter in Bend. I was a cabinet maker. I lived out of my truck."

He eats his fruit snacks and shoulders his pack. I wish I could hike with him, but my water is just beginning to boil. HairTie, T-Rex, and Rocky are asleep in the shade.

"See you down the trail," he says and walks off, his trekking poles stabbing merrily at the sand. He looks so free, with his tiny pack. And this is his second long trail. He must be fast. Wait, I think. Take me with you.

It's five pm when I set out with HairTie to hike again. Our next water source is Deep Creek Hot springs, in ten miles.

We pass mile 300. 300 miles, I think. What is distance, what is time.

We try to imagine what the hot springs will be like. We picture a big parking lot, cracked cement pools, soda cans rolling in the wind. Drunk locals and boom boxes and badly pitched tents.

We've been walking along the dusty hills all day, looking down at the ravine where the creek is. Following it downstream. Now it is dark and the trail looks down at a bright sandy clearing next to the water. We see the light of little headlamps clustered in a pool

"HairTie! Carrot!"

It's T-Rex's voice, but where are we? There are no people here, no parking lot, no boom boxes or tents or piles of trash. There is just the white sand, the creek where it pools among the huge boulders, and, apparently, hot springs.

The hot springs pool is deep and clear and lined with smooth stones. It's the four of us in this magical pool and two other hikers, who hand around a plastic soda bottle of wine they packed in. Above us are the stars.

Our sore bodies melt into the water.

"This is the best thing in the world," I say.

There is a man there, stoned out of his mind, and a gentle dog named Green, or maybe Queen. The dog stands close to the pool and lets us pet her with our wet hands. There are never any dogs on the trail- we miss dogs in an aching way, animal friends, pets in general. One day HairTie and I spent an hour, while walking, just talking about hamsters. The dog's person sits on the edge of the pool, fully clothed, with his feet in the water, and doesn't speak. Later he will spread his sleeping pad on the rocks above the pool and in the morning we will pass him, still sleeping, in his bright red sleeping bag.

I emerge from the springs more relaxed than I can ever remember feeling. I stumble barefoot through the sand to the flat spot where I've dropped my bag. The spine of something sticks in my heel and I rip it out and look at it. There is a little blood there but I don't feel any pain. The calluses on my feet are getting thick.

The sand where I spread my sleeping pad is soft and flat and warm. There is the warm air and the sound of crickets and the burbling stream. My second full twenty-mile day. And tomorrow we'll do another twenty miles, along the Mojave River and beyond into something I can't even imagine. And on and on and on, I think, into forever.

***

I wake; I eat bits of food with my quilt wrapped around me. My food bag is huge- it must still weigh six pounds. I brought way too much food. It's so hard to know.

The hot sun comes out and we hike up the hills above the hotsprings and follow the creek downstream, looking down longingly at all the beautiful turquoise swimming holes. The creek ambles lazily among the boulders, along the little white beaches and under the cottonwoods. We are high above it in the scrubby desert. There are no trails to the swimming holes, no footprints on the little beaches. We are in a sort of wilderness here, and it is wonderful to look down on this wild water. It lifts our spirits. And yet in a way it is an illusion, all of this. It is a little strip of habitat for us to navigate, hidden in the mountains between the sprawling endless cities.

"Where are we?" we asked some young men in fashionable clothing who appeared yesterday at our swimming hole beneath the bridge. "We walked from Mexico and we don't know where we are."

"San Bernadino County," they said.

After a few hours we turn a corner and the illusion of wilderness is broken. The hills peter out into a valley cut with roads; in the space below us is a massive concrete spillway. The river disappears inside it.

It's very hot on the spillway, and the air is filled with dust. Beyond the spillway the trail dips down to where the remnants of the river are, a little clear water running over a riverbed cut with jeep tracks.

We cross the clear water and sit to rest on the sand beneath some bushes, where there is a little dappled shade. We fill our water bottles and eat handfuls of things from our food bags.

There is a rustle near T-Rex; a giant rattlesnake is making its way through the leaves two feet behind her. We stand up and watch the snake wind its body into a coil, its little rattler sticking out.

"Why?" says T-Rex. "Why when I'm trying to eat my lunch?"

We saw another one earlier in the day, curled up on a rock next to the trail.

Suddenly HairTie appears, her leopard-print blouse blowing in the wind.

"I had a standoff with a rattlesnake," she says. "It was across the path and I threw rocks at it, but it wouldn't move. I finally got around it by climbing up onto the boulders."

The others want to rest in the shade. It's still morning, and I want to get farther before the crushing heat of noon, so I set off on my own. After a few hours I find a stream, which has slowed to the point of being just a pool across the path. The bottom of the pool is a gelatinous tangle of frog eggs. I dip my bottles into this pool and then drag my things beneath a scratchy oak tree, into a sandy patch of shade just big enough for my body. I curl up on my side to nap, but I can't. Small insects crawl over me, but they don't bite. I've become part of the desert.

I hear the others pass after a while, and I pack up and head out. I find them after a mile or two, sitting on the trail in the slanting light.

"Hey, you guys," I say, but nobody smiles.

Apparently, they've had a rough couple of miles- Rocky's knee is killing him, and T-Rex's foot pain has grown intolerable. HairTie's shoes are too small and so her feet have recently turned to hamburger.

We're having a low moment.

We'd planned to make it all the way to a lake before dark, but I'm the only one that can walk, right now, without excruciating pain. HairTie takes off her shoes and puts on her flip flops, and the two of us mince slowly down the trail. Rocky and T-Rex don't yet know what they'll do- they want to sit for a moment in the long light and talk it over. We hike with heavy hearts, hoping they can make it to the lake, hoping everything works out.

HairTie and I reach the lake at dusk, a big flat water ringed with mountains. The sun is setting over everything. We walk around the lake to a boat-in picnic site with half a dozen little gazebos. Each gazebo has a picnic table. There are no other people, there are no boats on the lake, there is no one anywhere. Why does it always feel this way? Like we're in some sort of post-industrial collapse? I decide that as thru-hikers, we inhabit a different layer of reality than other people. That's why we never see other people on the trail, why the parks and campground are always empty for us, even in beautiful weather. Why the rest of the world seems so far away.

I dunk myself in the lake and then clamber out, freezing. I rinse my socks in the lake. I pick a bouquet of flowers and stick it in a blue glass Budweiser bottle that I pull from the spilling-over trash. Rocky and T-Rex arrive, sad and quiet, and we all cook our dinners around the table in the dark. While we cook there are surprise gusts of wind, which scatter our food and bits of tin foil across the ground. HairTie's sit pad flies into the lake, and she jumps in the water to retrieve it. And suddenly we are laughing, uproariously, at everything.

***

I wake before dawn and lie in my sleeping bag, watching the sun rise over the lake. I can see HairTie, wriggling like a larva in her sleeping bag a little ways away. Rocky and T-Rex are still fast asleep in their tent on the edge of the water.

Rocky, T-Rex, and HairTie are injured, but I am not. I love hiking with them, laughing with them, camping with them. But we're on a long walk and today, they cannot walk. What is there to do?

In the end I set out into the mountains alone, leaving my friends behind. They'll hitch into Wrightwood on the highway, and once there they'll rest, buy new shoes, and give their injuries some much needed attention. It's a huge relief to know that they're taking care of their injuries, and I'll see them again when I arrive in Wrightwood in two days.

There is a McDonald's on the PCT. Today I walk quickly through the desert, knowing that the junction to this McDonald's is only sixteen miles away. If I can reach McDonald's by one o'clock, I can hide there during the hottest part of the day, eating cheeseburgers.

Cheeseburgers. My stomach is upset this morning, and I feel a little nauseous while I walk. I had stomach pains in the night that woke me up. I've been eating all sorts of crap, lots of processed foods and crazy amounts of sugar. I need to eat better. I need to feel good, so that I can finish the trail. But it's hard. I burn food so fast that hunger is like a monster inside me, overriding any rational thought. I'll eat anything. Absolutely anything.

I won't get any cheeseburgers at McDonald's today, I decide as I walk. I'll get, like, a salad. That's what I really need. Vegetables. I try to visualize this salad, in order to make it more real. But the salad I visualize is the worst salad imaginable. I imagine eating this terrible salad while all my friends eat cheeseburgers. I want to cry.

A few hours later I round a corner and there is a massive freeway. It is the freeway that runs through the desert between L.A. and Las Vegas and it is packed with cars going crazy fast.

I suddenly feel as though there is a tear in my reality, and another reality is leaking through.

Then I see the side trail to McDonald's with its etched wooden trail sign- *McDonald's, .4 miles.*

It's one o'clock. I made it!

The side trail dumps me onto a paved road that parallels the freeway. It is painfully hot on this road, and the air is thick with exhaust. Up ahead are the McDonald's and a gas station, and then the desert again, forever and ever and ever.

A group of hikers are already inside the McDonald's, sitting in a plastic booth. They are surrounded by spent chicken nugget cartons. I drop my pack, wash my hands in the clean bright bathroom, and plug my phone into the outlet below a huge flatscreen TV that is blaring fake news. There are lots of other people in the McDonald's, and I stand in line with these people. I am red from the sun and my clothes are filthy, but the people ignore me. People from all over, transported here via the freeway. I feel as though I am in an intergalactic space station.

I order two double cheeseburgers, a large order of french fries, and some weird lemonade made with fake sugar. I sit with the other hikers, who have been eating for hours. One of them glasses the menu board with his binoculars and reports on his progress.

"I've eaten three thousand calories," he says. "Not counting the several liters of coke."

After finishing my burgers I order a Reeses McFlurry, which has something like seven hundred calories. I eat the icecream slowly, staring in horror at the flat-screen TV. Evil-seeming people and incomprehensible, brightly colored images flash across the screen, accompanied by garbled, too-loud talking. None of it, as far as I can tell, has to do with finding water or navigating mountain ranges on narrow dirt paths. I get up and poke the TV until I find the OFF button.

Fifteen minutes after finishing my icecream I order two more double cheeseburgers. I take the patties out of one burger and add them to the other burger. I give the leftover buns to the hiker with the binoculars, and he eats them. I look down at the unwieldy sandwich as I eat it.

"Fuck,"   I   say   after   I   have   finished.   "Fuck."
I leave the McDonald's in the afternoon and walk back to the PCT, which crosses beneath the freeway in a dim, cool pedestrian tunnel. The underpass is long and dark. Inside, the walls drip with secret water. Then there is a square of light crowded with bright green, like a portal to another world. I emerge through this square into a tangled wood, a clear little brook running along the edge. I hop across the brook on stones and climb out of this lush, secret green place, back into the desert. As I walk into the dusty hills I look back at the freeway and shake my head.

How am I ever going to integrate back into the regular world.

I only feel sick for the first two hours of hiking. Then I dig a hole, take a massive dump and immediately feel better. How efficient my gut is, on the trail. I drop out of the hills to a little valley with cactus and in the center of the valley there is a water cache. The next fourteen miles after the cache, I know, is uphill.

There are a couple of broken plastic lounge chairs at the cache and a small group of hikers- it's Spark, and the other dudes who were singing Papa Roach in the dark at the picnic table. They have paper bags of beer and they're happily drunk. Their safari clothes are stained with sweat and dirt and their hair is tangled from the wind.

"We're the Winfrey boys," says Spark. "We were thinking Oprah Winfrey could sponsor us. We figured she'd buy each of us a car." He had a Gatorade bottle full of Carnation instant breakfast and whey protein mixed with water, and he's shaking it up. "You want to try it?" he says, when he sees me looking at it.

"Nah," I say.

"It's my birthday," says another one of the hikers. He looks to be about seven feet tall, and his hair is in two long braids. "I'm sorry, is that annoying?"

"No," I say. "Happy birthday." I'm painfully sober, and after a moment, the boys forget that I am there. So I fill up my water bottles and hike on.

The trail climbs steeply up the mountain, and there is nowhere flat to camp. At last, at dusk, I come upon a little grassy patch in a dry streambed. The spot is just big enough for my sleeping bag and it feels secret, hidden from the trail. I drink some water and eat some almonds then brush my teeth, spitting onto the dusty ground. I spread out my sleeping pad- it just barely fits beneath the thorny, overhanging branches of a low bush. I lie under my quilt, feeling as though the mountain is cradling me. The sky is hazy with thin, transparent clouds. I live here, I think. In the nature. I walk on the nature and eat on the nature and sleep on the nature.

I am safe.

***

I dream it's raining and I wake in the dark to feel the smallest raindrops on my face, like a cloud is falling on me. The mist-rain doesn't seem too serious so I go back to sleep.

In an hour, a little light is leaking through the clouds. Don is coming, I think. I sit up in my bag and pat it. It's wet, but not all the way through.

I get up, pack my damp things away, and hike in the cold dawn. I am in the cloud and the cloud is all around me. Next to the trail the land falls away to forever, but I cannot see it. Today I will climb for fourteen miles.

I find a flip-flop on the trail. When I reach the water cache halfway up the mountain a couple of hikers are there, sitting in the dirt jeep road, playing music on a little speaker. Their sleeping bags are laid out on the grass to dry. The sun has just begun to peak through the fog.

"Did you lose a flip-flop?" I say.

"Yes!" says one of them.

I cook a meal at the cache on my little alcohol stove, and then hike on. The desert, like it likes to do at high elevation here, turns to beautiful pine forest. Suddenly I am slow, and I feel dizzy, and there is pain in my lungs. Altitude sickness! There isn't enough air in this air.

The higher I climb and the more beautiful the forest becomes, the sicker I feel. Soon I am barely crawling up the mountain. By afternoon, I am nauseous, grumpy and sluggish. I trudge along, lifting one foot in front of the other. Mountaintop-itis, I think. That's what this is.

At the summit of the mountain is a ski resort, closed for the season. It's eerie here. The creepy gondolas are shrouded in fog and there is a big, fenced-off reservoir half-full of brackish water.

Now the trail begins to descend, and steeply. The trail here is like a ditch, filled with rocks, tipping steeply down the mountain.

I am tired and dizzy and irritable and the rocks hurt my feet and I stumble, trying to get to the bottom of the mountain. In just a few hours I'll be in Wrightwood, a little town where I have never been, in a room that T-Rex and HairTie and Rocky, who are already there, have rented. There will be a shower, and I will be able to wash my clothes. There will be a store with wonderful wilted produce and cheap deli potato salad. I will lie in a real bed.

I obsess over these things as I descend with my altitude sickness, wanting them more and more and more. When I finally reach the highway, I am in an awful mood. How will I get to town? Just then a woman appears with three huge malamutes and puts me in the windy bed of her pickup truck. *I was out walking my dogs,* she says.

Wrightwood is a little tourist thing, a couple of shops and restaurants all clustered together next to the highway. People walk along the street and music plays from the doorways of bars. Our room is at the Pines Motel, which is right next to everything, because everything is right next to everything. It's a dim room, cobbled together in some sort of trailer painted to look like a cabin, and the inside walls are thin cardboard-like material painted to look like bricks. HairTie and T-Rex and Rocky are all there, talking loudly, rested and freshly showered, being excited, opening beers. I've been listening to nothing but birdsong for days and staring at the trail, and I feel suddenly, acutely overwhelmed. The music coming from the street is attacking me, the light is attacking me, everything is attacking me. At the store on the way to the motel I bought strawberries, oranges, a roast chicken and a tub of potato salad. At the motel I drop my things on one of the beds (I have a bed!) and shut myself in the bathroom. If I can only shower, I think. If I can only shower then I'll feel all right.

The bathroom is old and dirty and the fixtures are fastened to the tub with what looks like toothpaste. I take off my clothes and jump in the shower and fiddle with the nobs. I turn on the hot water and it's scalding, so I turn on the cold and the water becomes freezing. The hot water, it seems, doesn't work when the cold water is on, and vice versa. Fuck, I think. I've never encountered a hotel shower this awful. I'm wet and shivering, and I turn on the hot water and the it scalds me. I start to cry a little.

After my terrible shower I climb into bed, pull the scratchy comforter over my head and cry a little in secret. The others are laughing and exclaiming, but it's dark and warm under the covers and I just wish I were alone, in a quiet room far away from everything. I want it to be quiet so badly I start to panic. Anxiety anxiety anxiety, coursing through me. I hate being in town. I hate it I hate it I hate it.

After a while, the storm passes and I come out from under the covers, feeling calmer. I sit on the couch with a blanket around me and eat potato salad and strawberries. Rocky is talking about dramatically jumping through the fake brick wall, into the room next door.

"We should do it all at once," he says. "With our arms held out like this." It's time for bed and we pull the janky curtains over the bent and twisted curtain rod. In bed I'm warm and there's a good down pillow, and after a while I sleep.

***

We go to breakfast at the Evergreen Cafe with some other hikers, and during breakfast I fret about whether I should leave. Town stresses me out and I don't really want to take a zero here- I feel strong and I'm not injured, so it seems as though I should keep hiking. But all my friends are here and if I go ahead I won't see them until the small town of Agua Dulce, eighty miles away.

The Evergreen Cafe is a greasy spoon. There are soft focus photographs of children posing with farm animals on the walls and fake daisies hang from the ceiling. I look at the menu with its eggs and pancakes and decide to order a salad. I am going to do it, I think. I am going to order a salad and actually eat some vegetables right now.

When my salad arrives, it is a little plate of romaine lettuce with chicken and bacon and stale tortilla chips on top. There is barbecue sauce instead of dressing. I take a bite and it tastes like almost nothing. Everyone else has big, hot ceramic plates of meat and eggs and hashbrowns. They are spreading jam onto their toast. T-Rex's pancakes are so fat they hang off the edge of her plate.

I finish my salad. Rocky and HairTie and T-Rex and the other hikers eat until they are painfully full and then there is still food left over, hashbrowns growing cold and toast and pieces of sausage. I eat all of this and then I am happy and satisfied too, salad and grease and potatoes all mixed up in my stomach.

I should really stay and take a zero.

Back at the motel we lounge around, our objects spread across every surface. A boy appears in the open doorway- he tells us he lives at the motel. The boy wears Levis and has long blonde hair. He comes over again throughout the day, asking us if we want to play something called "hula hoop wars" with him.

"Do you have any pets?" I ask him.

"Three dogs and five puppies," he says. He runs off and reappears with an armload of dusty, bloated puppies. The puppies are squealing and clawing at him. He drops them on the floor and they crawl away from us. I pick one up and put it in my lap and wrap my jacket around it. The puppy has red fur and floppy ears and its forehead is wrinkled with worry. It smells of dryer sheets. The other puppy is dirty white and has a cut above its eye. The white puppy crawls under a folded cot in the corner of the room, pushes itself into the corner and cowers there.

In the evening, we spread our food across the table and have a feast. Roast chicken, potato salad, romaine lettuce, salami, cucumbers, avocado. A pint of cheesecake icecream has turned to milkshake in the fridge and we pass it around, dipping lettuce leaves and broccoli stalks into it. I finally feel relaxed, like really relaxed. I am clean and warm and well rested and eating vegetables dipped in icecream. We are laughing so hard it is difficult to breathe at times. I am so happy I stayed. And yet, I can feel Canada calling me, like a whisper. *Canadaaaaaa.....*

***

At seven thirty, a trail angel named Carol meets us at the brightly painted gazebo in front of the motel and we crowd into the back of her pickup truck for a ride to the trailhead. We've resupplied, sorted our food, put the things we don't want into a piled-up hiker box and left it in front of the hardware store for the other hikers. I walked to the grocery store and got an orange, which I peeled and ate in the sunlight.

This morning the trail climbs way up to the top of Mt. Baden-Powell. Our crew spreads out and soon I am alone, huffing and puffing past the day hikers, feeling strong. I feel good today. I feel like I could climb forever.

Fourteen miles into the day, I reach a beautiful little spring in a tangle of vegetation just off the trail. The water pours from a pipe in the earth directly into a basin made from half a steel drum. Around the spring are seats made of split logs, and the sunlight is gentle through the trees. I fill my bottles, feeling happy. In just a mile is a campground, Little Jimmy Camp, where I'll sit and make lunch and wait for the others. I'm up on top of the mountain in the forest again, and it's cool, and the path is soft.

At Little Jimmy Camp I sit at a picnic table under the ponderosas and happily assemble my dinner- freeze-dried ground beef, dried carrots and cabbage, a packet of instant rice noodles. I'm still eating the freeze-dried ground beef that I ordered in bulk and repackaged for my resupply boxes. It tastes awesome, and I love making it in my little vegetable soups each night. I open the ziploc baggie and dump the beef into my pot. I pour in water and set the pot over my stove. While the soup cooks I watch the dappled shade move across the pine needles on the ground. My plan is to go six more miles today, after eating, and I hope I can convince the others to do the same. It's eighty-four miles to Agua Dulce where we'll resupply, and if we do twenty-mile days, we'll get there in four days. I have just enough food for four days, and so do the others. But I wonder what sort of mood they'll be in after climbing Baden-Powell and if they'll want to go farther. I might have to go on by myself. I frown. I like hanging out with the others, HairTie especially. I don't really want to hike by myself. But I know I've got to average eighteen miles a day to make it to Canada before the snow flies. What to do.

I eat my dinner and then the others arrive, and they are tired. We all talk at once about mileage and food and the infinite possibilities of the universe, and when the dust settles they are staying, and so am I. Fourteen miles, I think, as I spread my sleeping bag on top of a picnic table. I've been at the campground for hours- I could've easily hiked the other six miles by now. Now we'll have to do twenty-three miles for the next three days to make it to Agua Dulce before we run out of food. Twenty-three miles is my hiking edge right now- the point at which I get sore and cranky. The point where my joints start to hurt and I stop having fun. Currently twenty miles is awesome, but twenty-three miles is rough. Sometimes hiking with a group is hard.

"We'll be asleep by seven," says T-Rex. "We'll get up at four and hike." But at nine they are still talking and laughing, making noise in their tent. I'm cold on the picnic table, contorting myself in my bag in an attempt to stop the drafts. It's dark and I can't seem to get comfortable, and my stomach has begun to hurt. I could've done twenty miles, I think. Thirty miles. A thousand miles. A million miles. I can hike forever, I think. I can.

***

I wake in the middle of the night from dreams of bears. I'm freezing on the picnic table and my stomach is aching, some sort of burning sensation. I turn onto my side, but the pain won't go away. What? I'm so confused. I jump off the table and run to the edge of the clearing and throw up in the leaves. I feel like there is more inside me, trying to come out. My stomach clenches. Maybe now it's over, I think. Whatever it was. Maybe now I can sleep.

But I can't get warm in my bag. Why is it so cold? Why do I feel so cold? An hour later, I don't make it to the edge of the clearing; I lean over the side of the picnic table and vomit. I lie back down in my bag. The freeze-dried ground beef, I think. It must have been the ground beef. I hadn't thought that it would go bad after I repackaged it, but I suppose it had.

I hate vomiting! I rinse my mouth out with water and try to sleep. My stomach is still burning; I still can't get warm. Drafts come up from under the picnic table. This night is so impossibly cold! If morning would just come, I think. Then maybe everything would be alright.

At five I get up with the others and pack my things to hike. I'm exhausted. I haven't slept more than a couple hours, but I've puked so I should be better now, right? I fill up my water bottles at the spring and set off blearily down the soft path. I'm in my down jacket- the sunlight has not yet made its way through the trees. Walking feels all right. Maybe I can do this!

In a few miles we reach the Islip trailhead, which is a windy, waterless parkinglot at the base of the mountain. There is a pit toilet there. Now we'll climb several thousand feet to the top of the mountain and then down the other side. We sit at a picnic table eating handfuls of things for breakfast. I ate little bits of all of my food before vomiting, so now I don't want any of it. I stare forlornly into my bright yellow food bag. HairTie gives me a granola bar, and I eat this. It hits my stomach like a truck, and I feel the bile rise up in my throat. Oh no, I think. No more vomiting. I shouldn't have eaten. I guess I can't eat.

I set off up the mountain, one foot in front of the other. I am freezing in the sun in my down jacket, and I am unbelievably fatigued. I begin to fantasize about lying in a bed, blankets piled over me- I have never fantasized about lying down so hard in my life. Maybe I shouldn't do this. Maybe I should turn around. No, I tell myself. You threw up, you should be fine now.

When I am almost to the top of the mountain I sit down on the path. Rocky appears.

"Are you ok?" he asks.

"I think I'm gonna turn around," I say. It's difficult for me to speak. I want to lie down right there on the trail and go to sleep. I want to pull the hood of my jacket around my face and sleep.

The hike downhill back to the parkinglot seems to take hours. Once there I sit at the picnic table and lie my head on its wood top. The wind batters me. I'll stay here, I think. I'll just sleep for a little while. But there is no water at this trailhead. So I'll hitch somewhere- but where? I look at the highway that runs past the trailhead. It is a narrow mountain road and there is no traffic. It's still too early for day hikers.

I sit on a large rock between the parking area and the highway and wait for traffic with the hood of my down jacket pulled over my face. I am so fatigued I can't even sit up straight. I try to stand to hitch, but this feels impossible. Not that it matters. There are no cars. I sit on my rock and listen to the wind and try to feel warm.

A man in a little hatchback pulls into the parking area and I wave at him.

"You need a ride?" he says.

His name is Bill, and he's a retired schoolteacher. He's section hiked most of the PCT in California.

"This trail goes all the way to Canada," I say.

He looks at me, amazed at the idea.

Bill takes me ten miles up the road, to a campground on the other side of the mountain where my friends will stop for lunch. There is water there, and I can set up my little shelter, lie beneath it, and rest.

Bill gives me a bottle of pink-lemonade Gatorade and half a granny smith apple wrapped in cellophane.

"I hope you feel better," he says.

I walk down a steep road to the campground. It's empty- my friends are not yet here. I fill up my water bottles at the spigot, find a flat spot next to a big ponderosa, and set up my shelter in the full sun. I crawl inside of it, lay out my sleeping pad, and pull my sleeping bag from its stuff sack. I'm so cold. So so cold. I lie down and pull my sleeping bag up to my chin as the sun slowly transforms my tent into an oven. I just want to be warm. I just can't get warm. I even have my down jacket on. Eventually I fall asleep.

I hear voices in my sleep, shouts, the sound of vehicles, people walking by. I wake and everything is silent- and it's incredibly warm in my tent. The warmth feels good, like food. I open the pink lemonade Gatorade and drink the entire thing. I look at the granny smith apple but my stomach turns over.

I walk to the other side of the campground and there in a patch of dappled shade are Rocky, T-Rex, and HairTie, curled on their sides in the dirt. I sit at the picnic table and look at my sleeping friends. Rocky's watch goes off, and he sits up.

"Carrot!" he says. T-Rex wakes up and rubs her eyes.

"Rocky's sick too," she says. "He's been throwing up."

I lay my head on the picnic table. I'm cold again.

"I'm over there in that other campsite," I say. "I think I'll stay at this campground tonight. I can't eat yet."

Rocky also cannot eat, and lies back on his sleeping pad on the ground, looking pale, his ghost-white sleeping bag liner pulled up to his chin.

The plague. The plague has reached our village.

I return to my tent and fall into a bit of a fever delirium. I wake and sleep, baking in the sun, unable to get warm. The afternoon passes with excruciating slowness. Since when are there this many hours in a day? HairTie brings me Gatorade powder and ginger tea, and in an act of unbelievable hiker generosity even loans me her pillow. Eventually it is evening and HairTie goes to sleep too, cowboy camping in the clearing next to my tent.

My fever breaks in the middle of the night and I wake, soaked in my own sweat. I tear off my down jacket and drink the rest of the Gatorade. I get out to pee and look at the stars. Hallelujah, I think.

***

In the morning when I wake I am hungry, and I eat a few almonds and don't feel like throwing up. The sun is shining and I feel so happy I can't stand it.

"HairTie!" I say. "Good morning!"

We hike. We all hike. There is a climb in the heat, a walk on a dirt jeep road, and then a large amount of poison oak. Suddenly we are in a burn, the whole world has been burned. I am tired but my morale is high. I've slept an entire day and the thing inside of me is dead! My body cooked the shit out of it, and now it's dead! Thank you, immune system, I think as I hike. Thank you thank you thank you.

I eat little bits of food throughout the day. I don't feel very hungry but I don't feel like throwing up, either. And now that I have no appetite, I don't have to worry about running out of food. It's funny how things work out. I poke around in my food bag. I have jerky, dried fruit, salami, nuts. Stuff to cook for dinner. I pick up my tube of peanut butter and frown. Nope. I never want to see peanut butter again. I'm not too excited about the dried mango either. And the freeze dried beef is gone, into the trash.

In the afternoon we reach a windy ranger station at the edge of the burn. There's water here and we fill up our bottles. I can only go a few more miles, I say to HairTie. I'll just go a few more miles and look for somewhere to camp. I'm still a little dizzy, and I feel weak. T-Rex and Rocky hike on ahead- they want to get to the Saufley's place in Agua Dulce as soon as possible. Donna and Jeff Saufley run "Hiker Heaven," an oasis for hikers. There are cots there, and showers, and even loaner clothes. I'll get my box there, to resupply for the next section.

A few miles after the ranger station I find a lush patch of oak forest that has, miraculously, been spared by the fire. It's flat and grassy there and hidden from the trail and there is no wind. HairTie and I set up our sleeping bags and watch the sun set over the mountains to the west.

The Big Dipper comes out swinging, right above us. I lie in my bag and look at the stars and try to feel peace, try to feel some sense of largeness come over me. Instead I feel nothing, just a general anxiety in my heart.

There aren't any answers. Usually there are answers but tonight, they're just not there.

***

The Station Fire burn is large, although I'm not sure just how large. It's large enough that when we come to the top of a mountain it's all we can see, stretching on and on and on- these folded mountains with their forests of blackened oaks. The understory is a riot of flowers and poison oak, overgrown onto the trail. We push our way through it, wincing as it brushes our bare legs. What can you do? Nothing, really. After a while, you just give in.

Mid-morning we stop to eat at a small stream. All I have left is salami and a bar of dark chocolate with raspberries. I carefully prepare my tools of salami dissection- small swiss army knife, wet wipes, plastic ziploc, trash bag. The salami is literally oozing with grease, and if I am not prepared before I cut the plastic open, it is a disaster. Then I have to peel the casing off the thing, which is its own messy chore. It's a lot of prep work to do while sitting in the dirt in the woods, which is why the salami is always the last thing left in my food bag.

After eating, we hike on. Parts of the forest are not burnt, and here and there are pale dry grasses and dappled shade. Bright yellow flowers grow along the trail. We climb up and up, and my gut aches where my hip-belt presses against it. My stomach is having a hard time with the salami-chocolate combination.

Then the forest is gone and we are walking through chaparral desert on top of the world and it is hot, hot, hot. Stretching away from us in every direction are rumpled dry mountains- "Dinosaurs Under the Covers Mountains," HairTie calls them.

I hadn't expected it to be so hot. Our goal for today is the KOA, a campground in the valley. Right now twenty-three miles is a lot for me, and in the heat it's even worse. It's hot and we're pounding, pounding, pounding on the dusty path. Way down below us we can see the valley with its cluster of green trees, but hour after hour it doesn't seem to get any closer. My back is drenched in sweat- everywhere else is sweating too, but the wind instantly dries my skin. By the end of the day, parts of my shirt will be stiff with salt, like cardboard. Ugh.

I stop to pee and fall behind and walk on by myself, feeling grumpy. When I'm in this kind of mood, hot and tired and grumpy, I tend to find a negative thought and fixate on it, in a loop. It's interesting, the things my brain will do when I walk for twelve hours without distractions. At this point, a month into the trail, I've exhausted almost all of my loops, the good ones and the bad ones. And I have no music.

There is a little store at the KOA that closes at four. We won't make it, but Rocky and T-Rex are ahead of us, and they promise to buy us bottles of Gatorade. I think about this gatorade for the last hour of my hike. Fruit punch flavor. The red kind. Gatorade Gatorade Gatorade. I also think about the shower I will take at the KOA. Will the shower be uncomfortable? Will the showerhead be too short? Will the water temperature be difficult to control? I imagine all possible experiences of showering, in an attempt to exhaust them. Shower shower shower, I think. Gatorade Gatorade Gatorade.

At last we are down the mountain and into the valley, and we pass through a cool, narrow forest with a dark little stream running through it. Then we are in an empty lot filled with debris- piles of scrap lumber and trash. There are some faded, shuttered motorhomes, and then the KOA, which is a massive, sun-baked parkinglot next to the freeway. Huge RVs are parked there, their swamp coolers blasting.

"Hiker camping" is on a stretch of grass next to some picnic tables. Other hikers are there, but I've no time to talk to them.

"Where are Rocky and T-Rex?" I say. "Where are our Gatorades?" Rocky and T-Rex are soaking their blisters in the pool but they've left their packs in the grass, and we find our Gatorades there. I drink mine so fast it hurts my stomach. The Gatorade is lukewarm, and I don't really taste it. Then I march resolutely towards the shower building.

The showers, it turns out, are special magic showers descended straight from heaven. They are single showers and each stall has two little rooms- one room with the showerhead and the other room to take off your clothes and hang them so they don't get wet. The shower is white and clean and the showerhead is high and the temperature is perfect. I stand under the water for what feels like a long time. Next to me, another hiker is having a similar experience. She is literally moaning with pleasure.

I wash my clothes in the shower, squeezing Dr. Bronners onto them and rubbing them against themselves. Since I have nothing to change into, I put my wet shorts back on, along with my down jacket, and carry everything else outside and lay it on the concrete to dry. Lots of other hikers have spread their clothes there, and the wet flattened clothes look like some sort of still-life art project. I sit at the picnic table and allow myself to relax just a little bit.

In the morning it's just eleven miles to Hiker Heaven, where we'll pick up our resupply boxes. I have no idea what to expect there, but I'm sure it'll be strange and wonderful, just like everything else so far.

The sun sets, and we spread our sleeping bags on the grass. There is a streetlamp buzzing above me, and in the distance I can hear the freeway. It's cold now, and I am snug in my bag, but I feel very awake. The moon comes up and an ant crawls over me. I look at what I can see of the stars through the light pollution and think of the endless possibilities of the universe, sprawling away into forever.

***

I wake before dawn to the sounds of other hikers, hurriedly packing away their things. There are plenty of cots at Hiker Heaven, but only a few beds. So it's a race, I think, as I brush the frozen condensation off my bag. A race to the beds. I don't care though. A cot sounds like heaven to me.

The sun comes up as I hike over the bright, dry hills. Then there is a freeway and we pass under it via a long, dripping tunnel. I am walking with some other hikers and I joke about the tunnel.

"The tunnel alternate!" I say. "Would you do the PCT if the whole thing was a tunnel?"

Hiker Heaven is in Agua Dulce, a town so small it doesn't even have a post office. The PCT goes right through it. Once in town I stop at the grocery store and buy an icecream bar and a bottle of Gatorade. I wander the little produce section, poking the wilted lettuce. I select some romaine and a cucumber. I feel inexplicably relaxed. How wonderful, to just walk into a town! As though cars don't even exist!

At Hiker Heaven I push open the gate to find a magical paradise of wonder. There is a concrete patio, and several dogs are sprawled across it in the sun. There is even a chihuahua! I squeal and hold out my arms, but the little dog scampers away. Inside the open garage door is a mailing station. There is a cork board with trail info, a box of PCT bandanas, a stack of water reports, and a postal scale. Huge shelves are stacked high with resupply boxes. I pick up the food box that I mailed to myself. I am already growing sick of nearly everything inside, but no matter.

Next to the garage door is a little covered area with laundry baskets and loaner clothes. The clothes are folded and sorted into bins- t-shirts, sweatshirts, pants, shorts. All of the clothes seem to be from the mid-nineties, and the hikers wandering around look like as though they dressed from a costume box, which is amazing. I choose a pair of pleated shorts and an old, stained t-shirt that is soft. I put the clothes on, luxuriating in the feel of cotton against my sunburnt skin, and am overwhelmed with relief and gratitude. Who are the Saufleys, these angels who want to help us on our way? Who set up their entire property for us, dirt-covered layabouts walking to Canada for no reason?

There is a long, sloping lawn that ends in a horse corral. Inside the corral are a regular horse and a pony. On the sloping lawn are rows of big canvas screen tents, and inside the tents are cots. I find a tent with a few empty cots and drop my pack on one of them. HairTie claims one of the others.

There is a double-wide trailer that is just for hikers. It has a kitchen and living room. In the dim living room sunburnt hikers are sprawled on the couches, watching Top Gun on VHS. In the kitchen people are drinking hot cocoa. I put my name on the shower list on the bathroom door. I just showered yesterday at the KOA, but I am going to do it again. I feel unbelievably rich.

In the afternoon, I catch a ride to the store and get junk food for the next section to add to the healthy food I sent myself- Fritos, mini Reeses peanut butter cups, another bottle of Gatorade. When I get back it's evening, and the hikers have acquired many cases of beer. They are sitting in camp chairs around a firepit and are in the process of becoming as drunk as possible. I plan to leave in the morning, though, so I decide to go to sleep. My friends are all going to stay another day, but I've decided that it's time for me to H my own H. (HYOH is a hiker saying that means Hike Your Own Hike.) I really, really want to get to Canada before the snow flies, which is usually around the end of September. T-Rex, Rocky, and HairTie are great to hike with, but I'm starting to get anxious about finishing on time. I don't think I can stand to dally any longer.

I think about the thing I have with HairTie. What do we have? What even is it? I don't know.

I pick up my clean laundry from the garage. It is unbelievably clean, and carrying it in my arms feels like Christmas. I even washed my down jacket, which has been flat as a pancake since I soaked it with my fever sweats. Now the jacket is puffy and good smelling and new again.

The screen tent with our cots is far from the drunk hikers and their shouting (it's someone's birthday, and they are singing "Happy Birthday" over, and over, and over again) and I make my little bed there, contented. Other than the fact that I have eaten my weight in sugar today, I feel pretty good. The next section, I know, is supposed to be hot, but then they say that about everything, at least in the desert. Almost to Kennedy Meadows, I think. Almost to the Sierras. What does that even mean? The Sierras. Big granite mountains. I try to imagine them, but I cannot.

***

I wake in the dark hour before dawn. *Time to wake up!* Says my brain. But it's so freaking cold out there. I wrap myself in my sleeping bag and walk to the trailer.

It's icy feeling, even in the trailer, even in my down jacket with my sleeping bag over me. I put on some water for tea and poke around on the shelves. Why do I have such trouble staying warm now? I wonder if it's because I'm losing body fat. Aye, I think. I don't want to be one of those people who is cold all the time.

I make a cup of green tea and sit in the dark and watch the courtyard slowly lighten. When the sun comes up I eat the last of my salami and cucumber and pack away my things. The others are up- they're headed to the bakery for breakfast. I wonder when I'll see them again. They are such clever, friendly, hilarious people- what will it be like to not see them every day? How rare and special is it to find a group of people that I can laugh so hard with and feel so comfortable around? Is it worth it to do more miles, I think, if everything is boring and I'm all by myself? I feel as though everything is about to change. Well, I think. Well.

It's sunny today, but it's breezy and not too warm. I'm officially in the "transitional zone," between the desert and the Sierra, and sometimes there are beautiful oak forests and soft waving grasses, and flowers. My pack is heavy- I have a pound of potato salad in there, and a liter of Gatorade, and a hundred miles' worth of food. The Andersons, who also host hikers, are twenty-four miles down the trail. I plan to make it there by nightfall.

I feel good today.

By mid-day I'm descending to the oasis cache, the cache tended by the Andersons. It's the last cache, six miles before the road to their house. I'm plodding along and then suddenly there is poison oak, grown all over the trail. Oh no, I think. Not again. Like museum lasers, I think, as I attempt to edge my way around it.

At the Oasis Cache, there are camp chairs and big bottles of water, and I take off my pack to rest. In a cooler there is ice, and soda, and Natural Light, which I haven't had since I was a teenager. Well, all right, I think, as I open a beer and put it in the cupholder of my campchair. Beer usually makes me feel sleepy and awful, but I had a nice experience with a PBR a few weeks back. And this is just what people do at this cache, right? I hear another hiker approach- it's Toyo! Toyo sits in the campchair opposite me and I hand him a beer.

"Is this water?" he says, after taking a drink.

"Cheap beer," I say. "The very cheapest of all the beers. The number one cheapest beer."

"You gave me mango once," says Toyo.

"Do you want mango again?" I say. I pull the package of dried mango from my food bag. It was one of the things I ate before throwing up, and I still can't eat it, even though I have a fresh package in every food box. I give it to Toyo.

"You look Greek," Toyo says to me.

"I look Greek?"

"You are beautiful," says Toyo.

"Thank you," I say. It feels like it means a lot, a seventy-one year-old Japanese thru-hiker telling me I'm beautiful.

Some other hikers appear.

"You know what Natty Light is?" says one of the hikers. "They make the regular beer, and then they make the Natty Light from what's left over."

The beer does not make me feel good. Afterwards I am sleepy and sort of sick, and it's difficult to hike. A little ways down the trail I need to dig a cathole, but there are no flat spots- just the narrow path, hugging the mountain as it winds around. At last there is a small wash, and I push my way through some greenery to a spot away from the trail where I can poop. Not poison oak, not poison oak, not poison oak, I think as I carefully check each plant before pushing it aside. I squat, and after a moment I notice some short poison oak, growing up from the sand beneath me, just brushing my legs. Great, I think. Just great. I stand up, and my head brushes something. Poison oak, hanging over me in vines. Goddamit, I think.

I reach the road at dusk. It's two and a half miles to the Anderson's, and I'm pretty sure it's too late to hitchhike. I'm tired and thirsty, and I really want to take a shower. Poison oak, I think. Poison oak all over me. I start to walk, and just then a minivan appears, and makes a u-turn.

"Are you hiker trash?" says a woman.

Her name is Little Steps, and she thru-hiked another year. This year she's at the Anderson's, helping ferry people from the trail.

We pull up in front of a small house on a residential street. There are bright lights in the yard, and couches clustered in a circle. There are many, many people in the yard, standing and sitting on the couches. Maybe thirty people? All of the people are wearing Hawaiian shirts. When the van pulls up everyone starts to cheer and clap. I get out of the van and squint in the bright lights. I feel overwhelmed, and sort of terrified. Aside from the bright lights in the driveway, it's dark, and I can't really see anything. There are empty beer cans everywhere, and lots of shouting. It feels like I've just arrived, thirsty and exhausted, at a chaotic, Hawaiian-themed house party.

"Where's the water?" I ask someone. He points to a spigot on the side of the house. I turn the spigot on and it sprays me. It's dark, and I can't figure out how to adjust the pressure. Who are these people, and who can help me? And is this really where I'm staying? I want to cry.

In the back of the house, though, is a surprise. After a short lawn there is a manzanita forest that, apparently, stretches on into forever. Narrow little paths wind through it, and there are dozens of small flat spots tucked away among the trees for camping. Ah, I think. I understand now. This is beautiful. I wander through the manzanita labyrinth and soon I find the perfect, peaceful little spot for my tent. I pitch the tent quickly and for a moment I sit inside. Back here in the forest you can't hear the party at all. It's ok, I tell myself. You're not really at a Hawaiian-themed house party. You're actually camped in this nice peaceful manzanita forest.

In front of the house they're serving dinner. There are something like fifty people waiting, and the line goes way out into the street. I stand at the back. I wonder if there will be enough food. How could they possibly cook enough food for this many people, and why would they want to? It's ok if they run out, I tell myself. I can always cook my own dinner.

Some drunk people are shouting at me.

"You just got here!" they are shouting. "Go to the front of the line!"

"What?" I say. "I can't do that!" I want them to stop shouting at me. I want to be invisible.

The van pulls up again, and another hiker gets out. The crowd erupts into cheers.

"Go to the front of the line!" A stranger is tugging on the sleeve of my jacket. "Go! Go! Go!"

"Ok!" I say. I move to the front and am yanked into position. There is an outdoor kitchen of sorts there- a stove, a table, a big metal cupboard where everyone puts their food so mice don't get it. On the table, beneath a bright outdoor lamp, is the most incredible spread-

Taco salad! I think. Holy shit, taco fucking salad.

Lined up on the table are massive bowls and dishes and pots of food. There are several industrial-sized bags of tortilla chips, a pot of refried beans that a smaller hiker could probably fit inside of, a pot of nacho cheese just as big, a massive pot of ground beef, and unbelievable quantities of lettuce, tomatoes, onions, olives, peppers, and sour cream.

Holy fucking shit, I think, as I watch the people in front of me load up the most massive plates of food. There is really enough food here! I can make a big plate of food too, just like those people, and eat it!

Thank the universe for the Andersons.

There is even a spot on the couch for me, once I have my taco salad, since I was towards the front of the line. I sit and slowly consume my taco salad, mesmerized. It is kind of like nachos and kind of like tacos, and it is incredible. There is so much lettuce mounded onto it, and ground beef, and nacho cheese. It is very large, almost spilling off the plate, and I have a hard time finishing it. But I do. Once the plate is empty I rest my fork on it and look up, my eyes glazing over. I will remember and long for this taco salad, I realize, for the rest of the trail. Maybe the rest of my life. I look at the hikers around me- I don't know any of them. And then I realize that Spark is there, sitting right next to me on the couch.

"How are you doing?" he asks, pausing midway through his own massive plate of food.

"Better now," I say.

After eating, I go looking for the shower. It's an outdoor shower and I find it in the backyard- a little wooden platform with flimsy plastic curtains zip-tied around the outside. I take off my clothes and step inside, shivering. But the water seems to be off, and there is a complicated-seeming propane heater that I can't figure out. Poison oak, I think. Poison oak poison oak! I cry a little, standing naked in the shower. Then I put my clothes back on and go to my tent, where I immediately feel better.

It's warm in my tent, and I feel safe and cozy. I have my sleeping bag up around my ears, and I am gazing through the mesh, out into the forest. I lie there as waves of anxiety wash over me, alternating with waves of sleepiness. I miss HairTie, and wonder when she'll arrive. I don't have reception, so I can't text her to see where she is, or when they plan to leave. It's ok, I tell myself. It's ok.

***

I sleep well (I actually manage to sleep past dawn!) and in the morning I do feel better. I get up and carry my sleeping bag to the front yard and sit on one of the couches, eating almonds from my food bag with the sleeping bag wrapped around me. The hikers I do not know are around me on the couches, yawning and looking hungover- most of these hikers are faster than me, and so they've been a day or two ahead. But now they've been at the Andersons' for a few days, "sucked into the vortex," as they say, and so here we are, all in the same place. It's nice to listen to them talk while I eat my almonds. People to hike with? I think. New friends? Except now they are packing their bags, getting ready to leave. And I can't leave yet, because what if HairTie is just about to arrive? Maybe she stayed at Hiker Heaven another night? I try to imagine my friends hiking; I wonder how many miles they've gone. Where would they have slept? How fast are they moving? When they get here, will they want to stay? Then the other hikers are gone and it's just me in the yard, with a handful of people I don't know at all. These people are drinking beer, and smoking weed, and eating candy, and shouting, and watching videos on their tablets. Where am I? What universe is this?

By three in the afternoon, I can't wait any longer. I could be here forever, waiting. Plus, I'm eating all my food. I fill up my water bottles and Little Steps gives me a ride back to the trail. As I walk away from the road, my heart fills with sadness. Am I doing the wrong thing? Should I turn around and wait for my friends? Why is it so hard for me to compromise for other people? The people who started this morning will be a day ahead of me, and at this rate, my friends will be a day or two behind. I'll be stuck in the middle this whole section, with no one to talk to. Why do I do this to myself?

I don't want to hike after dark so I stop at the first water cache, eight miles in. It's nice there, with big trees and a picnic table. I pitch my tent in a flat spots in the grass. I am going to sleep so good tonight, I think. I am just going to have the best night's sleep ever.

And it's true.

***

I wake from a dream and lie in my sleeping bag with my eyes closed. I'm imagining my hand pressed against HairTie's clavicle.

"This is what I live for," I imagine myself saying. "The moment when the true value of a thing becomes apparent." In my imagination, she looks concerned. "Don't worry," I say. "We all die alone. What you have, you couldn't give it away if you tried."

Like an explosion, I think. Through time and space in every direction. Then I am awake and I sit up, and drink the rest of the water in my Gatorade bottle. I text HairTie-

I miss you, I say.

I wait a few moments, but there is no response.

My plan for the day is to hike twenty-five miles- Hikertown is at mile 517, and I want to get as close as possible before camping. Hikertown is a place I can't say I really understand, but it's listed as a resupply point. I'll get close today, I decide, and then arrive early in the morning.

Today, much to my delight, I walk through magical, softly lit, un-burnt oak forest for the entire day. A real forest! I think, as I trod happily on the leafy path. An actual forest, that goes on and on! I am up in the hills, and just before Hikertown I will drop down, down, down, into the valley. But not just any valley- the Mojave. The last stretch of desert before I climb into the Sierras.

Each time I leave the forest for a ridge, I can see the Mojave down below me- it is the flattest thing I've ever seen. It's like a non-place, or a place where only the wind lives. I shudder a little. No big deal, I tell myself. I've already hiked through five hundred miles of desert- what's a little more desert?

The water sources today please me immensely. Instead of caches, I draw water from these clever contraptions hidden behind clusters of scrub oak, designed to catch rainwater during storms. They're called "Guzzlers". Their roofs are corrugated tin, and you crawl underneath the roof, unscrew a lid, and there is cool, clear, magic water inside. From the trail you wouldn't know the guzzlers are there at all, except that they're on my maps. This water is from the last rain! I think, as I fill up my Gatorade bottles. The water is yellow with the tannins of leaves, and it tastes amazing. What clever, generous soul put these here? I wonder, as I lounge in the shade, drinking water.

I listen to an audiobook for most of the day. I know that this will drain the battery on my phone, but I don't care. I'm so tired of my thoughts that I can't stand it. I've thought every thought! Absolutely every possible thought! The audiobook helps a lot, and the miles fly by. Soon I am at the edge of the mountain, and I begin the descent into the valley.

Suddenly the oak forest is gone. Now it is just rocks, and the blackened husks of burnt-out trees.

And then, the wind appears. Just a little bit of wind, at first. Not too bad.

It is so windy! I think. My stars!

I'm almost out of water, but in a few miles there's a cache that's maintained by Hikertown. "Water in a barrel," is what my water report says. I reach the barrel right at dusk, and lift the hose. It's empty.

No water, I think. Huh. It's ten more miles to Hikertown, the next water source, and I've already gone twenty-three. No bueno, I think. No bueno. And besides, it's almost dark.

I jiggle the barrel, which is lying on a stand on its side. Nothing. I open and close a nozzle. There is a little standing water in a bucket- it's opaque brown, and there are dead insects floating in it. Someone probably washed their clothes in there. Finally I think to tip the barrel, and water comes out. There are still a few liters left inside, it seems- just not enough to reach the hose unless you tip it. I fill up my bottles, purify the water, and drink. It's warm, and tastes like plastic. Di-hydrogen monoxide, I think. Hallelujah.

The wind is stronger now, and the land is steep and rocky on both sides of the trail. Now I just have to find somewhere to camp. I walk a few miles, my pack heavy with water, and then there is a little dry streambed, trampled flat. It's sheltered from the trail (and the wind!) by a cluster of burned oaks, and it's quiet and peaceful there. I happily pitch my shelter. No such thing as cougars, I think as I push the stakes into the sand. No such thing as cougars. I'll have a cozy happy bed, and tomorrow I'll get to Hikertown, whatever that is! And then after I'll set off across the Mojave. This trail sure is easy, I think, as I wet my hanky with a little water and use it to wipe the sand from my feet. Easy peasy! Little do I know that this innocent-seeming thought is reverberating out into space, against all the known possibilities of the universe, and stirring the Wind Gods into an angry frenzy. The sun is setting behind the burnt oak trees, and some crows are playing in the wind, way up in the sky. Woo woo woo! I can hear the wind in the treetops. Yep, easy, I think, as I do my stretches, unfold my sleeping bag, and prepare for bed.

HairTie texts me right before I fall asleep.

I miss you too, she says. *But to be honest, SunCat has been gaming me, and I'm kind of into it.*

What the fuck? I think. *Gaming?* What does that even *mean?* I remember SunCat- he shared a screen tent with us at Hiker Heaven. Young, Australian, kind of stoned all the time. I remember lying on a cot with HairTie, spooning her. My sleeping bag draped over both of us, and beneath it, I'm running my hand over her skin under her shirt. While we lie there, she chats with SunCat, who is sitting on the other cot. They're talking about... music. They both love music.

I close my eyes. Why don't I love music. I mean I like music, but I don't *love* music. You know? But it doesn't matter. I wanted to hike faster, didn't I? Isn't this what I wanted? I roll over onto my side on the hard ground. I feel so alone. I don't understand anything anymore.

***

My sleep is solid and deep in the quiet, empty desert. I wake at dawn and sit up. It isn't even very cold! I pull out my gallon ziploc bag of trailmix and stare at it. It's almost empty. I send myself all sorts of dried fruit and nuts in my resupply boxes, and they all end up in this bag together. So far it's the bulk of my snacks, and snacks, of course, are the bulk of my meals. I only have time to cook once a day, and even that feels like a luxury. And now I'm almost out of trailmix. Well hell, I think. My system is obviously not working.

It's fifty miles until my resupply in Tehachapi. I'll need some more snacks. I think about Hikertown. What is Hikertown, anyway?

I remember HairTie's text from last night. There's something inside of me now- disappointment? Loss? I don't know.

It's seven miles to Hikertown, and the trail hugs the mountain for most of that. Then the trail drops down, onto a jeep road that cuts forward across the valley, where BAM! the wind hits me like a balled-up newspaper. I struggle forward, clutching my hat to my head. The wind is howling across the dead-flat dusty valley. Woo woo woo. I am walking along a property boundary- beyond a wire fence there are piles of electronics, slowly corroding in the sun. Here is a pile of smashed computer monitors; there is a jumble of coffeemakers. Everything is covered in dust.

I pass a series of properties. In the center of each property is a small cluster of ramshackle buildings. Freight containers, old RVs, wooden shacks. Since it's the desert, I can see everything. I peer at the buildings as I walk in the wind and try to guess what's inside them.

I reach the highway and see that the trail continues on the other side of it. Across from the trail is a square, wind-swept property surrounded by a chain-link fence. Inside the fence is a row of tiny outbuildings, each built to look like a storefront in the Wild West. Saloon, bank, corral, they say. Like a set for a children's play.

This, I realize, is Hikertown.

I let myself in at the gate. The little wooden doors of the saloon swing open, and a woman appears.

"Good morning," she says grumpily. "Come with me, right this way. Set your pack down in here, here's the lounge."

The woman leads me to a buttercup-yellow garage. She pries the door open, steadying it against the wind. We scoot inside, and the door slams shut behind us. Bang, bang, bang, goes the wind on the outside of the door.

One side of the garage has been converted into a kitchen. There's a sink, a fridge, a stove, and a long countertop. The other half of the garage is like a living room- big couches, easy chairs, and a dining room table. I lean my pack against the couch. On the couch is a handsome red dog. The dog raises his head and looks at me.

"Whew!" I say. "That's some wind!"

"You want to take a shower?" says the woman. "You want food? You can order food. We got anything you want."

I pick up the trail register.

"Thirty people here last night," says the woman. "Just left this morning." I read the list- Spark's name is one it! It must be the fast people, then. I look at my watch. It's 9:30 a.m. I just missed them! All those people, just ahead of me!

"I'd love to take a shower," I say.

The woman leads me to another building, and through a sliding glass door.

The building is the same buttercup yellow as the garage. Inside the building there is no furniture, and the beige carpet is covered in stains. There are stains on the walls, too. In one end of the building, which I think is maybe a trailer, Is a cramped bathroom. The fixtures in the bathroom are coated in dust. The woman hands me a fluffy pink towel.

"Thank you," I say.

There is no soap in the bathroom, but I have a little bottle in my pack. In the shower, there is a window, and in the windowsill a little bird has built a nest. The nest is made of tufts of fiberglass insulation, and there are two blue eggs inside.

After my shower I battle the wind across the clearing to the garage. I've washed a few things in the tub, and I hang them to dry on some two-by-fours in the yard.

"Those'll dry fast in this wind," says the woman, whose name is Debbie.

"Yeah," I say.

I ask her if there is a convenience store nearby.

"About eight miles," she says. I think about hitching eight miles on that freeway, in this wind. Then I see the hikerbox, sitting in the corner. It's piled with food.

I dig through it- I find a bag of peanut butter cookies from Trader Joe's, some granola, dried black bean soup, prunes, and a bag of tortilla chips. I eat a couple of the cookies.

"I think this is good," I tell the woman. "I think there's enough food here."

"You hungry?" she says. On the counter are the remains of a big breakfast-cold sausage links, bits of scramble, pieces of ham. Debbie hands all of these things to me, and I sit at the table and eat them.

"This is awesome," I say. "This is so awesome."

"You want something else to eat?" Debbie asks me.

"A salad?" I say. "Do you have that?" Debbie makes me a massive salad of lettuce, avocado, cucumber, red bell peppers. And then she turns on an actual grill and fixes me a burger. I give her money for all of this, and the shower too.

Debbie takes me on a tour. We go in the little building marked "Bank." Inside the bank there is a tall stack of resupply boxes. Around the boxes are cat beds, cat towers, and opened cans of cat food.

"How many cats do you have here?" I ask.

"Just three," says Debbie. "We had more, but the dogs got 'em."

I kind of wish I could open everyone's boxes, like Christmas.

By the time I'm ready to set out again it's two thirty. It's seventeen miles from Hikertown to the next water source, a faucet on a creek (what does that even mean?) on the other side of the Mojave, so I know I'll be doing some night hiking. I average two and a half miles an hour, so I can usually kind of guess, at this point, how long a stretch of miles will take me.

"I guess I'm off to walk the aqueduct," I say to Debbie. This part of the Mojave is all tracts of private property, so instead of having its own trail the PCT just follows the Los Angeles Aqueduct, which is buried underground. The route is winding and indirect but then, so is the whole trail. If the trail were as the crow flies, it'd only be half as long and then, of course, it would be over too fast.

Already I wish I could live here forever.

Outside, it has not gotten any less windy. If anything, the wind has increased. On the upside, I tell myself, it's not very hot. I climb up onto the concrete aqueduct and start the long walk across the valley. My pack is heavy with water. I listen to my audiobook for a while, and then my phone beeps at me. It's almost dead. Damn, I think. I can't actually afford to let it die. All my maps are on my phone.

Then it's just me and my thoughts, walking across the Mojave in the wind. Windmills march along the horizon, their red lights blinking in unison. I have nothing left to think about, and I begin to fidget from boredom, tugging at my pack straps. I try shouting, then I try singing. I am so bored I want to stop hiking and just sit down in the dirt. Anything, I think. Anything would be better than this.

Now and then, the wind picks up a bunch of sand and flings it at me, scouring the backs of my legs. The wind tries to tear the hat off my head.

The wind causes the straps on my pack to whip me in the face. The wind blows dirt into my water bottle when I open it to drink.

I am walking past big flat properties, each one with a rusted fence and a couple of old RVs. Who lives here? I feel like I'm in the first episode of Breaking Bad. Scattered across the land are Joshua trees, being weird like they do. In the distance I can see some low mountains rising up. The foothills of these mountains are dotted with more windmills. Clouds are pouring over the lip of the mountains and then dissolving. Tomorrow I walk over those mountains. I wonder what the wind is like up there?

The sun is setting. The light is changing every minute, in the dirt and the sky and the Joshua trees. It's beautiful out here, I think, as the wind harangues me. I imagine of all of the people ahead of me, and all the people behind me. Why am I hiking alone? A bit of an Eagles song has been stuck in my head for weeks. Just one little part, playing over and over and over. I sing it as loud as I can, to the wide open air and the Joshua trees.

We may lose, and we may win
But we will never be here again
So open up I'm climbin' in
Take it eaaaaaaasy

I realize that singing makes me thirsty, so I stop. I have enough water for seventeen miles but still, there's no point in wasting it. It's dusk now, and the landscape is slowly disappearing. The blinking lights of the windmills are closer, and even more eerie. The moon is big, but won't be up for hours. I take out my headlamp and then remember that it's almost dead. It's too dark to change the battery now, even though I have extras, so I just focus the thin wavery beam on the trail.

At 9:30 p.m. I reach Cottonwood Creek, which is actually invisible. The ditch where the creek should be is empty. The creek is underground somewhere, but the city has installed a concrete box with a faucet on it. When you turn the faucet handle creekwater comes out. Across the dry creekbed I see the flickering light of a headlamp. Friend! I think. Fellow hiker! I cross the bridge over the creek. The windmills loom above me, making their howling sci-fi sounds. The wind is howling too. I walk down the bank.

"Hello?" I say, using my creepy witch voice.

"You looking for water?" says the hiker, who cannot see me in the dark. I realize I have startled him.

"No," I say in my normal voice. "Just looking for a place to camp." I'll never make friends at this rate. I pick my way down the bank, shining my light on the ground. The dirt is littered with shotgun shells, and there is broken glass everywhere. Well, I think. Well.

I set up my tent and the wind immediately blows it over, so I stuff it away. I sit on my sleeping pad and cook a little pot of food, positioning rocks all around my windscreen to hold it in place. By the time I'm ready for bed it's after ten.

I lie in my bag and look at dark sky. There is a momentary lull in the wind. Maybe the wind is over? I curl on my side to sleep. That wasn't so bad.

***

I am almost asleep when the wind returns.

Bam! it says. Bam bam bam bam! The wind rushes into the opening of my sleeping bag, puffing it up like a sail. Fwap fwap fwap fwap! goes my sleeping bag. I pull the bag up over my face, but then there isn't any air. Goddamit, I think. I just want to sleep. I curl onto my side and grip my sleeping bag and drift off. An hour later, the wind wakes me again. Bam bam bam bam! I peer out of my bag. The moon is up, hanging like an egg between the windmills.

Maybe I should just hike? Bam bam bam bam! answers the wind. No, I think. I need to sleep. For at least a couple of hours.

I roll onto my other side and am woken, in a few minutes, by the wind. Bam bam bam! I stick my head out of my bag, and am rewarded with a faceful of sand. I curl up again, and manage to drift off. Bam bam bam!

This goes on throughout the night. No wind, then WIND WIND WIND! Like some sort of psychological torture. At last it is the gray hour before dawn and I sit up. The inside of my head feels grainy and slow. Dark stormclouds are tumbling across the horizon. Great, I think. Just great.

I'll climb up, today, for most of the day, into these windy mountains and then at the end of the day I'll go back down, to the highway. I sleepily set out, hiking up the bare hills. The windmills are churning all around me, and then it begins to drizzle. I put on my rain jacket. Fwap fwap fwap fwap! goes the wind in my rain jacket. The wind is beating against my ears, and I pull the hood of my jacket over my face. Soon I am too hot, and sweating in my jacket. The drizzle has stopped, and there's a rainbow. I put my jacket away. Bam bam bam! goes the wind through my t-shirt. Now I'm cold again. Just hike, I think blearily. Just hike and you'll be warm. I'm hungry but it's cold and the wind is everywhere- there's nowhere to stop and eat.

The next water is in eight miles. According to my water info, it's a creek, a real actual physical creek, down in a canyon. I just have to get there, I think, as I hike up through the windmills. Maybe I can rest there, and eat something. The wind is coming from all directions now, BAM BAM BAM! and it's difficult to put one foot in front of the other. I reach the top of a ridge and the wind punches me in the face, almost knocking me off the trail. I plant my feet to steady myself. I stumble a few steps, using all the muscles in my legs to stay upright. Forward, I think. Forward forward.

I climb up and up and up on switchbacks and exposed ridges. The higher I climb, the more intense the wind becomes. I am so hungry I feel weak, but there is nowhere to stop. I eat my last handful of almonds, which I have stuffed into my pocket. I'm dizzy. I'm so hungry.

I reach the creek at ten. It's way down in a crevice between the mountains, and the wind is less there. There is even a pile of downed oak trees and I sit behind them, which cuts the wind further. Here the wind is gentle puffs- puff puff puff! And the sun is shining warmly. The stream is clear and burbly. I fill up my water bottles and sit on my sleeping pad. I rub the sand and grit from my face. Jesus Christ, I think.

I decide to cook a little pot of food. I pile rocks around the windscreen and my stove hisses merrily. I can still hear the wind, bam bam bam! way up above me. After eating I spread my sleeping pad in the dappled shade of my little hidden area and lie down. It's time for a nap.

A wake a few hours later, feeling better. There are just seventeen miles left to the highway- I can do this, I think. I can totally do this. I eat some chocolate. Seventeen miles, I think. Just seventeen more miles.

As soon as I leave my sheltered little canyon the wind is there, waiting for me. The trail today follows the ridges, one after the other, as they go up and up. Up on the ridges the wind is a howling, inconceivable monster, battering the living daylights out of everything. The wind yanks at my pack, the wind scours at my face. I plant my feet a certain way and the wind suddenly changes directions, almost knocking me to the ground. The wind smashes my hat into my face, which in turn smashes my sunglasses into my nose. The straps on my pack turn into little whips, fwapping me in the face. Even my shirt collar is out to hurt me. Fwap fwap fwap! it says, as its pointy edge jabs at my chin. The wind is so strong my nostrils are smashed, and it's difficult to breathe.

Still the trail climbs higher, and the wind becomes stronger. What is this, sixty-mile an hour winds? Seventy? I grip my hat and stumble forward. I feel angry at the trail for bringing me up here in the first place. For delivering me into danger. Why, PCT? I think. Why this mountaintop? In this wind?

Bam bam bam bam bam! The wind is a psychotic, howling monster, bent on destroying everything. Soon I am on a narrow path, clinging to the mountain way up high, and I actually, for the first time on the PCT, fear for my life. I could fall over the edge. The wind could blow me right over. Why, I think. Why why why. It is an unbelievable effort to keep climbing, and soon I am starving again. But there is nowhere to stop, nowhere to hide from the wind. The only thing I can do is keep moving.

I squat to pee with my pack on, and the wind suddenly changes directions, blowing the pee all over my shoe. Well, I think, looking at my soaked shoe. That's a nice touch.

At one point time disappears and it is just me and the mountain, and the wind. I have always been in this moment, I think, as I fight my way forward over the infinite, climbing path. And I will always be in this moment. Up ahead, on a bare, windswept ridge, there is a single tree. Someday, I think, I am going to be reincarnated as that tree. As punishment for all of the choices I have ever made.

Or as a reward.

Suffering is beautiful, I tell myself as I climb. All of this is beautiful. Bam bam bam! goes the wind. I feel like I am in a river, fighting the heavy current. I feel like I could be swept off the mountain at any moment.

"Why not?" I shout, to the universe. "Why not just fucking blow me off the mountain?"

At the top of the mountain there is a cache. I read about the cache on my water report- *Chairs and bottled water!* the report said. *Sign the register!* And I wondered about that as I climbed. Chairs? Why would there be chairs in a place like this? Now I am at the cache and the plastic lawn chairs are tumbled over, lying on the trail. I sit in the dirt, gripping my pack, and open the trail register, fighting with the wind for control of its pages. Even here, sitting on the ground, it's difficult to breathe. In the register I look at the names of all the people in front of me- twenty or more people, just passed through today! And yet I haven't seen a soul all day and I have felt infinitely alone. We're all here, on the mountain, and yet each of us is alone in our own personal, windy hell. I turn back a few pages in the register, and there is no mention of the wind. *It's hot!* Someone says. *Thanks for the chairs!*

I look at my watch. It's four thirty, and there are nine more miles to the highway. If I get to the highway before dark I can hitch into Mojave, to the Motel 6 where all the hikers stay, and I can get a room there.

The thought of a wind-free room with a bed almost makes me faint. Or maybe it's the hunger.

I have to get the fuck off this mountain.

The trail is no longer climbing, but the wind is no less brutal. At one point, there is a fallen log and I hunker down behind it, quickly eating a handful of sandy salami. There is a little flower there, growing in the wind. Oh little flower, I think. I do not envy you.

Soon I can see the highway below me, cutting its way through the flat desert. But the trail descends slowly, teasingly, following the ridges as they go almost imperceptibly down. Down, I think. Down down down! I want to fuck off this mountain! I want off!

BAM BAM BAM BAM! says the wind, in response.

I have been struggling in seventy mile per hour winds, I realize, for twelve hours. If a jeep road were to appear, a shortcut to the highway, anything, I would take it. But there is no shortcut, just the trail, and now the windmills again, sticking ominously from the earth. Woo woo woo, go their huge blades, as they turn in the sky. Their red lights blink in unison.

I have always been here and I will always be here. Forever and ever and ever.

I reach the trailhead at dusk. There is a small cache of water there, and a big plastic bin. I open the bin, and inside is a huge bag of stale peanut M&M's. I eat some of these M&M's. They taste incredible. Taped to the lid of the bin is a list of trail angels in Mojave and Tehachapi who give rides from the trailhead. I turn on my phone, and it beeps at me. Beep beep beep! Battery critically low! The screen is dim, and I type in the number for one of the trail angels. Work! I think. Don't die on me now!

I get through to a man named Ted.

"I'm at the corner of Willow Springs Road," I tell him, "and Teha, Teha, Teha-" I suddenly cannot remember how to say Tehachapi.

"Yes," he says. "I understand. I'll be there soon."

"Thank you," I say. "Thank you thank you thank you." Dark storm clouds are rolling in again, filling up the sky. It's freezing, and I put on my down jacket. All of my exposed skin is red and raw, and I can't stop shivering. There is sand stuck to my face, and in my hair. My legs are numb and aching. I just have to get to the Motel 6, I think. I imagine the thirty hikers ahead of me, all crowded into a single room. Friends, I think. Other humans.

Ted appears in a warm, windless Ford Fiesta. He's retired, and is part of the city council.

"This is my first year doin' this," he says. "We get a lot of hikers, comin' off the trail. Hurricane force winds, that's what you were hiking in today. Down in the valley they rerouted the interstate."

"Oh dear," I say.

"I guess you want the Motel 6?"

"Yes," I say.

I peer out the window. Mojave, as far as I can tell, is a sort of a nowhere place- just a highway crossing in the windy desert, some low buildings hunkered down close to the earth. Ted drops me at the Motel 6. It's dark outside, and the wind is howling with a terrible fierceness. The motel is large. All the doors are shut against the wind, the curtains drawn. Where are the other hikers? I think, a wave of loneliness sweeping through me.

The rooms are cheap and so even though my budget for the trail is very tight, I decide to rent one all for myself. I need this. I need this room. In a sudden decision, I decide to get the room for two nights. The room is small, bright, and clean, and I shut the door behind me against the wind. I latch all of the extra latches. Woo woo woo! I can still hear it, pounding against the facade of the building. I drop my things on the carpet and walk slowly to the bathroom. In the bathroom, I take off all my clothes and climb into the shower. I turn the water on hot and sit on the floor of the shower for a very long time.

***

During my zero in Mojave I leave my room just once- to buy roast chicken, canned chili, fruit, vegetables and Gatorade at the grocery store across the street. Outside is how I imagine Mars to be; dusty and flat and the wind is screaming. I also buy razors, to shave my legs. I haven't shaved my legs since I was nineteen and I realized that I didn't *have* to shave my legs but now, since I'm using my legs so much, I want to see them. While shaving my legs on the floor of the small shower I discover that my calves have become strangely hard, as though they're made not of flesh but of something else. Wood maybe. What am I, I think. Some sort of athlete?

I eat the entire roast chicken, wash my clothes in the sink, clean the trash from my pack. I listen to trains rattle by in the desert. All day the wind continues to pound. As I lie in bed that night I remember what someone said the other day- that once this storm was over a heat wave would come through. I wonder what that person meant by "heat". I contemplate the subjective meaning of "heat" until I fall asleep.

***

In the morning I eat a granola bar and pull back the heavy curtain and peer at the bright outside world. The wind has gone, and everything is still. I call the ride angel who picked me up at the trailhead, but only reach his voicemail. How will I get to Tehachapi, I think. I gather my things from all over the room, pull my clothes off the furniture where they've dried stiff. I fill up my water bottles and stuff everything into my pack.

Outside the sun is hot and bright. There's a hiker named Dog sitting against the wall of the lobby.

"I'm waiting for my ride," he says. "He's taking me to Tehachapi."

"You think he'd take me too?" I ask.

I've only eaten a granola bar, but there's no time for anything else. Dog's ride appears- it's a man named Hawk, retired from the US Coast Guard, driving a sedan with tinted windows.

"I'm looking for a ride to the post office in Tehachapi," I say. "I also need a ride to the trailhead. And I need to get denatured alcohol somewhere, for my stove. I can give you gas money."

"You want to go to the Home Depot?" says Hawk. "I've got some errands to run."

We drive up a few feet in elevation and around a hill and there is Tehachapi, a cute little strip of a town with actual real trees. Trees!

At the Home Depot I wander the wide cement aisles, confused and disoriented. I'm clutching my water bottle and my skin is sunburnt a deep russet color. I keep asking employees where the denatured alcohol is, but they have no idea what I'm talking about.

"What's it used for?" They ask.

"I don't know," I say. "I use it for my backpacking stove."

At last I find it in the paint section, in a huge metal can. There are no smaller cans so I buy the big one, along with a couple of packages of beef jerky. I eat one of the packages of beef jerky while leaning against the car, waiting for Hawk.

At the post office I tear open my general-delivery resupply box and dump it onto the counter as though I'm about to do a timed drill. Ready, set, *resupply!* I paw through the pile of food, pulling out the things I still like to eat, dropping some other things into the hiker box that the post office has set up in the corner. The section I'm about to start is the longest section so far- 130 or so miles until my next resupply- and my food bag, when I'm finished stuffing things into it, is massive. I fill up the plastic bottled-water

114

bottle I use as my fuel bottle, and put the remaining denatured alcohol in the hiker box. I find a couple of good bars there, and add those to my stash.

Hawk is standing by, picking up empty plastic bags and putting them in the trash, waiting for me to finish.

"You want a bar of really dark chocolate?" I say. For some reason I've sent myself three. He unwraps it and takes a big bite.

"This is different," he says.

Hawk, in his incredible generosity, then drives me all the way back to the trailhead. I pull my pack from the trunk of his sedan and sling it on- it's super heavy, the heaviest it's been in a while. I have six days' worth of food and seventeen miles' worth of water in there.

I wave goodbye to Hawk and begin to walk. The trail climbs up into the hot, dusty hills, and the sun is painfully bright. I'm sleep deprived and I still, in a way, feel exhausted from my trek through the windstorm- seventeen miles, I think. I just have to make it seventeen miles.

I see no other humans all afternoon, and it is dark when I reach the bend in the trail where the spring will be. It's damp here, and the forest is all around. I swing my headlamp back and forth and its wavery beam exposes the other hikers there, crouched on the ground over little pots of food. I say hello, but I cannot see their faces.

The spring is a little drizzle of water running from a plastic pipe into a trough. I fill up my water bottles and pitch my shelter next to the trail. The wind has picked up again and I can hear it way above us- woo woo woo! But it cannot reach down into the sheltered hollow where we are. I crawl into my shelter, spread out my sleeping pad, and collapse into my bag. Outside I can hear the rustle of other hikers on their tyvek. Other people, I think. Hallelujah.

***

Usually I wear my down jacket while I sleep, but it's so warm that I sleep in just my t-shirt. Uh oh, I think, when I wake in my tent in the morning. It's supposed to be cold in the desert at night. What does this mean?

I pull myself from my tent and see that while I was asleep a dozen other people arrived and spread their groundsheets in the small clearing around the spring. These people are just beginning to wake, and sit up in their bags. Their hair is tousled and their faces are smeared with dust. It's seven, late for a hiker morning. Everyone must've night hiked like I did, to beat the heat.

It's completely still, and the sun has not yet found its way into our little canyon. I fill my bottles and hoist my pack. It's so heavy I almost stagger- I'm still tired and I've packed nineteen miles' worth of water this morning. Nineteen miles to the next water source, another spring flowing from another pipe. And between here and there, what? And so I begin to hike up, and up, and up. All morning I climb up through a burn. This is the most recent burn I've seen; it looks as though it happened just yesterday, or as though it's still burning at this moment. This land is on fire, I think, as I slog through the hot sand, past the twisted ghosts of trees. There is no shade anywhere.

I was drenched in my own sweat just a few hours after setting out in the morning, and that sweat dried, and my shirt hardened with salt. Now my shirt is drenched again, a second time, as I slog with infinite slowness up the mountain on the sun-baked path. The spring, I think. I just have to make it to the spring.

I reach the spring in late afternoon and there is no one there. The spring is a bit of water flowing from a pipe into a slanted meadow filled with nettles. Below the meadow are large flattened spots for camping. I've been so hot for so long that I am exhausted, and I set up my tent right away, on the edge of the clearing. I'm going to camp here, I think. Fuck it. Nineteen miles but I feel like I've gone twenty-six. I cook a little pot of food and get my chores done and then climb into my tent to rest. A handful of other hikers arrive- I can hear them outside my tent. They gather wood for a fire in the big firepit nearby. Everyone is camping here, it seems. Everyone is exhausted by the day. I listen to their voices, their talking and laughing. Then they are all around me, covering the clearing with their crinkling groundsheets. I think I recognize some of their voices, and I climb out of my tent- it's Spark, and the other fast people.

"Hello?" I say.

"Come hang out with us," says one of them.

It's night now and the group of us huddles together in the clearing, our headlamps set to the red setting out of respect for the dark. Across from me is Spark, blowing on a small pot of ramen, the last of the alcohol burning white in his popcan stove. Next to me is Track Meat, a tall man with a long beard and sun-faded short-shorts. Track Meat wears thick seventies eyeglasses and as we talk he pushes them up on his nose. There's also Instigate, sprawled on her stomach on her sleeping bag. She's twenty-two years old, and just graduated from Oberlin College. Her greasy down jacket has grown ambiguous with dirt- is it gray? Blue?

"All my gear is borrowed," she says.

"Word game," says Track Meat. "Twelve letter words that start with P."

I know that some people say that the PCT is crowded, and they don't like the crowds. But at this moment, at the end of this hot and lonely day, I love it. Sitting at this spring with all these strangers. These are my people, I think, later that night, when I'm in my sleeping bag, almost too happy to sleep. These are my people, and in the morning we'll all wake up here, side by side, and then we'll set out together into this great hot desert, the Mojave's last hurrah.

***

I wake before dawn, like I've been doing. I'm tired, but I can't sleep anymore. Too excited for hiking, I suppose. Well, I think. What else is there.

Outside the cowboy campers are spread in the dirt, their sleeping bags pulled up over their heads. Instigate is half out of hers, her sleeping pad askew. Various objects are arranged around the sleeping hikers- water bottles, shoes, things in dirty ziploc bags. Pieces of gear that would look, to an outsider, like bits of trash.

The morning is hot, but I'm in the forest and it's shady. I reach the first water source after a few hours- it's a clear, beautiful spring, flowing via pipe into a trough among the ponderosas. I want to stay near this beautiful water forever; I want to put my whole body into it. But I can't, so I fill my bottles and hike on.

I climb up out of the forest and onto an exposed hillside. My plan had been to hike for another hour, find a patch of shade, and take a siesta. But it is only hot sand and sagebrush beneath the bright, merciless sun. I'll hike to the next cache, I think. It's at the bottom of all of this; there will be shade there, and I can rest. I just have to get to the next cache.

After a few hot exposed hours, I round a bend and there is the cache-plastic gallons of water, tied together with string and piled in the dirt. And not a single tree for shade.

After a few minutes Spark arrives, and we sit on the burning sand and eat handfuls of things from our trailmix bags, chocolate melted over everything. The sun is making us woozy so we pull our sleeping pads over our heads to create a bit of shade. Instigate arrives. Her hair, which hangs over her face, is streaked from the sun. There's a bounce in her step, as though she has springs in her shoes.

Up on the hillside is a single Joshua tree. We want to wait out the heat of the day and we realize that this tree is our only hope for shade.

Joshua trees consist of thick, scaly trunks that end in poofs of spiny leaves, like an agave plant. Basically they are Dr. Suess trees that will stab you in the face if you walk into them. Their convoluted trunks create bands of shade. More hikers show up until there are seven of us and we contort ourselves on the hot sand. In the end, each of us has a little patch of shade that is almost, but not quite, big enough. Someone checks the thermometer on their pack strap; it is 96 degrees beneath the Joshua tree.

"You know my dad thru-hiked the PCT in the seventies," says Instigate. "I always wanted to do it." She pulls an empty peanut butter jar from her pack and fills it with something dried from a ziploc bag. She adds water and stirs this with a plastic spoon.

"What's that?" I say.

"I worked at a co-op last winter," says Instigate. "We'd make big pots of food in the deli- curried chickpeas, lentil soup. Whatever was left at the end of the day I'd take home and dehydrate."

Spark tells the plot of a YouTube video, then someone tells another. It's like we're all sitting around the internet, together. Except we're not. We lie there under the Joshua tree in the bands of shade, watching the empty sky, fidgeting. We sweat; we move as little as possible.

Around four it is still hot, but we can't wait any longer. We set out in a group. The shadows are long and I climb, sweating profusely; I fall behind. I have no idea where the others are. Then I turn a corner and they are all there, curled in the shade of another Joshua tree.

"You guys didn't make it far," I say happily, as I drop my pack in the sand. Track Meat is there, stretched in the sand, reading a scifi paperback. He pours some instant lentils into his cookpot, adds water, and sets the pot in the sun to rehydrate. Instigate holds out a ziploc bag of gummy bears that have melted into a single warm, gelatinous mass. We take turns touching the bag and laughing.

I feel buoyed by this company, by these strangers in the desert. Here we all are, on this expedition. Here we all go, towards Canada. Will we even make it.

We hike. The light fades completely from the sky and the stars come out. We make a train, hiking close together, and we do not turn on our headlamps. We reach another pass and drop our packs. Track Meat pulls a glow-in-the-dark star chart from his pack and holds it up, pointing out the constellations in the sky.

"Let's camp here," I say. There is a flat, sandy clearing and we spread our groundsheets there, beneath the Joshua trees. Instigate recites an epic poem from memory- it is long and full of drama and I feel as though it has been written about us, right now. I have *Best American Short Stories* on my phone so I read aloud about a woman working in the Midwest and a man named Mangus who lives in a trailer. Afterward the world is absolutely quiet; I had forgotten how silent things were without the wind. The stars wink on above me. Thank you, I say to the universe. Thank you.

***

In the desert, the water dictates the miles. Today there is a twenty-one mile stretch between water sources; the stretch begins just eight miles after we wake. This gives us a twenty-nine mile day, unless we want to dry camp, which would require that each of us carry a few extra liters of water, in addition to the four, or five, or six we're already carrying.

On top of that, the trail climbs for most of the day. I carry five liters; in the heat I know that even this will not be enough, but I do not want to carry more. All day I ration water.

Also, the water report is extremely vague about the water source at the end of the twenty-one mile stretch- there is a campground there, says the water report, but the faucets are turned off. The small cache, says the water report, is empty. Down the trail, however, on a faint trail through the brush, is a series of cisterns. The first cistern is empty; the second cistern is empty; the third cistern has had water in previous years, although no one has reported on it so far this year.

I think all this over as I hike up in the heat through a burn, rationing my water. Twenty-one miles with no water source, and then there might not be water at the end? Well, I think. Well. I walk side by side with Instigate on the wide, dusty trail. We talk about misogyny, about cities where we've lived, about how to make a meaningful life. Instigate's hair swings free over her shoulders. Now and then the wind blows it in her face.

"Dammit," she says, pushing it back. "I whittled a hair stick, but I lost it. I have to whittle another one." She pulls out a clif bar, a seasonal flavor, and looks at it thoughtfully. "This one was on sale."

I run out of water two miles before the campground. I'm thirsty but it's dusk, and cool, so I'm alright.

Instigate tells me about her years of running in highschool, on the track team.

"Our coach would make us run in the heat until we threw up. We'd ask him for water and he'd say 'No, just suck on a rock if you're thirsty.'"

I'm not gonna die but still I can't help obsessing, those last two miles, about the water source. Water water water, I think. Rest rest rest. Shade. But then, I think, what if there is no water? The next reliable water is eight miles after the campground. Could I do a thirty-seven mile day, if I really had to? What would that even feel like?

Then we're coming down off a ridge, Instigate and I, and we can see the campground below us. The campground is empty but then at the edge of it is an RV, and a white tent ringed in what looks like prayer flags. Trail magic? I think. Root beer floats? But no, I tell myself. That's probably just some campers.

"I bet it's just campers," I say. "Maybe they can give us some water."

"Yeah," says Instigate. "Let's not hope for anything else. Just in case it's not anything."

As we near the tent we see people in the road playing frisbee. From where we are it looks as though their shirts are filthy, but I can't really tell for sure. Then, suddenly, I realize that those aren't prayer flags around the tent- they're PCT bandanas! And then, suddenly, we're standing in front of the tent looking at a table laden with bottles of water, Gatorade, and burgers. And our friends are there too, sitting in plastic chairs, stuffing their faces. And other hikers. And all of it, all of it is for us.

I can't believe it. I fill my liter bottle with cold blue Gatorade and chug the entire thing. Then I put a burger patty in a plastic bowl with scrambled eggs on top- the eggs are leftover from breakfast- and cover the whole thing in mustard. I sit in a folding camp chair and eat this. I'm so happy I could burst.

"And in the morning," says one of the trail angels, as she picks up plastic cups, "there are pancakes. From 6 a.m. until people stop eating them."

What even is this. I can't believe it.

Dark falls and all the tired hikers carry their packs into the campground and spread their groundsheets in the dirt beneath the huge oak trees. We have "storytime" again, although this time there are more hikers listening. I sit in my sleeping bag and read a story aloud from *Best American Short Stories* about a man in Texas working on the set of a Hollywood movie. The story is dirty and random and makes us all laugh but then nothing happens for a while and I realize that the story is incredibly long and so I stop reading, halfway through, and then realize that everyone is already asleep. I put down my phone and pull the sleeping bag up over me.

And tomorrow, I think. What wonders will tomorrow hold.

***

We wake to the sunrise. I sit up in my sleeping bag and look at the others, sitting up in their sleeping bags. I rub the dust from my face. The sun is warming us, warming everything it touches. It's good to be alive, I think. Really, really good.

I think of all the weeks I've spent in the heat, of all the various incarnations of desert I've seen. I never knew there were so many different kinds of desert. So many variations of light and heat and sand. Tomorrow I'll be in Kennedy Meadows, the start of the Sierra. The water report ends just fifty miles after that. "Water is plentiful after mile 750," say my maps. I try to imagine what that would even be like, to have water everywhere.

We climb in the heat all morning, up and up and up. Midday we stop for lunch at a spring that runs through a fold in the dusty hills. Everyone is sitting on a slant in the dirt, the contents of their food bags spread around them. Stale nuts, melted candy bars, smashed cheese in dirty ziploc bags. Carnation instant breakfast. We resupply tomorrow, in Kennedy Meadows. We are eating what's left.

We climb and climb and climb, and when we're at the top we go slowly down, on a dusty path through sad burned hills that stretch away into infinity. Kennedy Meadows is out there, the Sierras, the end of the desert- but as I round each corner, all I can see is more burned hills. I feel sick to my stomach today. Just a little bit, but still it makes me slower than the others. They say that lots of hikers get sick in this section- I wonder if it's the water? I purify all my water, but still, there are so many people around, so few water sources, so many chances for contamination. Well, I think, as I walk through the burn, watching the light play in the little clouds that have gathered in the sky. I'm only a little bit sick. It's not like it's giardia. It'll pass.

Four miles before Kennedy Meadows is the Kern River, the first real river of the PCT. We've been anticipating this river for days. Fifty miles to the river, we've said. Thirty-seven miles to the river. Almost to the river! There are, according to the water report, swimming holes there, and our plan is to camp at the river tonight and hike the last few miles into Kennedy Meadows in the morning. Now I push myself through the burn, faster and faster. Must get to the swimming holes, I think. Must catch up with the others.

Just as I arrive at the river, it begins to rain. The river is slow and marshy, and there aren't any places to camp.

"Have you seen a group of people?" I ask some day hikers.

"Yes," say the day hikers. "They came through here and kept hiking."

I look at the rain where it lands on the water. I'm hot and dusty and I'd been looking forward to getting into the water all day. But now nothing is as I expected it to be, and I feel a little bewildered.

I take off my clothes and get in the river in the rain. The river is warm and shallow and filled with muck. Afterward I hike half a mile and find my friends, calling out to me from on top of a bluff.

There is a large clearing on top of the bluff and everyone has set up their shelters- it's like a village of ultralight tents. I put mine up too and then the rain stops and we all sit in the dirt, cooking little pots of food on our stoves. On the other side of the clearing someone is playing guitar and singing and then night falls and it's hiker midnight, 9 p.m. I crawl into my tent and look out at the clearing through the mesh. Tomorrow, I will have hiked seven hundred miles. I'll be at Kennedy Meadows. The promised land. The Sierra. The end of the desert. Everything.

Part Two: The Sierras

June 6 to June 30

Mile 698 to mile 1018

***

I wake in the dark, but morning has not come. The night is black and still and it's cold, so cold. Colder, even, than it was in the desert at night. I scrunch down into my sleeping bag and pull it up over my face. I try and will myself warm.

At last there is a little light and I sit up. I dig through my pack with cold fingers, extract my toothbrush. Afterward I eat a few handfuls of almonds and pack my things away, the big items stuffed into my pack with force and each small item in its special place until my meager possessions are all bundled up just so. It's time for another day.

My friends are still asleep, but I can't wait any longer. Kennedy Meadows, I am thinking. Kennedy Meadows Kennedy Meadows. The Sierra Nevada Mountains are a place I've never been- there will be water there, they say, water everywhere, and tall granite spires. We'll stay up high, around ten thousand feet. All I know, so far, is the desert- the heat, the sun, the gently sloping trail. The desert is my entire world. Now, apparently, everything is about to change.

As I hike the light spills over the mountains and already the landscape is shifting. The valleys are softening and in the distance, the horizon hints at greatness. Oh, the promised land!

I reach the Kennedy Meadows General Store before it opens and press my face against the glass. Shelves of food, cases of soda, racks of postcards. All of it dark and locked up. I sit on the wooden deck, watching the light grow stronger. At last the little bell tinkles and I go inside to get the boxes I mailed myself. Food, new shoes, a bear canister, trekking poles- there are so many boxes they fill up my arms and I stumble with them onto the deck and dump them onto one of the tables. I assemble the poles and lean them against the railing of the deck to admire them. Look at my new trekking poles! I will say to my friends, when they arrive. Don't be jealous! Then I tear open my food box and begin to sort things into ziploc bags. It's warm on the wooden deck and country music is wafting from some speakers.

My friends arrive and get their boxes too (we all have so many boxes!) and then the deck is crowded with people and things and someone turns the music up. I can smell meat cooking on a grill and I order a double burger and it comes out wrapped in iceberg lettuce. I cover the burger in mustard and grease runs down my forearms while I eat it. A woman hiker is sitting across the table from me, putting olive oil in her long hair. She explains to me the best way to acclimate to high elevations. Go slow, she says. Drink lots of water. I finish my burger, wondering what the world will feel like at thirteen thousand feet.

Fitting my bear canister in my pack is a pain. The bear can is required in the Sierras but first of all, I can't even fit all my food in there. And second, the thing is large and awkward. And do I even have enough food? It's a hundred miles until my next resupply, plus Mount Whitney, which you can summit from the PCT. They say that your mileage drops in the Sierra, and your appetite goes up. So six days, seven days- how much food should I pack? And will I really be that hungry? It's hard to imagine doing *fewer* miles and being *more* hungry. It's so hard to guess how much food I'll need, I think, as I shove the canister into my pack.

***

The next night the condensation descends on us like a ghost and when we wake in the dawn our sleeping bags have been dampened and then frozen stiff. I pull my clothes from the bushes; they are rigid with ice. Everything is covered all over in sparkling frost. We're fourteen miles from Kennedy Meadows- we hiked out the day before and camped beneath a bridge stuffed with swallows' nests, beside a slow clear river.

This would never happen in the desert, I think, as I pull on my icy sports bra. In the desert wet items of clothing magically dry, even at night, and there is no condensation. So then, we are out of the desert!

Today we begin our climb into the Sierras. We will climb and climb and climb, for days and days, and each day we will be a little higher. Ten thousand feet, eleven thousand feet, twelve thousand feet! Until what? I think. What is even up there, in those mountains?

We climb slowly, each of us feeling the altitude a little bit, in our own way. We stop for lots of breaks, and laugh and eat. I'm already hungrier than usual, and at one break, sitting against a warm hunk of granite, I examine my gallon ziploc of Fritos. Will it be enough? Would any amount of Fritos be enough?

"Let's all get an apartment together," says Spark, "after the trail." He's eating dry ramen, breaking it up and dipping it into the flavoring packet.

"A small apartment," I say. "A very small apartment. And we can spread our sleeping pads on the floor."

Instigate is picking the raisins from a bag of trailmix.

"I don't want to own any possessions," she says. The world around us is very still.

At dusk we camp in a flat quiet forest on top of the mountain. We spread our groundsheets out just as dark falls and I lie there, looking at the stars. Ten thousand feet, I think. Ten thousand feet and counting.

***

The next afternoon we reach a lake- Chicken Spring Lake. It is our first lake. It is clear and shallow and it sits in a little hollow at the base of some gravelly slopes, sparkling like glass. Track Meat and Spark lounge on the green grass in the bright yellow sun like scared baby chickens while Instigate and I take off our clothes and jump into the water. The water is hypothermia-cold and we gasp as we paddle around. Then we lie on a warm flat rock in the sun to dry.

"I'm so happy," I say. "So happy."

Another hiker arrives and we shout at him until he jumps in the lake too.

We sprawl on the grass until dusk, telling stories, laughing, and cooking little pots of food. It's a fun adventure, every day, to get in and out of our bear canisters- they're difficult to open and I regularly put things like gatorade powder in the bottom and then I must, in the middle of the day, struggle to open my canister. Spark jokes that they're our regulation nightstands-

"In the Sierra," he says, "all necessary sleeping objects must be elevated above the ground."

***

All night it's cold. I wake every hour and tug at the corners of my sleeping bag, trying to keep in the heat. When dawn comes it's a relief, but still it's too cold to get up. Twenty-eight degrees, says the thermometer on Spark's pack. The others are cold too and we stay buried in our sleeping bags and have storytime for a while. Other hikers walk by on the trail that passes our campsite, headed to Mt. Whitney, and we holler at them.

"Good morning!"

"Hello!"

"I love you!"

At last we get up and pack our things away and start to hike. It's eleven miles to Crabtree Meadows and then another eight miles on a side trail to the top of Mt. Whitney, the tallest peak in the Lower 48. Fourteen thousand five hundred feet high! Apparently, pretty much everyone on the PCT climbs Mt. Whitney. You're so close, they say. You're in the best shape of your life. You may not ever get another chance.

I don't feel like I'm in the best shape of my life. All day I feel nauseous and weak from the altitude, like I can barely hike at all. It sucks. I was feeling so strong, and now this. My morale bottoms out. The tilt-a-whirl! I think. Today I'm riding the tilt-a-whirl. I want to cry. This isn't what I wanted, this unrelenting nausea. The group stops every few miles and we sit in the grass, eating snacks. Instigate finds wild onions and gives them away to everyone. By the time we reach Crabtree Meadows it's afternoon and there are thick gray clouds tumbling over the mountain.

"Let's wait until morning to climb the mountain," we say.

We set up our shelters and cook our little pots of food and then lie on a big flat rock in a cuddle puddle, laughing and farting. We are all low on food and we hungrily watch a group of deer as they browse on the other side of the meadow.

"How could we get that deer?" I say.

"Run it off a cliff, maybe," someone volunteers.

Bits of cloud race across the sky. Someone produces a bag of trail mix that has cocoa puffs in it and we pass it around. Dinner.

I'm pretty sure I don't have enough food for this section, but I might if I skip Mt. Whitney. If I skip Whitney it's only thirty-two miles to the next resupply- twenty-three miles plus nine miles of side trail to the Onion Valley trailhead. And I feel so awful from the altitude. Hey, I think. Maybe I will skip Mt. Whitney. And then there is Forester Pass, the highest point on the PCT. Thirteen thousand feet, almost as high as Whitney! But everyone else is climbing Whitney, so I should do it too. Right? I can't decide.

The light dims and our cuddle puddle breaks up. Everyone's arms have fallen asleep. We crawl into our shelters and I lie in my sleeping bag, feeling vaguely ill. I can do whatever I want. Right?

***

At five a.m., I hear Instigate walking around in the cold. It's twenty degrees outside.

"Time to climb the mountain!" she says. The others are rustling in the dark, but I stay in my tent. When I do get up there is only Track Meat, clipping the hip belt of his pack, and a bunch of bare spots in the dirt where the others camped.

"I'm not gonna climb Whitney," I say to Track Meat. "I just don't feel up for it. I'm gonna hike out."

"OK," says Track Meat, and then he's gone.

I feel sad.

It's early, though, and I have Forester Pass ahead of me, and that feels good.

In a normal year, Forester Pass is blanketed in snow.

Wait, let me back up.

When you're hiking towards Forester Pass, all you can see is a little trail that winds between alpine lakes and in the distance, a huge wall of rock. Nowhere in the huge wall of rock does there seem to be a "pass." There are some little notches in the huge, sheer wall of rock, but those seem precariously, impossibly steep. So all there is to do is walk forward on your little trail between the clear, sparkly alpine lakes, and assume that at some point there will be a "pass".

In a normal year the huge wall of rock is blanketed in snow, and at some point you would just start climbing, sort of kicking steps, up the snow towards the very smallest notch in the rock, which is actually the pass. This year, though, the snow in the Sierras is very low and so I just walk, and walk and walk, through bright green meadows and past marmots on their rocks, and little burbling streams, and the air grows thinner and thinner, and I eat lots of dark chocolate, and I feel fantastic, and the huge wall of rock grows closer...

And suddenly I am switchbacking up the rock, looking down as the green meadows and the burbling streams grow farther and farther away. I am huffing and puffing but I do not, somehow, feel as though I am going to throw up. And I have enough food, since I didn't climb Whitney! And I'm out here on my own, in this great beautiful wilderness! I am a free agent! And then I am on top, gazing down at everything in both directions, the kingdom I have just traversed and my new kingdom, to the north.

Forester pass, the highest point on the PCT.

It's cold on the pass, so I hurry down the other side. There are a few patches of snow, but I just hop right over them. My pack is so light, seeing as I'm almost out of food, and I feel like I'm flying. No altitude sickness! Just like old times! I think of the desert, how I could walk for as long as I wanted. How my body made energy. How my blood carried oxygen. Maybe the Sierras won't be so bad? Maybe I'm acclimating?

A little ways down the pass there is a clear, burbling stream bordered in spongy green meadow and I sit in this meadow and eat a snack. The sun is golden, the temperature just right. I fill my plastic Gatorade bottle with the best-tasting water in the world. Why can't I feel this happy every day? Why isn't life always like this?

I continue to descend, away from the rocky crags and into a seemingly infinite meadow of unbelievable beauty. Wow, I think, as I watch the afternoon light play on the little flowers in the grass. John Muir wasn't exaggerating. There are scattered trees now, and between them the light is broken into warm yellow bands. Little lakes, round and aquamarine, glitter in the sunshine. The air is soft and perfectly still. I just want to lie down in a meadow. I just want to lie down in a meadow and sleep for a hundred years.

I pass groups of day hikers, headed up. Their packs are huge, and my ego puffs up.

"Hello!" I say to them merrily. They frown at me- they are in pain. They wanted to go backpacking, but now they are in pain.

At the bottom of the valley the grass is tall and thick and the mosquitoes are out in droves. I stop to drink and they land on my legs, my arms, my face. Well hello, mosquitoes, I say. It's nice to see you at last. I keep hiking and the trail begins to climb. It's evening, and I'm tired. I huff and puff. I pass a ranger, scattering stones at an illegal fire ring.

"You must be a PCT thru-hiker," she says.

"How can you tell?" I ask.

"You PCT hikers are always so tan," she says.

"Uh huh,"

"And your packs are so small,"

"Uh huh,"

"And you hike so fast."

"Ah." My ego puffs up even larger.

"Can I see your permit?" She says.

I dig it out of my pack and present it to her. My first ranger! She squints at it and hands it back.

"You got a bear canister in there?" She says.

I rap it with my knuckles.

I reach the junction with the Kearsarge Pass trail. This trail will take me out over Kearsarge Pass, and down into the town of Independence. Out of the Sierras and back into the hot, flat desert. There is a little flat spot to camp at the trail junction, and a stream burbles through the grass. I set up my tent in the dusk, stuff my food into my bear canister, and set the canister in the dirt a little ways away. I climb into my tent and arrange my

133

shoes and remaining water around me. I eat some almonds and a few handfuls of Fritos. Just nine miles in the morning to the trailhead. Then resupply. I turn on my phone, but it beeps at me and turns off again, dead. I don't even care. My first section in the Sierras is finished! I lie in my sleeping bag and listen to the water running through the grass. I'm ready to recharge.

***

I wake in the cold morning and crawl out of my shelter and squat in the dirt to pee. I retrieve my bear canister (each night I feel as though I am setting a "trap," and each morning I am slightly disappointed that I didn't "catch" anything) and sit in my sleeping bag, eating the dregs of my food from dirty ziploc bags. Almond crumbles, the dust of crackers. Just nine miles to the trailhead!

I hike past several beautiful, twinkling lakes and then climb up and up and up, to Kearsarge Pass. On top of the pass, I sit on a rock and look out at the world. I've been in the High Sierra for a week and now, sitting here, I can see the desert floor way down below me. The trailhead is only a few miles from me but the towns where I'll resupply, Lone Pine and Bishop, are all the way at the bottom, via a long winding road. The desert! It never left. It's been here all along. I realize for the first time how high up I am. The valley down below is all hot, flat sand, stretching away. But way up here in the craggy peaks is a wonderland of water and light. Lush meadows and little flowers! Soft pine forests full of deer! What magic is this.

I leave the pass and switchback on the steeply descending trail, towards the valley floor. The trail descends seemingly forever, a winding staircase of rock. The switchbacks are strange and labyrinthine, and sometimes it appears as though the hikers descending are actually coming up.

"Like we're in an M.C. Escher painting," says one day-hiker who passes me, headed down. At last I am at the bottom, at the trailhead, and I drop my pack onto the pavement. I drink some water and assess the situation. Lush, craggy peaks tower up around me and day hikers lean into the trunks of their cars, organizing supplies. This trailhead is the end of the road, and everyone seems to be going into the mountains, not coming out. How will I get to town?

I am sitting on a metal bear box at the edge of the parking area when a little pickup truck pulls up next to me.

"You need a ride to town?" says the man inside. He is small and tan. His has silver hair and he's wearing Ray Bans.

"Yes," I say.

"I was just in the area," he says, "and I thought I'd come by and see if any thru-hikers needed a ride."

The man's name is Yawn, and he hiked the PCT a few years back. He takes me to the main road and drops me off and I stick my thumb out; within a minute a car stops, a little sedan. Wow, I think. I've forgotten how easy it is to hitch when I'm by myself. In the car are a woman and a pug, on their way to a funeral somewhere east. The woman chatters at me in a soothing voice. The pug sprawls on its bed in the front seat and eyes me sleepily. Its head rests on a bag of pistachio nuts.

I look out the window as we drive through the desert. Sand and heat, sand and heat. And the air is as thick as pudding.

The woman drops me in Lone Pine, a little stagecoach town that looks like a movie set for an old western. I pick up my resupply box at the post office and then get a private room at the hostel- it has two sets of bunk beds. The room is clean and filled with light. I open the window to let in the good desert air with all its heady oxygen and take off my clothes and put them in the tub. After showering I put my clothes back on wet. I know they'll dry in the time it takes me to walk to the store and back.

The store is small and messy and there is a gaping hole in the chip aisle where the Fritos should be. I can't really find anything I want to eat. I buy some potato chips and an apple and return to my room, disappointed.

A little while later, I get a text from Track Meat.

"We're at the trailhead. We're coming to Lone Pine? There are seven of us."

"I got a room." I text back. "The store has no Fritos."

I barely have time to lie on my bed in a clean white sunbeam for a little while, spacing out and staring at the ceiling, before everyone arrives. Their shirts are filthy and they're clutching cases of beer. Track Meat tosses me a bag of Fritos he found at the gas station, officially bonding us for life. The door of the room is propped open to let in the good evening air and we all take off our shoes and sprawl on the landing to drink. There is a Rock Paper Scissors tournament and footrub exchanges and then we sit, watching the little stagecoach town go dark. After a while, we are hungry and we bound down the stairs and set out into the warm, empty street. We check the dumpster behind the pizza place but there's nothing there. We all pull our pants up real high.

"Who feels like *only skipping?*" says Spark.

As we skip down the dark sidewalk another hiker runs by, slamming into us with his shoulders.

"Juice! Juice! Juice!" he says. It's a game of his invention, and only he knows the rules.

Carl's Jr. is the only thing still open and we order burgers and watch Ciara videos on my phone while we eat. Afterwards, back at our room, Track Meat and I watch the video again and try to copy the moves, but it is impossible.

***

I can't sleep in a bed anymore. I wake up at some indeterminate hour of the night and step over my sleeping friends, who completely cover the floor of the room. I go out onto the landing and watch the sky lighten and look at things on my phone. Things! On my phone! The internet, the whole world, everything! I have no idea what's going on in the world right now. Shootings? Uprisings? Industrial collapse? Kittens being funny? I wouldn't know.

The sun rises and the street is filled with long orange light. Others come out onto the landing, put on their ratty shoes, and set out for the coffeeshop across the street. I go to Carl's Jr. again for breakfast. They have a burger that's wrapped in iceberg lettuce, for people who don't eat gluten. Really big thick pieces of crunchy iceberg lettuce, going all the way around the burger. And there's tomatoes on the burger, and red onions, and pickles and mayo. I've decided that it's the best lettuce-burger I've had. I get sweet potato fries too, and eat them while I'm walking down the street, peering in the windows of the closed-up shops.

After breakfast we all pack up our bags and hitch to Bishop, fifty miles away. Bishop has a big grocery store, so we can resupply there. Hitching in a group is hard and we spread farther and farther apart on the hot, windswept highway until I'm standing in the narrow shade of a single telephone pole, hitching by myself. I can't tell if the people in their cars think I'm completely insane or not. No one in this valley seems to know what the PCT is- they just see a bunch of filthy homeless people trying to hitchhike, all at once, and I'm sure it's terrifying for them.

A van swerves onto the shoulder. Track Meat and Instigate are already in the back, and Spark is in the front. It's a work van and the back is an empty cargo area, with little cardboard boxes of parts flying across the metal floor. There aren't any windows and it's hot back there. Track Meat has a crossword puzzle he's cut from the newspaper, and we try to help him fill in the clues. It gets even hotter in the back, and I start to feel carsick. Then we're in Bishop and the doors are opening and light and cool sweet air are rushing in.

Bishop is an old stagecoach town too, but it's longer than Lone Pine. Spark, Instigate and I walk to the local pizza place. Today is the last day of the California State high school rodeo championships, and all the young cowboys are here, in the pizza place, in their oversized rodeo vests, playing arcade games. I challenge myself to assemble the largest salad bar salad ever. I put potato salad on it, and hardboiled eggs, and bacon, and baby corn. Spark eats an entire medium pizza. The young cowboys stare at us, the dirty homeless people with packs. One of them is carrying a lasso.

We walk to the big grocery store and wander the aisles, stupefied. We lose each other in the vastness and then find each other again, in unlikely places. I buy an inordinate amount of food, the most I've ever packed for a 120-mile section. I also buy fried chicken, vanilla icecream, and a blueberry pie. We congregate with our carts in the Starbucks seating area of the store and unpack our bags, spreading our dirty things across the tidy little tables. We pull out our bear canisters and stuff food into them. I eat the middle of the blueberry pie and half the pint of icecream, and then I feel sick.

I start calling the hotels, but they're all full because of the rodeo. A couple other hikers have gotten a room in a little inn down a side street and so we wander there, through the bright warm alleys of the town. The room has a small vintage kitchenette and one single, huge bed which spreads from wall to wall. It's the biggest bed I've ever seen. There's a screen door that opens out onto the street and the room is filled with light.

Soon everyone is there, all ten of us. There is talk of camping but then everyone decides to stay, all together in the little room. I eat fried chicken and raspberries in the bed and then night falls and Spark, Instigate, Track Meat, and I decide to go exploring. We find a western-themed bar with real swinging doors and order whiskey and I sing along loudly and off-key to all the country songs. The bartender tells me that I look underage and I tell her I live someplace where it rains all the time. Someone says it's Father's Day, but then we don't know for sure if that's true. We pretend that Track Meat and Spark are our fathers. It's really funny for a little while.

It's late when we get back to the room and we collect all the furniture, besides the bed, and stack it in the corner. This leaves floor space for people to sleep. A couple of people collapse on the bed, some others spread their sleeping pads in front of the door. I push mine against the wall, and Track Meat disappears mysteriously into the crack between the bed and the window. We reach a general consensus to keep the path to the bathroom clear, and then I put in my earplugs and go to magical, peaceful earplug land. I barely slept the night before in the hostel, on account of being in a bed, and I am exhausted. It's really comfortable where I am on the floor. Isn't life strange.

***

I wake up on my sleeping pad on the floor and everyone is gone. Their packs are there, but the hotel room is empty. Warm sunlight is filtering in through the window. I look at my watch- it's eight o'clock. I slept until eight o'clock! I can't believe it. I shuffle into the little kitchen and pull my fried chicken from the fridge, and sit on the bench outside to eat it. I text Instigate. We're all at the bakery, she says. Be back soon.

I use the opportunity to organize my pack. Around half of my food will fit in my full-size bear canister; the rest of it fills a stuff sack to bursting. Once everything is shoved inside my pack, I can barely close it. It's full all the way to the top. But it's not too heavy, now that we're out of the desert and I don't have to carry tons of water. Fritos sure take up a lot of space, I think, as I swing the pack onto my back.

The others return and the room turns into a whirlwind of packing and organization. Mid-morning we set out in little clumps toward the road. It's a long hitch back to the trailhead, and then we have the massive climb back up over Kearsarge Pass. We are not looking forward to it.

Eventually, by way of many long waits and short hitches, we make it to the trailhead. I have imagined the hike back up Kearsarge Pass to be so grueling that I am pleasantly surprised when I am, suddenly, at the top. The trail is nicely graded, and I feel good again. Back in the mountains! Back in the land of wonder! It's evening by the time we are down the other side of the pass, and we decide to camp at one of the little lakes along the trail.

Dark comes on and there is only the sound of the wind in the pine trees and the Milky Way, unfurled across the sky. One hundred more miles through the Sierras, I think, as I pull the sleeping bag up over my face. And what will this next section bring?

***

My sleeping bag is wet when I wake, and the condensation on the outside has frozen into a hard crust of ice. It's late for a hiker morning but the sun still hasn't made its way over the granite mountaintops and we sit, our wet sleeping bags wrapped around us, and wait for those magic yellow rays. At last they arrive and we rise stiffly and stuff everything away, dip our Gatorade bottles into the lake to fill them. It's so good to be back on the trail!

We begin to climb Glen pass. It's not a crazy high pass and it's morning, so I feel good. I fall to the back of the group and when I reach the top there they all are, lounging around. Track Meat, Instigate, Spark, various other hikers. There's another pass after this one- we'll descend all the way to eight thousand feet and then climb, over seven miles, back to twelve thousand feet. Pinchot Pass. I cannot really conceptualize a climb of this nature, being new to the Sierras and all. But I feel great.

A few miles later, there is a string of lakes- Rae Lakes. The lakes are like little turquoise mirrors that sparkle in the lush green valley. We stop for lunch on a huge, sun-warmed rock next to one of the lakes. Instigate, true to her name, jumps into the lake and paddles around, gasping. But she cannot persuade anyone else to do the same. There are more lakes, we say.

We'll swim for real in a few miles.

After the lake I fall behind the others and walk through the fragrant pines and bright green meadows by myself, feeling kind of tired. My altitude sickness has kicked in and even though I'm descending, I feel like I'm on a bit of a tilt-a-whirl. Then I see the others clumped in a patch of sun next to a noisy stream, swatting mosquitoes. We've missed our swimming opportunities, somehow, and now there is only climbing, for the rest of the day. My feet are wet from stream crossings, and everyone seems sort of grumpy. I eat some trailmix in the roar next to the stream. I cannot hear what anyone is saying.

We begin to climb and soon we have left the forest behind, the lush green meadows, the sun-warmed rocks. Soon I am at the back of the group, dragging myself up the trail towards the rocky crags in front of me. I feel dizzy, nauseous, weary, as though I'm about to puke- the whole thing. I can barely lift my legs, one after the other down the trail, and I know I have several thousand more feet to go. And it's already evening.

So this is what I'm in for, in the Sierras. This is what it's going to be like. Me at the back, feeling like I'm gonna puke, dragging myself up the trail. I wonder how long I'll be able to keep up with the others who are all, it seems, faster than me. I have to keep up with them, I think, as I drag myself along the trail. I have to keep up. This thought makes me feel sort of panicky.

The sun is dropping behind the rocky crags and I can feel the others getting farther and farther ahead. I'm shivering, even though I'm climbing. I put on my down jacket. Is it really that cold? Why can't I keep myself warm?

Stop hiking, says a little voice inside me. Stop hiking and just camp on this side of the pass.

But I can't, I think. I don't want to camp in the dark by myself. I have to meet up with the others. They could be miles ahead by now!

Stop hiking, says that little part of me. Stop hiking stop hiking stop hiking.

Then I see Instigate, sitting on a rock in a field of boulders. The light around her is gray. The sun is setting over the peaks.

"Oh my god," I say. "I'm so glad you're back here too."

140

We set out together towards Pinchot pass, lifting our leaden legs, gasping for air. We are both weary, exhausted, depleted, for reasons we both can and cannot explain. In the normal world, if you're tired, you can just exercise less, or not at all. I won't go for a run today, you can say. I won't ride my bike very far. But not on the PCT. On the PCT, you have to hike. Whether you want to or not. And in the Sierras, you have to HIKE.

I leave the trail for a while, via my brain. I have this thing I do- I construct elaborate fantasies of situations that would make me happy and I play them over and over in my head, changing little details each time. In this one it's the end of August, a week before my birthday, and I am in Portland. I go to Seamus' house and all my friends are there. There's a huge spread of pot roast, kale salad, and other non-trail foods that I can no longer fathom. There are dogs there too, and I sit on the floor and let these dogs jump all over me. The dogs have bad breath, but I don't care.

We reach the top of Pinchot Pass a little after eight. The moon is out, and the last of the light is draining from the edges of the sky. It's freezing up here, and we hurry down the rocky trail on the other side. Before us are a series of bare hills and down beyond that, a couple of lakes. Where have our friends gone? To the cold lakes? To the lush forests at lower elevations? We cup our hands over our mouths and make strange noises as we descend, echoing them off the rocky crags. We hear nothing in return, and soon it is completely dark. Then I see a little flicker of something, a headlamp in the fold of a little hill, down below the trail. We cup our hands over our mouths and make strange noises again.

"Ay ay ay!" comes the response.

We find Spark and several other hikers on a small shelf below the trail, their alcohol stoves flickering in the dark. Nearby a stream burbles from the edge of a snowfield. It's cold, and we can all see our breath. I set up my shelter. My sleeping bag is still wet almost all the way through from the condensation the night before, and I prepare myself for Maximum Insulation. In my shelter I spread out my sleeping pads, and then climb into my bag with my long underwear, my down jacket, my warm hat, and my rain jacket on. I pull the two hoods over my hat and cinch them tight. I snap the special snap at the top of the quilt that goes around the back of my neck, the one I just discovered that makes the bag extra warm. I lie down, peering out of the mesh of my tarp. The landscape is dark except for the light of the moon reflecting off the rocky peaks, and the Milky Way is unbelievably bright. I am exhausted but I am so happy to have found my friends and I am, incredibly, warm.

***

My legs wake me up in the night, aching like they do. I pull my damp sleeping bag around me. It's cold, fifteen degrees, but I'm just warm enough in my shelter. My legs are aching, though, and I can't fall back asleep. Why, they seem to be saying. Why did you hike over two twelve-thousand-foot passes in one day.

The sky lightens and I sit up and watch as the bright rays of yellow sun make their way down the rocky crags to the little fold in the mountain where we are camped. The air is bitter cold but I know that hiking is the only thing that will make me warm and so I shiver into my running shorts, stuff my things away, and set off down the trail towards the valley below, with its lakes glittering in the morning light.

The trail is steep and rocky, and it descends for miles. My left knee, for some reason, feels stiff today, kind of like a squeaky hinge that needs to be oiled. It's a little swollen and it's difficult to bend, and I imagine it making creaking noises as I step my way down the difficult trail. I've injured my knee before, back when I used to bike a lot, but this doesn't feel like that. Mystery pain, I think. That's what happens when you hike over two passes in one day.

At the bottom of the descent, there is a rushing river, and next to the river is a big flat rock, baking in the sun. We drop our packs on this rock, pull out our wet things and spread them on the rock to dry. I eat jerky and tiny snickers and shout at the others over the noise of the river. Instigate has some arnica gel and I rub it on my knee.

When it's time to go I pack up my sleeping bag, now dry and fluffy and warm! And take a few steps on the trail. Whoah whoah whoah! says my knee. It's difficult to walk, and I'm leaning on my trekking poles like crutches. Dammit, I think. What have I done.

After the river, the trail is steep; we're climbing up towards Mather Pass, at twelve thousand feet. I hike slow, way in the back, mincing up the trail. I can feel the others getting farther and farther ahead and then my altitude sickness kicks in and the trail tips beneath me, the ol' tilt-a-whirl. Dammit,

I think again. I have to keep up with the others- but how?

I see no-one else on the climb up to the pass. Instead of feeling awesome, like I sometimes do when I hike by myself, I just feel really, really alone. What if I never see my friends again? Now that there's something wrong with my knee, what if I can't keep up? What if I have to hike the rest of the Sierras by myself?

I reach the top of the pass and a couple of hikers are there, sitting on a granite ledge, eating lunch. I am overjoyed to see them and I sit and look out at the valleys and lakes and forests way down below, on the north side of the pass- our new kingdom. We will descend down into it, walk through it, and then we will climb out of it, up and over the jagged granite mountains to the north. It's beautiful but it's a lot of work, and I am starting to really understand why mileage drops so much in the Sierras.

I inch my way down the other side of the pass, stepping carefully on the jumbled, rocky trail, leaning on my trekking poles when I can. Then there are the places where the trail crosses melting snowfields that cling to the mountain- the snowfields are about half the size of normal in this low-snow year but still steep and a bit sketchy, and I step carefully into the footprints that are already there and kick steps into the snow when there aren't footprints, hoping that I don't slip or posthole (that's when you sink down into the snow). I am acutely grateful, in this moment, for the awesome, cleat-like tread on my shoes, and I think of Instigate, whose tread is worn almost completely off. How is she doing? Where is she even at? Squeak, squeak, squeak, says my knee as I inch my way across the snowfield. Should I even be hiking right now, with my knee like this?

A little farther down the mountain I find myself in a field of large boulders. I hop from boulder to boulder, balancing with my trekking poles. Below the boulders is snow, and beneath the snow is running water. I feel like I am in a video game. Again, I am thankful for my trekking poles and for the fresh tread on my shoes. If I get out of the Sierras without breaking my foot, I think, it will be because of them.

After the boulders, the trail flattens out for a while and winds its way through bright green grasses alongside a clear, aquamarine lake. The sun is shining and there are little flowers and I feel like I'm in a dream. I sit next to a stream and feel myself relaxing into the earth. I want to fall asleep in the grass. I could stay here forever.

But I can't. I'm way behind, again! And I have to keep up with the others; I have to get to where they're camped before dark or I'll have to camp alone, in bear country, with more food than will fit in my bear can. I don't understand the bears around here. I don't know how many there are, or what they're capable of. If I camp by myself I'll spend half the night awake, staring out into the dark forest, imagining horrible things. So I get up from my nice spot in the grass next to the stream and pack my things away. I have to catch up with the others.

A mile later the trail turns complicated again- steep switchbacks of jumbled rock, winding their way down the mountain. Don't break your foot, I think, as I ease myself down. Skree, skree, skree says my knee. The lake turns into a river, and the river crashes down the valley in a series of waterfalls. The trail follows the river, lower and lower and lower, and at last I am in another valley, this one cloaked in forest, and the path is flat again. It is dusk, and I walk as quickly as I can. Walking and walking and walking, trying to beat the dark. Through the long flat woods with the river on my left, the trail soft and loamy beneath my feet. Just when I feel like I can't walk another mile there is the smell of woodsmoke and then everyone is there, sitting on logs around a campfire in the gathering dark.

Hallelujah.

I spread my sleeping pad next to the fire and stretch. It feels good to stretch. I can feel all the muscles around my knees loosening, the little tendons and bits of things. Stretching, I think. Maybe all I need to do is stretch.

Hiking twelve hours a day and I don't even stretch. What are we thinking.

I drift off to sleep staring out the mesh of my shelter at the darkened woods. Maybe my knee will be better in the morning. Or if not I'll just have a short day and rest it. I was so strong in the desert, so full of energy, and now everything feels so fragile, like I could just break. Which is it, I think. Am I strong or am I not. And what will the future bring.

Of course there isn't any answer.

***

In the morning I'm excited. We're going over Muir Pass today! I have no idea what that means, but my knee pain is gone and so I'm just sort of stoked. I set out happy. I hike! From eight thousand feet to twelve thousand feet, my altitude sickness drowned in dark chocolate, sliding on soft snowfields, losing the trail, climbing over awkward boulders, the angle of the earth constantly changing. What is the angle of the earth? What is water, snow, boulders? Everything is jumbled, where is the trail? Following the person in front of me, so far ahead she's a dot, watching her posthole, shouting at the person behind me.

"The trail's over there!"

This is fun. Today I'm having fun.

There are many false passes and I drink straight from a raging river that erupts from a mountainside blanketed in snow. The water tastes like life, the world, everything. At the top of the pass is Muir Hut; Instigate and I reach the hut at the same time and there is Spark, asleep in the sun next to the hut, his hat over his face and a book on his chest. We take off our packs and creep towards him on the rocks.

"Let's see how much of his gear we can steal before he wakes up," says Instigate.

We are almost there before he startles, mumbles something unintelligible.

"Are you still asleep?" I say.

"Yes," says Spark.

I explore the inside of the hut; it's made of brick and shaped like a honeycomb. On the mantle above the fireplace is a sort of altar to John Muir. Then some other hikers arrive and we sit in the sun eating lunch, the hut sheltering us from the wind. A young southbound JMT-er named Phoebe appears.

"Do you know the lyrics to that Miley Cyrus song?" we ask her.

"No," she says.

"What about the lyrics to that Avril Lavigne song?"

"No."

"Damn," we say. Those songs have been stuck in our heads.

145

"Are you hiking with other people?" asks Spark.

"Yeah," says Phoebe. "They're still climbing the pass."

"If we see them on our way down, should we tell them to hurry up?" I ask.

"Sure," says Phoebe.

We leave the pass and start our descent through snowfields, across boulders and rushing streams, under the deep blue sky. O kingdom, my kingdom! I look down at the glittering land that stretches before me. I am at the back of the group and then I see one of Phoebe's friends, readjusting her pack in the snow on the side of the trail.

"Phoebe says to hurry up," I say as I lope past her.

"Screw her," says Phoebe's friend. I realize that I am most likely the fifth person to relay this message, and I laugh.

There is a lake that is impossibly clear and dream-like and colder than ice. Instigate and I are incapable of resisting and we take off our clothes and jump in. Afterward we stand shivering on a rock. There is a little bit of a wind. By the time we're dry the sun is long and we put on our clothes and race down the valley. I hop across a painfully beautiful stream on stepping stones (there are stepping stones everywhere, over everything- a practice of moving through life/mountains/space via stepping stones) and grow hungry. I sit next to the stream to eat and become impossibly weary; I have only gone sixteen miles but I could just sleep, sleep, sleep. Instigate by this time is far ahead. Up and down, I think. Up and down. Climbing and descending and climbing. I could just lie down right here and sleep.

No! If I were by myself, maybe. But then would I, really? Hiking the PCT is not about relaxing. It is about walking to the point of exhaustion. The world a blur, the satisfaction of passing out in the dirt beneath the Milky Way, your hard foam pad like heaven beneath you. And in the Sierras I hike so slowly, over the boulders and passes and clear perfect waters, that there is even less time for breaks. Less time. Less less less.

Instigate talked of doing twenty-three miles. Twenty-five? I can't remember. It's evening now and I know I won't make it that far. I don't want to camp alone, though; all of this is still so new to me, this isolation in the great wilderness.

Just then I pass NoDay and MeHap, a couple of other hikers, sitting on a rock next to the lake eating Oreos. They're going just a few more miles.

I can do that, I think. I can make it a few more miles.

The tilt-a-whirl makes me so slow. This slowness in turn makes me feel sad, and this sadness washes over me. The sadness is all intertwined with a feeling of basic aloneness; the aloneness, I realize, that pervades all life. I haven't seen Spark and Track Meat since the morning. What am I trying to do here? Am I trying to keep up with people? Do I expect these people to wait for me? Are we all together? But no, we are each of us hiking our own hikes. So of course I am alone. Sometimes I will be alone.

And yet, tonight I do not want to be alone. Tonight I wish that there were one special person who was waiting just for me. Do other hikers feel this way? I don't know. Tonight I am feeling small. Where is my strength? I am feeling small and weak and tired.

Tonight the forest is suffused with a deep melancholy.

I find NoDay and MeHap crouched around a dead fire ring, eating dinner in the dirt, black mosquito nets over their faces like shawls. I've been crying a little bit and I feel awkward and strange, needy for no reason I can explain. What do I need? Who are these people to me? What are we to each other? Where even are we? What even is this? I can't place myself, anymore, in the universe. I set up my tent, hurrying in the last of the light, but still I don't know where I belong.

***

I wake up in the dark before dawn, stick my finger in my crotch, and realize that I'm bleeding. My period... and the relief that comes with it, like the pressure dropping when it finally starts to rain.

Everything is going to be ok.

I fall back asleep for a little while and when I wake it's light. I sit in my sleeping bag and eat trail mix, picking out the parts I like best. I wasn't expecting to bleed. I'd been losing weight and my period was two weeks late and I figured I might not get it at all- bleeding on the trail is random at best. But then here it is.

I put a raisin in my mouth and crunch down on something hard. I pick the hard thing out of my mouth, brush the smashed raisin off it, and turn it around in my hand. It looks remarkably like a piece of a tooth! I run my tongue along the inside of my mouth. There is now a strange, jagged hole where the side of one of my molars should be.

Jesus fuck, I think.

At least there isn't any pain. I shiver out of my sleeping bag and into my hiking clothes. My next resupply is Mammoth Lakes- will my mouth last until then? And what is Mammoth Lakes?

There's a climb and a long descent today and as soon as I'm on the trail I feel it- fatigue, dizziness, and cramps underneath everything, dulled by the ibuprofen. A short day, I think as I hike. I'd give anything today to have a short day. I stare at the trail. I can see Spark and Instigate's footprints, which I know by heart. I wonder where they are?

I ford Evolution Creek. The water is bitingly cold and comes up to my knees and I wade across in my shoes, bracing myself with my trekking poles, and then shake the gravel from my trail runners on the other side.

All I want to do, today, is sit in a patch of sun and rest. I feel worn out, depleted, empty inside. Like I've got nothing left. I'm sitting on the warm ground at a trail junction, soaking up the sun like a lizard, when MeHap and NoDay appear. We've been hearing a rumor that there are hotsprings down a side trail somewhere, and we decide to try to find them. We hike down into a dry valley carpeted in lush green grasses and trickling everywhere with water. I wander through the woods, feeling lost. Then I hear strange noises.

"Carrot! Carrot!"

Through the trees is the deep sparkling river and at the edge of the river, sitting in the long grass, are Instigate and Spark. Their shoes are off and their faces are red from the sun. They've been lounging in the sun all afternoon and now they shoulder their packs to hike out, but not before I convince them to do just a sixteen-mile day.

"I know," I say. "Less than twenty miles is wild. But there's a beautiful lake there!"

Soon we are all in agreement and my dear friends hike away, cupping

148

blades of saw grass in their palms to make duck noises. I feel ecstatic that I've found my friends again; it's as though I've been lost in the wilderness for a hundred years.

I cross the river barefoot; the water is deep and the current is strong and the rocks hurt my feet. On the other side of the river, MeHap, NoDay and I find a stretch of forest and a hot, grassy meadow. There is a bathtub-sized hole in the grass filled with murky, steaming water, bubbles rising up from the mud floor. We lower ourselves into this water until we can't stand it, then lie on the grass and let the sun bake us. NoDay produces a bit of weed and a tiny pipe to smoke it in. I'm really sensitive and afterward I lose track of space/time and know only that it feels awfully good to slip into the hot water and that MeHap is passing around his titanium pot, in which he's combined Oreo pudding mix with stream water to make a thick gray mass. Soon my heart is racing with sugar as I am very, very high. And then, of course, it's time to hike.

I put one shoe on and then look out across the meadow. How do things fit inside my pack? And then I'm at the river and crossing it, staring down at NoDay's legs in front of me. The current is quick and cold; I'm not sure how any of this river-crossing business is going to work out except it already has once, so I suppose it will again. NoDay's legs are tanned and streaked with dirt. After the river we climb a spiral staircase up the mountain. MeHap is making fun of Spark.

"I love whey protein," he says in Spark's faint Georgia drawl. "I wash my clothes in whey protein." I'm laughing so hard on the steeply climbing trail that I feel as though I might asphyxiate. MeHap declares himself in excellent cardiovascular shape.

"I'll climb up the passes behind day-hikers," he says. "While singing. And I'll twirl my trekking poles like batons."

It's almost dark when we reach the lake. Instigate and Spark are there, along with a smattering of other hikers. They've built a fire and are huddled around it, eating dinner. I boil some water for my dinner and set up my shelter; it's cold at the lake. But of course it's always cold at lakes. We sit around the fire and talk until it's too dark to see each other's faces and then we drift off to bed, starlight just beginning to shimmer off the surface of the water.

***

A lone coyote calls out in the night next to the lake. Yip yip yip! When I wake it's frigid cold. My bag is covered in condensation and my toe socks are frozen. Putting on frozen toe socks, I think, as I ease them onto my feet. Every day a new sensation.

I'm cold today. Cold all day and I can't get warm. Sunbeams, hiking, my down jacket. Nothing can warm me. Walking through the forest, stopping to rest in little clearings, drinking stream water. You know you're a tired thru-hiker, I think, when you sit down to eat a snack in a patch of sun and you almost fall asleep. I have to make it, though. I just have to make it to Mammoth Lakes.

My phone is dying, so I keep it off. I can't see how fast I'm hiking. Little bits of my tooth break off as I walk. I'm out of tampons so I'm just letting myself bleed, and sort of brushing the blood away when I notice it on my legs. Because I'm feral, you know? Soon I have the beginnings of chafe on my inner thighs. Blood is salty. Salt crystals are sharp, and they will cut you. This is what chafe is. I'm a dirty hiker and my own blood is cutting me, making a searing, cracked rash where the inseam of my shorts rubs my thighs. I don't have the time or the energy to try to take care of it, though. Also, I'm more or less out of food. I'm bleeding, and hungry, and dreaming of vegetables. I'm thinking about the motel room I'll get in Mammoth Lakes. What is Mammoth Lakes? I walk through clear burbling streams. I balance on logs. I'm sick from altitude, sick from everything. I turn my brain off.

Evening finds me camped beneath the granite mountains, feeling another frosty night come on. I lie in my sleeping bag in the cold clear air, dreaming of heat. The hot powerful sun, the desert. Aye, the desert! I miss the desert. I wonder what Northern California will be like. No one talks about Northern California. Hikers talk about the desert, the Sierras, racing through Oregon, the rain in Washington. Maybe Northern California will be beautiful, I think, as I snuggle down in my sleeping bag. Maybe it will be perfect. I imagine myself flung forward like a stone from a slingshot, free of my three-pound bear canister, breathing easy in the low, oxygen-rich air.

I just have to make it.

***

I dream that I'm choking, and I wake in the night coughing. In the morning I sit in my sleeping bag, eat breakfast, and immediately feel nauseous. Don't throw up, I think. Don't throw up don't throw up. Oh, altitude. Oh, camping at eleven thousand feet.

It's twenty-three miles to Red's Meadow. I don't know what Red's Meadow is but there's a store there, and a campground, and that's where the road starts to Mammoth Lakes. If I can only get to that road today, I think, then anything is possible.

Even though today's altitude is not as high as the previous days, my altitude sickness has seemed to reach a sort of fever pitch, like a joke. The earth is tilting away from me, and the fatigue is overwhelming. My body, today, is made of lead.

All I have left to eat today are a few handfuls of almonds and some Fritos. The Fritos are stale and I don't want to eat them but I do, sitting at a glittering lake on the other side of the pass. I feel numb to the beauty of the lake. I poke at the chafe between my thighs. The skin is red and rippled, textured like an elephant's skin. There are cracks in it. It stings like a motherfucker.

It's afternoon and I've only gone twelve miles. Word on the trail is if I make it to Red's Meadow by seven, I might catch the last shuttle to Mammoth Lakes. If I can catch the shuttle then I can get to Mammoth Lakes *tonight*. I am exhausted, and my chafe stings like fire when I walk, but something happens as I stare at the lake, eating my crumbled Fritos. I can do it, I think. I know I can do it.

After the lake the path is flat and smooth, the first flat trail in what feels like days. So far in the Sierras it's been climbing over rocks, or picking your way around water, or down steep slopes; the path is never just *flat*. One can never just *walk*. Forward movement is complicated, laborious, exhausting. Now the trail is smooth and tidy as it cuts through the forest in a straightforward way. I clip my pack on and I pick up my trekking poles and I walk.

At 6:30 I reach a bunch of little wooden sheds and a dusty pen with horses inside. The trail splits at a narrow dirt road and I follow my friends' footprints. MeHap, NoDay, Instigate. All of them ahead of me. And every now and then I see one of Spark's. The only print I don't see is Track Meat's; the soles of his old road-runners are so smooth and worn that I'm not sure he has a footprint at all.

I reach the Red's Meadow store at six forty-five. I push open the door to the little wooden building, making the bell jangle. Inside the clerk is shuffling around, getting ready to close.

"Is there a shuttle to Mammoth Lakes?" I ask.

"Shuttle doesn't start till Saturday," says the clerk.

"What day of the week is it?" I ask.

"Thursday."

"Can I charge my phone in here?"

"Sure," says the clerk. "I'll be here till eight. There's an outlet over there next to the couch, behind the icecream cooler."

I buy two cans of chili, two apples and an icecream bar and plug in my phone. I sit on the couch, eating icecream and texting people.

"How do you get out of here?" I text to Spark, who is in Mammoth Lakes.

"Hitching seems pretty easy," he says.

"There's a campground just down the trail," says the clerk, who is sweeping in front of the beer cooler. "There's a site for backpackers there. You'll see all the little tents."

The campground is dim and forested and there are bear boxes and a couple of RV's there, with entire living rooms of outdoor furniture set up in the dirt. In the bathroom I twist the tap and watch in reverence as cold running water spills into the sink. Dear god, I can finally clean my chafe. Afterward I change into my long underwear, take off my shorts and wash them with hand soap in the sink. The water runs brown-gray and finally clear.

"Is this the hiker site?" I ask a group of men, who are wearing expensive base layers and cooking dinner at a picnic table.

"Sure," they say. "You can camp here too if you want."

They're John Muir Trail hikers and they have big, heavy packs. They limp a little as they make their way around the campsite. I feel for them, but I also envy their luxuries. Camp shoes! A double wall tent! I heat my canned chili over my alcohol stove and we sit around, chatting about nothing. I finish my dinner with the two apples, and then it's time for bed. I unfurl my magic spaceship tent at the edge of the campsite and the dudes look on, envious.

"Twelve ounces?" says one of them. "Really?"

"Yeah," I say. "With the stakes and everything."

It's nice to have my ego puffed up in this way. Soon the JMT and the PCT will split again and the JMTers with their heavy packs and their overuse injuries will be gone, and it'll just be thru-hikers and the occasional day hiker. Everyone's packs will be at least as small as mine. So I've got to get it while I still can.

It's warmer in the campground than it was last night, when I was camped way up by the pass. It's so warm I don't even need to sleep in my down jacket, which means that tonight I have a super awesome fluffy pillow. I snuggle down into my hard, wonderful bed. I feel happy, and my stomach has finally calmed down. And tomorrow I'll be in Mammoth Lakes!

***

In the morning, a friend of one of the JMTers gives me a ride into Mammoth Lakes, which turns out to be an off-season ski town, stuffed with gear shops and restaurants, sidewalks crowded with tourists eating ice-cream cones. I wander bewildered from motel to motel; most of them are full but the Motel 6 has a room for $120. I drop my things on the floor and text everyone I know. *I've got a room if you want to come crash here. And split the cost.* Then I flip through the phone book, looking for dentists. Two of the three dentists in town have no openings until next week.

"We can squeeze you in today," says the third. "If you can be here by noon."

I look at my watch; it's eleven thirty-five.

Good thing I'm already wearing running clothes.

I arrive at the dentist flushed and sweaty but on time. I dread going to the dentist; I'm terrified of needles and so the numbing is often traumatic and the dentist, for some reason, always seems drunk to me. When I'm in the chair, I'm usually either arguing with the dentist about the dangers of amalgam fillings or choking on my own saliva. I sometimes take a valium beforehand to calm me down (which my last dentist actually prescribed to me) but today I have nothing. I do not know this random dentist from the phone book and I am in a strange town. I have no idea what to expect.

It is the best dental experience of my life.

The dentist is quick and surprisingly sober.

"What do you want me to do?" he asks.

"Pull the tooth?" I say.

"No need to do that," he says, poking his fingers into my mouth. "There's plenty of tooth left here. I'll add some more filling material to what you've already got, and then smooth it down. You'll still need to get a crown at some point, but it should last a couple years."

"Amalgam filling material?" I say.

"No," says the dentist. "We don't use amalgam in this office."

"What?" I say. The dentist glances at me over the tops of his glasses. His face is weathered and avuncular and he has a New York accent. The dental assistant is lining up small shiny tools on a tray. A ray of sunlight from the window lands on her shoulders, making her look like an angel.

"Composites have really come a long way," he says. "They're just as good as amalgam now."

The whole process is over in forty-five minutes.

"How soon can I eat trail mix?" I ask the receptionist on my way out.

"As soon as you're not numb anymore," she says. My mouth is barely numb. I'm not even drooling.

"You mean I can eat anything?" I say.

"Yes," she says.

There's a Carl's Jr. on the way back to the motel, and I stop and order a lettuce-burger and sweet potato fries. All I've eaten today is a bag of mini snickers, and I'm starving. I chew the burger carefully; I can only taste it on one side of my mouth. But that side of my mouth tastes amazing.

Back at the motel room, I find NoDay, MeHap, and several other hikers. Spark and Instigate and Track Meat are at a bluegrass festival, a hundred miles away. In the room there are packs everywhere, gear explosions, the beginnings of resupply organization. I peek in the bathroom- dirty towels are mounded next to the toilet, and the tub is lined in a thick gray film.

"The shower drain is clogged," says one tall male hiker, as he runs his fingers through his long, curly hair. "I don't know how that happened."

A mound of trash fills one corner of the room. Someone finishes their beer and adds it to the pile of trash. NoDay opens a bag of granola and the granola explodes, showering oat pieces over the carpet. Then everyone is gone, out to run errands, and it is only me.

I lie down on the smooth bedspread and close my eyes.

I remember reading somewhere that there are only two possible prayers: "help me" and "thank you."

"Thank you," I say to the universe, before I fall asleep.

***

There's a free shuttle that goes towards Red's Meadow, where I'll get back on the trail, and two days later I pile on with a bunch of hikers that I haven't yet met. I feel infinitely recharged from my zero in Mammoth Lakes, during which I did nothing but eat and sleep, and I'm really excited to get back on the trail. The other hikers on the shuttle have small packs and they're all very tan. My pack is heavy with my bear canister and six days' worth of food. The bus winds its way up into the mountains. It's overcast.

I hike alone all afternoon, watching the light move in the forest. At dusk, I reach a little flat spot next to a stream at the edge of the mountain and pitch my tent there. It's cold and I put on all my layers and make a pot of instant refried beans. I eat the beans with Fritos, sitting on the ground staring at the first few stars. I'm camped by myself in bear country, which still makes me nervous. But I think I'm starting to understand the bears here; they're clever, but they're terrified of humans. As long as I keep my food secure I'll be fine.

I wake a few hours later to the sound of rain on the fabric of my shelter. Light rain, almost like mist. I pull out the extra bit of cuben fiber that covers the mesh in my tent and put it up. Now I'm completely enclosed, and the space is small and warm. This will be the first time I've slept in my tent in the rain. Sleeping in the rain, hiking in the rain. I guess we'll see what that's like, I think, as I drift off again.

***

In the morning the world is cold and drizzly, and it's hard to get out of my bag. At last I'm up, packing my wet tent away, feeling the tiny rain alight all over me. How do I hike in this? I stuff my things into my trash compactor bag pack liner and start to hike. The cool drizzle clings to me, but it's not too bad.

I look at the footprints as I walk. NoDay, Instigate, MeHap. They left Mammoth Lakes before I did, and the tracks aren't very fresh. I figure they're a day ahead. I'm becoming an expert tracker, I realize, of my friend's running shoes. Isn't life strange.

It's beautiful at the top of the pass but too cold, and I hurry down the other side. Only I can't hurry- the trail is steep and slick and then suddenly it's gone, disappeared beneath a snowfield. There aren't any shoeprints on the snowfield, so I know that's not the way across. There's another route, a better route, and I just have to find it; I have to find the footprints.

Only there aren't any footprints. There is just a field of huge, wet boulders, tumbling steeply down the mountain. I follow what I think are footprints but the snow, when it first disappears, leaves chunks of trampled ground that look just like they've been walked on and soon I'm standing on a big hunk of something looking down at nothing, shivering in my rain jacket with no idea where to go.

Ok, I think. You're not a fool. You've been relying too much on this well-marked trail. You have a brain, so use it.

156

Below me is the valley I'm about to traverse, and to the north where the valley meets the slope of the mountain I can just make out a bit of trail. A little ways up from that I can see where the trail cuts into the mountain, and if it continues on its course that would mean that I could find it in the clump of trees to my left, across a steep ravine. I shiver in my rain jacket, feeling tired and cold and small. I'm so used to following the trail, to being stuck to it with an almost magnetic force. Well, I think. It's not going to hurt me to find my way cross-country. It's just a mountain after all, here under my feet, a thing made of stones and mud and earth. I know how to do this.

I retrace my steps up the slippery boulders, cross a stream swollen with rain and snowmelt, pick my way over rock slabs the size of cars, traverse the sodden grass and mud, climb a slope into a copse of trees and then there it is, that tidy strip of trampled earth, wending its merry way as though nothing was the matter at all.

I stick it with my trekking pole.

"Trail," I say. "I have found you."

A moment later I realize that I am shaking with hunger. I haven't eaten a snack in hours, and the effort of climbing up and over the pass in the rain has exhausted me. I crouch on the wet grass and eat a handful of damp trail mix, but it's too cold to sit still for long. Well, I think. I'll be down in the valley soon. I can eat then.

According to trail lore, the next ten miles before Tuolumne Meadows, a place called Lyell Canyon, is major "problem bear" territory. Phoebe, the southbound JMT-er we met on top of Muir Pass, slept in Lyell Canyon and a bear pawed her pack while she was cowboy camping, tearing little holes in it with its claws. She had to chase the bear away. I am by myself and I know that if I camp here I will sleep terribly, even if there isn't any bear. I will lie awake in my sleeping bag, attempting to make out the shapes of the trees in the dark.

Well hell, I think, as I shiver my way down the mountain. I am cold and exhausted and nothing sounds better right now than stopping, pitching my good little tent, and crawling into my warm dry sleeping bag. But I have to make it all the way to Tuolomne Meadows, because of the bears. There is a campground there with bear boxes, and I'll sleep much more soundly. I look at my watch; at this rate, I'll get to Tuolomne Meadows after dark.

Night hiking, I think. In the rain. Eleven more miles, and I'm so tired already.

A few miles into the valley, I find a dry patch of ground beneath a huge pine tree and stop to cook dinner in the rain. While I'm sitting there, a couple of other thru-hikers pull up. Their names are Scat Tracker and Unicroc, and they're planning to camp right here in Lyell Canyon.

A little later I finish eating and hike on. I can barely walk, I am so tired at this point, and it feels like a really bad idea to try and night-hike to Tuolumne Meadows. Like the worst idea ever, actually. I see Scat Tracker and Unicroc, setting up their tent in the trees a little ways from the trail, and a few minutes later I find a similar spot, in a little cluster of trees in the meadow. Fuck it, I say, as I fill my Gatorade bottles in the glassy stream. I pitch my little shelter and crawl inside happily, pulling off my wet things and unstuffing my sleeping bag. I've placed my bear canister in the dirt a stone's throw from the tent, where I can watch it from where I'm lying. Bear TV, I think. If it comes to that.

I lie in my fluffy sleeping bag and feel my blood circulating. I'm warm for the first time all day, and it feels incredible. The simple things, I think. These small things have such tremendous value. Like being warm and dry. What pure and perfect heaven is this.

The light is fading from the sky, and the trees around me are becoming indistinct. My sleepiness is overwhelming, and I feel myself drifting off. No bears, I think. Bears don't bother me tonight.

***

My mosquito bites wake me in the middle of the night. I react like crazy to the mosquitoes here, for reasons I don't understand. Each night the bites that riddle my legs wake me and for a while I lie curled in my bag in the dark, scratching like a junkie. Dang, I think, as I scratch at my knees. It's like I'm ten years old again.

In the morning it's cool and the rain has stopped. I've slept late- seven o'clock. I crawl out of the tent and check my bear canister; it's in the same place that I left it. Huh, I think. No bears. I'm tired this morning, hungover from crossing the pass in the cold rain. I feel cold and lethargic but the thought of civilization pushes me forward down the trail- I think of the little store in Tuolumne Meadows, the possibility of seeing my friends.

The valley is beautiful, water on water on water. A flat stream winding through squishy green grass under an overcast sky. I imagine stripping off my clothes and jumping in, swimming in the turquoise water under the cool gray clouds. The water would make me new again.

And then there are day hikers, in their clean bright clothing, gripping bottles of water and looking as though they're all either too hot or too cold. I can smell their shampoo.

The Tuolumne Meadows Store is a big white canvas tent alongside the highway. There's a picnic table below some trees next to the parking lot and all the thru-hikers are there, eating snickers bars and drinking beer, their sleeping bags spread in the grass to dry. The clouds are beginning to break but I'm still cold and I wander in and out of the store, buying bits of food to eat. I buy a burger in the cafe, then some french fries. I eat two bananas. It's nice to be around other hikers again, sitting watching the tourists come and go. There are hikers here I haven't seen in weeks, people who I thought were ahead of me, people who I thought were way behind. We're all swirling around in time and space, crossing passes in the wilderness, totally unaware of each other.

And then Track Meat and Spark show up! Track Meat gives me a beer and I buy a cup of chamomile tea, and all the possibilities of the universe are proposed, and then it's decided that we'll hitch down to Yosemite Valley, where NoDay and MeHap and Instigate are.

We stand on the side of the bright highway next to a meadow of heartbreaking green. None of the tourists stop but eventually a man named Crow who works in the valley and his friend, Lindsey, offer to drive us to Yosemite Valley. The road is long and winds past clear lakes and convoluted granite cliffs. Crow tells us about his hometown of Salinas, California, and shows us pictures of his baby daughter.

"It's her birthday tomorrow," he says. "I'm going to throw her a party."

We round a bend and there are the tall granite walls of the valley, a waterfall falling in slow motion from the cleft between them.

"Wow," I say. "This is really beautiful."

We park and stand in the dusky road between rows of dark wooden houses.

Other employees appear. They have beers and they're wearing their blousy weekend clothes. We walk together beneath the towering trees to a little grocery store, the granite walls of the valley all around us, and buy ginger beer and a bottle of Jack Daniels. We walk to a sandy beach on the riverbank. The river is shallow and clear and runs over smooth round stones. We sprawl across the sand and drink our whiskey and watch the night fall. The air is smoky where it moves above the water.

I take off my shoes and wade into the water. Someone has a guitar and is singing. There are sour gummy worms and then the ginger beer is gone, and the whiskey too. There is a little path that winds through the trees to a secret spot where the staff like to camp and we spread our sleeping pads in the dark there. I eat dinner by the light of my headlamp, listening to Spark snore in his bivy. It's balmy and warm and there is a single mosquito, but I don't mind. I lie in my bag on the warm sand, staring up at the stars. I can smell the trees all around me, and the river nearby. The dark is soft and comforting, tonight, and I watch the silhouettes of the trees move against the sky. Of course this is all there is, I think. Of course this is all that matters.

***

After a zero in Yosemite spent eating and being weird we're back on the PCT- just the PCT! It's not the JMT anymore. This morning we pass other PCT hikers, and no one else. Our packs are tiny, we are very tan, and at this point, we are all very, very hardcore.

I am strong. I feel strong! When did this happen?

Today the world is a lush impossible green, there is water everywhere, and the air is warm and bright. We cross tumbling streams on wet stones and there are mosquitoes, but only in the shade. We climb for a while and I feel sick from the altitude, but only a little. Just a few more days of this, I think. Just a little while longer. Then the long drop into Northern California, after which we'll never go above nine thousand feet again.

We stop and swim at Mirror Lake. It's cold and there's a yellow scrim on the water. Pollen? I look at the little floating particles. There are flowers everywhere, beginning to explode.

The summit of the pass is unexpectedly easy.

"What a gentle little pass," I say, when I reach the top and find NoDay and Instigate there, eating lunch. A harbinger of things to come? I can see it now- The Gentle Rolling Passes of Northern California. No long approaches through sparkling, airless meadows, no monolithic rock walls and wicked, Escher-esque switchbacks. Just gentle sun and gentle climbing, forever and ever and ever. And I won't even have a bear canister!

***

At dawn the next morning I brave the mosquitoes to fetch my bear can. I unscrew it and sit in my tent, eating handfuls of things for breakfast. A handful of this, a handful of that... I am getting so tired of my trail food. Oh well, I think. That's the way it goes. Sometimes eating is not for fun. It's just for food.

A few miles into the morning we stop to eat second breakfast on a stretch of granite in the sun, where the mosquitoes are not so bad. Another hiker is there, and I watch enviously as she sprays herself with DEET, creating a magical force field that the mosquitoes cannot breach.

"Do you think I can use some of your deet?" I ask her. She hands me the little bottle.

"Dark magic," I say, as I spray my legs. "I am so thankful for this dark magic."

NoDay takes some too.

"We've crossed over to the dark side," I say. I watch as the mosquitoes do not land on me. "And it is so awesome."

We climb all day through beautiful flowery meadows and on granite staircases running with water. I'm tired, sort of woozy, and I stop a lot to rest. Why am I tired? A question that has no answer.

As the afternoon progresses I become even sleepier, until it feels as though I'm hiking underwater. I run into Instigate on a little sandy beach next to a cold, glimmering swimming hole and we jump in and then lie on the warm sand to dry. It's midday so the mosquitoes are hiding on the undersides of things, nowhere to be seen.

"I could just go to sleep right now," I say. The sun is warm on my skin and black flies are landing on me and then flying away, landing and then flying away. "I could just go right to sleep."

NoDay is in front of us somewhere. We'd talked about going twenty-three miles but my pace today is pathetic, like I'm wading through pudding. And then around five o'clock the shadows get long and the mosquitoes rise again from their resting places. We are walking through a long meadow when suddenly the mosquitoes are very, very bad.

I stop to take a drink of water and immediately twenty of them are buried in my legs. A handful are clustered on the underside of my hat, one is climbing into my ear, and a couple are trapped beneath my sunglasses. I swat at them manically, and shove the water bottle into my pack. I haven't managed to drink any water. I walk as fast as I can, trying to outpace them, but I cannot. I start to run, my pack bouncing awkwardly against my back. I'm swearing and swatting and stumbling, panic rising. At the same time, some little part of me wants to succumb- to just lie down in the meadow and let them have me. The DEET I put on this morning has long since worn off.

There's a wide deep stream ahead and I wade out into the middle of it and stand there, heart pounding. There are fewer mosquitoes out here, and I slowly begin to calm.

Instigate appears on the trail, marching towards the stream.

"It's better out here!" I say. She plunges into the stream, not even stopping to take off her shoes. I can see the cloud of mosquitoes around her. Once in the stream they drift away, like smoke.

We stand in the stream until another hiker appears. His name is Brown Bag, and we met him earlier in the day.

"Do you have any DEET?" I shout at him, before he is even at the stream.

"Sure," he says. "You want some?"

"Yes," I say. "You like beef jerky? I can give you beef jerky!"

How fast can you get it to me, I want to say, but I don't. I feel like an addict going through withdrawals. I'm being eaten alive and my salvation lies in that tiny, clear bottle. I watch as Brown Bag calmly sets his pack on the bank of the river and begins to rifle around inside it. Oh, dark magic! I think. That you would happen faster!

After we're all deeted up Instigate and I sit on the riverbank and calmly drink water and eat snacks, crucial tasks we've been avoiding for the last couple of hours. I feel deliriously happy, almost euphorically so. I'm just sitting on a rock here, in the good evening light, just casually, as though I don't live on a tragic, inhospitable planet. Like I could just sit down on a rock and eat! My mind has officially been blown.

"Let's just go a few more miles and camp," says Instigate. "I feel like all my strength has been sucked out through a million tiny straws."

We walk until we find a flat spot next to a beautiful clear stream and then we set up our tents and collapse. I'm so sleepy, so so sleepy. Maybe it's the DEET? I think vaguely, as I lie in my sleeping bag staring at the darkening sky.

***

I wake up in the middle of the night to pee, per usual, and the mosquitoes are still there. I can see them in the bright moonlight, swarming my tent. Dang, I think. The mosquitoes here don't even go to bed. What to do?

I pull an empty gallon ziploc bag from my pack and squat over it. It's kind of the perfect size, actually. After I've peed I seal it, and open the zipper of my tent just enough to stick the closed bag outside in the dirt. Why didn't I think of this before?

I wake to the hot sun on my tent. I turn on my phone and see that we've slept in; it's almost eight o'clock. I guess I was tired. I sit in my bag in the warmth, eating my stale trail food. Eventually I extricate myself and pack my things away. The mosquitoes are sparser now, in the full sun on this warm granite slab where we've camped. Instigate is moving just as slowly as I am, and by the time we're hiking it's nine o'clock. We look at the footprints on the trail, wondering if anyone has passed us while we've slept. NoDay is half a day ahead of us by now, and Spark, as far as we can tell, is still behind us. He wanted to hike out of Yosemite Valley on the JMT, and we're not sure when he got back on the trail. As we hike we make bets as to when he'll catch up with us.

"If we average two miles per hour at the end of the day, and Spark averages three miles per hour, then that means that every hour, he gains a mile on us. So if he left Tuolumne Meadows in the morning the day after we did, that would put him twenty hours behind us..."

And so on.

We drop down into a meadow and suddenly, mosquito hell strikes again. They are swarming, swarming, swarming, and we cannot walk fast enough, and we cannot swat fast enough, and we are trying to do everything at once, and I am panicking. Then we see some day hikers, coming towards us from the other direction.

"Do you have any DEET?" We ask them, desperately. They do, and we smear it on our legs and our clothes. Then the swarm is gone and we stand, the sun shining down on us. We are finally able to breathe.

I sit for a minute at a stream and drink some water. When I stand up to hike again the world tips, and fatigue falls onto me like a lead blanket. I walk slowly across the meadow, lifting one foot in front of the other. What? Why do I feel this way? I'm dizzy and slow, and hiking seems impossible. How will I ever finish the thru-hike, I think, if I feel this way?

I come upon Instigate, sitting at a stream.

"It's the DEET," she says. "The DEET was making me woozy. You have to wash it off."

I wipe the DEET off my legs with a hanky and some water and then sit for a while in the sun. I start to feel a little better.

"Dang," I say. "No wonder the mosquitoes don't like it."

Instigate is staring spacily across the meadow.

"I'm pretty sure it was poisoning me," she says.

It's midday now, and the mosquitoes aren't so bad. That's nice. As I hike on, my energy begins to return. Then I check my data and see that there's a water alert- a short waterless section is coming up in a few miles, and after that, water becomes more scarce. No water? I think. How can that be? There's water everywhere. Unless...

I climb up onto a ridge, turn a corner, and it happens. The landscape dries up. The forest is no more, the lush grass is gone, the streams have disappeared. The sun is bright and the hillside is littered in slabs of granite. The air smells of sagebrush.

And the mosquitoes are nowhere to be found.

Hallelujah.

The best part, though, is the trail. The trail is not convoluted, mucky, running over with water, or climbing up or down through complex piles of things. The trail is flat, sandy, and evenly graded. And I can see it in the distance along the ridge, just going along casually for miles and miles.

Northern California!

My heart sings out with joy. We did it! We really did it!

I fly through the next few miles. The trail is so easy, it's like there's no limit to how fast I can go. I pass the marker for mile 1000. Of course I can do it! I think. I'm doing it right now! Soon I reach a footbridge over a stream and find Instigate there, happily eating lunch. We are both ecstatic.

"Northern California!" I say. "We're done with the Sierras!" My heart feels impossibly light.

We lounge for a while, staring at the light in the trees. Then someone walks across the bridge. It's Spark.

"Y'all must be slow," he says, "if I've already caught up with you."

"You must be slow," I say, "If you've only just caught up with us. Happy Birthday!" I toss him a bag of bacon jerky.

Spark has already hiked twenty-three miles. We've done thirteen. It's four o'clock. In fifteen miles is the highway, where we'll hitch to Bridgeport, our next resupply spot.

"What if we night hiked?" I say. "What if we go all the way to the highway?"

Instigate is down.

"It's your birthday," I say to Spark. "You should probably do a thirty-eight mile day."

"Yeah," says Spark. "Ok."

We climb up, up, up onto a gravelly ridge. The trail is steep but the path is smooth, and we huff and puff. We turn at the top and suddenly we can see everything, going on and on and on. The whole world! It's dusk, and the light is stretched on the ridge in long yellow bands. We jump up and down and spin around. There's a snowfield, and Instigate makes a snow angel. Sonora Pass!

For the next seven miles, the trail follows the ridge. It's a bare ridge, composed of just gravelly rock and the occasional tiny, brightly-colored plant. On either side of us, the gravelly slopes sweep away into nothing and then rise up again, like ocean waves. The waves of the mountains are every shade of brown and dusky blue, and looking at all that space makes our eyes ache, as though we're looking at an optical illusion. We walk and walk, and the yolk-yellow sun goes down and comes up and goes down again, depending on where on the ridge we are.

"This is my favorite pass so far," I say, when we're sitting on the trail eating jerky. The sun is setting again, for the fifth time tonight. "I love this pass."

Then the sun sinks for good and we walk single-file in the dim gloaming, reluctant to pull out our headlamps. We traverse a series of steep, slippery snowfields, and I try not to look down as I cross them, try not to see the way the earth plunges away. The light that has gathered on all the surfaces begins to dissipate and soon we can see only shadows, and the vague shapes of the mountains. We walk closer together, guiding each other, moving in and out of darkness, trying not to trip over rocks. And then the light is gone entirely and the stars come out and we are on a tiny strip of trail suspended over nothingness. We are traversing on foot across infinite space.

Don't fall off the trail, I think, imagining myself plummeting down into the nothingness. Just don't fall off the trail.

There's a lightning storm over the most distant ridge, in what must be Nevada. Flashes of yellow crack the darkness and we stop and stare, amazed.

By the time we begin to descend towards the road we are exhausted. Little streams trickle out of the earth, and we stop to fill our bottles in the dark.

The air grows warm and balmy and soon we reach a stand of trees, clustered on the side of the trail a half-mile from the highway. There is a flat, sandy spot of ground among the trees and we spread our sleeping pads there and fall into them, no energy left in our bodies. It's eleven o'clock.

Part Three: Northern California

July 1 to August 4

Mile 1018 to mile 1685

***

I wake at dawn and look at my friends sleeping on the ground and walk to the sandy hillside and watch the sun rise. The land is warm and soft and dry and I can see for miles. I eat some almonds, and then stop. I'm so hungry, but I don't want to eat any more almonds. No more almonds! Instigate and Spark sit up in their bags.

"Are you pooping?" says Instigate.

"No," I say. "Just watching the sun rise."

We walk to the road and there is Track Meat, standing on the asphalt in the long bands of light. He stayed in Bridgeport the night before and is headed back to the trail. I haven't seen Track Meat in a while. He's torn the sleeves from his t-shirt and has a new, tiny straw hat. Track Meat does bigger days than I do; I watch the sun rise behind him and wonder when I'll see him again. Goodbye new friend, I think.

A little sedan pulls onto the shoulder. He says he can fit Instigate, Spark and me and we stuff our packs into the trunk and climb inside the car. The man is on vacation.

"What do you do for work?" we ask him as he drives us to Bridgeport.

"I'm an FBI agent," he says. "Counter-terrorism."

Bridgeport is a single street of old, whitewashed hotels and inexpensive diners. Everything is star-spangled; Fourth of July is just two days away. We get breakfast at a greasy spoon and then I sleepily gather my resupply boxes from the post-office and carry them to a motel that rents travel trailers. Instigate and Spark come with me and sit outside on the porch swing.

"Room stacking," says the motel clerk, "Is an arrestable offense."

"They'll just leave their packs in the trailer," I say. "They won't sleep there. I promise." I take a mini snickers from the little glass bowl on the counter.

The rental trailer is about twenty feet long and from the nineties- the interior color scheme is gray-blue with splashes of white. I turn on the A/C that blows from the ceiling.

It starts to rain while I'm at the laundromat. There's another hiker in the laundromat, sitting in the corner charging his phone. We look out the window and watch big fat drops falling on the dry streets.

"Petrichor," he says. "That's what that smell is called."

I go to the small general store with its western false-front and buy a head of iceberg lettuce, some roast beef, and mayo. Back at the trailer I assemble my little meal at the dinette and then sort my resupply. Really I just want to lie on the big bed in back and stare at the flat white ceiling, but there are chores that need to be done.

I re-pack my bag without my bear canister. We're out of the required area now, and I can mail the giant plastic canister away! I picture myself flying through the hills and forests of Northern California, my backpack as light as a helium balloon. In the desert we carried huge amounts of water, in the Sierras it was the bear can. Now what will happen?

***

In the morning, Spark and I are the last ones left in town. We get coffee at the "Coffee Cafe" across the street from the motel. The cafe is cluttered with ceramic cats and scrapbook art. On the counter is the flier for Bridgeport's 151st annual Fourth of July parade. There will be a turkey shoot and a greased pole race. Outside, marching band music is piping from the be-ribboned courthouse.

At the post office I ship away my bear canister and bounce ahead my stove and some of my warm clothes. I've got a peanut jar for soaking my dinners and I'm gonna try and go stoveless for a while, just to see if I like it. If I go stoveless I won't have to carry a stove, or a pot, or a windscreen, or a stand, or a bottle of fuel. And my dinners will be fast- just mix the food with water in my jar and carry it until it's time to eat. Instigate has been stoveless since the start of the trail, and she's always spooning lentils out of her little peanut butter jar while I slave over my popcan stove. I'm feeling inspired.

After the post office I go to the burger barn and order a burrito bowl.

"I'm excited for the turkey shoot," I hear some locals say.

172

The sky curdles, thunder cracks, and suddenly there's rain. I eat my burrito bowl outside under an overhang, watching the bits of trash blow across the road. Spark texts me; he's holed up at the coffee shop, reading sci-fi.

"Maybe it'll blow over," I say. "And then we can hitch."

A marine and a man on holiday shuttle us to the trail and by afternoon we're winding up through bright meadows of false hellebore and yellow mule's ears. Every mile or so a clear little stream burbles out of the earth. After an hour and a half we're standing on a rocky outcropping on top of our last ten-thousand-foot pass, looking down over everything. Our last ten-thousand-foot pass, I say to Spark. I can't believe it. After this we won't go above nine thousand feet, not for the rest of the trail.

The Sierras were beautiful, but damn, now that I'm out of them and there's all this oxygen I feel great.

The trail is flat and fast and easy after the pass and we hike until eight-thirty and camp next to a little stream. I eat my rehydrated instant pinto beans from my plastic peanut butter jar. They taste amazing.

***

The condensation comes down thick and heavy and we wake in the cold dawn, our bags soaked almost all the way through. We shiver into our clothes and pack away our now-heavy sleeping bags and are hiking by quarter after six. The sun has not yet made it over the mountain.

Later there is a sunny spot and we take a break and spread our sleeping bags on the warm rock to dry. I have Les Miserables on my phone and I read a chapter aloud, about little Gavroche in his elephant and some rag-pickers. Afterwards the trail rolls for hours along the ridgetops, through what looks like someone's unkempt flower garden. I keep expecting to see a little picket fence, an old woman bent over her roses. It's July and the flowers are everywhere, exploding.

On either side of the ridge the mountains roll away. They grow hazy and soft in the distance.

It's hot and muggy in the afternoon and stormclouds curdle, once again, on the horizon. Thunder cracks- BOOM -when I'm right on top of a little pass.

Lightning flashes and fat warm raindrops begin to fall. I hurry down the rocky trail that hugs the mountain, the red stones glistening with wet. The air is loose and soft and elastic around me, and the warm raindrops fall on my shirt and then dissipate, fall on my shirt and then dissipate. On the slope of the rocky, mossy mountain grow old, twisted juniper trees, like giant bonsai trees. They stand against the stormy sky, convoluted and glowing. They are beautiful.

I lean against one of these old trees and close my eyes. My body feels electric.

"What do I need to know?" I ask the tree.

"You're doing everything just right," says the tree.

An hour later I find Spark, sitting on a dry patch of ground beneath a ponderosa. I plop down and eat a snack and we play "tell the plot of a movie you like" while we wait for the last of the storm to pass. I tell the whole plot of Brokeback Mountain, which is one of my most favorite movies *and* one of my most favorite short stories. Then we press on down the beautiful canyon, towards the future and whatever lies beyond it.

I fall behind and then there is a small road and a trailhead, and a cooler with a rock on it. Trail magic! We haven't had trail magic since before the Sierras; I thought there wouldn't be any more. In the desert we were so spoiled, I think, as I open the cooler. The cooler is empty, no sodas or beer. But I don't care- just the thought of trail magic cheers me. I open the log book and happily flip through. I read-

Instigate lost her boobknife, NoDay is having trekking pole problems, and MeHap wants beer.

They're just ahead! I wonder when we'll see them again.

It's dusk when I climb down into a canyon and follow a stream into a little valley, where I find Spark sitting on a log eating Cheerios (dumping the bag into his mouth, actually) in the last of the light. I assemble my cold dinner of soaked instant refried beans, olive oil, and Fritos. When I climb into my tent I feel happy and light. I've gone twenty-nine miles today, my longest day ever. Ever ever.

***

Today it's hot and muggy and there are many small passes all overgrown with bright yellow flowers. I climb these passes with Spark, feeling sleepy and sort of dreamy. At the tops of the passes we hold onto our hats to keep them from the wind and look down at strings of twinkling lakes. In the afternoon the sleepiness grows until it consumes me entirely and I drag myself over the last pass by sheer force of will. I have eaten some strange combination of my trail food, or I have eaten my trail food in the wrong order, and my stomach hurts and I cannot wear my hip belt and I drag myself up the pass, sweating profusely. After the pass is the Carson Pass trailhead, with pit toilets and a parking lot and the highway. I find Spark there, sitting on the ground against a wooden sign. There's a family eating a picnic at the wooden picnic table, which they've spread with a red and white checked tablecloth. It's the Fourth of July.

"I got these three bars," says Spark. "From a day hiker. I already ate one. You want one of the others?"

"Do you think if we sit here long enough," I say, "that family will give us their leftovers?"

"I bet they have watermelon," says Spark.

We sit against the post for an hour and then one of the women walks up to us.

"You two want some fruit salad?" she says. She's holding two paper bowls of grapes, cantaloupe, and watermelon. All wet and mixed together.

"Oh my god," I say. "Fruit with all the original fluid still in the cells!"

"There's watermelon in there!" says Spark.

The woman goes back to the table and returns with a plate of sandwiches.

"You two want these chicken salad sandwiches? How about some potato salad?"

"Oh my god," I say again. The chicken salad is homemade, and tastes like vinaigrette. "Oh my god. Thank you. No one has ever enjoyed these foods," I say, "as much as we are enjoying them right now."

The family folds up their tablecloth and packs up for the drive home. We

175

sit against the wooden sign until dusk.

"Let's just hike a little longer," says Spark. "Until we find a place to camp."

"Yeah," I say. "Like maybe twenty minutes?"

"I'm pretty tired," says Spark.

"Yeah," I say. "Me too."

After the highway, the trail climbs up over a hill and then drops down into a wet, swampy meadow, heavy with green, and golden in the last of the light. The mosquitoes are thick as mist in this damp place and we walk as quickly as we can, swatting at them. There is nowhere to camp and we cannot stop walking and so we hike and hike and hike, as the light slowly drains away and we are left at last with only shadows. Finally the trail climbs out of the meadow and up into the dark forest and nearly all the way to the ridge there is a little flat spot in the pine needles, beneath a cluster of ponderosas.

A man named Jug walks by as I'm setting up my shelter. He has no trekking poles and in one hand he carries a plastic cranberry juice jug full of stream water.

"I'm gonna hike till I get to a place where I can see the fireworks," he says.

"Godspeed," we say.

I climb into my tiny tent and arrange my things around me- headlamp, hanky, warm hat, two liters of water. Spark is in his bivy with the mesh part closed, hiding from the mosquitoes.

"Can I read more Les Miserables?" I say.

"Ok," says Spark.

I read another chapter but it's convoluted and hard to follow and features none of the main characters.

"I kind of want to stop reading," I say, but Spark is already asleep.

I lie in my sleeping bag and then-

BOOM! BOOM! eeeeeeeeeeeeeBOOM!

It's the fireworks in Lake Tahoe, too far away to see but close enough to hear. I'm so glad I'm not in a town right now; there's no better place to be, I think, than bedded down on some pine needles in the dark woods, especially on a night like this. I wonder if Jug got close enough to watch them.

eeeeeeeeeeeBOOM!

***

I wake in the morning to my tent, going FWAP-FWAP-FWAP-FWAP-FWAP in the wind.

"Tent!" I say, and I tear it down. It's ten miles to Highway 50, where we can hitch to Lake Tahoe. After an hour or so of hiking I stop for second breakfast and another hiker appears, a woman; she camped just a few miles before us, in mosquito hell. I sit with her in the sun while she boils instant coffee, offering me some from her tin pot.

"It's decaf," she says. "I accidentally bought decaf."

Afterwards I hike on, and when I reach the highway, Spark is not there. There's a text from him; he waited for a long time for me before hitching. Dang. As I'm standing there, staring at the cars flying by, a little sedan pulls up on the shoulder. The doors pop open and NoDay, MeHap, and Instigate pile out. They were just up the road at Echo Lake, picking up a box, and now they're back at Highway 50 to hitch to Tahoe. We've caught up to them with our twenty-nine-mile days.

It's good to be reunited and within minutes, we've all got rides to town. Instigate and I get a ride in the same car with a man and his young son, on holiday.

"You guys smell bad," says the boy, as he cranks the window.

The man drops us off at El Nido Motel but the door to the office is locked so we sit on the concrete stoop, waiting. It's Friday, the day after the Fourth of July, and all the motels are full. We'd heard that El Nido might have something and so we sit on the stoop, watching the traffic congestion on the main drag, wondering why we wanted to come to Lake Tahoe in the first place.

177

"Ugh," I say. "It's awful here."

Instigate has a violin she's sent herself and she unwraps it, rosins her bow, and begins to play. A door pops open and a woman wanders over.

"You want some ice water?" she says. She hands us two sweaty plastic tumblers. The ice hurts my teeth but water is amazing. I haven't had any water since right before the highway.

"You know where the manager is?" I say.

"Nah," she says.

Eventually the manager arrives and tells us that the motel's all full. And then he tells us that we shouldn't hang out on his stoop, because we look like riffraff.

"We were only hanging out here because the office was locked and we were waiting for you," I say.

We walk up the main drag in the direction of the post office, which is apparently about a hundred miles away. The road is hot and loud and the wind smells like exhaust. We pass a motel, the Bear's Den, with a VACANCY sign and I stop into the office. They have a room, they say. Just one bed. Can I put five people in there? Sure, but there's no air conditioning.

I drop off my pack and set out for the post office. By the time I get there, I'm thirsty and exhausted, and I wait in the long line for my packages. Finally I get my boxes and I can go back to the hotel. Except instead of walking, I think, I'll take the bus this time.

I wait at the bus stop for what feels like an hour. I'm hot and dehydrated and the cars keep blowing by, vrooo vrooo vrooo. As I wait I can feel the day ticking away, those few precious moments that I have to do a million little things. When I finally get back to the hotel, I am near panic. I drink a liter of tapwater and stand in the cold shower for a long time. Then I lie facedown on the rickety mattress, feeling paralyzed. I need a week, I think. I need a whole week to get everything done.

Instigate, Spark, MeHap and NoDay arrive with beer and we all sprawl around the room, wilted in the heat.

178

It's hot and crowded in our hotel room. Spark takes a shower and while he's in the bathroom, NoDay puts his clothes in the freezer, along with all the towels. Then MeHap puts on NoDay's town dress, and NoDay puts on MeHap's hiking outfit. Spark comes out of the shower, naked and angry, and we laugh as he tears the room apart, looking for his clothes. Eventually he finds his clothes and we set out into the evening, which is beginning to cool, to find some dinner.

The Thai place is crowded and the pizza place is too expensive, so we end up at a little Mexican joint where we order massive plates of salty food. Then we stumble back to the motel room and arrange ourselves the best we can- two people on the rickety bed and the rest of us on the floor. The floor feels good and comforting underneath me; I don't sleep so well in beds these days. All the windows are open and outside, I can hear the sounds of traffic. I think about how no place is how you expect it to be, and the best thing to do is to not want things in the first place. But it's so hard to do that. So hard.

***

The next afternoon we find the lake- that aquamarine miracle on the edge of all this awful, traffic-choked sprawl. Lake Tahoe. We carry beer onto the beach, walking barefoot along the edge of the water, and lie in the last of the scalding sun, having storytime. There is a little chihuahua there, named Lucy, wandering in the sand. I pet her and she trembles. Where should we stealth camp? we wonder. We look at the wooded mountains that rise up at the far edge of the lake.

"Let's walk in that direction," I say.

We walk along a residential street, with big houses set back in the woods. We go stomping through a patch of woods that seems especially expansive and find a little cemetery there, with a tomb that's shaped like a small chapel. We pay our respects and then walk beyond the tomb to a prickly stretch of ground beneath some ponderosas. We spread out our groundsheets as best we can. Next to us is a golf course, and the sprinklers have just come on.

It's balmy tonight, and the stars are out. Instigate takes out her book of constellations. I feel safe here, in this little patch of pine needles among my

179

friends.

I wake in the pine needles in the long golden light of the morning. The air smells resinous and good. Coyotes yipped all night long.

We get breakfast at Denny's, pushing open the jangling glass door to the smell of bitter coffee and bacon grease. We crowd into a leather booth, pulling cords from various outlets so we can steal the outlets for our phones. I order decaf coffee and a skillet thing. Instigate gets a vanilla milkshake, and MeHap and NoDay have blueberry pancakes. We are some of the first customers of the morning.

"I used to work graveyard shifts at Denny's," I say, stabbing at the greyish sausage on my skillet. "When I was seventeen. I had long, blacklight-reflective yellow hair."

After breakfast I stick out my thumb and walk along the sprawling thoroughfare, trying to get a ride back to the trail. Spark is hanging at the coffeeshop for a while, and the others forgot to fill the tiny bottles of bleach they use to treat their water, so they're doing that. A woman picks me up. Her four-year-old daughter is in the back, watching a Disney movie on the built-in TV. The woman is from New Jersey originally. There is a traffic jam, but the woman knows how to get around it. We tear through narrow side streets and then she drops me in the sun on the edge of town. Another ride, a couple of wealthy tech industry people from the Bay with "a house in Tahoe," takes me right to the trail.

I reach the rickety cabin that is Echo Lake Resort shortly after setting out and park at the little picnic table out front. It's one o'clock. I eat two icecream snickers bars and text the others.

"We're having trouble hitching," they say.

It's hot and there are day hikers everywhere. I'm thirsty after my icecream, but they won't let me fill my bottles at the store.

"We're on a spring," they say, "and the spring is almost dry."

I look at the oily sheen on the lake. Well, I think. I guess I'll wait until the next stream in five miles.

I don't think of myself as a fast hiker, compared to other thru-hikers. It takes me from morning to sunset to "do the miles" and I can only really go "fast" in the evening, for a couple of hours. But today there are day-hikers everywhere, and regular backpackers too, with their big packs and their heavy boots, headed to the lake in eight miles or to the one after it, and I am *flying* past them. Even the day hikers who carry nothing but bottles of water. Even on this long, hot, rocky ascent. I am passing them and passing them and passing them. Not even their dogs can keep up.

My god, it's happening, I think. I am getting strong.

I reach Aloha Lake in the afternoon. The lake is set among granite walls and glitters with a thousand tiny lights. The edge of the water is clear and I space out, eating snacks and staring at the little creatures that swim around in there. When I get back on the trail there are familiar footprints ahead of me. Oh no, I think. Did my friends pass me while I was taking a break? Are they ahead of me now? Well, I think. I'll just have to catch them.

I summit Dick's Pass. I wish Spark were here to make an inappropriate joke but it's just me, sitting on the windy summit looking out at the light and the folds of the land. Then I race down the other side of the pass. Gotta catch them before dark.

At dusk I am exhausted and I still have not found my friends. I pitch my tent on a little flat spot next to the trail in a dim, scratchy forest that, to be honest, gives me the creeps. I don't know why it gives me the creeps, but it does. The mosquitoes are bad too, and I duck into my tent as soon as I can. I do my little nighttime chores (stretching distractedly, washing my feet with my hanky, making notes on everything that happened that day) and then lie in my bag, waiting for sleep. There's a stream nearby, and through the noise of the running water I can just make out the sound of sticks breaking in the woods. It's just animals, I say to myself. Animals acting out their little dramas. The whole forest is full of invisible dramas of which I know nothing about.

Crack, crack, shuffle, goes the noise in the woods.

Go to sleep, I think.

And then, rustle rustle rustle.

That's my tent, says my half-asleep brain. My half-awake eyes see the fabric of my tent move. Then I am awake. My tent! Something is pawing at my tent!

"Hey!" I say, and clap my hands. Then I clap them again for good measure. I can't really tell above the sound of the water, but I think I hear more sticks break as something moves away into the woods. It's pitch black outside, and I can't see anything.

Goddammit. I lie back in my bag. I hate camping in the woods alone. I lie there, watching the moon rise through the fabric of my tent, straining to hear every little noise.

***

All night I sleep and wake, sleep and wake, startling at every little sound. By dawn I am exhausted. The mosquitoes are thick, and I wave at them. Well creepy campsite, I say. Goodbye.

Just around the corner I see where two other people are camped. It's not MeHap and NoDay. Maybe that's whose footprints I've been following, I think. These strangers. Maybe my friends aren't ahead of me after all.

All morning I climb through the flowers in the sun towards Barker Pass. At the trailhead there, I find a styrofoam cooler and there's an orange inside, floating in the water among the empty soda cans. Trail magic! It doesn't even matter when they're empty; it's just nice to see coolers again. I think I'll still salivate every time I see a cooler, long after the PCT is done.

I take the orange to the tilted picnic table in the shade and sit there to eat it, along with my plastic jar of rehydrated instant refried beans. As I eat I brainstorm possible PCT calendar ideas. Here's what I've come up with so far:

Weird Rashes of the PCT

Burns of the Pacific Crest Trail

Thru-Hikers Sleeping

Instigate walks up while I'm crumbling Fritos into my refried beans.

"You're not in front of me!" I say.

She tells me that she walked until after dark last night, trying to catch me. She tells me the mile where she camped- about a half mile before my spot. MeHap and NoDay, she says, camped at the pass.

"We were all chasing each other," I say.

Instigate busts out her peanut butter jar of dehydrated lentils and we quietly spoon food into our mouths and then hike on, grateful for the company. We're walking through the dry pine forest, hugging the mountain just below the ridge. At one point we turn a corner and the air is hazy and yellow with smoke and we can see a plume of something, way off in the distance by Tahoe.

"What if we turn a corner," I say, "and there's, like, a wall of fire? What would we even do?"

"I'm not sure," says Instigate. The PCT abhors dull moments, and the instant you feel like you're coasting it will throw new obstacles and challenges at you. I joke that a "wall of fire" would be just the sort of thing the PCT would throw at us on a nice day like this.

I forget to check my maps and then we're in a seven-mile stretch without water, and my bottles are empty. For so long, in the Sierras, there was water everywhere- sprouting from every rocky crevice and pooling into hundreds of glittering lakes. I'm still getting used to the fact that Northern California is dry, and that I need to pay attention to my maps. We book it down the mountain, towards the stream, and when we get there we find a half dozen other hikers, congregated. A hiker watering hole! Just like in the desert! I've missed this- walking towards a water source, knowing that other hikers will be there. I've missed the company of it and the structure it gives to my day. I fill my bottles and sit, eating snacks and listening happily while the other hikers chat.

Before we fall asleep, Instigate and I place bets on when the others will catch up with us. We're not sure when Spark got out of town, but we figure he'll catch us the next evening. MeHap and NoDay, though, we might not see until Sierra City, the tiny mountain town where we'll resupply in sixty-eight miles.

***

The next day is more Northern California magic- sunshine and gentle passes all covered in flowers. It feels like we're really in summer now, a floral ecstasy, the bright fever of July. Five miles into the morning we stop and have second breakfast, sitting on a ridge slugging water from our Gatorade bottles, eating crumbled potato chips and jerky. Spark appears on the rise, holding his trekking poles in one hand like he does.

"I accidentally did a thirty-four mile day yesterday," he says.

We walk along the ridge for hours, looking down onto the tops of everything. We take a break and Instigate plays her violin on the mountaintop. Then there is a steep, difficult descent, big slabs of rock twisting around like a staircase. I fall a bit behind. At the bottom there's a paved road, and next to the paved road, trail magic- water and cherries and PBR. Instigate is already there, sitting on her ground sheet in the dirt. I get a text from Spark; he's hitched into Soda Springs, four miles away, for burgers and beer. Come hang with me, he says, but we want to keep hiking.

Meet us at the shelter at mile 23, we text back. There are only a handful of shelters on the PCT, and tonight we get to sleep in one. How exciting!

First we hear I-80, a wall of sound, and then we cross beneath it in a long, cool tunnel. We never actually see the thing, just thick green woods and then the tunnel. That seems right- less disruption of our fragile thru-hiker habitat. At the other end of the tunnel a couple of hikers are clustered around coolers- more trail magic! There is a cooler of cream soda, a stack of bottled water, a sack of Little Debbie snacks, and a cooler of Coors Light. I sit on one of the coolers and eat three Little Debbie snacks- the strawberry cream rolls, which are actually my least favorite kind. But right now they taste pretty fucking amazing. Instigate takes out her violin and begins to play a sad, lonesome song, taking advantage of the acoustics in the tunnel. I open a beer.

By the time we hike on, I feel sick. We climb a few miles up to a pass, pause to take in the warm breeze and the expansive view, and then we rush down the other side. At the bottom is a lush green meadow and at the edge of the meadow is the shelter, tucked back into the trees. It's a little stone cabin with a tall pointed roof, and inside is a dark, dusty room, with a single beam of light coming to rest on the carved-up wooden table.

Upstairs is a loft and a window that I manage to open onto the good evening air. It's stuffy inside.

"Let's sleep in the loft!" I say to Instigate. The other hikers here are camping out back because they think the shelter is creepy. We spread our bags on the smooth, creaky boards of the loft and lie out. Immediately my eyes begin to itch.

Around ten I think to take my phone out of airplane mode. There's a text from Spark.

"Where the fuck is the shelter?"

I text him back but there's no response.

"I think Spark is drunk," I say to Instigate. I hear the sound of tiny feet skittering on the wooden boards, and then a mouse runs over my bag. Go away, mouse, I think. A moment later, I hear the mouse downstairs, chewing at something. Crinkle crinkle crinkle.

***

In the morning, we hike half a mile and there is Spark, sitting in his sleeping bag among the trees, looking bleary.

"I think I might be a little hungover," he says.

Today the stretches between water are longer. We're easing into the hot part of Northern California, and now our water comes mostly from springs. One of the sources is listed in my data as being about a quarter mile before a dirt road- but I get to the spot and the spring isn't there. It's the only water in a long dry section so I drop my pack on the trail and set off on an off-trail adventure to try and find the water. All I find are many dry streambeds, and I return to the trail discouraged and confused, and even thirstier than before. And then when I get to the dirt road the water is there, and all the hikers are clustered around it. Spark and Instigate have been there for a while, just casually eating lunch while I tromped around in the woods, looking for water. I fill up my bottles, feeling mad at the world. And then I tell myself that I'm being a whiny baby. I sit in the shade and eat my refried beans and drink a liter of water, and then I feel better.

Instigate has a little book of topics that she's studying, and one of them is driving, which she hasn't yet learned how to do. And so while we sit next to the water eating our lunch she has me give her "verbal driving lessons," which she writes down verbatim in her book. Spark draws the pictures to illustrate.

In the evening I somehow get ahead of my friends and after a time I reach a paved road and a campground and a grated metal bridge over a stream. I climb down to the stream, take off my shoes and socks, and soak my feet. It feels luxurious to do this little thing, to sit next to the stream soaking my feet all alone, watching the sun sink in the sky. Afterward I fill my bottles and hike the last few miles to our campsite, a beaten, eerie-seeming clearing next to the trail. The clearing is in a spot where the trail cuts between two steep, wooded ridges, and at one end of the trail I can see the flame-orange of the setting sun, captured in a sort of "V." In the morning it's just eleven miles to Sierra City, where we'll resupply. I wonder what Sierra City will be like. Sprawling? Hot? Expensive? There is never any way to know these things.

Spark and Instigate arrive just as the light is almost gone, and throw up their shelters against the mosquitoes. Then the three of us sit out in the warm night for a bit, talking about nothing. I tell them about the last summer I spent in Alaska, the loneliness and the isolation. I am feeling a bit of that loneliness now, for reasons I don't understand. But then again, maybe I'm just tired.

***

When I wake, I meditate on the way a creepy clearing becomes a peaceful clearing when others are around. It's all the same, I think. The same forest. The same the same. I resolve to talk myself out of it next time I think that a campsite is creepy. Not creepy, I'll tell myself. Peaceful.

Then we're up and it's a race down, down down to Sierra City, or rather to the narrow paved road that leads to it. We're rushing thousands of miles down in elevation, on long narrow switchbacks, down the trail that is sandy, then covered in pine needles, then finally slippery with last year's oak leaves. And at the bottom, at the bridge, when I'm aching and starving and thirsty, there is, fantastically, a swimming hole, a reward for all my hard work. Spark and Instigate are already there; Spark sitting on a rock,

186

Instigate splashing around in the frigid water. I join her in my underwear and jump off a slick boulder into deep aquamarine water that is almost, but not quite, the temperature of ice.

Homeostasis resets and we cross the bridge and stick our thumbs out to hitch the mile and a half to town, because any amount of road walking, to a thru-hiker, is too much road walking. We get a ride right away and cram inside, our packs on our laps. The man drops us off moments later in a one-street mountain town that looks like it's straight out of Little House on the Prairie.

Ah, Sierra City!

There is a big, white painted general store, and I rush inside to order a burger from the deli. I stand at the counter, but the woman behind the counter just stares at me. Why is time moving so slow?

Finally, I order my burger. It's a Sierra City "Gut Buster" burger- made with an entire pound of ground beef! They say they'll wrap it in lettuce for me, instead of a bun since I don't eat gluten, and I rush next door to the post office.

"I have packages," I say to the woman behind the counter. There is a tall stack of boxes behind her.

"Huh," she says. She turns and pokes at the boxes, but does not lift them. She moves to another stack of boxes, and finds one of my packages there.

"That's it," she says.

"No," I say. "I have one more. With stickers all over it."

"That's it," she says again.

I run back to the general store, but my burger is not yet ready. The woman who makes the burgers is standing on a stool, calmly pouring more eggs into the big glass jar of pickled eggs.

I move to get her attention but then I see that she's having a conversation with a man in a trucker's hat. The man is wearing suspenders. They're not currently speaking, but one or the other of them seems about to, and I don't want to interrupt. I go out onto the porch and sit for a while. A young man is breaking down boxes. Then he stops breaking down boxes and crosses the street to the bar, which is painted red and looks like it belongs in an old western. The young man sits down on a bench on the front porch of the bar and lights a cigarette. A Jack Russel terrier appears and the young man picks up a bit of trash, and throws it into the street. The dog goes after the trash.

"That dog fetches dimes," says the man in the suspenders. He's standing right next to me, eating an icecream cone.

I run back to the post office.

"I really do have a package," I say to the woman. She frowns at me and bends over, groaning in pain as she lifts the boxes.

"Usually I have a boy who does this," she says.

"I'm sorry," I say.

She finds my package and heaves it onto the counter. I thank her and run back to the general store.

My burger is not yet ready. I sit on the porch and stare at the street, eating one of the snickers from my resupply box. I ate the last of my food hours ago, and I'm starving.

About an hour after I originally ordered my burger it appears before me, swimming in its own juices in a little paper boat. It's the biggest burger patty I've ever seen, there are vegetables piled on top of it, and I eat the whole mess of it very quickly. Afterward an inexplicable sleepiness descends on me and I wander lazily down the street (the town is two blocks long) to an inn which is, apparently, just for hikers.

I feel like the whole town is just for hikers. There are no cars, half the businesses are closed, and locals sit out in front of the storefronts on straight-back wooden chairs, watching the day pass by.

In the evening I go back to the general store for my second gut-buster burger. Instigate orders a blackberry shake and gives me half of it, and I give her half of my burger, which I cannot finish. Two pounds of ground beef in six hours, it turns out, is just a tiny bit too much for me. While I'm sitting there eating, MeHap and NoDay finally roll into town.

Around dusk, we claim a corner of the backyard behind the inn and roll out our sleeping bags for cowboy camping cuddlepuddle storytime. It isn't really a cuddlepuddle, more like sardines, but it's nice and warm this way. Instigate reads aloud to us, using all the funny voices we've grown to love. All around us, other hikers are tucked away in their tents sleeping, and from the canyon comes the rushing sound of the river.

I'll be hiking out in the morning; I don't want to zero. My plan is to not zero for at least a few hundred miles. I wonder how that's gonna go, I think, as I drift off to sleep.

***

In the morning Spark and Instigate make friends with a local and set out to another town to look at some old ruins. I pack my bag and walk to the general store to order my third gut-buster burger in 24 hours. I get some soft-serve icecream, too, and a pint of raspberries, and eat the icecream and raspberries all stirred up together as I walk down the street in the long morning light.

I sit at a table on the empty deck and study my trail data for the next section.

"Belden is creepy," is the description of my next resupply stop, a hundred miles away.

In the afternoon, I hitch to the trail with MeHap and NoDay. The trail climbs, and climbs, and climbs up through the leafy, dappled forest, out of the river valley towards the top of the ridge, which is the way of the PCT in Northern California. Up to the ridge, down to the river. Up to the ridge, down to the river. It is an enormous climb and I am sleepy today and there is a pound of ground beef in my stomach.

In the evening we reach the spring on top of the ridge and sit by the water, watching it burble out of the leafy ground. A mile later we find a campspot on a small shelf above the trail and I pitch my shelter there, MeHap and NoDay spreading out their groundsheets for cowboy camping. It is absolutely quiet. Before we fall asleep we talk about life after the trail, which is a topic that fills me with dread. How does one return to regular life after five months of this? How can something so simple and wonderful be anything but the most real thing ever? Why isn't the PCT a real "place" where I can "live"?

189

***

I sleep the sleep of dreams and wake late- nearly eight o'clock.

After an hour or so of hiking we reach a dirt parking area and see a bunch of mountain bikers- not the actual mountain bikers but a bunch of vans with racks for bikes and two dudes, sitting in folding camp chairs in the dirt, drinking beer. We joke with them for a while.

"If you bike on the PCT, you have to carry breakfast burritos," I say. "And throw them at hikers."

They offer us beers and MeHap and NoDay each take one and sit down in the dirt to drink. I decide to keep hiking but it doesn't really matter- It's hot and I'm sleepy and slow anyway. I could've just stopped, I think, as I pull myself lazily through the scratchy, third-growth forest. I reach the mountaintop and there's reception so I sit and text people, looking out at the hazy green mountains. By evening I've only gone twenty-two miles, and I start looking for a place to camp. I don't want to camp alone but then I turn a corner and see a couple of tents, pitched in a dusty clearing next to an old jeep road. I don't know these people. Lights are out; everyone's asleep.

I pitch my tent and climb inside. I can hear someone snoring. It's just beginning to get dark.

This clearing sure is peaceful, I think, as I lie in my sleeping bag, staring out at the dark forest.

***

Crash crash crash, CRUH-CRASH!

It starts right as I'm falling asleep.

CRASH! CRASH! CRASH!

The sound is coming from the other end of the clearing, where some people are camped. Some big animal, stomping around in the woods around their tent.

A bear?

Silence.

Oh. The bear has gone away.

I'm about to drift off when it happens again, this time closer.

CRASH! CRASH! CRASH! Shuffle shuffle shuffle. Step. Step. Step.
CRASHCRASHCRASHCRASH!

The animal is circling the clearing now, behind the tents.

CRASH! CRASH! CRASH!

The animal is coming closer to my tent.

Shuffle. Shuffle. Step. Step. Step.

What the fuck *is* that?

I pull out my headlamp and shine it through the mesh of my tent. A huge
brown mass crosses the dark gulf between two trees, and disappears.

CRASHCRASHCRASHCRASH!

It's a deer.

Just a deer. I lie back down in my sleeping bag and shut my eyes.

CRASHCRASHCRASHCRASH! goes the deer, as it circles the clearing.
Step! Step! Step!

The deer is coming closer to my tent. The deer is circling, moving into the
clearing. The deer is not afraid.

The deer is insane.

"Go away, deer!" I shout. I just want to go to sleep. The deer startles and
runs into the trees.

CRASH. CRASH. CRASH. The deer is coming closer again.

Step. Step. Step. The deer is approaching my tent. I roll over, determined
to ignore the deer.

Slurpslurpslurpslurpslurp. The deer is eating the sand where I peed.

Salt. The deer wants salt. The crazy deer wants salt.

CRASHCRASHCRASHCRASH. The deer runs into the trees again.

Crash. Crash. Crash. Crash. The deer is circling the clearing. And circling the clearing. Again, and again, and again.

Oh my god, I think.

***

In the morning, I'm red-eyed and tired.

It's hot and I walk slow, stopping often. The water sources are all off trail today, little wooden signs nailed to trees indicating such-and-such a spring, at such-and-such a distance, often with a note tacked below from a hiker saying how much elevation loss and whether the water is in fact worth it. The note itself is usually written on a bit of one of someone's map.

I'm at one such spring, a "seep" actually, crouched in the alders coaxing water into my Gatorade bottles, when Spark arrives. A minute later Instigate appears, and the gang is reunited once again. We hike slowly all morning through the dim, scratchy third-growth, leap-frogging each other, popping out of the woods now and again onto a ridgetop blanketed in mule's ears, the earth sweeping away into forever.

In the afternoon, there's a steep descent, long switchbacks on slippery pine needles down, down, down to the Feather River. At the bottom, we find smooth granite bowls filled with warm aquamarine water, the water flowing from one bowl to the next like some sort of swimminghole dream. We pull off our clothes and play like otters in the deep water until the sun sets and then we spread our groundsheets in last year's oak leaves, unroll our bedrolls. We sit beneath the trees in the warm air, Instigate, Spark, and I, eating our dinners.

"I guess we're hiking together now," says Spark. "The three of us."

It's true; Track Meat has gone ahead, MeHap and NoDay are behind. There were six of us and then, slowly, there were just three. We didn't talk about it; we didn't acknowledge it was happening. We just hiked together. And waited for each other. And hiked late to catch each other. And left each other notes.

"Yeah," I say. I pour a little water in my peanut butter jar and shake it up to wash out the last of the lentils. I tuck my spoon into its special place in my pack.

Later I lie in my sleeping bag, watching the stars through the boughs of the trees.

This is where we live, I think. This is the way it will always be. Right?

***

In the morning, we climb for seven miles away from the magic river until we break through the trees into the sweeping hazy soft stretching rolling view that goes on forever. Instigate and I sit on the dirt and play "what's in your food bag." Instigate has Lara bars, powdered hummus, an unidentifiable dinner, and some other bits of things in dirty ziploc bags. I am almost out of food but today there is a road walk alternate that goes through Buck's Lake, a little strip with a convenience store and a bar. I think I'll go there, and get some more food. The road walk is two miles longer than the PCT part but there will be icecream!

I get to the bright paved road to Buck's Lake after Spark but before Instigate and set out in the heat. The sun is overhead and there is no traffic and the forest rises up, soft and impenetrable, on either side of the road. I start to sweat and my trekking poles go clack, clack, clack on the pavement. It's hot and the sweat is dripping inside my clothes, making me chafe. The hot hard road hurts my feet. Icecream, I think. Icecream icrecream. At least the road is downhill.

After a mile I realize I've been walking down the road in the wrong direction. Goddamit. I turn around and walk back up the way I came, past the trailhead and then further, towards the town. It's so hot I can't stand it but there's nowhere else to go. I have to get more food. There's no traffic or I'd hitch. I'm out of water but I'm too impatient to stop and get some from the streams that run below the road. My lips are chapped and the sweat drips down my body. Oh, chafe. My asscrack feels like it's full of sand. Clack, clack, clack go my trekking poles.

I'm bleary and dehydrated when I reach the crowded little convenience store and I wander around, touching things on the shelves.

"You seen any other hikers today?" I ask the clerk as I pile food onto the counter. Barbecue potato chips, icecream, a can of peas with a pop-off lid, a giant Rice Krispies bar. I unscrew the top on a bottle of fruit punch Gatorade and drink the entire thing. My face is as red as a beet.

"No other hikers," says the clerk. "I always notice the hikers." She looks at my pile of food. "They usually go for the Little Debbies," she says, nodding at the rack in the corner. "Cheap and full of calories."

"This is good enough for me," I say.

I eat the icecream and walk up the road, feeling wild from sugar. I reach a little bar, and the bartender remembers Spark.

"He was here at noon," he says. "Got a burger and some beer."

Outside the bar I see an older man loading things into a pickup truck.

"You hiking the PCT?" He says. "Can I buy you an icecream?"

"No thanks," I say, "but I do need a ride to the trail."

"Hey Phineus," he shouts over to a young man getting into a hatchback. "Give this lady a ride to the trail?"

Phineus speeds me to the trailhead in his rattling hatchback, windows down, pack on my lap, no seatbelts. He says he owns 120 acres outside of town and sometimes PCT hikers come stay with him and never want to leave. I look out the window at the hot road, what little there is to the town. He drops me at the trailhead and I wave goodbye and there is Spark, asleep in a patch of shade on the piney ground.

There's a note from Instigate pinned to the wooden trail sign.

Gonna do a 30 today. Didn't go into Buck's Lake. See you soon!

Spark and I climb five miles back up to the views (up to the ridge, walk the ridge, then down- Northern California Style) and in the evening we find Instigate, taking a break in the dusky light. She tells us she saw three bears, points out an interesting mushroom, adjusts the violin on her pack, and we're off. We camp just before dark on some uneven ground next to a stream and I eat a Reeses peanut butter cup and an entire bag of jalepeno potato chips for dinner. Afterward I lie in my sleeping bag and listen to the sound of the water, tired from another almost-thirty-mile day. I wonder when I'll actually make that thirty-mile milestone. Maybe in Oregon I'll be able to do thirty-mile days. Maybe I'll do them *every day*. They say that Oregon is the fastest section. But why?

***

It rains randomly for five minutes in the middle of the night and then it's morning and we're up and it's a race to town. Ten miles downhill hearing the highway in the distance and then seeing the brown river, hitting the dusty bottom and crossing the railroad tracks in the bright sunshine, the crunch of ballast under my trail runners, back into the forest and then walking into the cluster of shuttered buildings which is Belden, population nine. I sit in front of the bar/restaurant/motel and frantically pick at a bag of cheese puffs from the hiker box. I sent a resupply box here but the post office has closed permanently and now I don't know what to do.

Spark already hitched into Quincy to resupply. Instigate has enough food for the next section and sits next to me, offering ideas. Then Brenda Braaten, the local trail angel, pulls up in her little sedan, dropping some hikers off at the trail. Her house, called Little Haven, operates as a sanctuary for thru-hikers one month out of the year. We gratefully pile into her car and she shuttles us to her tilted property, where chickens peck at the blackberries and one part of the house, a sort of apartment, is just for hikers. Against the wall in the apartment is a stack of boxes.

"So if I mailed a box to the post office in Belden and the post office is closed," I ask Brenda, "do you know where it would end up?"

"It would end up here," she says. "All the boxes sent to the post office come here."

Hallelujah, I am saved!

There are also loaner clothes, an epic hiker box, a kitchen stocked with giant bags of Cap'n Crunch, a shower, and two bedrooms with real beds. The apartment, which was apparently on the verge of collapse when the Braatens first acquired it, has a beautiful "abandoned house from the seventies" aesthetic and I wander from room to room, touching the appliances and stroking the bedspreads.

"The linoleum!" I say to Instigate. "Can you believe the linoleum!"

We rifle through the loaner clothes and put on hilarious outfits- Instigate looks straight out of the sixties and I look like my mother in 1992- and then we walk the quarter mile along the muddy river to the RV park, which has a restaurant and a laundry. I order a burger and Instigate orders a coffee milkshake and the locals stare at us, but not in a mean way. Then we walk back with our clean wet clothes and hang them on the line to dry and sit inside out of the heat, eating Cap'n Crunch and sorting our food. Brenda brings over a plate of homemade peanut butter cookies from her side of the house and I eat too many of them and descend into a glutenfog. A moment later about a thousand other hikers arrive and we say man, we gotta get back to the trail.

Brenda gives us a ride back to the trailhead. We don't know where Spark is but then we hear him shouting and see him way across the river on the deck of the bar, a beer in his hand.

"What are you doing?" he shouts, waving his free arm in the air.

"Trying to get to Canada," says Instigate.

"Why?" he says.

It's hot climbing up out of the river valley but at least it's evening. We stop to take a break a few miles in and Spark materializes, trucking up the trail behind us. The three of us hike a few more miles until dark and then beyond, me tripping over the rocky trail but Instigate and Spark confident with their magic night vision, until we find a flat spot in last year's oak leaves, just big enough for the three of us to cowboy camp.

***

The mosquitoes wake me throughout the night and then we wake for good in the dim morning, all scrunched together in the leaves. We sit up, eat unappetizing food, and start our morning with a nine-mile climb. The going is slow and rocky, through bushes and stream crossings. At one point I hear crashing along the trail and think it's Spark, coming back from pooping but it's a black bear, lumbering along like duh doh duh doh duh doh and then it sees me and is like, Wah? And then it turns around and flash! There is no bear. On top of the mountain I take a long break, eating and googling varieties of California ticks, and then the sluggish humid afternoon takes me up and down, up and down along the ridge. Camp is a flat bench that looks out at the aching yellow sunset. We spread our groundsheets in the sand. We eat dinner watching the sun dip lower, lower, lower, setting the world on fire.

***

Animals step softly through the forest all night, waking me up. Aye, I think. Why do I ever try to cowboy camp. On the plus side the Milky Way is smeared above me like butter on toast and it almost makes me dizzy, looking up there into everything. In the morning the sun rises big and golden and we pack up with excitement; today we'll reach the halfway point! Instigate and Spark are off like a shot and I plod along behind them, thinking about all sorts of things. There's only one spring in the first fifteen miles, down a little side trail, and when I get there I know they've missed it; their footprints aren't there. I fill up an extra liter in case I catch them but I know I won't. "Carry no water and hike as fast as you can" is Spark's motto.

I reach the halfway-to-Canada monument and it's a short, awkward concrete pillar in a clearing of trampled dust. It's so ugly I don't even take a picture. Instead, I drag the trail register into the shade and read it like a book while I eat my lunch. People ahead of me, people even farther ahead of me. And I never get to see the ones behind me.

Halfway to nowhere never felt so good.

After lunch I'm sluggish and tired, and I make my legs go up and down, up and down. I reach the highway and there's a note from Instigate; she and Spark hitched into Chester to get dinner. There's trail magic at the highway, some of the best trail magic I've seen, via "Piper's Mom." Three coolers full of soda, bottled water, boxes of snacks. I am overcome with gratitude and delight. I eat a strange pre-cooked packaged beef and rice dish, a couple of little Butterfingers, and finish it off with a can of Pepsi. The Pepsi makes me feel incredible and I take down Instigate's note, replace it with my own.

Drank a can of pepsi, feel like I can do anything. Ima do a 30.

I race through the woods, feeling as though I'm turning the whole earth beneath my feet. I see no one and I hike up and over the convoluted surface of the planet and then down, down to the second fork of the Feather River. It's dusk when I reach the river. I don't want to camp alone, at least not next to a river with its loud noises that mask the sounds of night-monsters, so I hike on and in a mile I reach a peaceful clearing at the junction to a little spring. The last of the day's sunbeams are gathered here, loose on the ground, and it's absolutely quiet. I pitch my tent and eat my dinner in the dregs of the light and then lie down, watching the moon rise through the fabric of the tent. I've finally done a thirty-mile day. My first.

Oh glory, I think. Sometimes the forest can be so good.

***

I dream I'm asleep in a cathedral, long rays of light coming through the colored glass windows and when I wake it's morning, yellow light filtering through the trees. I lie in my sleeping bag and let it wash over me, this peaceful feeling so far away from everything, here in this little clearing next to the trail.

I'm stiff today; I'm still adjusting to the way these long NorCal days make my body feel. My body feels hungover, and this morning I use my trekking poles like crutches as I stumble down the trail. At least I'll be at Drakesbad Guest Ranch soon, which is, according to trail lore, a middle-of-nowhere heaven where they welcome filthy hikers with open arms and grant you access to their reasonably-priced lunch buffet. And Spark and Instigate are somewhere behind me, having hitched into Chester for the Mexican food yesterday, so I should be seeing them soon as well.

It's hot in the woods and the trail splits and branches as it circles its way around various thermal attractions. There's a little geyser that I don't see and then there's a "boiling lake," which looks like a vat of bubbling soup.

Around noon the trail breaks free of the forest and there are the small cabins of Drakesbad Guest Ranch, spread out in the valley below me. At the main building there are a number of wrought-iron tables arranged on a big wooden patio. There are white tablecloths on the tables and wealthy people in crisp new outerwear sit there, laughing while the remnants of their salads wilt in the sun. I stand on the deck, feeling dirty and rumpled, and wait to be noticed. A staff member is wiping down a big glass dispenser filled with ice water. There are lemons floating in the ice water. The man ignores me and then the phone rings, and he goes inside to answer it. I sit down at a picnic table next to the deck. Drakesbad is not what I imagined, but I have to admit I had a hard time imagining a legitimate business that would actually *want* thru-hikers at their buffet.

I see a woman in an apron and talk to her. She tells me that there isn't any food left, or that the food that's left is for the staff. The man gets off the phone and I talk to him.

"There isn't any food?" I say.

Just then Spark appears.

"If it's only the two of you," says the man, wringing his hands and peering out at the trees as if a group of hikers might suddenly materialize, "then you can go through the line. As long as you clean up first."

We wash our hands in the little bathroom behind the building, then grab small white plates and pile them with cucumber salad and large, elaborate sandwiches which we assemble at the sandwich bar.

"Don't eat everything," says the woman with the apron. "The staff has to eat too."

"I thought you said there wasn't any food," I say.

"I was only joking," says the woman, staring at me.

"Maybe our lunch is free?" I say to Spark. "Or discounted? Since it's a buffet but they're telling us not to eat the food?" There's a big silver desert tray with just a few brownies left, and I don't take one.

"Your lunch will be fourteen dollars," says the man as he passes our table, carrying a pitcher of ice tea.

Spark tells me that Instigate is a few miles behind; she's having foot pain. The staff begin shutting down the buffet. I assemble the tallest sandwich I can, layers of meat and cheese and meat and cheese and meat and cheese, and surreptitiously slip it into an empty potato chip bag that I have folded in my pack. I'll give the sandwich to Instigate later, when she catches me.

Spark is gonna sit on the patio for a while and read sci-fi while his food digests. I shoulder my pack and set out into the afternoon heat.

The road back to the trail is dusty and then I'm climbing, up and up in the hot sun to a ridgeline. I've eaten a lot and I'm hiking heavy. After the climb is a long burn, pink fireweed among the blackened trees, the sun heavy and yellow, sinking. Instigate still hasn't caught me and I think of the sandwich, wrapped in a foil bag on the outside of my hot pack, growing warmer. I imagine the lettuce wilting and the mayonnaise turning to oil. I eat the sandwich next to a stream, watching the tea-colored water move over the stones. It tastes better than anything I've ever eaten in my entire life.

Tomorrow I'll reach Old Station, a little cluster of buildings next to the highway. I have a resupply package there. And then, after Old Station, there is the "Hat Creek Rim", a thirty-three-mile waterless stretch that guidebooks compare to the Mojave but which I can't conceptualize at all. Why is the creek named after a hat? And what part of a creek could be called the "rim?" And why is it so hot there?

***

I wake to the sound of thousands of insects chewing. It's a subtle rasping sound, coming from all directions. The insects are living in the blackened trees, and they're eating them. Rasp rasp rasp rasp.

I sit in my sleeping bag and eat my breakfast- a handful of trailmix, a handful of granola, a piece of jerky, all from dirty Ziploc bags spread in my lap. I shake a packet of emergen-c into the last two inches of water in my Gatorade bottle, and gag a little as I drink it. The lake where I filled my bottles yesterday had a bunch of dead creatures in it that I failed to notice. They're some sort of invertebrate- they look like the sea monkeys I had as a kid, and I can feel them on my tongue.

I pull my shoes onto my feet. I'm tired today. The moon was like a spotlight all night, shining through the fabric of my tent, and I didn't sleep well. But Old Station is in thirteen miles, and there's nothing to do but walk.

I think about Old Station as I hike. What will be there? Gatorade? Ice Cream? Something wonderful I can't imagine? Air conditioning? It's already hot, and there isn't much shade in this burn. There also isn't any water for six miles, and I'm thirsty. Finally there's a stream, cool and fast, and I fill up my bottles. Then the sandy trail is cutting through dappled ponderosa forest, and I have to shit. I drop my pack on the trail and stomp through the woods, looking for a place. Afterward I walk back in the direction of my pack and... the trail isn't there.

Of course. Of course I would get lost leaving the trail to take a shit.

Only I would do something like this.

The forest is flat and looks the same in all directions. There's no way to orient myself. I walk in a big circle, feeling like a fool. I wish I could call to my pack. I am getting a little bit panicky and then the trail appears, a miraculous little strip of sand in all this nothingness and my pack sitting there, looking so innocent. What is the lesson here, aside from the fact that I am a fool? That I should only shit in uneven terrain? Or take my phone with me so I can use the GPS?

Old Station consists of an RV campground, a post office the size of a children's playhouse, and a busted-looking gas station next to the highway. The gas station is expensive and out of almost everything; there are only empty places on the shelves where the food should be. And they only have the little bottles of Gatorade. The rims of my Gatorade bottles are thick with chapstick residue and some sort of slime that seems to be living, and I wanted to replace them. But I'll just wash them in the bathroom sink instead.

I buy an icecream bar, a bag of barbecue potato chips, and a little Gatorade in the "blue" flavor. A bunch of hikers are clustered around a picnic table in front of the store and I join them, eating my icecream bar and watching the traffic on the highway go by. It's crazy hot.

Spark and Instigate appear, sweaty and red from the sun, and procure a six-pack of beer.

"I made you a sandwich yesterday," I say to Instigate, "but then I ate it."

I buy a shower in the RV campground and wash my clothes under the cool water. Afterward there is still dirt caked onto my calves, although I swear I washed them- will I never be clean again? The laundry room that's attached to the showers is cool and there are outlets and long counters for folding laundry. I plug in my phone and my steripen to charge and then sit on one of the counters. Spark and Instigate join me, and we pretend that the counters are bunkbeds. We formulate a plan for the Hat Creek Rim; we'll hang out until the cool of the evening and then night-hike the first part, with plenty of water. I drink a Pepsi I bought at the store, shaking the ice in the cup. If I'm going to night-hike I may as well caffeinate. Another hiker joins us and curls up under one of the counters to sleep.

Around five, a maintenance guy appears and tells us that we're kicked out.

"I've got to lock the laundry room," he says. "People are complaining."

We move our operations to a picnic table at the edge of the campground and then finally head out. There's a last water stop a few miles down the trail, a spigot next to some pit toilets, and we fill up our bottles. How much water to bring for thirty-three miles? I wonder, as the cool water spills over the mouth of my platypus. Five liters? Five and a half? It's night now and we walk to a flat, sandy spot below the rim, which looms above us in the dark. The rim is a bluff. That's what it is. A tall bluff above Hat Creek. I lie in my bag and watch the stars come out one by one. Tomorrow we'll go up onto that rim and follow it north. There won't be any shade, and there may or may not be a water cache.

***

I wake in the night to the full moon hanging above us, the landscape draped in watery silver. So this is the sun's light, reflected off this ball that pulls at us, this mass of regolith and solid iron. The sun's light turned inside out. It's cold now, and I draw my sleeping quilt up to my chin. The irony of the desert- so hot in the day, so cold at night. I fall asleep again and when I wake, it's six, pale yellow light bleeding across the ground. Time to get up.

"Forty-eight degrees," says Spark, looking at the thermometer on his pack. I don't want to leave my warm sleeping bag. Finally I eat a little breakfast and extricate myself. I'm only wearing running shorts and a tank top; I know the cold is temporary.

We climb up to the bright, treeless rim and then we're looking down on everything, down on the hazy valley and the creek way below. We're in a heat wave so it's even hotter than normal today but I don't mind. I have really good cell service up here, not a thing in any direction to interrupt it, and there's plenty of sun to rock my solar charger. This means that I can listen to music, something I haven't yet been able to do.

I haven't listened to music in almost three months.

And music, it turns out, is incredible.

I'm pumped. I'm so pumped I don't give a fuck about the heat. I feel like I'm flying. And besides, I like the desert. I like the flat sandy path. I like the challenge of racing from water source to water source. I like the sun.

I'm so happy.

The cache is called "Cache 22" (a play on words I won't get until much later) and it consists of a sort of cave made from interwoven tree branches, like an overturned basket, and in the dappled shade of this shelter there are a couple of plastic chairs, a trail register, and dozens of gallon water jugs. There are already a handful of hikers there, sweating in the plastic chairs, and all of the water jugs are empty except for two. Instigate, Spark and I walk down the hill to where an oak tree throws some solid shade on the dry yellow grass and spread out our sleeping pads to wait out the heat.

"A hundred degrees in the shade," says Spark, checking his thermometer again. We all take off as much clothing as we can and pull our food bags out to eat snacks. I read *The Adventures of Huckleberry Finn* aloud from my phone and we watch as the other hikers set out from the cache, one by one, into the afternoon heat. A pickup truck appears, rumbling up the dirt road. A man and a woman step out. They're holding a galvanized metal tub of apricots.

"We're here to stock the cache," says the woman. She offers us the apricots. The apricots are soft and overripe, right off the tree. We eat as many as we can stomach and then we pile the water jugs into a little red wagon and haul them up to the bird's nest. The couple also has watermelon, beer, and a cooler full of ice. I put some ice in my hat. The ice melts, and I put more ice in my hat. At last the cache is stocked, our bottles are full, and our stomachs are aching with fruit. It's time to set out.

We hike a few more miles along the rim as the sun melts into the horizon. The path is sandy and smooth but there are lava rocks jutting from it, here and there where you wouldn't expect them. I keep tripping over these rocks and almost falling on my face. It seems that my legs have a setting for "forest floor with tree roots" and "flat sandy path," but that they cannot acclimate to a flat sandy path with root-like rocks sticking out of it. At dusk we find a small clearing next to the trail where all of us can sleep. A woman named Egg is with us; we've been seeing her on and off for a while. Egg is short, wears a big white hat in the sun, and hikes in a cornflower-blue yoga dress. Her pace is "slow and steady" while ours oscillates between fast and lackadaisical. At the end of each section, however, our averages are the same, and so we see each other often.

Instigate takes out her violin, rosins her bow, and plays *Wayfaring Stranger* to the last of the setting sun.

***

We wake late on the warm grassy bluff overlooking everything and sit in our sleeping bags, rubbing the dust from our eyes. This morning I'm having bacon jerky and some caffeinated fruit snacks for breakfast. Caffeinated fruit snacks sometimes make me feel like I'm flying and sometimes give me awful stomach pain. Today it's the stomach pain and I clutch my guts and complain to Egg and Instigate as we hike the last thirteen miles to Burney, the town where we'll rest and resupply. Undoing the hipbelt on my pack helps a little with the pain, but then the weight is all on my shoulders, which is annoying. At least I'm almost out of food, so my pack is super light.

It's a hundred degrees again today and I'm hot and caked in layers of dirt, my clothes stiff with dried salt, my pack wet with sweat. There isn't any shade just the bright sandy trail with the volcanic trip-rocks protruding from it and we're plodding, plodding, plodding, trying to make it.

A few miles before the highway there's a fish hatchery and a big mucky lake ringed in thistles. A log sticks out into the lake and Instigate and I walk out onto the log, strip off our clothes and dip our legs into the water.

I ease off the log until I'm standing in the water. My feet are buried in muck, and muck from the floor of the lake rises up around me. The water smells like salt and fish and there's bits of trash in it. I reach into the lake and pull a small brown bottle, like an old-timey medicine bottle, from the muck.

"Look at this cool thing I found," I say. I turn the bottle over. The underside is coated in flat black worms.

204

"Leeches," I say. "Leeches!"

"Ugh!" says Instigate. I pull myself back onto the log and rub the muck from my skin. We look into the water and now we can see all the leeches there, swimming around happily, flexing and contracting like they do.

We join Spark in a patch of thistley shade next to the trail and put our shoes back on our wet, dusty feet. Then it's the last hot, thirsty miles to the highway, where, according to the data, "one of the most difficult hitches of the trail" awaits us. But of course everything is always the opposite of the way you think it's going to be and the first car that goes by stops for all three of us. It's a red-eyed smoke jumper in a busted civic and he speeds us to Burney, windows down radio blasting static, shouting a conversation with Spark in the front seat.

Burney is a perfect town. There is one street and everything is there, all clustered together. We get a room at the Charm Motel, where they give us a hiker discount and generously allow us to cram five people into one room. Our packs explode across the floor. The room smells terrible and then Egg finds two empty tuna packets in the bottom of her pack, rotten from the long days in the sun. We laugh- we'd wondered, for a moment, if the smell was coming from us. We shower, wrap ourselves in hotel towels and haul our dirty things to the coin-op laundry downstairs. We lie on the beds in the sunbeams and drift in and out of sleep while our clothes wash and then we put on our wet clothes, slightly cleaner than they were before and walk to the all-you-can-eat pizza and salad buffet, no sidewalk but the hot car-wind blasting us dry in minutes. Other hikers are there, crowded into a booth with their packs all around them, playing card games and drinking gallons of soda. I pile a small plate high with iceberg lettuce, ranch dressing, potato salad and hardboiled eggs. My body wants vegetables and for now, this will have to do. Spark and Instigate eat a few slices of pizza and then sit quietly, waiting for their small hiker stomachs to allow them to eat more pizza. I walk across the street to the Safeway, where I am overwhelmed. The bluish fluorescents, the sounds echoing in the aisles, the mountains of cheap food. I feel as though I am being buried beneath mountains of harsh, empty plentitude. I buy blueberries, chocolate Haagen-Daz and a roast chicken. Back at the room I eat my icecream at the little table. The other hikers rent the room next to ours, buy a bunch of beer and turn the TV on loud. Soon it's dark, the soft light of the streetlamps coming in the windows. I brush my teeth, staring at my reflection in the mirror- sunburnt, overly tan, wild hair- and then crawl into one of the palatial beds, pulling the scratchy hotel comforter up to my chin. I lie there on the weird soft mattress, looking at where the light from the street leaks around the curtains. In the distance, I can hear a train. I am restless and my whole central nervous system is buzzing, as if on fire. I know I won't sleep much tonight- I never do, in hotel rooms- but I also know it doesn't matter. Town stops are for taking care of business. I can rest when I'm back on the trail, sleeping on the ground. I can rest when I'm hiking twelve hours a day.

***

In the morning, I walk to the post office but my box is not there. So I resupply for the next ninety miles at Safeway, pulling things off the shelves that I might like to eat, not really sure what to buy. Banana chips, almonds, jerky… what else? Granola bars I guess. Trail food is so weird. I don't want any of it, and yet I need to pack around four thousand calories a day or I'll be hungry. Sometimes I end up with too much. Sometimes I have too little. And when I'm truly hungry it all tastes amazing.

I buy another pint of chocolate icecream and some blueberries and walk along the road towards the edge of town. Spark and Instigate are at the library; they'll head out later. As I walk, I look at my reflection in the store windows. Why is my pack so big? What is even in there? Can I bounce all my stuff, aka mail it forward? I play this game with myself often. Spark, Instigate and I like to joke about it. We call it "packorexia"- thinking that our packs are huge, even when they're not. Spark is the worst; his pack is the size of a pea and yet he's constantly complaining about how heavy and/or big it is. I mentally go through all the items in my pack. What can I bounce? What can I go without? Where is my edge?

A man in a pickup pulls onto the shoulder as I'm passing the McDonalds. He has silver hair and a red plaid shirt. I saw him at the grocery store, where he'd introduced himself; he gives rides to thru-hikers. I put my pack in his truck and then turn and notice another hiker jogging up. The hiker has wild dark hair and a thick mustache. He's carrying an overstuffed Osprey pack.

"Thanks," the hiker says to the driver, as he tosses his pack in the back with mine.

It's shady at the trailhead. I look in my plastic sack at the weeping carton of chocolate icecream.

"Hey," I say to the other hiker. "You want to eat this icecream with me? It's melting. And I've got blueberries."

"Ok," he says. He tells me his trail name is Ramen.

"It's sort of silly," he says. "But I just wanted a trailname. I figure it could be worse."

We sit on the damp ground and eat the blueberries and the half-melted icecream, and I learn about Ramen's life. He's a firefighter in the summer and in the winter he works in Antarctica. He's from North Dakota. He studied forest ecology in school. His parents are archaeologists. He's twenty-five years old. I watch him eat the icecream; much of it ends up in his mustache.

"How are you liking the trail so far?" I ask him.

"It sucks," he says. "I've been having this foot pain."

"I'm sorry," I say.

"Motherfucker," says Ramen, as a spoonful of icecream lands on his shirt.

When the icecream is gone we hike. The excitement of chatting with someone new has worn off- Ramen seems to be in a foul mood and I wonder if he's always like this, or if it's just today. But no matter; after just a couple of miles we find ourselves in a small clearing with the most incredible cache that either of us have ever seen. There are lawn chairs, picnic tables, big jugs of water, and a six-foot long cooler that I open and then shout in surprise- it's full of ice, soda and candy. I grab a cream soda and a handful of Reeses peanut butter cups and sit in one of the lawn chairs. How is a person supposed to get in the miles when there are caches like this?

Please leave a joke, is written on the first page of the trail register. I carefully scrawl my favorite thru-hiker joke:

Q: How can you tell if a thru-hiker is on her period?

A: She's only wearing one sock.

(Later, in Washington, I'll get a text from Instigate- *I'm only wearing one sock.*)

In the evening the trail crosses a creek that forms a series of deep, tepid pools. It's the best swimming hole that we've had for a while and I clamber into a pool that's shaped just like a Jacuzzi and let the cool water run over me. Ramen jumps in the water downstream and then sits on the smooth rock bank and consumes an entire sleeve of Oreos. Spark and Instigate appear on the footbridge above me, meowing, and we walk another quarter mile to a dusky campsite in the trees. I set up my tent and crawl inside, feeling sleepy and drained. Why am I so slow sometimes? I lie in my bag, feeling the night cool all around me. And what can I do to be faster?

***

I'm the first one to wake and I rustle through my food bag, looking for breakfast. Spark calls this the "Carrot alarm clock"- plastic bags crinkling, opening up and closing. I put some boring food into my mouth- tortilla chips or something- and then I'm packed and hiking by seven. I'm determined not to be lazy today. They say that the way you do one thing is the way you do everything, and that's definitely true for me. So far I'm like a two-step- quick quick slow, slow, quick quick slow, slow.

The morning is mercifully cool and overcast and I'm climbing, climbing through the wonderful dappled forest. Then I'm ridge walking, way on top of everything, through the pink fireweed with the mountains rolling away into forever. I miss a water source in the afternoon and I'm thirsty, hiking with Ramen. Ramen's telling me about his travels in Eastern Europe. This seems to make him happy; he's not in such a foul mood today. And listening to Ramen tell stories full of colorful detail helps the time pass- I hardly notice my thirst. The stream's at the end of a little side trail and we find Spark there against a big downed log, his food spread out all around him, assembling dinner. Instigate is there too. We rest, let the sweat cool, eat. I wash my chafe.

Dusk finds Instigate and I night hiking, stepping carefully over roots in the trail, Spark ahead of us. We don't want to turn our headlamps on. We talk loudly about everything, watch the moon rise in the trees. At last we're at the logging road that apparently leads down to the stream where we'd all

208

agreed to camp. We stumble down the dark path and find Spark sitting on the abandoned road eating cinnamon raisin bread, his white tyvek groundsheet glowing in the moonlight. Around him the logging roads spread out in every direction, like spokes in a wagon wheel.

"The stream is hard to find," he says. "Go east and then north and then east and then south." He points his hand in a general direction. "Whatever you do, don't go west."

"Um, ok." I say.

Instigate's sense of direction is much better than mine and I follow her down the faint path that's beaten in the tall, damp grass. It's spooky down here in this no-man's land of overgrown logging roads and I can't help but think of mountain lions. If this is the only water source for miles, wouldn't mountain lions come here to drink? And isn't it likely that they'd come here to drink *at night?* I swing my pathetic little headlamp around in the dark but it barely makes any light at all. Instigate's is no better. Eventually, through some navigational magic on the part of Instigate, we hear the sound of running water and then find the stream, moving clear and shallow below a steep grassy bank. Instigate grips the bough of an overhanging tree and suspends herself on the bank. I toss her bottles to fill and whip my headlamp around, watching for giant, sadistic housecats. Our bottles full, we set out to walk back the way we came, but of course we're lost.

"Where's the trail?" I say.

"I'm not sure," says Instigate.

"Whoop, whoop," I say into the dark night. I think I hear a whistle in response.

"That way?" I say. "I think Spark is that way?" We retrace our footsteps back to the stream and discover a grassy fork that we'd overlooked- the way we came in. A little while later we're in the clearing with Spark. It's cold now, and there's condensation on everything.

"Did you hear me whooping?" I say.

"No," says Spark.

I set up my tent, spread out my sleeping pad and explode my sleeping quilt, which I've taken to calling my fluffer puff, from its stuff sack. It's the

209

warmest, driest, loftiest thing in the world and tonight I am so grateful to climb inside of it.

***

Somehow it's nine o'clock by the time Instigate and I get hiking in the morning, which is pretty embarrassing by thru-hiker standards. If nine p.m. is hiker midnight, then nine a.m. is hiker noon. To make things even more awesome we can't find the path back to the PCT, and end up bushwhacking through thick manzanita up on the ridgeline, pretending we're bears. At last we stumble onto the trail, that magical gently-graded path, that light-speed freeway through the wilderness.

It's hot and we're climbing up, up, up. And then we're ridge-walking, and then we're going down. Hot, sweaty climbs and long, leafy descents- it's the Northern California way. At the bottom of this ten-mile descent is the McCloud River, and I am racing down the switchbacks, passing everyone, thinking about jumping in that cool water. I pass Ramen resting next to a stream.

"Is that you who pees right on the trail?" he says.

"Yeah," I say. "So what?"

"You don't pee right on the trail," says Ramen, morose.

"Ok," I say. "I won't."

I pass Spark and Instigate having lunch on a leafy bench next to the trail. I am dehydrated and hungry and I am pounding downhill as fast as I can. It hurts my body but I don't care. All I want is to take off my clothes and lie down in the river.

At lower elevations the forest is lush, streams trickling out of everywhere and poison oak crowding the sides of the path. The trail dumps me onto a road, and on the other side of the road I can hear the river. There's a footbridge there and below it the slanted sun puddles on the jumbled rocks. I pull off my clothes and step into the shallow water. The water is achingly cold- the flow is from the bottom of a lake, via a dam upstream- and it hurts my tender feet so bad that I cry a little but still I dunk myself into the water, once, twice, three times. As far as tolerance to cold water goes, mine is pretty high. I grew up in Alaska, swimming in frigid lakes. I didn't swim in a warm body of water until I was nineteen.

I rinse my shorts and my shirt in the water and spread them on the rocks to dry. Egg is on the other bank, reading a book in the shade, and I wave at her, then cross the bridge in my underwear and join her. Instigate, Spark and Ramen appear after a little while and we all eat dinner together, shouting at each other over the sound of the water. I am unbearably sleepy now.

My goal is thirteen more miles and so I pack up my things and set out. Instigate is going even farther, and Spark has fallen asleep. I'm climbing again, back up to some awesome ridgeline overlooking everything, after which I'll probably descend to another river. The forest is so dense now and the trees are so tall that I feel like I'm *inside*, which is unusual for California. Sweeping views; that's what the PCT is known for. I think of Oregon, of the thick wet forests of the Pacific Northwest. Home.

I call it quits around nine at a loamy little campsite tucked into a fold in the mountain. The dark is impossibly black and nearly impenetrable down here, under the canopy of the forest, and it spooks me. I wish I wasn't camping alone- but so it goes sometimes. I set up my tent and crawl inside. I pull my sleeping quilt over my lap and eat my rehydrated instant refried beans and tortilla chips. I love not having to cook my food. It was nice to have a stove in the Sierras, where it was fifteen degrees at night and I needed something to warm up my core, but overall I've found cooking on the trail to be more hassle than it's worth. After eating I brush my teeth, take my daily notes and then lie in my bag, listening to twigs break in the darkness. I think of Instigate- is she night-hiking still? And did Spark make it any farther than the river? At some point the stick-breaking starts to feel more companionable than threatening, and the blackness of the forest lulls me to sleep.

***

I wake once in the night to pee, and don't want to get out of my tent. It's so black out there! I pull a gallon Ziploc bag from my pack and squat over it. If you're a guy you can pee into an empty bottle or whatever, but if you're a woman- the gallon Ziploc bag is where it's at.

Unless, of course, the bag has a hole.

I watch the bag fill and then zip it and set it outside the tent. Tonight there are no holes. And I didn't accidentally knock the bag over onto the floor of my tent, either.

I guess I forgot to tell you about that.

When I wake again it's seven, a little light filtering through the dense canopy of green. I eat breakfast, pack up, and try out my legs. Ooof, I'm stiff today. During the six-mile climb to the top of the ridge I almost cry from fatigue and then I realize why I'm so tired. I haven't taken a zero day since Sierra City, three hundred miles ago. In nineteen miles I'll be in Mt. Shasta, a little hippie town at the base of the big white volcano. I've never been there and I have no idea what it's like, but I already know I'm zeroing there.

The only thing left in my food bag today is a package of salami and a little baggie of raisins. I'm sick of salami because I packed too much of it this section, and just thinking about it makes me want to hurl. I wait until I'm shaky from hunger, sitting on top of the ridge and then I eat it, rolling each slice around a few raisins. It tastes pretty good that way. Afterward my stomach is upset, and it makes hiking in the heat even more miserable. No more salami after this. No no no no no.

I arrive at the highway sweaty and exhausted and gritty with chafe. There's a cute note from Instigate taped to a post at the trailhead-

I   *went*   *fasta*
and now I'm in Shasta.

It's three-thirty and I have to make it to the post office in Mt. Shasta by five, to pick up my resupply box. Tomorrow is the weekend, and the post office won't open again until Monday. I walk onto the 1-5 onramp, where there isn't any shade. I shake my water bottle- empty. There's no traffic, either, just a busted pickup every ten minutes or so, driving by on the frontage road.

An hour later I say Fuck It, and walk onto the freeway. It's a trick I know from my hitchhiking days; it's illegal to hitch right on the freeway and the cops will kick you off, but not if you get a ride first. There's a mess of stormclouds tumbling over Castle Crags to the west, blocking out the sun. An SUV pullls onto the shoulder just as the first fat drops begin to fall. A fucking saint. He's a highschool teacher. He has his two-year-old son in the backseat along with another hiker who was stranded in Dunsmuir. The teacher speeds us to the post office in Shasta and I get there at 4:54, banging on the locked door. The postal clerk lets me inside. Inside the post office things move achingly slow, as if I've entered another realm of space-time. Finally the postal clerk pushes my tall stack of boxes across the laminate counter- my food resupply, an awesome care package and new trail runners to replace the ones I've been grinding down for the last seven hundred miles. I carry my loot across the street to Shasta Base Camp, the outdoor store that's letting thru-hikers camp in the grassy lot out back.

I pitch my tent in the grass and put my boxes inside it to protect them from the rain. Other hikers are there, tarptents spread across the lot, coming and going with beer, snacks, armloads of gear for their morning summit of Mt. Shasta. I recognize Instigate's tent and find her inside, asleep.

"I'm gonna start a load of laundry," I say. "You want to give me your clothes?" She pulls off everything, digs the dirty socks from her pack and pushes the stuff out the door to me in a little pile.

"Now I have to stay in here until the laundry's done," she says.

I walk to the Laundromat and start a load, our filthy things barely filling the washer up halfway, and then cross the street to the health food store where I buy lettuce, strawberries and sliced roast beef. I eavesdrop on the hippies as I wait in line at the checkout- the hippies here, so far, are more like hippies than any hippies I have ever seen. Apparently there are hippies here who worship the mountain. They believe that a race of tiny, sacred people lives beneath it. The couple in front of me is wearing loose, blousy clothing and they're barefoot. They're buying yogurt and honey and some sort of exotic, expensive fruit and they seem to be flirting with each other. Watching them interact this way is deeply satisfying, for some reason.

I walk back to Base Camp with a big, stupid smile on my face. Everyone is crowded in the lot there, staring at the sky; there's a huge double rainbow, arching from one horizon to the other. One bearded, elvish hiker in particular is excited-

"The bottom one is inverted! The bottom one is inverted!" he keeps saying. Instigate emerges from her tent, wrapped in her sleeping bag. Spark appears, carrying a six-pack of beer, and joins the party. He's been in Dunsmuir all afternoon, eating pizza.

213

A little while later I carry my things down the street to the motel and get a room for the night, so that I can use the electricity to charge my phone and water purifier. The stormy, dusky sky is doing wild things with the light, and I'm grateful to get out of the rain. My data listed this motel as "hiker friendly," but the woman at the front desk delivers a long, angry lecture about room stacking and then gives me the room right across from the office, next to all the noise from the road and a rattling refrigeration unit that stays on all night. The bed is squeaky and uncomfortable but the shower is glorious, and I explode my pack everywhere and then lock myself inside to rest. Everyone else is going to see the new Wolverine movie, but I just want to chill in the dark with the curtains closed.

***

I wake at four thirty and lie in bed, unable to sleep any longer. There's just too much going on- the streetlights bleeding in through the windows, the humming of the refrigerator unit, the trains rattling by in the dark. The Union Pacific route that runs from Portland to L.A. via Dunsmuir. I close my eyes, remembering. My first long train ride, twenty years old when I didn't know anything, didn't carry enough water and I lost my sleeping bag under the train. Going over the Cascades in February. We did make it to L.A., though, tongues swollen from dehydration, stumbled into a taqueria and ate and drank everything, built a house of tumbleweeds next to the tracks and waited for the train that would take us to Texas. Went to jail in Texas.

I sit up in bed, propped against a bunch of pillows, and do errands on my phone. After a couple of hours, the hiker hunger hits like its own freight train and I text Instigate and Spark; either they're still asleep or they're up and they've already eaten. I walk out into the bright morning and down the street to the Black Bear Diner. I find Instigate there, sitting at a table with a hiker named TeaTime, a quiet blonde man in a neon green hat.

"Have you eaten?" I say to Instigate.

"Yeah," she says. "But I'll hang out with you."

"You can have some of my milkshake," I say.

"Deal."

I order an enormous burger with fries and a blackberry shake. I consider ordering a bear claw, which is a special pastry that, according to the menu card, has more than three thousand calories.

"What if you did your whole resupply on these?" I say to Instigate, staring into the pastry case as I pay for my breakfast. "One per day. It would be so simple."

After breakfast we go across the street to Rite-Aid to stock up on all the travel size items (toothpaste, hand sanitizer, sunscreen) and then I wander through town, looking at all the crystal shops. There are so many crystal shops that some of the shops are directly competing with each other; there is a crystal shop in a remodeled gas station with a signboard out front advertising the "thirteenth crystal skull," and across the street is another crystal shop with a big sign in the window proclaiming that "the thirteenth crystal skull is a hoax."

I find Spark in a coffee shop reading sci-fi and I sit down next to him so that I can eavesdrop on the hippies some more. There's a hippie couple across from me wearing rope sandals and spooning honey from a mason jar into their giant mugs of coffee. They both have long dreadlocks and are disarmingly beautiful.

"Around the corner and down the street," says the one hippie to the other, "there's a chai shop. You don't have to pay; it's all based on donations. Tonight they'll be playing the gongs there, so I'm going to go and lie on the cushions and, you know, get gonged."

"And singing bowls," says the other hippie. "They do the singing bowls there too."

Afterward I walk through town some more, just taking it all in. There's an empty lot ringed in blackberry bushes and barefoot hippies are standing in the bushes, eating berries.

"Hey, sister bear," says one of them to me as I pass.

I also see train riders, who you can tell apart from the hippies because they wear more black and have cats on leashes and super mellow pitbulls. I assume they've trickled down from Dunsmuir, one of the best little railroad towns on the planet, and I stand at the tracks and watch longingly as a UP intermodal blows through headed south. Sleepy little one-street Dunsmuir, where I once stood at the public water fountain with my friends Kristi and

Finch, running my diesel-blackened hands under the cool water and a woman in a floral-print dress walked up and said

"You ladies just off the train?"

The thunderstorms roll in again in the afternoon and I retreat to the Black Bear Diner for my second giant meal. I order the pot roast, which comes on a giant ceramic platter with coleslaw, French fries, green beans, salad and bread. I also order a huckleberry shake, and then merrily destroy everything.

Later I lie in bed, feeling bored and lonely, leftovers propped in the cool air of the windowsill. It's raining hard outside, splattering off the concrete like birdshot. I think of Spark and Instigate, hunkered down in their tents behind the gear store, and I think of the lecture about room stacking. I text Spark-

You guys should come stay here. Room stacking schroom shtacking.

And then there's scratching and meowing at the door, and I let the feral cats inside.

***

I'm awake and it's dark and I can't tell what time it is. I step over Spark, who is sleeping on the floor, and begin to pack my food bag from the contents of my resupply box. Instigate sits up and looks at me.

"Was someone knocking on the door last night?" she says.

"I think so," I say. "I heard it too." The hotel clerk, maybe, coming to yell at us for room stacking? And then there was the refrigeration unit, humming and clicking on and off. And the patter of the rain.

I walk to the curtains and throw them open. It's full daylight, and the rain has stopped.

After checkout I head to the Black Bear Diner for my third and final meal there, which I'd ordered to go. The restaurant is crowded with hikers and locals and I take my burger in its Styrofoam box and sit on the stone bench outside. Spark and Instigate pass by on their way to the highway onramp and I wave at them. Afterward I make my way to the onramp and they are still there, standing tall behind their cardboard sign. I join them and dance around on the grassy shoulder, doing a bad job at hitchhiking. I feel good today.

A man in a rattling sedan gives us a ride to Dunsmuir and drops us at the little grocery store, where the manager loads our things into his shiny new pickup and drives us the rest of the way. Then we're at the trailhead, yanking and pulling at our packs, nothing to do but hike.

We're climbing for sixteen miles and it's muggy as hell. Oh, Northern California. I am drenched in sweat, my shirt like a wet plastic bag, stopping to rest at clear, stream-fed granite pools, plants overhead green and bright, everything in the throes of summer. We climb well past the point where we would like to stop climbing. We climb because we have to and, in the end, because there is nothing else to do. At last we break free of the trees and there is the ridgeline stretching away and the granite spires of Castle Crags, making drama out of empty space.

The evening is cool, the sky coagulated into clouds. We shiver in our damp clothes. We find a flat spot a few feet above the trail, behind a big silver fir. The spot is reminiscent of a tree fort and will fit the three of us if we arrange our sleeping pads just so. We gather water at the nearby spring and lay our groundsheets down. My stomach is upset and Spark gives me a ginger teabag to put in my water bottle, which helps almost immediately. Spark has taken to carrying several varieties of Yogi tea, and we have a good time making fun of the sayings on the teabags every time he pulls one out. They read as though written by a random word generator stocked with super overused new-age words and are almost insultingly cliche.

"Ok," one of us will say. "Three words. Blank your blank."

"Faith? Hope? Peace?"

"Starts with L."

"Love."

"Love your soul."

"Oh my god."

Tonight we sit in our sleeping bags, eating little bits of dinner and listening to the night coalesce. The set dims, the sky is clouded, the stars are absent.

217

The others are asleep and I am not. I am listening to the stick-breakers, acting out their dramas at the edge of the stage. Their parallel worlds, laid so neatly over mine. Their hopes and dreams and fears.

***

Today the air is hazy with fires and there are smoke jumpers, falling from the sky. The whole world is trying to burn. I climb fourteen miles without water to a beautiful spring that pumps from the earth and sit there, filling my bottles and drinking.

"Spark and Instigate were just here," says an elfin, silver-headed hiker who carries a jewel-blue backpack. "You just missed them."

Then I'm ridge walking for the rest of the day, as fast as I can. I pass a little blonde girl, plodding barefoot on the trail.

"Your pack is small," she says. Her father appears, carrying another baby on his back.

"Thank you," I say.

Night falls when I'm three miles from camp and I fight the dark back with my dying headlamp. I tend to spook myself while night hiking, swinging my headlamp back and forth, looking for the green eyes of animals in the understory. As I walk I weigh the fear of camping alone against this fear of walking in the dark. My fear of camping alone is stronger, and so I soldier on. Still I am jumpy as I hike. My world is not meant to overlap with the world of the stick-breakers.

There's an opening with a trickle of water and I see another headlamp, bobbing in the dark. I meow at the headlamp and the headlamp meows back. My feet take me forward along the dark path and then there are Spark and Instigate, in their sleeping bags in a little flat spot next to the stream. I set up my tent behind them, shivering in my tank top. It's cold now; it's always cold at night on the PCT. Almost always.

***

I dream I'm resupplying in New York City, but also trying to find someone to date. Only no one will date me, because I'm wearing my dorky hiking clothes.

I climb all morning in the smoke-hazy heat and eat lunch by myself at Nine-Mile spring, sitting in the shade watching water trickle out of the ground. So many springs in Northern California- will it stay this way into Oregon? Oregon! We're almost to Oregon. They say that Oregon is the fastest part of the whole trail, and people do big miles there. But why? We joke that as soon as we cross the border in Oregon there'll be a moving sidewalk. "The moving sidewalk of Oregon." We can just stand on it and pick huckleberries as we're propelled north.

I find Spark and Instigate posted up in the shade next to a paved road. There are a couple of shuttered RVs there, and some camp chairs lined up in the dirt.

"Trail magic?" I say.

"Not yet," says Spark.

I pull out my peanut butter jar of instant refried beans and a bag of broken tortilla chips.

"I'm making my own trail magic," I say. "It's called lunch."

Spark reads his book and Instigate naps in the dirt. The RVs remain still and lifeless; there are no hotdogs, no coolers full of cheap soda.

I'm exhausted after lunch, and my stomach hurts. My stomach's been weird lately, lurchy and off. The other day I filled up a water bottle at a stream and then forgot to treat it with my steripen- I wonder now if I caught something. Spark and Instigate have magic stomachs that allow them to drink untreated water without getting sick- it's like a superpower. But I know that if there's a waterborne parasite within a mile of me, I'm likely to catch it. I unclip the hipbelt on my pack as I climb. Ouch, ouch, says my stomach.

I reach the saddle where we're camping right at dusk, a pretty little sandy spot looking out at everything, green mountain ridges fading into smoke. The last of the light seems to pool on the bare ground here, and I pitch my tent and sit inside, eating my dinner and watching it fade into night. I'm feeling lonely again tonight. Tomorrow we have just twenty-six more miles to the highway where we'll hitch to Etna, our next resupply town.

219

According to my data, Etna is one street long and "consistently ranks as everyone's favorite trail town." What does that even mean? And then there's the smoke from the wildfires. There's been a drought, and the whole forest is burning. The smoke grows a little thicker every day, a little harder to ignore. How many fires are there now?

As if in response, lightning streaks across the eastern horizon. Boom! goes the sky, but there isn't any rain.

My stomach gurgles audibly, its own sort of thunder.

***

I sleep well and wake on the gravelly saddle overlooking everything, the light returned around me. Spark, Instigate, and I sit in our sleeping bags rubbing our faces, and I eat a few bites of breakfast-

Pow, says my stomach. I stare at the food in my lap- almonds, jerky, dried banana. *Bang*! says my gut. I lie back down in my sleeping bag and cover my face with my hands. I feel hot all over, as though I have the flu. What is the appropriate course of action in this situation?

The answer, of course, is brilliant in its simplicity.

Hike.

I drag myself along the ridges all morning, the horizon churning with clouds, smoke and thunder and lightning. From the valleys below come the sound of cowbells and in the afternoon there's a rainbow. Instigate and Spark are ahead, and I see no other hikers all day. It's just me, alone with the drama of my insides and the hot feeling in my head that comes and goes like a mirage.

Fatigue overtakes me in the afternoon and I lie down in a campsite next to the trail to nap. But I can't seem to fall asleep and I stare instead at the scratchy canopy, the patches of light, dark thoughts flashing and then slipping away. I know that something's off when I feel this way- I don't get stuck in negative thought loops on the trail anymore. It's a surprising and wonderful result of having had nothing to distract me from my own brain for months. The negative things I used to obsess about are just sort of gone. I seem to have worked through all of them while pounding out miles

220

in the desert, worn them down like worry stones until there was nothing left at all, just sand that slipped through my fingers and away.

I give up on trying to nap and push myself fast down the trail towards the highway. I'm hungry, but my gut won't let me eat. And now I have diarrhea, too. The trail follows a rocky outcropping and way down below me is the most beautiful valley- that must be where Etna is- but I just hurry on. Gotta get to the road.

At one point there is a small scrap of paper at the edge of the trail. So small only a thru-hiker would notice it, the clean whiteness of the paper against this landscape of broken rock. I bend down to retrieve it, carefully moving the stone that holds it in place.

Brewer's Spruce, it says. *One of the rarest trees in North America*. I look up and see a strange conifer below me on the slope, its boughs like lanky pipe cleaners. Who wrote this? I turn the scrap of paper over in my hands. I close my eyes. Ramen? I picture him with his mustache full of icecream. He'd seemed so dark and strange. But he studied trees in school, didn't he?

One of the rarest trees in North America.

I imagine Ramen a day ahead of me, walking alone with his big pack, noting the names of the trees along the trail. Thinking of the ways they're interconnected, the patterns in how they grow. Recognizing them by their shapes. It's so different from how I hike- staring at the trail for hours, noticing very little. Trying to go as fast as I can. Thinking about miles, numbers, where I'll camp that night. Snapping a picture now and then on my phone, just because I feel like I should.

I smile at the little scrap of paper in my hands, and then replace it carefully beneath its rock.

I reach the highway right at dusk. A hiker I don't know is there, laying down his ground cloth behind a pile of rocks.

"Have you seen Instigate and Spark?" I say.

"They just got a ride into town," says the hiker. "Fifteen minutes ago."

"You come from Etna?"

"Yeah. The women who dropped me off are still here. Right over there."

He waves at an outcropping of rock where four blonde women are perched, watching the sun set. I approach the outcropping, suddenly conscious of how dirty I am, of the way I smell.

"Hello," I say. The women smile down at me. They are young and radiant, backlit by the setting sun.

"Would you like to watch the sunset with us?" they say. I drop my pack and climb up onto the rock.

"I'm hiking the PCT," I say. "I think you gave another hiker a ride to the trail?"

"We did," says one of the women. She has long, carefully braided hair and her skin is glowing. Small gold crosses twinkle in her earlobes. "We can give you a ride into town if you'd like. It's on our way."

"Thank you," I say.

"We work at a Christian summer camp down the road."

"That sounds like a nice summer job."

"It is."

The women smile at me in unison, their teeth flashing white. It's impossible to tell how old they are. Sixteen? Seventeen? But no, all of them are in college. Anthropology, journalism, religion; they tell me their majors as we speed carefully down the mountain road, smashed together in the tiny sedan. The woman with the braided hair is sitting next to me, being a good sport about how dirty I am, how literally caked in dust my legs and clothing are. She keeps telling me how wonderful it is to meet me, how inspiring my journey is.

One of the women in the front says something cross to the woman with the braided hair. The woman with the braided hair furrows her brow.

"I'm sorry," says the woman in the front. She turns and reaches over the seat, taking the hand of the woman with the braided hair. "You're beautiful, and you always make me laugh, and I love you."

The women drop me off at the Hiker Hut in Etna. The Hiker Hut is a small, square building behind a beautiful, sprawling bed and breakfast, and it's where the thru-hikers stay. It's dark now and I wave goodbye to the

222

women and then stumble down the gravel drive. The door of the Hiker Hut is open, and golden light spills out. Inside there are two sets of bunkbeds, a little kitchenette and a couch, where Ramen and another hiker sit watching TV. *One of the rarest trees in North America.* I sit down next to them, dropping my pack onto the floor.

"Did you leave the note about the Brewer's spruce?" I say to Ramen.

"Yep," he says.

"You seen Spark and Instigate?"

"Yah. They went to the brewery."

There's a shelf next to the couch with loaner clothes, and I rifle through them. I find a pair of shorts and a tank top almost exactly like the one I'm wearing now.

"Is there a shower here?" I say.

"Yeah," says Ramen.

The TV mumbles evenly, the screen a pale sepia. It's some PBS documentary.

"This is the calmest TV show I've ever seen," I say.

After showering I hunt for my resupply box in the mountain of thru-hiker boxes on the darkened porch. When I find it I tear it open- candy, jerky, dinners, bars. I realize that I'm shaking with hunger so I eat some of the bars. It's too late to go to the grocery store now, and the restaurants will be closed. Everything will have to work itself out in the morning.

I get a text from Instigate; they're stealth camping at the edge of town, and will make their way over in the morning. Suddenly exhaustion settles on my limbs like sand, and I drag myself across the damp grass of the yard to a bare spot where I can pitch my tent. I climb inside, arranging all my things around me- water bottles, resupply box, shoes. I snuggle down into my sleeping quilt and stare out at the dark yard. Etna's a small enough town that the stars are visible, even with the smoke, and I watch as the night deepens and the Milky Way comes into focus, unfurling so soothingly across the sky.

***

Five thirty and it's cold and dark and I'm awake, lying in my sleeping bag waiting for the light to come. Golden dawn finds me walking down Etna's single street, sunrise shining off the closed-up store windows. The only other people out besides me are the old ladies with their paper cups of coffee, blinking in the empty road. I peer in the glass door of the drugstore and the bell jangles, a sleepy woman in a red apron holds it open.

"You can't want icecream this early," she says.

"No," I say.

The grocer is sweeping the lot in front of the little grocery store. I'm the first customer and I wander the aisles, feeling dazed. Pork rinds, wilted lettuce, packages of hot dogs with bright orange price stickers. *Reduced!* Dusty cans of aerosol room spray. I put lettuce and a can of chili in my basket. Tortilla chips and jerky to supplement my resupply. An avocado. There's a flat of huge, ripe peaches, swarming with fruit flies, and I grab one of those too. The whole store seems too small inside, as though it was shrunk.

Back at the Hiker Hut I start a load of laundry. The other hikers are stirring, packing their things away. Some of them are headed back to the trail. Instigate and Spark arrive- they've been up for a while, drinking coffee and eating pastries.

"I can't believe it's August already," I say.

"I know," says Instigate.

I post up at the little table in the Hiker Hut to do things on my phone. Instigate writes emails, and Spark naps. Soon it's afternoon, and some new hikers have arrived.

"The smoke up there is crazy," they say. They show us photographs- huge plumes of yellow, rising up over the ridges. Engulfing everything. Outside a pale haze has settled on the town. "Seven new fires since yesterday," say the hikers.

"Dang," I say. It's as if the whole world is trying to burn.

Instigate, Spark and I borrow loaner bikes from the Hiker Hut and bike to

Bob's Diner for dinner. My bike is an old, rusted mountain bike with a seat that's way too low. It makes me feel like I'm ten years old. We wind back and forth on the empty main street, pretending we are the neighborhood children.

"Let's go throw rocks at cats," says Spark.

The waitress at Bob's Diner is mean to us but later her mood improves. I eat one of the most underwhelming lettuce burgers of the trail. I propose the idea of hiking out after dinner.

"I don't know," says Instigate. "The smoke makes me feel kind of sick."

Instigate is really affected by smoke, and she's been trying not to show it. It gets hard for her to breathe. Our post-dinner bikeride is a solemn one; the smoke outside has grown even thicker. It appears to be pooling in the valley, inversion style.

Back at the Hiker Hut Instigate curls up in a ball on the couch. We shut the doors and windows in hopes of keeping out the worst of the smoke.

"I definitely can't hike in this," says Instigate.

"Maybe it'll be better tomorrow," I say. "Up on the ridges where the trail is." But I wonder if that's true.

In the evening I pitch my tent in the dark in a new corner of the yard, next to a hammock and a little creek with a footbridge over it. Hikers come and go as I lie in my bag, waiting for sleep. Someone is smoking nearby, and I can see the cherry of their cigarette. I'm exhausted, but I also feel overstimulated, and my stomach is still being weird. Only a hundred and twenty miles until Ashland, where we'll stop for a couple of days so that we can make our resupply boxes for Oregon. Oregon! I can't believe how close I am. All I have to do is make it through this smoke. And whatever else comes next.

***

I wake to Spark and Instigate rustling in the dark. It's five thirty.

"We're gonna go get coffee and donuts," says Spark.

"Alright."

I pack up and stand on the dim gray roadside, my stomach rumbling from lack of breakfast. But it's important to get back to the trail as fast as I can; everyone is worried that they'll close the trail because of the fires. Rumor is that there's an arsonist setting the fires.

There's little traffic on the road and after a time Instigate and Spark return, cruising on the loaner bikes. A moment later two retired schoolteachers in a long SUV pull onto the shoulder and we all pile in, our packs on our laps. The schoolteachers grew up in Etna, as did their parents before them. We talk about time and family and generational differences and staying where you are vs. moving away. The couple is only driving to the other end of town but in their incredible generosity they ferry us all the way to the trailhead. We breathe deep as we climb out of the car. Up on the ridge the air is much clearer and we can see the smoke below us, pooled like yellow cotton in the valley.

"We were in that," I say.

There's a trail register a half mile in and I dawdle there, reading the entries. Then I need to eat handfuls of tortilla chips and fiddle with my phone while I walk, and before I know it I've lost the others and it's just me, wandering along the ridges in a daze. I feel lazy and tired and that spirals, somehow, into nausea, and then I feel as though I'm going to throw up. What is going on with my guts? I don't want to fall any further behind so I switch into Zombie Hiking mode, plodding along empty-headed trying not to focus on my misery. Instigate and Spark had talked of doing thirty miles or more, but I know I'll be lucky if I get twenty-five today.

By the time I reach the little stream that is my last water source for the day I feel ready to collapse. There's a dank green clearing here with a boarded-up forest service cabin where I'd thought of camping, but now, as I squat in the stream filling my water bottles, chills run up and down my spine. It feels as though the tangled brush is full of animals, watching me.

"Deer," I say to myself. "It's probably just a deer. Like, one single deer."

I look at the elevation profile and see that the trail climbs up for the next several miles and so I set out again, daydreaming of dry ridgetop campsites looking down over everything. When I'm camping by myself, those spots are always where I feel the safest.

226

After two and a half miles, I find my campsite- a flat sandy clearing on top of the ridge, front row seats to the sunset. There are a couple of really good tenting spots and also some of what Egg calls "furniture"- logs placed here and there to serve as benches. I pitch my tent, don my down jacket against the cold, pull my dinner from my pack and then sit on one of these benches to watch the light show. It's better than I could have imagined and I have it all to myself, which is bittersweet. I crawl into my sleeping bag and lie awake, waiting for the internal battle between my fatigue and my fear of camping alone to run its course. And at last, because we live in a merciful universe, it does.

***

The hike today is nine miles of ridgewalking followed by a twenty-one mile descent to the Seiad Valley, way down in the bottom of everything. There's a store there in the valley, and a café, and maybe Instigate and Spark will be lazy and dilly-dally there, and maybe if I go fast enough I can catch up with them.

I think about the store as I hike. A store with cool Gatorade and icecream snickers bars. A store with chips that I need to supplement my dwindling food supply in order to make it through the rest of this section. A store thirty miles away.

A store that closes at seven.

I haven't done thirty miles in twelve hours before but today, I decide that I will.

As soon as the trail turns from sandy ridgeline to long, leafy switchbacks, I begin to jog. I'm listening to Light Asylum on my phone, Magnetic Fields, Patti Smith, and I'm racing, racing down the switchbacks, hard ground pounding at my feet, trees rushing past, the earth slanted down, down, down never far enough down. *Glooooria, G-L-O-R-I-A. Glooooria.* I'm out of water but I don't care, I'm thirsty but I don't care, I'm leaping over streams and hurtling down the trail, making my whole body ache. Pushing as hard as I can. No thoughts. *Horses. Horses. Horses. Horses.*

I turn a corner and there's Egg, eating lunch at a little stream.

"We've got to get to the store before it closes," she says.

"I know," I say, and then I am gone.

At the bottom of the long descent is a campground and then a strip of narrow blacktop that cuts across the valley. The two-mile roadwalk to the store. I stop at some pit toilets to collect myself, sitting on the rocky ground. I'm hot and sunburned, damp everywhere from sweat, dehydrated. I feed a chocolate probar to my aching, fussy stomach. *Here stomach*, I say. *Shhhhh.* Egg emerges from the woods and I raise my trekking poles in the air, triumphant.

"Road walk!" I say. "How excited are you?"

"At least the blackberries are ripe," she says, leaning into the brambles that edge the road.

"We're gonna make it!" I holler.

The narrow blacktop joins a slightly wider road and then we see, in the distance, the object of our desire- a ramshackle white building next to the highway that can be nothing other than The Store. I twirl my trekking poles in the air manically.

"Weeeeeeeeee are the champions," I sing. "Weeeeeeeeeeeeeeeee are the champions, of the world."

It's six forty-five.

We reach the store and shake the door, but it won't give. *Store closes at six p.m.*, says a paper sign scotch-taped to the glass. My heart fills slowly with despair. So my data was wrong. I am pressing my face against the glass, gazing mournfully at the cases of Gatorade inside, when a man in a rattling pickup pulls up.

"You ladies need to buy things?" he says.

"Yes," we say.

"I was just at home, wanted some icecream." He fits his key into the door's lock. "I'm the store's owner."

Despite my promise to the store owner that I would "buy all the things," inside there is surprisingly little that I actually want to eat. Six passes around the store and all I have in my basket are tortilla chips, salt and vinegar chips, and half a watermelon. Egg has had better luck- some

228

lemonade and a pint of Ben & Jerry's ice cream, "red velvet cake" flavor. Afterward we sit on the grass in front of the RV park and share the icecream and the watermelon, although I get distracted and eat almost all of the watermelon myself.

Egg is staying to camp on the lawn of the RV park with the other hiker trash but I walk up the highway towards the trail. I've learned via interrogation of the other hikers that Spark and Instigate left just a little while ago, to "hike to a spring a mile up the trail," and I mean to catch them. I'm crossing an overpass above a mucky streambed when I hear the sounds of feral cats. I look down and there they are in the shadows, meowing up at me.

"You guys didn't make it far," I say.

"Nah."

"You camping down there?"

"No, too many mosquitoes."

But the unkempt mini-storage lot next to the creek, it turns out, is perfect. We unroll our sleeping pads on the dirty gravel. A stack of freight containers, all grown over with blackberry brambles, shield us from the road. We sit on the ground and eat our dinners in the dusk. Spark makes "double dinner," wherein he cooks two pots of Knorr pasta sides, one after the other, and Instigate eats her peanut butter jar of delicious rehydrated curried lentils. I have my instant refried beans and tortilla chips and then after dinner I think to go fetch Egg, so that she can camp with us. Egg joins us behind the freight containers and soon after, a cat appears. It's a thin black barely-grown kitten with a white face and little white paws. The cat acts shy at first, and then it allows me to pet it, and then it graduates to grabbing bags of snacks from Instigate's food bag and running off with them. Spark is allergic to cats, and he holds out his trekking pole whenever the cat comes near-

"Back!" he says. "Back!"

It's all very cute until we decide to sleep, at which point the cat walks across all of our sleeping bags, one after the other. I decide to name the cat Anus Face from Outer Space and I lie awake for a while, petting it and trying to push it under my quilt but it always pops out, like a balloon from underwater. At last I am too sleepy and I shoo it away, and it goes.

At least one of us is almost all the way asleep when the mosquitoes appear. The mosquitoes are light enough to ignore, kind of, and we take turns being the one who is almost all the way asleep until some indeterminate hour of the night when we all rise and fumblingly erect our tents as best we can in the gravel. Instigate's tent has no bug screen and so she simply stays the way she is, puts the square piece of mesh that she carries over her face, and begins to snore. In the safety of my poorly erected tent there are neither cute animals nor mosquitoes and so I, at last, can sleep as well.

***

When we wake Anus Face is there, perched atop a pile of wooden pallets, watching us.

"Anus Face!" I say, and he pads over to me and rubs the length of his dusty body against my sleeping bag. I sneeze.

We're all red-cheeked and bleary eyed, exhausted from our long night of wakefulness with the mosquitoes. Some of our tents have collapsed. Mine looks very drunk. We pack up our things and head over to the Seiad Valley Café, after a conversation that goes like this-

"I think we should get an early start."

"The café opens in an hour."

"There are a few things I need at the store."

"I think I'll get breakfast."

"Coffee sounds good."

It's an indirect style of communication characteristic of thru-hiking feral cats like us, and is heavily influenced by unspoken mutual affection and, also, a fear of abandonment.

The café is a little room crowded with tables and light. The kitchen is along one wall, behind a low divider. The menus are sticky and we order big, greasy breakfasts. I see something about gluten-free biscuits.

"We're all out of those," says the woman who is scrawling our order onto a pad of paper. "But I can make you gluten-free pancakes."

"Really?" I say.

"Yeah."

Generally in the world I never get to eat pancakes, unless I make them myself. I can't believe that this woman, in this hot little valley far from everything, is about to make me gluten-free pancakes as if it's no big deal. What magical universe have I stumbled into?

After taking our order the woman stands at the stove in the back of the room, pulls a stick of butter from its paper and smears it across the grill, and starts frying eggs. It feels as though we are in a real house, and someone is cooking breakfast for us. A few minutes later our table is covered in big, hot platters of food.

My buckwheat pancakes are golden brown, lightly speckled, and each at least an inch and a half tall. Sitting atop them are my two over-easy eggs. There is also bacon.

"Oh my god," I say, as I pour cheap syrup over the entire mess. I am about to be so happy.

After breakfast I go into the little store and wander the aisles until I find a bag of catfood.

"You got a cat?" says Joyce, the checkout clerk.

"Not really," I say.

"You feedin a cat?"

"It's a stray. In the mini-storage lot on the other side of the creek. We camped there last night. It's a really friendly cat. Kind of a kitten. Black with little white paws. It has a notch in its ear."

"You gonna leave food out for that cat?"

"Yeah. I think it lives there?"

"You name it?"

"Anus Face from Outer Space."

The woman looks at me.

"Or Oreo."

"You know what," says Joyce. "I'll feed Oreo for you."

Back at the mini-storage lot, Anus Face is nowhere to be found. I walk in circles, calling, not sure what noises to make. I peek inside a couple of the freight containers, which are busted open- inside are mountains of tumbled furniture, all hung over with cobwebs. Whose stuff is this? How long ago did someone lose everything they had, only to have it end up here, gathering mice and spiders in this empty lot outside of time?

I pour some catfood onto the top of a blue plastic barrel. The barrel is high enough that the mice would have a hard time reaching it, and it's right next to where we camped last night. Back at the store I push the remaining catfood across the counter to Joyce.

"Thank you," I say. "Oreo's fate is in your hands."

It's mid-morning now, and hot. We're about to climb four thousand feet in eight miles, one of the steepest climbs on the entire PCT, and the air is hazy with the yellow smoke of the fires in Northern California and now the fires in Southern Oregon, too. And we'll be hiking through a burn.

It is a burn of epic proportions. Charcoal-black snags and lifeless, ash-covered earth. Steep, merciless switchbacks and below us, the yellow smoke puddled in the valleys.

It feels as though we're hiking through Cormac McCarthy's *The Road.*

We reach a short spur trail to a spring. The wooden sign for the spring, now burnt an impossible black, has been propped up in the dust. We walk to the spring and tip our bottles under the trickle of clear, miraculous water that still, somehow, pours from the earth. The sun bears down on us. Back at the trail I find Instigate, curled on her side in the dirt.

"What's wrong?" I say.

"I don't know," she says.

"Can you hike?"

"I don't know."

"What should we do?" I say to Spark. The smoke has been bothering

Instigate since we left Etna and the steep climb seems to make everything worse.

"Do you want to go back down?" I say to Instigate. "I'll hike with you if you want to go back down."

"I don't know."

"Do you need to eat?" says Spark.

"I don't know."

I pull out my dirty food bag and rifle through it. I hand Instigate some dried banana and a piece of my precious jerky ration. She chews the food slowly and then sits up, brushing her hair off her cheek and leaving a smear of ash in its place.

"I think I can hike now," she says.

We hike on with the hope that Instigate will feel better once we get to the top and are no longer climbing. At last we reach the ridge and, thankfully, she does feel better; her mysterious smoke-caused illness is gone. Soon after the burn ends abruptly and we are catapulted into a world of green, living trees, lush grasses and bright wildflowers. A stream runs languidly through a bright meadow and we collapse in a bit of shade there, exhausted.

Lunch is consumed, and then snacks. Shoes come off and books come out. Each of us eyes the others, waiting for some sign of movement. None of us wants to keep hiking.

And yet we do. Elevation drops and now we're in the forest again, but it's a living forest. A side trail leads us to our third water source, a shallow spring that runs across the trail. On the trail to the spring is a giant doug-fir, the first big one I've seen, and I lean my body against it. I rest my forehead on its bark.

"Hello big tree," I say. I look down at my feet and see a medium-sized rattlesnake, coiled against the base of the tree. Hiding.

"Hello rattlesnake," I say as I step carefully away.

Just seven more tired miles to camp, and then three tired hikers eat three underwhelming dinners and collapse on three wonderfully uncomfortable bedrolls. Six shoes come off, one sun sets and through the smoke several dozen stars come out. Instigate draws her finger in the air, forming constellations. I am all for the renaming of constellations, for the forming of new worlds. Like the world of the PCT. I close my eyes. Does any of this even exist?

***

I wake in the middle of the night, shaking with fever. My whole body aches and I can't get warm. I put on extra layers and burrow down into my sleeping quilt. I haven't felt sick for a couple of days, and now this. What the fuck is wrong with me? In the morning I lie numbly awake, staring out at the light that's spilling across the meadow, listening to the others get ready.

"I can't hike right now," I say the through the wall of my tent. "You guys should go ahead."

"You need anything?" says Instigate.

"No," I say. And then they are gone.

I drift in and out of sleep until ten, when I drag myself from my tent and have awful, split pea soup-like diarrhea in the woods. Afterward I discover that I am out of water. We'd camped next to a boggy meadow in hopes of gathering water from the little pools there, but they'd been too shallow and fouled by cows to be of any use. Now I turn on my phone and look at my maps. It's five miles to the next water source, and I am dizzy with fever. You can do it, I think.

Five miles has never felt so difficult. I walk and rest, walk and rest, trembling under the hot sun. I feel as though I'm in a delirium; everything is both brighter and softer than it should be. I round a bend and find myself amongst a pack of coyotes; there's a cacophony of yipping and then the pups race across the meadow to join the adults. I stand perfectly still, entranced by the action. What is this magic? I hike on and at last I am stumbling along a jeep road below the trail, following the tracks of cows to where clear water trickles from the mountainside. After filling my bottles I unroll my sleeping pad in a bit of shade next to the trail, put on my fleece shirt and pull my sleeping bag over me. I'm so cold. What is this fever. I wish someone would show up- another hiker, a friendly face. Maybe it's just the fever getting to me but I feel suddenly so, so lonely. For some reason I think of Ramen, walking along in his own world, reciting the names of the trees. He's a day behind us; he stayed in Etna to visit a friend. Now I wish he would appear, just come striding around the corner. I don't know why, really.

I fall asleep and then it's afternoon and the sun has clouded over. I feel a little better. A hiker named Stormy passes by on the trail and stops to chat. She and a number of other hikers skipped the section from Etna to Seiad Valley, she says. They closed the trail because of the fires.

I hike with Stormy into the evening. She started hiking just a few hundred miles back and is still working her way over the physical learning curve that happens to everyone in the beginning- stopping to tape her sore feet, complaining about her blisters. I try to remember the last time I had a blister. I can't.

The trail dips down into a beautiful meadow and there are cows there, milling around. I've been hearing their bells for miles.

"Hello cows," I say. A big black one stands on the trail, giving me the side-eye. I stare at it, feeling very small and vulnerable, until it thunders away into the trees. Then up through the forest, around a bend, and there's a wooden sign nailed a tree.

The Oregon/California border.

Stormy takes my picture and we laugh and dance around.

"The moving sidewalk!" I say. "We made it to the moving sidewalk!"

Dusk finds us on a peaceful, light-drenched ridge just twenty-five miles from the highway and Ashland. We quietly pitch our tents and say goodnight. I lie in my sleeping bag, so glad to not be walking any longer. I have no idea where Spark and Instigate are, or how many miles they did today. I know I'll catch them tomorrow in town but still, I miss my friends. It makes my heart ache to think of them pulling ahead, getting farther and farther away while I am sick. My trail family. They are my trail family.

***

I sleep hard and heavy, exhausted from sickness and walking. I wake and hike in zombie mode, pushing the earth beneath my feet, just trying to get it done. I feel better and then I don't, better and then I don't. Fast and then weary. Another day of shit like split pea soup, but there is less of it. I can hardly eat but then I don't have much food left so I break even in the end. Ridgewalking beneath a hot, smoky sun. Just trying to get there.

I can hear I-5 when I'm eight miles away, like a river in the distance. Then five, then three, then two miles. Then I'm picking my way through a messy shortcut to Callahan's Lodge, which sits next to the highway onramp. There's an abandoned building and some railroad tracks. The smell of creosote and overripe blackberries. A worker from Callahan's picks me up on the hot highway onramp. He's headed to Ashland; he's worked at Callahan's for twenty years. I sit on the jostling bench seat and stare at the dirt caked to my legs. I roll down the window a little. Heat, smoke, fever, a hundred and twenty miles without a shower. I don't know if I've ever smelled this bad.

"Where do you want to go in town?" He says.

"I don't know. The hostel?" I'm weak from hunger but I feel too embarrassed to go anywhere before I bathe.

At the hostel they sell me a shower for five bucks and I stand under the hot water for a little longer than I should, watching the brown water pool around my ash-blackened feet. Everything I touch comes away smeared with dirt- the shampoo bottle, the bright chrome fixtures, the white tiles. Even the towel I use to dry off is less than white when I'm done with it.

I find Spark and Instigate at a coffee shop, where they've commandeered the big leather couches in the corner. Their bags are propped against their legs and they're sprawled out unwashed in their still-filthy hiking clothes, drinking coffee and reading sci-fi and Isabel Allende, respectively. I am so proud of my friends and their disinclination to give any fucks. Instigate has found us a place to stay on the couchsurfing website but we can't go there until seven, when our host gets home from work. I leave my pack with my friends and wander to the co-op for sustenance.

Gluten-free pepperoni pizza, a dollar fifty a slice. Big plate of mixed baby greens with tahini dressing. Roast chicken leg. I eat at a little table in the dining area, drink a paper cup of water, buy a chocolate cookie and eat that too. As I eat I watch the other people eating, shuffling newspapers, talking all together so that their voices make a cacophony that comes together and breaks apart. A man rattles carts; a woman in a flowered dress selects a pear. I am completely overwhelmed with stimulus.

Back at the coffeeshop I buy a cup of peppermint tea and sink into the leather couch to google digestive disorders on my phone. I'm pretty sure I've caught a parasite from untreated water; I just don't know which one. It doesn't feel like any of the ones I've had before. And the symptoms don't really match giardia. Fever, for example. What parasite gives you a fever?

It takes about a minute to find my answer.

Cryptosporidium parvum, one of the most common water-borne parasites in North America. Infection is characterized by watery diarrhea and fever. Symptoms come and go. Can't be treated with antibiotics but tends to run its course in a couple of weeks. In 1993, a water purification plant in Milwaukee was contaminated and 400,000 people fell ill.

Bingo.

Just knowing what's probably making me sick brings a wave of relief. No antibiotics, so now what? Maybe the worst of it is over? Maybe I'll feel better soon? I imagine the parasite in my guts, swimming around, living out its little dramas. Changing into this or that, fighting for control of various corners of my intestinal universe. Upheavals, regime changes, revolutions. The swelling of orchestral music. Hopes and dreams and fears.

At seven we gather at a little yellow house on a quiet street near Lithia Park. Our host is a woman in her fifties who bike commutes to Medford for work, ten miles each way. Her house is furnished with plain, tidy furniture and beautiful rugs. There are cases of books and several nice guitars. An elaborate homemade quilt hangs on the wall.

For dinner we walk to a restaurant with big oak tables and order small, expensive plates of food. Spark and Instigate chat with our host while I stare forlornly at my salad, unable to join in the fun. I'm exhausted and grumpy and all I can think of is being horizontal in the dark, maybe a pillow under my head, my vertebrae releasing one by one onto the cool hardwood floor. I am a very poor sport. At last dinner is finished and we are walking the six blocks home through the smoky night air. Around us people are milling, having a weekend maybe (is it the weekend?), coming in and out of glass-fronted bars, carrying shopping bags. They are well-fed and draped in impractical clothing and their worlds are non-linear, spreading in all directions like spilled water. I feel overwhelmed.

At the house I sit in the dark and try to play the guitar. The one song I know how to play is *Papa Was a Rodeo* by the Magnetic Fields, but now I can't remember all the chords. Spark and Instigate shower and we start a load of laundry in the basement, all of our dirty socks together to make soup. There's a guest room in the house- it belongs to the woman's son who is now a firefighter in Montana- and it has a twin bed in it. Spark and Instigate give the bed to me, opting instead to sleep on the couches in the living room. I crawl into this bed at some awful hour long past hiker midnight and lie on top of the covers, waiting to feel sleepy. It's stuffy in the room and outside in the street there are sounds, regular town sounds, white noise that I have lost the ability to not hear. Every part of me feels stimulated, as though there is some great opportunity that I should at this moment be taking advantage of. Things to do, things to see, everything happening everywhere! But really there's nothing- just a smoky August night in this little Southern Oregon town that many people would describe as peaceful. But not me. I have been in the woods too long, I think. I am calibrated to the woods.

Part Four: Oregon and Washington

August 5 to September 23

Mile 1685 to mile 2660

Each friend represents a world in us, a world possibly not born until they arrive, and it is only by this meeting that a new world is born.

-Anais Nin

***

I sleep until nine-thirty and then sit on the living room floor, eating the melted-frozen dregs of a half-gallon of cookies and cream icecream we'd acquired the night before- walking in the dark to safeway and wandering under the buzzing fluorescents, opening the carton before we'd even cleared the parkinglot. Passing it back and forth in the crosswalk, two titanium spoons sticking out.

I turn on my phone and put in Ramen's number. I got it yesterday, from another hiker.

"Are you in Ashland?" I say.

"Yeah. I'm staying at the hostel."

I take a breath.

"We have a house off of couchsurfing. It's next to Lithia Park. You want to come over?"

"Ok."

After we hang up I pace through the rooms of the house- kitchen, dining room, living room. I feel nervous and jumpy. I wash the breakfast dishes and empty the dish drainer, wipe the crumbs off the countertops. Push the piles of hiker food in the living room around until they look less insane.

There's a knock on the screen door.

Ramen drops his pack and sits in the overstuffed leather reading chair. His green long-sleeve shirt is torn at the elbows and he smells like woodsmoke. I sit on the floor in front of my boxes. I hold up a bottle of hand sanitizer in the shape of a frog.

"My hand sanitizer is a frog," I say.

Ramen flips his straight dark hair. His mustache, I notice, is clean today.

"I got new boots," he says. "I've gone through five pairs of boots."

"You want to make out?" I say. The words float from my mouth, leaving me dizzy.

"What?"

"Do you want to make out? I mean, we don't have to."

"What? I don't know. Really?"

"Yeah. But it's ok if you don't want to."

"I don't know. I mean, I guess so. I don't know." Ramen looks at his hands. They're rough, and his nails are dirty. "Maybe a little bit."

"There's a bedroom," I say, standing. "In case someone comes home."

In the bedroom of our host's firefighter son, I push Ramen against the wall. I press my lips against his cracked lips. He's shaking like an old washing machine and making hissing noises through his teeth.

"I'm a virgin," he says.

"Ok," I say.

"No, I mean, I'm a virgin."

"That's alright."

"I don't have much experience with this sort of thing."

I bury my face into the shoulder of his long-sleeve hiking shirt, which is the color of old moss.

"You smell amazing."

"I haven't washed my clothes in so long."

"I think you should take off your shoes."

I push Ramen and he falls onto the bed. He's grinning and shaking and I climb on top of him. His hands are at his sides and he's putting his tongue in my mouth in a strange way, like a fish gasping for air. I pull up my shirt and press his hand against my skin.

"You can touch me," I say.

"I think I better go," he says.

"Ok."

At the door, he gives me a weird, quick kiss on the lips. He's wearing his pack and to do this he has to stick his neck out like a goose.

"See you around," he says.

I look at the blank wooden door after it shuts behind him. I hear his footsteps fall away.

Afterward I repack my bag and meet Instigate at the bus stop in front of the library, where she's mending her pack strap with dental floss. I sit on the grass next to her and eat a cold chicken leg.

"I made out with Ramen," I say between bites of chicken.

"You what?" she says, holding the floss in midair.

"I made out with Ramen." I stop eating. I realize that waves of shame are breaking over me. I think of his clenched fists, of his nervous gasping. Of his insistence on leaving.

"He's a virgin," I say.

"He's a what?"

"I feel sort of awful now. Like I did something really wrong. I don't know."

"I'm sorry," says Instigate.

"It feels like I made out with a straight girl," I say.

"I'm sorry," says Instigate.

It's time to go back to the trail.

Instigate scratches the letters P C T onto a piece of cardboard with a dying sharpie and we stand on the roadside in front of a pizza place, trying to score a ride.

"Y'all wanna get pizza?" says Spark.

"No Spark," I say. "We have to hitch."

***

When I wake the sky has clouded over and I lie in my sleeping bag, waiting for my memories to return to me. Half the time, when I wake up, I have no idea where I am, and it takes a minute for the world to resolve itself around me as though from a fog, for the details to fill themselves in.

Ah. I'm on the PCT. We slept on a jeep road. My body is oriented north-south.

And then I remember Ramen.

It's not bad, though. The shame of yesterday is gone, like smoke.

I fumble with my phone.

That makeout was hawkward, I text to Ramen. *Both hot and awkward. About 65% hot and 35% awkward.*

I put my phone down and rub my face. I don't know why I'm doing this. Then I send another text-

Maybe we should try again.

I feel good today and I hike fast. It's real, I think. The moving sidewalk is real. Every so often I turn my phone out of airplane mode to see if I have a text from Ramen. Nothing.

What if he doesn't text me back? I can't just keep checking- it will kill my battery. As the day wanes, cell service becomes more sporadic. Soon I only have it on the ridgetops, when I'm way up looking down on everything. This anticipation is killing me. What's he gonna say? Come on Ramen. Don't leave me hanging.

Evening finds me ahead of the others, hauling ass to make it to camp before dark. There's a developed campground next to a lake, about a half mile off the PCT, and we'd talked of camping there. I arrive to a cluster of rumbling RVs and then the rest of the campground, empty, stretching away into darkness. The lake glitters in the last of the twilight.

It starts to rain as I set up my tent. I pull the pitches taut and then wander around the campground, looking at the empty sites, the parking lot, the sandy edge of the dark lake. I stare at myself in the mirror in the fancy heated bathroom. *Is this what I look like?* Tan face, the ends of my hair bleached from the sun. There are coin-operated showers, but I don't feel

244

like showering.

Later I lie in my tent, listening to the gentle prattle of the rain, wondering how my friends fared. Maybe they couldn't find the trail to the lake? I used my GPS to find the trail, and they don't have GPS. And what of Ramen? I turn on my phone, but I don't have reception here. In a few days, if we make good time, we'll be in Crater Lake- and then Sisters, and then the Bridge of the Gods, and then Portland. I close my eyes. Portland! And yet, I don't want to be done with Oregon. I realize, suddenly, that I don't want the trail to ever end.

***

In the morning I stall in the warm bathrooms, brushing my teeth and staring at myself in the mirror, phone plugged into the outlet. When there's nothing left to do, I hike and find Instigate and then a mile later Spark, sitting on his groundsheet on an old logging road, his breakfast spread around him. Neither of them were able to find the campground and so each of us camped alone under the clouded sky, wondering where the others were.

We traverse the flank of Mt. McLaughlin and then I am alone in a gray forest of lodgepole pine, claustrophobic third-growth with only dry needles underneath, not a single sunbeam. It is dim and silent and I walk quickly. Suddenly there is a hot pain in my thigh and I see a wasp there, writhing on my skin. I shout and throw my trekking poles away and smack at it, and smack it and smack it, and now I can't tell the burning of the sting from the burning of my own hand. I grab my trekking poles and run through the ugly forest as quickly as I can, up and up and up on the switchbacks, until I find Spark and Instigate camped in a shadowy flat spot next to the trail.

"I'm so glad I found you guys," I say. "I hate this forest."

Dinner soothes my anxieties. I sit in my sleeping bag and wonder how long we'll be hiking through dry third-growth. I think of the wet part of Oregon, the mossy big-leaf maples and the tangled undergrowth, not a bare spot anywhere, everything growing and decomposing and growing. That's farther north and farther west, right before we get to Mt. Hood. Most of Oregon is actually pretty dry.

I close my eyes and try to think of the smell of the cedars. How much farther until the smell of the cedars?

***

I am walking fast today. There's a twenty-mile stretch without water and I am *flying* along the ridgeline, my backpack like a cloud on my back. There are the endless forests below me and in the distance some pointy spent volcanoes, Oregon style. I turn on my phone to see if Ramen has texted me back yet- he hasn't. I press my hands against my face. I wish I wasn't thinking about this so much but unfortunately, there is nothing else to think about. It's just me out here, trapped with my thoughts. Why hasn't he texted me? Did he hate making out with me? Am I too much of a freak for him? And I'm angry, too, but I won't let myself admit it. I push on grumpily, dehydrated and sore. I catch up with Instigate and we play "what if" while we hike. What if we night-hiked all the way to Crater Lake? What if we did a forty-five mile day?

The egg-yolk sun is setting in the ghost-white burn, throwing long bands of light over the fireweed. We're hiking and meowing, hiking and meowing, one mile then three then five. At last, we hear a short meow in response and find Spark in the flat, open forest, his tent pitched on the sandy floor. We roll out our bedrolls and eat dinner. Our feet hurt and we're tired. Crater Lake will have to wait until tomorrow.

***

My phone is dead. I can only imagine that Ramen hasn't texted. It's started to really wear on me now, a nagging dread that just won't go away. I can't seem to stop obsessing, out here with nothing to distract me. It's a curiosity I can't itch. What happened. What happened.

Instigate and Spark are tired of hearing me complain.

"You need to chase some other trail tail," says Spark.

We walk the road towards Crater Lake Mazama Village, which glitters like a temple in our imaginations. We arrive, we drink cold water from the shining fountains, we stare at the clean bright tourists who stare back at us. At the restaurant I pace the salad bar, my thru-hiker smell following me like a cloud of flies. I assemble a salad of the iceberg lettuce variety and also gather chili, cornbread, and lots of pieces of watermelon. Spark orders a family-size pizza and eats the entire thing himself. Instigate has a milkshake. Afterward we cross a big parkinglot to the store, where the other thru-hikers sit in the sun at a couple of flaking picnic tables. I start a load of laundry and feed quarters into the coin-operated shower until it bursts to life, washing all of my accumulated suffering away and making me new again.

Instigate's friend Ari arrives. Ari drives us to Umpqua Hot Springs, all of us crammed in her old sedan, pitching down a series of dark rutted roads. The gravel turnout for the hotspring is crowded with hippies; long-haired hippies spilling out of VW buses draped with tapestries, playing ukuleles. We follow the washed-out trail along the river to the hotspring pools, which have been scooped from the smooth rock. There are many small pools and we get a pool all to ourselves. We sink into the water, grateful, our bodies loosening like butter on a hot dash. As the evening passes, the other pools fill up and the night deepens, until there is only the flickering light of votives and what the stars can throw, shadows and disembodied voices and the roaring of the river.

When we're too hot to soak anymore we lie out on the wooden deck, our bodies steaming, and try to count the stars. We talk and we don't talk, we let our worries sink down towards the molten center of the earth. We're slurry with sleep and wonder and we've forgotten about linear time.

A mile from the pullout for the hotspring is a dark forest service road that dead ends in a burbling spring and we park the car there, thinking to camp. We're standing next to the car when we hear a man shouting in the dark forest. He's camped there, he says. We've woken him up and he's angry. We're too loud.

"We just want to camp here," says Instigate.

"You're a bunch of selfish immature assholes," says the man. It's not the worst thing I've ever been called but the man's tone is terrifying- as though he's trembling with rage, there in the dark woods. "You're a bunch of selfish immature assholes," he spits again, "and you need to leave right now!" I imagine meth labs, manic speed benders, homicide-suicide inducing psychotic rages. Confusingly enough, there's an Audi station wagon parked at the edge of the trees.

"You're the asshole," I shout. "We just want to camp here."

"Selfish immature assholes!" says the man again, and we see the white circle of his headlamp, bobbing towards us in the woods. Then he is standing next to his car, a hoodie up over his head, rifling through the contents of the trunk. When he looks up we can see his eyes, wild and red, and what appears to be a knife in his hand.

"Let's get out of here," says Ari. We do as we are told, crowding into the car and locking the doors. We stare out the windows as we pull past him and he stares back at us, eyes manic and bright, shiny thing clutched tightly in his hand.

We don't say much as we roll along the dark road towards Crater Lake. We don't talk about the man or the shiny thing or how scared we all were.

"I can't wait to get back to the PCT," I say. "I feel so safe on the PCT."

"Yeah," says Instigate. "If anyone tried to attack you, you could just outwalk them." She mimes a man with an upheld knife and another person walking just out of reach. Our laughter is like helium gas exploding and then we are deflated balloons, draped all over each other just wanting to be home. I remember when I was little and I fell asleep in the car and I had to be carried into the house. The tiny flowers on my dress, my thick stockings. My eyes are closing.

It's well after midnight when we pull into a forested campground along the road near Crater Lake. Most of the spots are empty and we pick one next to the burbling stream, big trees all around to keep us safe. I squat at the loamy edge of the stream to fill my Gatorade bottles, the water glassy in the flat light of my headlamp. I pitch my tent in the dark. Inside the tent, I am warmed by the spirits of a thousand geese and by thoughts of Ramen. The mystery of him hangs before me, a mirage. As I fall asleep the future branches and then splits into a thousand pieces; the pieces rain down into the ocean.

***

I dream that I'm trapped in a membrane and wake to find myself rolled against the wall of my tent, fingers stroking the damp fabric. I pull my fluffer-puff back up to my chin. It's six o'clock.

We're car camping this morning. We gather at the picnic table with our bags of granola and bits of dried fruit. Ari makes hot ginger tea in a mason jar and wraps the jar in her hat so that we can pass it around. The hat and tea together smell to me like collective houses I have loved, steamy windows and worn floorboards and early mornings with everyone else asleep, cumin and ginger permeating the painted cupboards.

On the drive back to Crater Lake we stop to stash apples and water in the woods. There's a twenty-seven mile waterless stretch today, and this way we won't have to carry such a crazy amount of water. But I don't want to carry any water at all; I'm tired of how heavy it is. I'm tired of everything today.

I cannot shake my sleepiness. I hike along the rim of Crater Lake, on the annoying trail that sometimes climbs into the trees and sometimes dumps you onto the road with all the cars and tourists. The lake itself is unremarkable today- wide, circular, hazy with smoke. There is an island ("Wizard Island") and the stillness of the water is cut by the wake of a single boat. The sunlight is too dull to make anything glitter.

I catch up with Egg, visible from a distance on account of her purple yoga dress and large white sunhat, and we hike together through a flat forest of blow-downs to a highway, on the other side of which there is supposed to be a cache. There is no cache and we sit for a while on a log next to the road, wondering what we should do. Finally, we decide to hike a little further and in a few hundred feet there is the cache- a modest pile of gallon jugs at the base of a tree. There's a good flat campsite there, too, and we set up camp. We're cooking dinner in the last of the light when Spark and Instigate arrive. Instigate is drowsy from Benadryl and she shows us her wasp sting; it's caused her upper arm to swell like a football. The wasps are everywhere, this time of year along the trail. They build their nests in the trail itself and when thru-hikers pass over they think that we're bears come to eat their grubs. They rise up in numbers, filling the air with their buzzing, and attack.

"I think I've fallen off the moving sidewalk," I say to Egg as I eat my dinner.

"Yeah," says Egg. "I was tired today too."

***

In the morning we hike fast through the waterless forest and reach the lake by noon, taking only one break, sitting in the leaf litter eating chocolate and talking about Garfield comics. At the flat, twinkling lake, we find Instigate's parents and her younger sister, Elena, who is a sort of teen version of Instigate. We strip off our shirts and wade out into the water, find the place where the ground drops off and paddle around in the cool depths, letting it sooth our hot mosquito bites, out thirst, our chafe.

It's a four-hour drive from the lake to Sisters, via a large circle around the state. We'd picked the lake as a spot to meet Instigate's parents because it had a campground and a road, not knowing that the campground could only be reached by a series of small, winding, very indirect highways that took one all the way west towards Eugene, south to a rushing river and a giant dam, and then east again to the open, dry ponderosa forest around Sisters.

In Sisters we flow like a dusty river into Instigate's aunt and uncle's house, which is bright and open and full of light. There are big windows that look out at the dry forest and in the distance the mountains, draped in smoke. Instigate's parents make three pans of lasagna, one of them gluten-free, and there is kale salad with sunflower seeds in it. We all sit around the big wooden table, wrapped in towels as our clothes are being beaten clean in the washing machine, and fidget with our forks like runners at the start of a race. Instigate's mother and father, who are a journalist and a painter, respectively, are both startlingly calm, as though real food was just a thing that you could have any day. After I have swallowed four helpings of lasagna Elena pulls a chocolate cake from the oven, frosts it and rests it on a white ceramic cake stand, and there is vanilla icecream and fresh raspberries to go with that. And beer and wine.

After dinner we collapse in the palatial basement, comatose with food. Spark sits next to the bookcase and runs his hands over the DVDs, and we talk idly of movies that we could watch. I convince Instigate to cut my hair, and afterward I feel melancholy. I think perhaps that I have eaten too much cake; I go upstairs and eat some more cake. We are all feeling this way, whatever it is- walking in and out of rooms, pulling objects from our packs and putting them back in, staring at ourselves in the mirror. What is it that we'd longed for so badly while out in the wilderness? In the end we watch cat videos on youtube, although there is something wrong with the volume or we can't find exactly the ones that we want, or they won't load. It's midnight when we turn out the lights and spread our sleeping bags on the smooth carpet, feeling vaguely dissatisfied. I lie awake for a long time, watching the small red and green lights blinking in the corners of the room- things charging and things humming, text messages incoming, the little blips and bloops of the sleepless world.

***

I wake at six to the light coming in the big windows and step over my friends to the computer, where I read hiking blogs until the others are stirring and it's a more reasonable hour, the whole world illuminated in daylight and the sound of pans clanking upstairs. For breakfast we sit at the bar in the kitchen and hold squares of cold lasagna in our hands like sandwiches, and finish that off with raspberries and icecream. Instigate's generous saint of a mother tips the last of the chocolate cake into a gallon ziploc bag, pushes it into my arms.

"For the trail," she says.

On the four-hour drive back to the lake I get a text from Track Meat. He's in Sisters with some other hikers. They've been four days ahead of us for weeks and we just crossed paths without knowing it, like ships in the night.

I wish we all could've hung out in Sisters, I text back. *Y'all should hike in slow motion for a week so we can catch up.*

Even if we hiked in slow motion you turtles would never catch us, says Track Meat.

Track Meat you are a fool who knows nothing, I message back. *Also we ate lasagna and icecream and we don't even miss you.*

But I'm lying. We do miss our friends. I think back to the High Sierra, when we were a big, unwieldy group of weirdos, our brilliance like sparklers in the dark. Laughing so hard it felt as if we would asphyxiate. Six of us, eight of us, ten? But how do you hike with a group that big? You don't. You break apart, you split up, you pull ahead and you fall behind. MeHap and NoDay four days back, Track Meat four days ahead. All of us kind souls spread out across the space-time continuum. Will we ever see any of them again? I try not to think about it.

251

At least I have Instigate and Spark. We're glued to each other with a special glue that holds feral cats together. Trust, loyalty, love, hard won over hundreds of miles. We don't say it, we haven't ever said it. Instead we say things like *do you want to camp at this lake* and *I'm eating pizza where are you.* But we know. Till Canada do us part.

At the lake we hug/wave goodbye to Instigate's parents and then stand at the edge of the water, using our fingers to scoop the last of the cake from the plastic bag. It's one o'clock and we all feel sick from sugar. We stagger forward dehydrated waiting to kick into gear, trying to muster some sort of wind. It takes hours for my pace to become effortless, to feel as though I'm riding my own legs, that special Oregon feeling.

My phone chirps.

Ok but I'll have to catch up, says the text.

It's from Ramen.

I pass Arnold, a grumpy, older thru-hiker who smokes pot from an aluminum can.

"Have you seen any other hikers today?" I ask him.

"Just Ramen," he says. "He's a few hours ahead of me."

A few hours ahead of me. Ramen left Ashland a day after we did, he hiked hard, and then he passed us when we were in Sisters.

Oh the irony.

"Thank you," I say.

Ok ready? I think to myself. Hike like you mean it. I pass Spark sitting next to a stream, pouring honey-nut cheerios into his mouth.

"I'm tired," he says.

"Can't stop now," I say.

I pass the side trail to Shelter Cove Resort. We'd stopped there on the drive back to the lake so that Instigate could pick up a box. Now I imagine that Ramen is there, doing his resupply in the little store. Will I pass him if I keep hiking? Or what if he's at the lake in five miles, over the top of the next pass? What if we keep leapfrogging each other, like, all the way to Canada? I look at the text again-

Ok but I'll have to catch up.

I'm racing uphill and the last of the light is bleeding from the forest. Dark, eerie dark, coming in like a ghost. Killing my will to night-hike. I turn a bend in the trail and there's Spark, his tent staked in a flat spot next to some blowdowns. I drop my pack, defeated and also a little relieved. No night-hiking for me. I pitch my tent and then sit in the dirt, muscles twitching, and spoon my dinner of instant refried beans. Instigate appears a moment later, spacey and strange, and stretches out on one of the logs.

"I just had the weirdest time hiking," she says.

"Don't forget to eat," I say.

"Yeah," says Instigate quietly, body draped over the log. We are all a little off today.

After dinner I lie in my sleeping bag in my tent, excitement crawling up and down my vertebrae. I know I need to sleep, but how? Suddenly sleep seems arbitrary and extraneous, like dusting or online shopping. I press the button on my phone and look at the text again.

Ok but I'll have to catch up.

***

I wake at six, my stomach in knots. I shake the Gatorade bottle that sits next to my head- empty. I guess I drank all my water in the night? Outside the soft morning light is settling on Spark and Instigate's tents; they're still asleep. I open my pack as quietly as I can and unroll the bag of tortilla chips. Crinkle, crinkle, crinkle. It's the Carrot alarm clock!

I'm the first one to leave camp and I hike the four miles to the lake fast. I'm thirsty. At the lake, long bands of yellow light stretch across the water and the section hikers are just starting their morning campfires. Ramen is not there, as far as I can tell. I fill my bottles, unroll my foam pad and sit at the edge of the water, spooning tuna from a foil packet. Second breakfast.

A few miles later there's a shelter in the trees next to the trail. It's a tall log cabin filled with light, a woodstove in one corner. I walk around, touching the things that hang from the rafters. Above me is a loft. I imagine the place in winter, the snow piled up in the woods. I want to come back in the winter, I think. With skis. I'm sitting outside the shelter eating yet another snack (Fritos) when Spark, Instigate and Egg catch up.

"Guess who camped with me last night?" says Egg. Egg pitched her tent a few miles before we did, on a little ridge just past the trail to shelter cove.

I almost choke on my Fritos.

"So he's behind us then," I say.

"We saw him at the lake," says Instigate. "He took off his clothes and jumped in the water."

"Your boy's got a nice butt," says Egg.

"Did you tell him I was here?" I say.

"No."

It's midday now, and hot. I hike on with the others, a sort of rushing in my ears. Something gets in my eye and I rub at it. The thing won't come out, and my eye begins to water. Soon it's hard to keep my eye open. What is going on? I feel anxious in an unfocused way.

There's some sort of trail race going on today- two runners fly past us, shining with sweat, quads bulging as they pound downhill. Then we turn a corner and there's an aid station- a dozen people sitting in camp chairs and a folding table with paper bowls of candy.

"Hello hikers!" says the woman tending the food table. "Welcome to the buffet!" She hands us plastic cups of flat Coke. Spark takes a banana from the table, and Instigate scoops up some Oreos. I eat grapes and peanut M&M's.

"Eat as much as you like!" says the woman. She's wearing an apron over her neon running clothes.

"Careful," I say as I palm Skittles, watermelon, packets of caffeinated sports gel. "You're playing with fire there." We settle onto a log next to the trail and eat our snacks, watching the runners trickle in. The ones we've seen so far are the ones at the very front, which is exciting. They're totally

254

going to win! After a moment a teenage boy jogs into the station.

"Water, water, water," he says. Someone hands him a paper cup of water and stuffs a packet of sports gel into the pocket of his shorts. The boy drinks his water and then he's gone. He's like third from the front!

"This is so exciting," says Egg.

Just then Ramen appears, wearing his green shirt and a green hat, stooped under the weight of his giant green pack.

"Welcome hiker!" says the woman at the food table. I look at him and then look away. He drops his pack and sits next to us, on the log.

We all have another go at the buffet and dawdle, watching the action. Runners pounding past, friends of runners, the people attending to the runners. I pretend to squeeze sports gel into Spark's hair. I get up to fill my water bottle at the aid table and when I turn around Ramen is looking at me. He's smiling.

Act natural, I think.

"TTH?" I say to Spark. "Time to hike?" I've been abbreviating everything lately- I claim it's a side effect of hiking an acronym. Spark shoulders his pack and we head out. Instigate has already gone on.

On the trail Spark pulls ahead and soon I'm alone, walking through the warm dappled forest by myself. A couple of elderly day hikers pass me, maps extended, and I try and help them puzzle out where it is that they're going. Ramen comes walking up, trekking poles clacking, and joins the party. After a while we realize that we can't help the women because they have no idea how to explain to us where it is that they want to go and so we wave goodbye, wishing them the best of luck. Then Ramen and I walk together, me in front feeling self-conscious of my pace (is it too fast? too slow?) talking over my shoulder, laughing. I stop to pee and we switch- he's in front now and I look at his back, at the irregularity of his gait, at the bands of muscle in his calves. He's wearing hiking boots and one of his feet turns out with each step. Soon we reach the lake where we'd all planned to stop for lunch, wide clear water twinkling in the afternoon sun. Instigate and Egg appear and we circle the water's edge, meowing, until we find Spark, his food spread around him in the dirt. Ramen makes instant mashed potatoes on his canister stove and Instigate and I strip and plunge into the water. Spark takes off his pants and wades in but stops short.

"Get your D wet! Get your D wet!" we shout. Spark is from Georgia and hates cold water. Finally he obliges and squats, plunging his crotch into the icy lake. I am in the water up to my neck, laughing so hard I sound like a dying mule. Spark puts his pants back on and splashes from the water. Instigate and I join him and we sit, shivering, in the long yellow light.

A bit later is Brahma lake, our campsite for the night. Instigate, Spark, Ramen, Egg and I sit in a circle on the dirt on our sleeping pads, too tired, now, to set up our tents. I mix up a disgusting protein shake in my dirty Gatorade bottle and dare the others to try it. The shake is from the health food store in Ashland and it tastes exactly like chalk. The shake is hard to drink without gagging, but I manage. Instigate has a protein shake too- hers is green and the consistency of slime. We pass the shakes back and forth, making faces and laughing until we cry a little. Egg knows all the songs to Les Miserables, and all day I have been trying to convince her to sing one. Now, as the mosquitoes gather around us and the sun sets over the flat, aquamarine water, she does. Dark comes and with it the cold Oregon night and I shimmy into my bag, exhausted and happy. I can hear Ramen rustling in his tent and see the light of his headlamp through the fabric. Instigate begins to snore, like a saw hacking at the night. Ramen's light switches off and yet I can feel him there, breathing and awake. Just a little ways away. I consider getting up, crossing the moonlit clearing and tapping on the fabric of his tent. What would happen then?

The moon is a bright disco ball, rising through the trees.

***

I sleep and wake, sleep and wake to the streetlamp moon. Instigate is tossing and turning saying *Brrrrr, cold, brrrrr, cold* like she does. It's how she got her trail surname- Brrrrrcold. Instigate also has a middle name, Sleeping Beauty, and in Washington she'll acquire another middle name, Baywatch, on account of a bright red sports bra. Instigate Sleeping Beauty Baywatch Brrrrrcold.

Spark got his name on his thru-hike of the Appalachian Trail. He started the trail with a flint sparker that he used to make fires. Spark doesn't have a last name but we call him SparkleMotion, SparkleToes, SparkleMagic and, recently, lil' Sparkums.

In the morning my tent is beaded all over with condensation and my sleeping bag is damp. It's fall in the mountains, already, and the nights are getting cooler. *Fall.* Where did the summer go, and how did it pass by so fast? It seems like just yesterday I was standing at the Mexican border, in spring. Chills run down my body as I sit in my sleeping bag, eating almonds and raisins. What is time? When I at last drag myself out of my tent I find a fresh, quiet world and ahead of me the soft narrow trail, stretching on into forever.

I hike fast, leapfrogging with the others, talking now with Instigate and now with Egg and then I happen upon Ramen, sitting on a log next to the trail spooning nutella into his mouth. I sit down next to him and unwrap a Probar. I bought a bunch for cheap at the Shop n' Kart in Ashland, and the chocolate ones taste like cake.

"You want to walk together?" I say.

"Ok," says Ramen. He has Nutella in his beard, and his hat is askew. I can smell him- like woodsmoke and salt.

"In Ashland when you told me you were a virgin," I say a little while later, walking behind him watching his gait, "I assumed you weren't a virgin on purpose. But are you? A virgin on purpose I mean?"

"I suppose so," says Ramen. "I was raised Catholic…"

"Are you, like, a practicing Catholic?" I realize that the concept is absurd to me.

"Yeah."

"So you're saving yourself for, like, marriage? To another Catholic virgin?"

"Yeah."

"Are there other Catholic virgins? In the woods, I mean? Or Antarctica?"

"I don't know."

I tell him that I was raised Catholic; first the hallucinatory Catholicism of my schizophrenic mother and then the strict, conservative Catholicism of my grandparents, who adopted me when I was fourteen. The poverty and despair of my youth; God, the devil, the Virgin Mary; the warmth of empty cathedrals when we were homeless, sunbeams coming in the stained glass catching dust motes. Little rooms full of votives and my thin, acrid-smelling mother, working a wooden rosary through her fingers. Speaking in tongues. *You've got the devil inside of you,* she said to me. *I should've let you die when you were a baby.* Then later my cold grandmother, bringing home the communion wafer wrapped in a paper napkin and forcing me to eat it when I had the flu. Lying on those faded sheets with the tiny flowers, bright desert sunshine making the curtains move. So sick I could barely swallow. *Body of Christ,* she said.

Ramen's parents are both liberal archaeologists.

"I think my experience of Catholicism was a little different than yours," I say.

The lake where we stop to fill our water bottles is full of copepods, the little propeller-shaped crustaceans that make their homes in the shallows. I hold my Gatorade bottle up to the light and look at them, swimming around. They're bright red.

"I'm sorry you have to die," I say as I stick my steripen into the bottle.

"They don't die," says Ramen. "It just scrambles their DNA."

"Well," I say, watching the eerie ultraviolet light of the steripen do its thing. "Well."

Soon we're at the trail junction to Elk Lake, a resort of sorts on the flank of Mount Bachelor. Ramen has a box at Elk Lake and so I hike the mile and a half there with him.

At the resort, there are people everywhere: barbecuing, drinking beer on blankets, sunbathing. The lake is stuffed with boats and ripples with the wake of jet skis. The lodge itself is unremarkable- sided in dark wood, tilting into the ground. On the porch of the lodge is a stack of clear plastic tubs- the hiker box. Shoes, discarded hiking clothing, toiletries, piles of food. I find a bag of Doritos and a cold bottle of Pepsi. Ramen and I split the Pepsi, sitting at a picnic table wiping the sweat from our faces. I set up my solar charger in the sun.

"This is nice," I say.

"Yeah."

The Pepsi restores my flagging hiking boner and soon we're back on the trail, cruising three mph. I know that for many hikers three mph is like no big deal, but it's a new thing for me, something that I've been working towards but haven't mastered until now, in Oregon. I love hiking this fast; the time it saves allows me to take real breaks and still get to camp before dark. And it makes me feel like I can do anything.

We pass a string of twinkling green lakes, Oregon style, and then we're crossing an enchanted meadow with South Sister in the distance, dramatic and beautiful. We see a little white tent and then Egg, standing on a patch of bare ground eating pomegranate gummi bears.

"You want these?" she says, handing us the bag. "I don't really like them."

We eat the bears as we cross the meadow, the shadows lengthening on the mountain. There's a campsite in three miles and we reach it right at dusk- soft ground, clusters of trees and a stream that burbles down the mountain. I pitch my tent and then sit on the ground around the dead fire pit, eating dinner and watching Ramen pound in his stakes.

"Do you want to cuddle tonight?" I say.

Ramen stands and looks out at the darkening valley below us.

"Yeah," he says.

I look into my refried beans.

"Ok."

Ramen has a long, narrow, single-wall tarptent with just enough space inside for two people's sleeping pads. I slide mine in alongside his and then toss in my water bottle, my dinky headlamp, my hanky and the little square of foam, cut from a hiker-box sleeping pad, that I use as a pillow. Everything else I stash in my tent. I'm relieved that Ramen wants to cuddle. I'm excited for the human contact, for the warmth and for the chance to replace the memory of our awkward, shame-filled makeout with something simpler and more innocent. I'm squatting in the cold now, waiting for Ramen to get settled in his sleeping bag so that I can shimmy into the tent. He has all sorts of crap around him- extra clothes, his maps, things in rumpled plastic bags I can't identify. I've just watched him brush his teeth and put on long, thick sleeping socks.

"Should I come in there?" I say.

"Yah," he says.

I crawl into the tent on my hands and knees and scoot around, pulling my sleeping quilt up over me. I button the bottom of the quilt into a footbox and lie down, tucking the sides around my body.

"It's so much warmer in here with two people," says Ramen. I can just make out his face in the light from the full moon.

"Yeah," I say, and then he kisses me. He pulls my body against his body and I feel our sleeping pads slide askew beneath us. He kisses me again and a wave of pleasure hits me like a brick wall. I feel myself loosening against him, onto the cold floor of the tent. I roll into him and he lifts my wool t-shirt up over my head, momentarily blinding me. He drops the t-shirt onto the floor of the tent and runs his hands over my skin. I bury my face in his neck and then pull off his shirt. He smells like earth, like wood smoke, like salt and he's hissing, the air moving in and out of his mouth.

"This isn't awkward at all," I say.

"No." The white of his teeth are like lights. My running shorts have bunched way up and he runs his hands along my thighs.

"Here is so soft," he says, touching my hip. He strokes my quads. "And here is like a rock."

"I'm a girl," I say. "Parts of me are soft."

"I like soft," he says.

"We keep our shorts on?" I say.

"Yeah."

"And I can't touch your cock?"

"No."

I press my skin to his bare skin and the heat between us is shocking, so stark against the cold night. I just want to lie against his face and breathe the air that comes from deep inside his body. This is it, I think. He's hissing again, gripping my sides so hard it's painful but I don't feel the pain and then he rolls me onto my back and rubs his rough palms along my goosebump skin. He kisses me so deep I feel like I'm drowning.

"I want you," I say. "I want you so bad."

"I can't do that," he says, but his voice is shaking. He climbs on top of me and kisses my face, my chest, my belly, my face again. I can feel his warm cock pressed against my thigh. It's cold or it's warm I have no idea, the tent is damp with condensation from our breaths, our manic breathing, our bodies.

"What if I came in my pants," he says. I wrap my arms around him.

He rests his head on my chest.

"It's never been like that for me," he says.

"What do you mean?"

"It was so hot. And that's the farthest I've ever gone." He lifts his head. "I've only ever made out with a girl twice. And I was drunk. I stopped drinking a year ago." He lowers his head back to my breasts. "I don't know."

"Do you feel bad now?"

"No," he says, after a moment. "I don't know."

We sleep at some indeterminate hour, wrapped up in our individual sleeping bags; I am still topless but warm, dizzy with exhaustion. I wake in the dark to find Ramen's fingers, searching in my bag. He locates my hand and then pulls it to him, presses it against his chest. We lie like that, me on my side looking at the whites of his eyes, the damp hair draped across his forehead, his warm animal smell around me. The moon is bright like a streetlamp and the fabric of the tent glows silver. I stare at his eyes and he stares back at me. We're just little animals in the woods. That's all we are. I wake again later and it's still dark and I've rolled away, onto my back. I look at the fabric of the tent, blinking as panic courses through me. Oh my god, I think. Oh my god.

***

I wake tired to the sun and Ramen does too and we roll over, peer out the vestibule at the lightening forest.

"You want to listen to Balkan pop music?" Ramen digs a bright yellow ipod from the pile of stuff next to his sleeping pad and pokes at the smeary screen. Tinny, happy music comes out. I pull Ramen's green shirt from the tent floor and put it against my face. The smell of it overwhelms me, like digging a hole in the loamy earth and putting my face inside.

"I haven't washed that shirt in a really long time." he says.

"No," I say. "You don't understand."

Ramen is just right there and so it makes sense to push our bodies together in the narrow strip of cold tent floor between our sleeping pads, to work my quilt down around my hips and press my skin to Ramen's skin, to kiss his mouth thick with sleep until that inexplicable thing is happening again, something there isn't even language for. I run my hand down Ramen's stomach towards his cock. He grips my wrist.

"I can't?" I say.

"No."

My fingertips are just touching his damp pubic hair. I can't remember ever wanting to touch a man's cock so much. The heat of it, the way it pushes against itself. Ramen rolls me onto my back and buries his face in my chest.

"Bite harder," I say. He clamps his teeth down on my nipple and a wave of cold-hot runs through me, like an electric shock. Then I'm drowning again.

It's nearly ten o'clock when we start hiking. I barely eat any breakfast- my stomach is in knots and I have to hike with my hipbelt undone. I feel tired but also not, hungry but also not; mostly I feel floaty, high but also numb, waves of panic bumping against the shores and then drifting away, feathery buzzing between my ears.

Ouch. My stomach hurts.

I catch up with Egg at lunchtime and we spread our sleeping pads on a bench above a waterfall. It's cool in the shade here and the ground is littered with bright pieces of obsidian. I lie down on my pad and put my hat over my face thinking to nap, but I can't. I'm humming all over, electric. Ramen arrives and drops his pack.

"You know anything about this place?" says Egg.

"I think it's an archaeological site," he says. "A place where people came to flake obsidian."

Some day hikers wander over- older women in coral-colored hiking clothing and men in clean, broad-brimmed hats. We're starting to see more day hikers- in the Sierra there were all the southbound JMTers but since then it's been only us, the arrogant thru-hikers racing against ourselves. Now we're in the Three Sisters Wilderness, the mosquitoes are over, the berries are poppin', and the weather is beautiful- and the day hikers are out, stretching their legs, breathing the good clean air and having picnics in the wildflowers. I have to remind myself not to feel possessive of the trail. It's ridiculous that I do at all- I come from the city too. We all come from the city. We are an urban culture. I no more live in the wilderness than a housecat does.

But I want to. And it's fun to pretend, at least for a little while, that I do.

I can't nap and I have to hike, so there's only one thing to do. I take out the packet of caffeinated sports gel that I pocketed at the aid station and squish it back and forth in my fingertips. The top of the packet has a little tab that you pull off in order to squeeze out the goo. The tab is shiny silver foil and about the size of a fingernail. We are always finding these tabs on the trail and picking them up. I most likely have them in every pocket of my pack; they are too small to remember to throw away.

I eat the goo and then retrieve my solar panel from the sunbaked rock where it's been charging my mp3 player. I hoist my pack and clip the mp3 player onto my hipbelt. Caffeine in my system and a steady supply of Foreigner; there's nothing I can't do right now.

"Your neck is covered in hickies," says Egg.

"Yeah," I say. "I know."

I leave the mountainside for a broad field of lava crumbles and soon there is no dirt, no shade, no water, just black lava crunching underfoot and the punishing sun beating down, beating down. My legs are smeared with black and I'm thirsty and windburned but I hike on, feeling happy and inexhaustible. The caffeine, the sleep deprivation, climactic classic rock, and Ramen, holding my hand in the middle of the night. All of these things swirling around inside of me, creating a magic, electrical cocktail that propels me quickly over the lava fields. I hardly feel the jagged stones beneath my feet.

Eleven miles later I am sitting beneath the wooden trail sign that provides the only shade next to the highway. The highway is a hot ribbon of fresh blacktop cutting through the fields of crumbled lava and there is no traffic, although there is a note from Spark- *Meow, meow, meow, meow* is all that it says.

Egg and Ramen arrive and we stand on the shoulder, waiting for the traffic that is not there. We dance around, clap our hands, make silly noises. When the sun starts to set in the faded sky and still we haven't found a ride to town, we start to lose morale. It's cool now and we stand with our arms at our sides, looking forlornly at the dimming road.

The pickup pulls onto the shoulder just as the last of the light is leaving. The door pops open and bad, thumping trance music spills out. There is no room in front but there is a futon in back, under the camper shell, and if we can squeeze in with the two malamutes then the ride to Sisters is ours. We twist our way inside, shoving our packs in before us and helping yank each other all the way into the bed. I lean back against my pack and one of the malamutes drapes itself across my lap. Egg and Ramen are squished at my feet, the other dog between them. The trance music begins to thump and we pull away, into the starry night.

After a few minutes one of the malamutes begins to growl at the other malamute. Then the other dog lunges and Egg has to grab it, wrestling it away from me. I can feel the throaty growl of the malamute on my lap. What is it that they say about dogs in close quarters? The less room they have, the more likely they are to fight? I should push the dog off my lap, but there's nowhere for her to go. The other malamute lunges again, and Egg wrestles it to the ground. The dogs are competing for ownership of the strangers.

Thump, thump, thump goes the techno.

Grrrrrrrrrrrrrrrrrrrr, go the big dogs at each other. And then we are in Sisters.

Our ride drops us at a gas station and I pace the blacktop, listening to the pealing in my telephone. Instigate answers- she and Spark are at her aunt and uncle's house, where we stayed before. Her parents have gone home, but this time her aunt and uncle are there. Instigate's aunt is on her way to pick us up right now.

Sisters, round two. With a different cast of characters. Instead of her mother and father and sister it is her aunt and uncle and twelve-year-old cousin. We take showers in the two glorious bathrooms and put our sweat-stiff clothes in the high-efficiency washing machine. We explode our packs in the basement. Spark and Instigate's cousin bond about Star Wars. Instigate's uncle grills steak and sautes spinach and mushrooms. There is corn on the cob. We eat on the back deck, freshly washed, the ponderosa night all around us. There is a single candle in the middle of the table and it illuminates us gently, our sun-red faces and clean, shiny hair. We all look aglow, as if lit from within. Ramen, especially, is handsome in a boyish way I hadn't noticed before- lean and wiry in his short-sleeve shirt, tilting his head to flip his hair out of his face. Eyes of some indeterminate color, half-closed with sleep.

I want to hold him. I want to give birth to him. I don't know.

I saw at my steak, which runs with blood. The mushrooms are swimming in dark brine.

It's the best meal I've ever eaten.

After dinner we are slurry with sleep and we wash the dishes under the hot, soapy water and then stumble downstairs to the basement, where we bump into each other like billiard balls until we each find our own little corner, bit of rug, or couch to sleep on. I am on my back on the hard smooth floor that feels so good against my spine. I am exhausted/awake, exhausted/awake, and then I am just exhausted. The window is open and outside the night creatures are singing.

There are only seven hundred miles left of the trail.

No, I think. *No no no no no.*

***

265

In the morning I stumble in the dark over my sleeping friends to the bathroom, where I discover that I've gotten my period. I feel relief; the electrical storm that was my PMS has broken, and general atmospheric pressure has stabilized. I feel great. I lie back down on the carpeted floor and stare at the lightening room, thinking. I can't sleep anymore but I can think all right. So I do.

Soon the others wake and we drag our rumpled selves upstairs and sit in a row at the bar in the kitchen where Instigate's aunt and uncle serve us bacon, pancakes and OJ. I feel like a little kid, sitting on a barstool being fed pancakes. Like Instigate brought home all the neighborhood kids. Instigate's aunt slicks up the griddle with a stick of butter and ladles out more pancake batter. I eat another four pieces of bacon. A gallon of milk appears, and Ramen and Spark take turns drinking right from the jug.

It's noon by the time we're packed and ready to go. Instigate's uncle drives us to the grocery store and I push a cart around in a daze, sleepless and weirdly alert, pulling bright packages off the shelf in some rough guesstimate of what I will and will not want to eat this next hundred miles. Afterward everyone else has more errands to run so I text Egg, and we walk to the highway shoulder to hitch. Egg makes a cardboard sign and I dance around. A run-down minivan with kayaks on top pulls off just as Ramen comes running up. The minivan drops the three of us at the lava observatory near the trailhead and we jog to the top, sticking our heads out of the castle-like windows which are oriented to various celestial bodies. Spark appears, and then Instigate.

Dusk finds us on the moon. Hills of crumbled lava, burnt forest and no water anywhere. Fireweed and an egg-yolk sun. There's a campsite somehow, a bit of earth swept bare in all these rock piles, and it's just big enough for the five of us to cowboy camp. We spread our groundsheets and lay down our sleeping pads, arrange our dusty objects around us. We eat our little dinners, pulling bits of food from foil wrappers and crumpled plastic bags, feeding the furnaces inside of us. My appetite is not good and I feel exhausted but sleepless, humming and alive. We laugh about nothing, look at each other's faces, burrow into our bags against the cold. Bats flap over us, pulling the dark after them, making a quilt of the night. The stars come out, little fires so far away. I am happy.

***

I wake in the still-dark to the sound of birds overhead and lie in my bag, watching the sky grow light. The others wake and I eat a little breakfast although I am still, for some reason, not hungry. It's cool this morning and the path is sandy and we all hike fast, me with my headphones in listening to Patti Smith, feeling good. I take the side trail to Big Lake Youth Camp to fill up my water; otherwise it's an ungodly stretch without. Instigate and Spark don't stop, that's not their style. They'd rather carry no water and hike fast, racing against themselves. But Ramen and Egg are there, on the porch of the main building with their resupply boxes spread around them.

Ramen plans to bushwhack from the youth camp back to the PCT, instead of taking the indirect side trail. He's got maps and he likes to use them. Also a compass.

"You want to come?" he says. We're standing next to each other on the trail and I'm looking over his shoulder at the map. I can smell his breath. He turns to face me and it's like he's gonna fall into me. But he doesn't.

"You want to come with?" he says again. It's open ponderosa forest, not any real way for us to get lost.

"Yeah," I say.

We slog across the ashy ground, climb over blackened blowdowns and then we're there, the trail back below our feet. It never ceases to amaze me, this eighteen-inch-wide highway to Canada.

My home.

I hike with Ramen through the afternoon. The huckleberries are ripe and we pick them as we walk, reaching our hands out grabbing fast before the stride of our legs carries us away, not wanting to slow down. In the afternoon Ramen's mood turns dark. He talks about women that he hates, says "you're mine, bitch" to each huckleberry as he picks it. I bristle and say nothing- he's only ever worked around men, I guess, it's just the way he knows how to talk. I don't know. I walk ahead and catch Instigate, tell her about it. I don't know, I say. He says these things. We're both tired and so we laugh, hiking uphill saying strange words in strange voices as loud as we can, and then quietly, laughing and trying to breathe all at once. We catch Spark at a murky lake surrounded by blowdowns and the three of us hike until dusk. We're standing on the shore of another lake, this one broad and clear, shivering as the sweat cools on our clothes, talking about campsites when Ramen pulls up.

"I think we'll go another two miles," says Spark.

"Alright," I say. "We'll catch up."

Then Spark and Instigate are gone and Ramen is looking at me square, his eyes some strange color like honey or olive I don't know.

"I want to make out," he says.

"Ok," I say. *No I don't know I don't know.*

Ramen pitches his tent on a flat spot in the trees on the other side of the cold lake and I sit on a log, assembling my dinner and watching the mist drift over the water. Spark and Instigate are ahead of us, camped somewhere a few miles down the trail and suddenly I feel lonesome for them. I don't want to be with Ramen, with his strange ways and strange eyes and angry words. My trail family, I think. I want to be with my trail family.

After eating I fill my water bottles in the lake, brush my teeth and spit into the dirt, climb into Ramen's tent alongside him. It's warm in here, the thin fabric trapping the heat from our bodies. Ramen kisses me and it's warm but I freeze inside, go cold.

"You know how it feels when you're in the woods," I say to him in the dark, "and there are predators, and you know the predators might be hunting you?"

"Yeah," he says.

"That's what it feels like to be a woman," I say. "Like you're being hunted. Like you could be prey."

"Ok," he says. "I never heard it described like that."

"Women want to feel safe. When you say 'bitch' and 'cunt', it makes me feel unsafe. If you want to hang out with women, you have to make them feel safe."

"Ok," he says. He's staring up at the ceiling of the tent. "No one ever told me that before."

268

"Just don't do it, I guess." Outside the moon has risen and there's a deer, stomping around at the edge of the water.

"Ok," he says.

***

The next morning the skies open up and it starts to pour. Cold rain, pissing rain, thundering down in the summer forest. There are doug-firs now, Oregon grape in the understory, usnea hanging from the tree boughs. We're transitioning into what I call "the wet part of Oregon"- the beginning of the true blue Pacific Northwest. My home bioregion. The forest that enchants me, my cathedral. That intoxicating mixture of dense understory, mossy nurse logs and dusty yellow sunbeams. Like I could lie down in a sunlit clearing and sleep forever. Let the forest digest me.

Ramen got ahead of me somehow and I come upon him leaning against the trunk of a big doug-fir, hiding from the rain.

"I just saw my first yellow cedar on the trail," he says. His eyes are wild and his cheeks are flushed. Water drips off his hair.

I lean into him, pressing my body against his. We kiss sloppy, there's snot running from his nose. The smell of the tree, the smell of his hair. His mouth tastes like pepper and the rain is running down all around us. I can feel his cock against my leg.

"I want to go to grad school," he tells me as we circle Mount Jefferson in the pouring rain, the trail a muddy slick. "I want to study the genetics of fire resistance in trees." Water puddles in every low place, sloshes over the tops of our shoes. Clouds tumble over Mount Jefferson and down, over the mountain and down. Weather coagulates on three horizons. We switchback up towards the pass; the rain pauses briefly on top and we take foggy photographs. I have my rain jacket hood up over my head for warmth and Ramen grips my face inside of it and kisses me. Then we rush down the other side of the mountain over patches of snow, the trail a route of tumbled rocks, hard to find sometimes. Dusk finds us at a flat spot next to a dirt road and Ramen eyeballs the level ground, imagining the coming storm.

"I think we'll be ok here," he says. He pitches his tarptent and we duck inside just as the rains return. We're trembling with cold/anticipation, the blood pooled at the centers of our bodies, hungry but not hungry. Tired but infinitely awake. We eat undercooked dinner and Ramen tells me about the orthodox churches he saw during his travels in Russia, the way he kissed the icons behind their glass, the small, old woman whose job it was the clean the icons with a cloth. I tell him about the illusion of linear time, how everything is really happening all at once on the head of a pin, now being all that there really is. I press my hand to his heated beating chest. Like now, I say. Like now.

"You're so amazing," he says. "Knowing you." He's talking as though he's alone. I run my fingers along the damp inside wall of the tent.

"Everything is so new for you," I say.

The storm opens up and the rain rattles the silnylon of the shelter. The dark is like a solid thing closing in everywhere and we are holding open this small triangle with the hotirons of our bodies. We're keeping life alive in this dark storm growing brighter, somehow, off of nothing, growing larger off of nothing, heat and light and something else, like a plant unfurling.

He lays his head on one of my breasts and cups the other in his hand.

"We should go to sleep," he says. I can feel his cock against me, again, through the fabric of his shorts. I want his small hard cock inside of me in this rainstorm in this dark dark forest, I want him to come in me until he's empty. I close my eyes and see the universe, spiraling away into everything. God.

***

Ramen wakes me in the indeterminate dark, hands pulling at my sleeping bag and I push it aside, press my naked damp skin against him. His hands, calloused from his trekking poles are on my body, my heart is beating I am alive and no other part of me exists. He's sucking air through his teeth, his cock a hotiron against my leg.

"You want to fuck," I say.

"Yeah." He lies on top of me, soft hair against my sternum. "I got blue balls."

"But you don't want to come."

"No."

"What do you do about it then."

"Just wait." He rolls off me and faces the tent wall and in the indeterminate dark I can see the knotted muscles of his back, his waist and the waistband of his tights. I scoot forward and spoon him, pull that warm back to my chest, kiss those shoulders that smell like the sea. He grips my hand in his hand and presses it against his chest.

When I wake it is light. I don't know how much I slept only that being awake is unbearably sweet. But now I have to hike.

Egg stops by while we're folding up the tent in the warm morning sunlight, trees sparkling with wet, sky an unbearable blue. I'm flushed and my neck is covered in hickies again but I try to act natural, chatting about such pedestrian matters as pack weight and inner-thigh chafe. This morning as the three of us walk we play inky-pinky, a silly word game that involves rhyming meaningless words and making the other players guess the rhyme. We stop for lunch at an aquamarine lake, ringed in moss and dripping with sunlight, and lie on the dry ground. I pretend I want to nap but I only want to put my hat over my face in the warm sun and dream about sex. Egg packs up and heads out and I crawl from my sleeping pad to Ramen's and take off my shirt.

"You're so beautiful in the light," he says. "I want to take a photo."

"You can," I say.

"No," he says. "I'll just have to remember it."

He rests his body on top of mine.

"I want to lose my virginity under a western red-cedar," he says.

"To another Catholic virgin?" I say. "After you're married?"

"Yeah."

I try to imagine this- the dress, the cake, the wedding and then a bumpy jeep ride to the wet forest, dim cedars and big-leaf maples cloaked in moss. Sunlight pooled in a clearing, the ground decorated with hemlock cones and trailing blackberry.

"I hope you have that," I say.

"Me too." He cups my tits in his hands. "This is just practice. Practice for the real thing."

"Yeah," I say. "Ok."

In the afternoon I hike fast through the cool forest, ecstatic at the beds of moss and the smell of the cedars, the way the light wends its way through the canopy. A man passes me, hiking south. He's got the usual- trail runners, running shorts, ultralight pack. But something about him is familiar.

"Are you Scott Williamson?" I say. Scott Williamson is the previous speed record holder for the PCT.

"Yeah," says the man. He's headed southbound, trying to break his own record. He's hiking forty-four miles a day and he has a friend with him. The friend has a little pouch hanging from his hipbelt and as we talk he surreptitiously eats handfuls of granola from this pouch.

"Good job on the light pack," says Scott Williamson, to me. My ego puffs up like a balloon.

"You really like to hike the PCT, huh," I say.

"I would live here if I could," he says.

"Yeah," I say. "Me too."

A while later I stop in a stand of big doug-firs and lean my body against one of them. The bars of yellow sun are scattered just so and I push my face into the deep rutted bark of the tree smelling the spider webs there, the dust, the hardened pitch. Big doug-fir, I think. What do I need to know right now.

I love you, says the doug-fir. *I love you so much.* I can feel the tree there, the tree underneath me the tree all around me, the tree inside of me. The trees holding each other holding the soil holding me. The trees more patient than anything, save the ocean. The trees with the long view. I can feel their pity- *Little mammal,* they say, *with your two legs. Running around saying Where Do I Belong. Making value judgments on the wind, the flowers in the springtime, the shapes of the stars. Little mammal with your trembling heart. I am your home and I love you and I will always be here.*

I start to weep, my face against the tree, snot running down my face. I have always felt this way about the trees; ever since I was little and I would walk out into the snow in my snowsuit and crawl beneath the laden boughs of the sitka spruce to find the little cave inside. Where the air was warm and the light was blue and dim. Where there was neither chaos nor screaming nor the smoke of Pall Malls. *I love you,* said the trees then, to me curled on my side smelling the new smell of the snow. *I love you I love you I love you.* Not a sound but a feeling in my body, in the very deepest part of my body. *I love you I love you I love you.*

I stop to fill my bottles at a mossy spring in the hillside and then hike on into the dusk, down down down to a little river with a footbridge and Egg, her white tent like a beacon in the gathering dark. I pitch my tent next to hers and then Ramen appears and pitches his and we all sit around assembling dinner with our headlamps, hungry and shaky with exhaustion, looking forward to the black hole of the night. Egg has wintersquash soup from home and she passes it around, the taste of real food with onions and seasoning like fireworks in our mouths. Ramen kisses me goodnight after Egg has gone to bed, me hunched over my bag of almonds, his kiss so firm it almost pushes me off the log. He scoots into his tent and I can see his headlamp bobbing around and I look at it, look up at the stars, look down at my goosebump legs. Tonight, I think. Tonight I'll actually sleep. The walk to my tent is nearly infinite and it takes me an epoch to brush my teeth but then at last it is the future and I am in my bag, fluffer-puff scrunched firmly around me, the quiet of the forest a lullaby.

***

In the morning I feel great and I resolve to hike as fast as I can; I want to make good time today. I pass Ramen and Egg and walk alone through the warm, dappled forest, wondering how far ahead Spark and Instigate are. A few hours? A day? The thought of not catching my friends fills me with despair. They are my cat pack; I have to catch them. I just have to.

At noon I reach a dirt road and next to it, a surprise- boxes of cookies and snacks, coolers of ice and soda, a ring of folding camp chairs. I sit in one of the chairs and drink a blackberry soda and eat a tangerine. I contemplate a sleeve of Oreos. Ramen and Egg show up, and then some other hikers. They all have boring conversation and I flip through the trail register, reading the entries. There's an entry from Spark dated the day before, with Instigate just below. So they're a whole day ahead of me then? My heart sinks.

Funhog, the woman who stocks this trail magic, shows up and sits in one of the folding camp chairs. She lives in Portland and she's wearing bright, color-coordinated hiking clothing, which brings me joy.

"Did you meet Spark and Instigate?" I say.

"Oh yes," she says. "They camped here last night."

So they showed up in the afternoon, ate snacks into the evening and then decided to camp here. Sweet relief! I might be able to catch them after all.

After the trail magic Ramen and I walk together in the afternoon light, which slants warmly through the cedars. There is a side trail to Little Crater Lake, a pit-like hole in the earth filled with aquamarine water, fallen trees suspended inside as if in jello. The light becomes more beguiling as we walk, more dusty yellow, the mossy nurse logs more enchanted. We turn off trail and stomp through Oregon grape to a small sunlit clearing and lay our sleeping pads down in the wild roses. I take off my shirt and lie back in the light and Ramen touches my body, runs his beautiful hands across my body, and I look at him looking at me feel the rasp of his hands until my breath comes quick and short.

"Fuck," says Ramen. He slaps his shoulder. There's a welt there, like a bug bite. "Fuck," he says again, and slaps his arm. "Little flies." They're not attacking me, or I'm not reacting to them. Ramen turns and lets me scratch the length of his wiry back.

"Do you want to put your shirt on?" I say.

"No," he says. "Fuck." He presses his chest against me.

I'd meant to hike fast today; I'd meant to catch my friends. Now time pools slowly outward like honey; I arch my neck and see the wild roses, Ramen's pack, a blue plastic rosary tangled on the ground.

"You're so beautiful," says Ramen. The light is behind him, sifting down through his loose dark hair. I don't know what time it is. Ramen is touching my face. He moves his hand down my belly and under the waistband of my running shorts. I gasp and lift my hips. I am drunk with anticipation.

"Is this how I do it?" he says. He is sort of touching the top of my pubic hair.

"No," I say. "You want me to show you how?"

"Ok," he says. I guide his hand down farther.

"Put just the tips of your fingers inside," I say. "And grip me. Like this. Like a hook."

He does as he is told. Connection, like tumblers in a lock. A current running through me running through him, running through all of time, the past and future falling away, one single moment. Everything, everywhere, happening all at once.

"Are you ok?" he says. "You're so red."

"Yeah," I say. "I'm ok."

Wild roses against my cheek, the indeterminate yellow light. The smell of moss. I'm convinced the whole forest is inside me. I'm spinning, loose, in space.

Ramen pulls his hand away.

"What," I say.

His eyes are hazel and green, hazel and green.

"I just went past my comfort zone," he says. "That's all." His voice is hoarse. "I'm gonna have to go to confession for this." He looks at his rosary where it lies tangled on the ground. "I'm gonna have to go to confession for this." He's still pressed against me, his chest on mine. "I was thinking we should break it off at Ramona Falls. I should be focused on the trees and I'm focused on you instead."

"What? Ramona Falls?" I feel confused, as though I've just woken from a nap. "How far is that?"

"Twenty miles I think," says Ramen.

I push him off me and stand up.

"Twenty miles?" I say. "Where's my shirt." There's a rushing in my ears. Ramen plucks my shirt from beneath him and I pull it on, stuff my sleeping pad into my pack. I hoist my pack and clip my hipbelt. My vision is blurring. I'm still spinning in space but now my eyes are filling with water. I'm drowning. I feel as though there are parts of me everywhere.

"I know this is just practice for you," I say. "But it feels real to me." I jab my finger at the forest floor, the tangled understory, the little flowers in the moss. "It feels more real than anything."

I leave him and hike; hike fast, my legs furious and my body buzzing with light. I haven't drunk any water, I haven't eaten, but I feel nothing inside, only a sort of weightlessness; only hiking makes sense. My legs like pistons, pumping as fast as I can make them. What a convoluted kaleidoscopic twisted universe we live in. What glory, what heights and depths. I want to hike until I fall apart.

I'm walking a narrow path along the steep forested mountainside. I'm crying; the dirt on my face is streaked with water. Mount Hood rears up in the distance. The light recedes, makes way for dusk. Spark and Instigate are at Timberline Lodge; if I hike until midnight I can reach them. A thirty-four mile day. The longest I've ever hiked.

Soon it's dark, the forest cloaked in blackness, the path climbing gently. My pathetic headlamp makes a wavery circle of light; the battery is dying. For once, I am not afraid of night hiking. For once, I have something stronger to fear. Tonight the trees are holding me. Tonight I know I am safe.

I sing softly to myself as I hike, my voice hoarse. I switch back and switch back, swinging my headlamp, wielding my dim circle against the infinite dark. In the void of this blackness, the smell of the forest blossoms; red-cedar and vaccinium and broken earth. I think of Ramen; I weep for the golden ball of light in his chest, bursting out into everything. I saw it, I saw it, I saw it. Goddamit shitbag motherfucker, I saw it. He's the forest, I think. We're the forest.

I break out of the woods; now I'm slogging through sand above treeline, way up high on Mount Hood. The trail cuts a faint path in the starlight; I can see the shapes of the ridges, suspended in space and across a great abyss the lights of Timberline lodge, burning yellow. It's just me up here on the mountaintop, between the earth and sky. It's just me, the sound of my breath as I push myself up to the ridge; it's just me, beneath the Milky Way. The stars are singing to me, the air that rises from the valleys; all of this is for me. There is a peace inside of me, a feeling of emptiness. Above me the galaxy is spinning, or I'm spinning, or we're all spinning. There is no time, I think. There has never been any time. There is only this.

I reach the lodge just before midnight and Instigate is there, waiting on the broad stone steps. I'd texted her on the ridgetop- *Are you still awake?* She's wearing her black hiking tights and the black tight-fitting shirt that together make her look like a superhero. I can smell her hiker smell- it's a little like Fritos, and more comforting than anything.

"Sorry to keep you up," I say.

"That's ok," Says Instigate. "We're stealth-camped in the trees below the gondolas." I follow her down a broad meadow filled with lupine to a chunk of forest, where she's spread her groundcloth on a flat patch of ground. Spark is there too, in his tent, and I roll out my sleeping pad among the blueberry pushes and unstuff my sleeping bag. I'm thirsty but I don't have any water; Instigate offers me half of her liter and I drink it, grateful. The muscles in my legs are popping like steel cables. I still haven't eaten but what is eating?

"What happened?" says Instigate.

"I don't know," I say.

I lie down on the lumpy ground and pull my sleeping quilt over me. Above me are the trees and through the trees, the sky, which has clouded over; in the distance are the low sounds of the lodge, the crunching of tires in the gravel lot, the restless movements of humanity. I roll onto my side and stare at the little plants. There is a roaring inside of me, like the sound of the ocean in a conch shell. I close my eyes. Sleep, I think. Just sleep.

***

At dawn it starts to drizzle. I pack up my stuff, feeling disoriented. How much did I sleep? I don't know. I shoulder my pack and walk up through the lupine meadow to the big stone lodge, inside of which I find a circle of couches around an ornate hearth and Spark, curled up with his sci-fi book, pack against the legs of his chair. The walls are beautiful wood and the lamps are low, the first gray light of morning sifting in through the big paned windows.

"This place is beautiful," I say.

"Yeah," says Spark.

"So clean, and really fancy."

"Yeah."

"I feel so dirty."

"The dining room doesn't open until nine," says Spark.

I make my way up some twisting stairs to the small, hot bathroom, where I brush my teeth in the sink and wipe the dirt from my face. What I really want, though, is a shower, and I ask the clean, sleek-haired woman at the front desk about it.

"We have a shower in the lower parking lot for hikers," she says. "Just walk down the hill and you'll find it."

A shower in the parking lot? I make my way downhill and in the lower parking lot I find a blue plastic port-a-potty and open the door. Inside, instead of a toilet seat there is a showerhead, and hanging from the showerhead is a rack with a bottle of shampoo, a bar of soap, and a bath poof. A towel is spread to dry optimistically on a rock outside. I turn on the water- it's frigid. *No hot water*, says a sign taped to the outside. Brrr, I think. I mean, I need a shower. But not that bad.

I hike back up to the lodge and join Spark on the couches, scrolling on my phone and waiting for the dining room to open. At last there is a clanking and a rattling and a woman appears, behind a little podium. We line up before her; filthy, unwashed thru-hikers with infinite, bottomless insides, and hold our breaths as the big oak doors begin to swing open. As we file past this woman we hand over our fifteen dollars. It is our ticket to the gates of heaven, aka the Timberline Lodge breakfast buffet, which we've been hearing about only for the last two thousand miles.

278

A broad, dark wooden dining room, diagonal tables with white tablecloths and bright silver, tall paned windows looking out at the gray misty morning. We sit at a big table in the middle of the room, Spark and Instigate and myself, and rest our dirty hands on the white tablecloth. A server brings us coffee and stemmed glasses of ice water. He looks to be about sixteen, and is obviously a snowboarder.

"Can we eat?" we ask him.

"Yes," he says.

The buffet consists of a long line of steaming serving dishes with gleaming steel lids. We walk down the line, lifting each of these gleaming steel lids in turn. Sausage. Bacon. Eggs. Pancakes. Grits. Fresh biscuits. Gravy. There is a shining tower of fresh sliced fruit, a crockpot of oatmeal, vessels of yogurt and honey, mountains of raspberries and blueberries. There are waffle irons and waffle batter for making your own waffles. Brown sugar. Maple syrup. Fresh whipped cream.

I fill my plate completely full, plus another small plate completely full, and take them back to our table and arrange them on the clean white tablecloth.

"All for me," I say to no one in particular.

We eat, and we eat, and we eat some more. And then we sit, us dirty hikers, gazing vacantly out the windows, our stained plates in front of us, waiting to digest so that we can eat again. At some leisurely hour the regular hotel guests stream in, and the dining room becomes a cacophony of mingled voices. We eat some more and the wait staff wanders by and tops off our coffee, understanding. They are used to this. We come in every year. I take an empty ziploc bag from my pocket and surreptitiously fill it with warm sausage patties. Also slices of cantaloupe. A server stops by and places a shot glass of fizzy liquid in front of each of us.

"What is this?" says Instigate.

"Apple cider vinegar," says the server. "For your digestion."

Fifteen minutes before breakfast is over Egg and Ramen appear, flushed and covered in raindrops. Ramen shoots a mournful look my way, and I smile warmly at him. I ain't mad anymore. Or sad. Maybe a little sad. Spark, Instigate and I lie prone on the couches in the lodge, idly going through our resupply boxes while Egg and Ramen stuff themselves. Are we going to hike today? I guess we're going to hike today. Only forty-seven miles until the Columbia River, the border between Oregon and Washington, and I-84, which can take us to Portland. We plan on spending a couple of days in Portland, making our resupply boxes for Washington. We pull ourselves upright and begrudgingly pack our bags. If we play our cards right, we'll get to the river before dark tomorrow, in time to hitch into the city.

I talk with Ramen outside on the wet stone steps before I go.

"Maybe I'll see you in Washington," I say.

"Yeah," he says.

Spark, Instigate and I hike away from Timberline Lodge in the cold rain and switchback down to a churning river and beyond it, a damp cedar forest. So beautiful, I think. It's so beautiful here. Like home. We ford the river and climb up in the mist to the ridgetop and then down again, across another swollen stream. Then up again to a series of campsites, which are full. Those darn day hikers! We shiver in our damp rain jackets, looking for somewhere to rest our underslept selves. At last there's a cluster of flat spots next to a rutted gravel road, near some parked machinery and the rumble of a generator, spotlights waiting to burst to life before dawn. Some sort of excavation in the forest. The three of us pitch our tents beneath the dripping trees and crawl inside, weary and grateful. I eat the last of my cantaloupe and lie in my sleeping bag, waiting for drowsiness to overcome me. Rumble rumble clack clack, goes the generator. I think of Ramen's ass in my hands, the weight of his body on my body. The warm smell of his hair.

***

The morning is gray and fog hangs like batting in the trees. Spark and Instigate are up and stirring, crinkling bags of breakfast, and then we're packing our things away, thinking about mileage and hours and miles per hour and what time dark comes. Can we make it to the highway by seven? Thirty miles. Yes. I think we can.

Hiking fast along the ridges looking at the beautiful soft-forested mountains rolling away, mist tumbling over everything, mist clumping up below us in the valleys. My hip-belt full of snacks so I don't have to stop and then those snacks are gone and I'm hungry again and I still don't stop. How long can I walk without eating? How far will the glucose that's already stored in my muscles take me? Drinking the dregs of cold stream water from my bottles. Rock hopping across a wide, shallow stream. I'll stop at the next one and refill. I'll stop at the next one.

We take a lunch break on a little flat patch of dirt next to the trail, stuffing granola into our faces and looking out at the hazy ridges. Spark takes out a sharpie and draws on Instigate's back, at the edges of her sports bra.

"What did he draw?" says Instigate, turning her shoulder to me.

"Um," I say. "A steaming pile of shit?" We're laughing so hard I almost choke on my granola.

We reach the Eagle Creek Trail and hike down, down, down on the soft path, soft green forest all around us; soft rocks soft nurse logs big-leaf maples cloaked in moss. Epiphytes! Life on life on life! We are singing in rudimentary Español; we are writing "PCT the Musical" in rudimentary Español.

Los pequeños osos negros!

En el bosque!

Son peligrosos!

Waterfalls- narrow rock trails above waterfalls, below waterfalls. Walking clinging to the wet rock behind waterfalls; day hikers in clean bright clothing, standing huddled next to waterfalls. Walking fast my feet achy, thirsty but not really hungry, hiking fast.

I reach the parking lot at the Eagle Creek trailhead, take a huge dump in the bathroom, stick my face under the water fountain and sit on a park bench in front of the interpretive sign, numbly eating almonds. Spark arrives.

"How long have you been here?" He demands.

"I don't know. Twenty, twenty-three minutes?"

"Well," says Spark, stabbing the ground with his trekking poles. "Some of us like to stop and look at the waterfalls."

"Oh my god," I say. "I actually arrived somewhere before you."

"Well," says Spark.

Instigate appears and we walk through the parking lot towards the Columbia River, our thumbs stuck out. A woman named Lou with a kayak on her roof rack pulls off and we pile inside her car.

"I can give you a ride to Portland," she says. As we turn west onto I-84 rain begins to pelt the windshield.

Lou drops us off at my friend AM's house in Portland and we stumble inside and collapse on the thick lush carpet, drink mason jars of tap water, tip our packs over pull all the objects out let our carefully ordered lives turn to chaos. AM sits on the floor with us with her beautiful tattoos, hair shiny and neat, laughing. We finally collapse at midnight on the various couches, lights of the city leaking in the windows, hearts racing from sugar. It feels as though there is no time; it feels as though I'm in a place outside of time. Oh the city, I think. Oh civilization. What am I ever going to do with you.

***

In the dark hour before dawn it hits me:

I'm in Portland.

All that's left is Washington.

The trail is almost over.

So, I think, curled on my side on the couch, my sleeping quilt pulled over me- what exactly am I doing with my life? I can hear AM getting ready for work in the kitchen, putting the teakettle on, running water in the sink. I pick up my phone and scroll in the dim light from the big windows, poking at things on the internet, the noise inside me growing louder. What am I doing with my life? WHAT AM I DOING WITH MY LIFE? *What?*

I know what's happening; on the trail, one doesn't have to think about the larger picture of one's life. On the trail, one thinks about walking, and about eating, and about acquiring food and making it to camp at a reasonable hour. It feels, in these moments, as though one's larger

282

existential problems have been resolved, as if some sort of transcendence has been reached, and one's previous worries are no longer relevant. But this is an illusion. One's existential problems haven't been resolved. In fact they're still accumulating at the regular rate, piling up and piling up and piling up like junk mail, and in moments such as this one, when one is lying on a "couch" in a "city" with birds and the sounds of dawn all around one, and "cars" in the "street" and water in "teakettles"- it is in moments such as this that one's backlog of existential problems come crushing down suddenly in a great roaring torrent and one can almost not catch one's breath for the noise of it all.

And now what does one have left? What?

Only Washington.

Washington, that reasonable, underwhelming rectangle of finite forests and knowable mountains. Just Washington.

Spark and Instigate are stirring now, sitting up in their sleeping bags staring out at the room with mushed faces. There is talk of coffee and pastries and there is the putting on of trail clothes. I can't go get coffee or eat pastries; I need to assemble my resupply boxes for Washington. Soon the house is empty and it's just me, kneeling on the thick carpet staring at the priority mail boxes I've lined up against the couch. I stand and wander around the house, look at the art on the walls, pick at the chocolate cake in the kitchen, peer into AM's light-filled office. Off the dining room is a guest room paneled in dark wood, a velvety spread on the bed, big rectangles of sun on the plush carpet. I lie down on this bed and gaze at an old painting; a pastoral scene of carts in a market, ramshackle outbuildings, village dogs. Outside the big window a pair of squirrels fights or makes love in a walnut tree; beyond the walnut tree the tempestuous Portland sky fights or makes love with the sun. Maybe I'll just lie here for a little while. Maybe I'll just lie here for a few minutes.

I wake two hours later to my phone, making noise. It's Ramen. He's just gotten into town, he's staying with a friend; he wants to meet up with the three of us for dinner. "Let's get Ethiopian," I say. I know of a place where for a few dollars you can stuff yourself until you feel like vomiting. After hanging up I rub my face and stare out the window; the squirrels are still in the walnut tree, running up and down. Ramen, I think. Ramen called me. Ramen's my friend and I care about him. The thought fills my heart with warmth.

My friend Seamus picks me up an hour later, dear Seamus, wearing a *psychic sister* sweatshirt and a crystal necklace, driving his bright new car blasting hip-hop. Seamus drives me to where all my stuff is stored, in my trailer behind a friend's house. I step inside the trailer, dear little trailer, with its wild print curtains and stale nag-champa smell, old linoleum, dusty milk-glass lamps that took me so many trips to goodwill to find- riding my bike in the dreary winter, thinking *what am I doing in Portland what am I doing in Portland.* I dig through the boxes stacked in the closet, boxes I mailed home from the trail, but I cannot find my box of warm clothes. I need those clothes, for Washington. Apparently it's cold and rainy every day in Washington during the month of September, although I cannot conceptualize this.

"Have you seen another box?" I ask Seamus. "There should be one more box."

"I haven't seen it," he says.

The missing box has my long underwear, my fleece shirt, my gloves and warm hat. Oh well, I think. How cold can it possibly be in Washington? The whole trail has been sunny and hot during the day. Why would it change now, in September? So for Washington I'll have my synthetic T-shirt, my running shorts, an ultralight down jacket, and a lightweight rain jacket. That should be enough, right? And if it's really cold I can just hike faster. *Right?*

Seamus and I drive to Dalo's, the Ethiopian restaurant in a rundown pink building that has been one of my favorite places to eat for over ten years. Ramen arrives with a buddy who lives in Portland. Ramen is freshly washed and in town clothes, clean hair swinging in the afternoon light. We commandeer a long, dim table in the restaurant and I order huge amounts of food, red lentils and oily spinach and lamb in berber sauce, and everything comes on big platters of injera, which we eat with our fingers. Spark and Instigate arrive and order honey wine. We are eating and eating and eating, and we are happy.

When the platters are picked clean we pay the bill and walk out into the evening light; I give Spark a piggy-back and we stumble as a herd to the rose garden nearby, where we all play on the swings until nine o'clock which is, of course, our bedtime. We say goodbye to Ramen, who is staying another day ("Catch up!" we say. "We'll see you on the trail!") and Seamus drives Spark, Instigate and I back to AM's house and I park myself on the floor and finally, finally deal with my resupply boxes. Spark and Instigate deal with a half-gallon of coffee ice cream and a bottle of wine and then fall asleep, half in and half out of their sleeping bags, Instigate sawing logs like she does. I finish taping the last box shut at midnight and then brush my teeth sleepily, staring at myself in the mirror- my wild hair, pink cheeks and sunburnt clavicle. I turn out the lights and at last I reunite with the glorious velveteen guest room, and settle in for Epic Portland Sleep Part II.

***

Sometime in the indeterminate dark AM comes into the guest room and perches on the edge of the bed.

"I'm going to work," she says. I sit up and hug her, but I don't know who she is. I'm actually still asleep. Who is this person? I think. It isn't until morning that I remember my weird dream and put two and two together- that was AM that I hugged. In my sleep. Thru-hiking does all sorts of strange things to a person's sleep patterns, apparently. Like enabling sleep-hugging.

For breakfast I make toad in a hole- two eggs fried in gluten-free bread with the center cut out. While the eggs are cooking I scrape the dregs of the coffee ice cream from the carton. I also saute some kale in a cast-iron skillet.

Instigate and Spark are at the coffee shop again. They like to drink a lot of coffee. On the trail Spark drinks instant coffee mixed with chocolate whey protein in a Gatorade bottle. He is always drinking this. Sometimes he lets me take sips of it, and it actually tastes really good.

I walk to the grocery store to get the final few things for my resupply boxes and stand in the bulk aisle, staring at the bins. I'm down to the last of my food money for the trip and so my Washington boxes are super simple- trail mix and granola, basically. A few packets of tuna thrown in. But I don't even care anymore. I've been eating this shit for so long that I've transcended the need to actually enjoy my food. No more desires. Eat to live, not live to eat. Walk as long as I can before I have to eat again. I wrap a twist-tie around another bag of granola. Is this new way of eating depressing? I can't tell.

285

A friend of Instigate's family lives in town and he picks us up late morning and takes us to his house in the Southwest hills to feed us brunch. Sausage, honeydew melon, homemade quiche. A flat of raspberries and blueberries that we pick at while everything cooks. We eat on the back deck, overlooking the sloping yard of plum trees and English ivy. After we've eaten all the food and gnawed the melon down to its rind this incredibly generous friend loads all our packs in his car and drives us forty miles east along the Columbia to the little town of Cascade Locks, where we'll cross over the bridge into Washington. Instigate's friend Sarah has joined us; she's going to hike with us for a week. Sarah is concerned that she won't be able to keep up with us, so she and Instigate set out as soon as we reach the bridge, in order to get a head start. I find Egg in a little plaza behind the post office, reading her book in the sun, and sit with her. I'm not ready to hike yet. Spark is at the house of the local trail angel, Shrek. The box of warm clothes he sent himself here won't arrive until morning, so he has to stay overnight. He walks so fast though, it doesn't even matter. He can catch up in like a minute.

A man appears with a pizza box.

"I accidentally ordered an extra large pizza," he says, smiling mischievously. He sets the box on a bench.

"Oh my god," we say. "Thank you."

My phone rings. It's Spark.

"They're grilling tri-tip at Shrek's," he says. "I think y'all should stay." It's evening now, and the sky has clouded over.

"Ok," I say.

At Shrek's we eat steak and roasted potatoes and sit in camp chairs around a bare fire ring. Other hikers are there, hikers I haven't met before, and it's fun to be around a new crowd. There's a partially finished treehouse and I plan to sleep in it but then it starts to sprinkle and so I set up my tent in the gravel yard, next to Spark and Egg. The ring of hikers are drinking beer and getting louder and louder and shouting over each other more and more, and then suddenly it's hiker midnight and everyone is collapsed partway in their tents, asleep. I crawl into my tent and lie awake, listening to the trains rattle by in the dark. There's a motion-triggered spotlight on Shrek's back deck and it keeps clicking on and off. Tomorrow, I think. Washington.

Washington.

***

I sleep hard and wake to a flat grey sky, sprinkles on my tent. I pack up and then fish the foil-covered plate of leftover tri-tip from the hiker fridge and stand on the back deck, eating cold rare meat. Other hikers are stirring, walking around, digging through the hiker box. Eating Payday bars and broken pop-tarts.

The post office doesn't open until ten, so Spark heads out to find some coffee. I fill up my water bottles and shoulder my pack. Washington, I think. It's time.

The Bridge of the Gods crosses the Columbia River, the wide, fat, slow river that separates Oregon from Washington. There is no room on this bridge for pedestrians, but the woman in the tollbooth is used to PCT hikers.

"Just walk against traffic," she says. "And stick close to the railing." I do as I am told, stopping in the middle of the bridge to look out at the misty gorge, the gunmetal water, the forested mountains rising up on either side. Traffic crawls by me, headlights on even though it's morning.

It starts to rain just as I reach the other side of the bridge. Big, heavy raindrops, drumming onto the ground. I take shelter under a stand of redcedar on the roadside, looking out at the rain from inside the hood of my rain jacket, waiting for it to let up. Water begins to sift down through the cedar boughs, and I hear it bouncing off my pack cover. Oh well, I think. At least it's not cold.

I climb up, up, up in the cloudy damp, wet thimbleberries brushing against my legs, good Portland pop radio on my little MP3 player. Eleven miles later I am way above everything looking down, the river a silver snake, the gorge like the earth broken open. I eat some trail mix and then Spark appears, bouncing up the switchbacks.

"What's up, homie?" he says.

"Oh, you know," I say, as I pick the raisins from my gallon bag of trailmix. "Nice day for a walk."

287

"Word," says Spark and then he's gone, disappearing around a bend. I will see him later, most likely, and maybe Instigate and Sarah too, depending on how far they hiked last night.

In the afternoon, I climb down in elevation to the sheltered folds of the mountain and suddenly the world is rife with epiphytes: life on life on life. Dank wet moss growing on big-leaf maples growing out of crumbling nurse logs. Yellow-green usnea like lichen crepe paper, strung over everything. Little streams burbling from the earth. I hike on and on into the evening, through these sheltered folds and around the contours of the mountain, until the light is fading and my hiking boner is gone, gone. Soon dark is draped like a blanket over everything and I still have not found Spark or Instigate. I'm hiking on fumes now, alone through the nighttime forest, my feeble headlamp keeping the ghosts at bay. Next campsite, I think. I'll stop at the next campsite. On the PCT, a "campsite" is just a little flat spot big enough for a very small tent; in some areas, it's surprising how rare these can be. Here in the rainforest the understory is especially convoluted, every square inch claimed by some strong, green, growing thing. Soon, I think, turning the quavery light of my headlamp on the impenetrable blackness of the forest. *Soon.*

I see a faint whiteness in the distance and there is Egg, her bright tent pitched on a little ledge.

"This is the best I could find," she says, her head sticking from the vestibule. "I was so tired."

"Sleep good," I say.

I hike on and cross a dirt road. I could camp on this road, but what if there was a car? Is it truly overgrown, or do people on ATVs come up here? In the darkness I can't tell. And where are Spark and Instigate?

Finally there is a little wash next to the trail, full of indigenous blackberry and sheltered by vine maple. I pitch my tent there just as the rain starts up again, hard. This will be my first night camping in my tent in the hard rain- Will I stay dry? I wonder, as I spread my saran-wrap-like groundsheet across the mesh floor of the tent and arrange my water bottles next to my head. I eat a little dinner and then lie in my sleeping bag, listening to the rain patter on the maples. I feel safe and sheltered in this little wash, with the green growing things crowded up against the fabric of my tent and the trees overhead and the foggy dark mountain all around. It's peaceful here, almost deliriously so. I drift off, drunk on exhaustion and happiness. The way it should be, I think, as I feel myself melt into the earth. Life.

***

The downpour lasts through the night but I stay warm in my cozy dry tent, deep in my sleeping bag. I wake at eight and stare at the forest through the mesh, watching the water drip off the Oregon grape. The rain intensifies as I'm packing up, stooped over in my rain gear rolling up the wet tent, digging for my stakes in the mud. I can't find one of the stakes and I poke around for a while, looking for it. I rarely lose things on the trail, and I'm feeling stubborn about it. Finally my hands are cold and wet and numb and I give up. Losing a tent stake, I think. There's a first time for everything.

I hike up through the damp foggy morning, warm rain dripping off everything, feeling groggy. I reach the top of a ridge- where are Spark and Instigate? A few minutes later something whacks me on the back of the head. I turn around and there's Spark, trekking pole outstretched. He is always doing this, sneaking up behind me and whacking me on the back of the head with his trekking pole.

"Where did you camp?" I say.

"On the dirt road," says Spark. "With Sarah and Instigate."

A mile later we reach a wide gravel road just as the sun breaks through the clouds. We pull our wets bags and tents from our packs and drape them across the ground, hoping this bright heavenly light will dry our things. I roll out my sleeping pad and lie back in the warm sun, hat on my face. Soon Instigate and Sarah appear, and spread their stuff across the ground as well. Sarah pulls off her boots and carefully unwraps and re-tapes her sore feet. I watch her, intrigued. I've forgotten what it's like to have blisters. Watching her suffer in her first few days on the trail brings back memories of my first five hundred miles- the blisters, the burning tenderness of the bottoms of my feet, the pain in all my little tendons. She smiles as she pokes at her feet, though. She's a good sport. And she's having fun.

We eat snacks, move our stuff around. The odd truck rumbles by on the gravel road. It's noon, and I've gone two and a half miles. I feel like I could stay here forever.

An hour later I'm still tired so I give myself the triple whammy-caffeinated fruit snacks, painfully dark chocolate and classic rock. Still I'm slow, like molasses pushing itself uphill. But no matter; as long as I keep walking I'll get there eventually.

I see a scrap of white paper on the trail- *wasp nest ahead!* is written on it in shaky pen, and there is an arrow made of sticks. I edge past, wondering where the actual wasp nest is. There's buzzing everywhere in the forest this time of year, insects flying around here and there, being busy. I don't see any wasps and then a half mile later there's another scrap of paper. *Wasps!!!* it says. Still the ever-present buzzing, still I don't know what are the wasps and what are the non-wasps. Still I don't get stung. A little later, there's yet another scrap of paper, stuffed into a ziploc bag. I sprint as fast as I can through the dappled shade of the trail. Never a dull moment on the PCT.

I stop to rest on a shaded bend in the trail, a little ways below a ridge. I dig the trailmix out of my food bag and snack for a while; my appetite is back, which feels good. I eat some more trailmix. Eating trailmix feels like shoveling coal into a coal furnace, like that scene in Titanic when the dudes in the bottom of the ship are shoveling coal into the engine. Shoveling and shoveling and shoveling, like they can't shovel fast enough. *More glucose!* They say in their thick Irish accents. *More glucose to the calf muscles!*

Spark catches up and then Instigate and Sarah, and I hike with them to the top of the ridge. We stop to break again at a little overlook and watch the sun sink over the folded mountains. Spark goes ahead but we gain Egg, who was just a little ways behind, and the four of us hike a little farther to a wide, mossy flat spot on the very top of the ridge, with views of the mountains all around and the last of the pink light fading like fire dying and the Milky Way coming in, sprawled overhead like ribbons unfurling. We roll out our bags for cowboy camping beneath the light show, lie down look at the stars talk about the nature of the universe, everything. It's cold, and my breath rises up from my sleeping bag in puffs. The stars twinkle obligingly above me and I realize all at once that I'm on a giant globe, spinning in space.

I think of Ramen, behind us in the wide dark forest. I wonder how he is.

***

I sleep hard beneath the spinning stars and wake in the bright morning, my bag soaked with condensation. I feel good today, sort of new. I'm the first one up, and I stuff some food into my mouth and pack my bags inside of bags inside of other bags. I'm ready to HIKE.

The trail runs right below our campsite, and Ramen comes cruising up just as I'm clipping my hip belt. It turns out he camped just a mile back, on the ridge where we stopped to watch the sunset- and now our sloth-like pace has allowed him to catch us, even though he left Portland after we did.

"Ramen!" I say. "You caught up!"

Ramen and I hike together through the morning, along the rolling ridges of the northern Cascades, the day clear and soft and warm. At noon we reach a mucky pond-lake, filled with "swimmies," and gather water as best we can. There's a blueberry-covered hillside next to the lake and we eat lunch there, moving our sleeping pads around chasing the patches of sun. Egg catches up and we all nap together, laying in the Oregon grape listening to the buzzing of insects, the air moving in the doug-firs. In the afternoon we accrue other hikers and walk together in a sort of train through the sun-drenched, swampy meadows, talking in rudimentary Spanish about berries and swimming and forest creatures and laughing at ourselves. We break at a deep blue lake thick with day-hikers and walk out to the end of a log to dip the clear water from the center of the water. We sit on the log and look at the day hikers. They have cumbersome gear and are wearing luxurious cotton items.

"Labor Day weekend," I say. "I think it's Labor Day weekend?"

In the evening, we're joined by a German thru-hiker named Burrito Grande who collects mushrooms in a big mesh sack.

"Steinpilze," he says as he cuts the thick stems with his knife. He doesn't know the English word for the mushroom.

Dusk finds the gaggle of us at a trail junction in a crowded, scratchy forest and we tramp through the woods to a semi-flat spot, where we arrange our sleeping pads in a row in the dirt. I volunteer to take the outside spot in order to protect the group from monsters, and we all sit watching the light fade as Burrito Grande cooks his steinpilze over the yellow flame of his alcohol stove. Soon every last part of the light has turned to dark and I'm awake in my sleeping bag, listening to my friends' nasally breathing and the dance of the stick-breakers.

Crunch crunch snap, say the stick-breakers. I clutch my quilt to my chin and my pupils dilate in the darkness but behind the darkness there is just more darkness, nothing to see.

Snap. Snap. Snap.

My friends are breathing evenly and I can imagine them, limbs hanging out of their sleeping bags, totally unafraid.

Go. To. Sleep. I say to myself. GoToSleep.

Snap. SnapSnap.

Go. To. Sleep.

***

I have a dream about Ramen- we're clambering along a steep, gravelly ridge, a whole big group of us, and one by one we have to rock-scramble over a particularly dangerous section. I make it across the rocks, as do our other friends, but then it's Ramen's turn, and I know he's going to fall. He's going to fall, he's going to fall, I keep thinking. I want to save him, but I don't know how. He teeters across the rocks with his big pack, balances for a moment, and then he falls.

I wake in the cold morning and sit with the others while we eat our underwhelming breakfasts. We pack up and hike through dappled forests, along scrubby ridgelines and through fields of fresasitas, everyone on their hands and knees gathering the tiny wild strawberries. I walk with Ramen and throughout the day he looks at me, looks at me with these *eyes* and I don't know what to make of his *eyes*. Why is he looking at me this way? I am still learning the ways of... dudes? And I don't know how to read him. Is he flirting with me? But he dumped me back in Oregon, before Timberline Lodge. I'm not a Catholic virgin. He is not allowed by his church and everything that he claims to believe in to flirt with me.

After seventeen miles we reach some trail magic stocked by a nearby Buddhist temple; a plastic trashcan of juice boxes and granola bars and a little wooden altar nailed to a tree. There are pine cones on the altar, bits of usnea. I eat a soft granola bar and then write one of my favorite Kerouac quotes on a bit of paper (THE VISION OF THE FREEDOM OF ETERNITY WAS MINE FOREVER) and tuck it into the altar. Just past the trail magic is the highway to Trout Lake, a little trail town I know nothing about. Ramen and I decide to hitch there and we get a ride in a pickup from a young rafting guide. Trout Lake is one block long, just a general store and a diner attached to the gas station, hot sun beating down. There's a big rummage sale going on. We eat burgers and then wander around the rummage sale, trying on hats. I buy a bag of barbecue potato chips and some Fritos at the general store, an ice cream Snickers bar. We get a ride back to the trail from a farmer who looks to be about 22, has bright teeth and sun-bleached hair.

"My pig just had piglets," says the farmer. He drops us a few miles from the trailhead and drives away, spitting dust. Ramen cinches up his pack and looks at me.

"Why are you looking at me that way?" I say.

"I think there's something special between us," says Ramen.

"But I'm not a Catholic virgin."

"As friends, I mean. As friends."

"Oh right," I say, laughing. "As friends." I stand and face the road, putting my thumb out. "So you're really going to marry another Catholic virgin? And follow all of those rules? It really means that much to you?"

"I'm not sure what I believe anymore," says Ramen. "I pray the rosary every day while I hike. But to be honest, these days, I'm just going through the motions. It's almost like a superstition."

There is no traffic on the road, and the sun is warm and gentle. A chickadee calls out- *Cheeseburger! Cheeseburger!*

"I feel like I'm either going to have an epic fall from faith," says Ramen, "or join an order, become a monk."

"So what do you have when you fall from faith, as a Catholic? What do you have after that?"

"Nothing," says Ramen. "I'd be an atheist. There wouldn't be anything. I'd be completely alone."

I turn to face him.

"Stop," I say. "Atheism is bullshit, and you know it."

Ramen sort of smiles a sad smile at me.

"No seriously," I say. "We're just mammals, living our imperfect lives on this three-legged dog of a planet. We fuck up for a little while, and then we die. But it's beautiful. So beautiful. And not because some organized religion tells you so but because you know it, in your heart. And nothing can ever take that away from you."

Ramen isn't smiling anymore. I turn back to the road just as a tractor-trailer slows and pulls onto the shoulder, churning up dust. There is just enough room inside for both of us, if we cram.

The evening is six miles uphill through a burn, blackened snags and pink fireweed, Rainier and Adams holding space on the horizon and in the distance the soft peaks of the Olympics, way out over the ocean. At dusk we search for a campsite on the ridge, finally settling for a lumpy, sloping place with a view of the sinking sun. We fire up Ramen's canister stove and make a pot of instant refried beans and eat them with Fritos, crouched on our sleeping pads watching the horizon fade from orange to pink to dark, the Milky Way winking on obligingly above us. Ramen is sitting next to me on the sleeping pad, his shoes off his big sleeping socks on, and we take turns passing the pot of beans back and forth, scraping the bottom with our titanium spoons. When the beans are gone I pour a little water in the pot, and clean it out as best I can. Ramen is digging through his pack, searching for his headlamp. I pull out my sleeping bag in its stuff sack and turn it over in my hands.

"We probably shouldn't make out, should we?" I say.

"I'm not opposed," says Ramen.

"But you broke up with me," I say. "I'm not a Catholic virgin, remember?" Ramen is quiet, looking out at the dark. "What is it that you even want?"

"I want someone kind of wild," says Ramen. "Someone who likes to have adventure and is really good at making out."

I laugh.

"Then what about me? Isn't that me? What is it. Tell me." Ramen holds his headlamp in his hands, fusses with it.

"There's no future in it," he says.

I unstuff my sleeping quilt and shake it out. We get ready for bed, sleeping pads side by side, brush our teeth, arrange our water bottles. I don't change into sleeping clothes because I don't have sleeping clothes, just the same running shorts and synthetic t-shirt I wore all day, down jacket if I get cold, wad it up and use it as a pillow if it's warm.

I'm sitting up on my sleeping pad, quilt wadded in my lap and I fall into Ramen, drape myself across his lap and he kisses me, pulls me back onto his sleeping pad and I roll onto him, pull my quilt over both of us, lie there with my head against his chest, hands knotted in his hair.

"Oh Carrot," he says. "I wanted this all day."

I press my hand to his chest.

"I don't know what's in your heart," I say.

"That makes two of us," he says.

I roll onto my back, pull my quilt over me against the cold night air.

"I have a proposition," I say. The Milky Way is above us, glittering like diamonds and I wave my hand in the air as if gather up the cosmos. "Life is suffering, yes? All of this is suffering. I say we do what we want and understand that afterward there will be some pain. There's no future for us, but so what? I feel like the sky is whispering at me, the cosmos, everything. *Do it do it do it.*" Ramen scoots up against me. I emerge far enough from my sleeping bag to wrap him in my arms. Soon his breathing is ragged, his body curled in sleep. I roll onto my back and stare at the stars again, look up at all of reality swirling away, time and space together. A ship hulks on the horizon, a great glittering ship, holding all of the suffering of my life. I can see it there in the distance; I can feel it. I close my eyes and paddle out towards it, paddle furiously in my small boat towards that ship, its column of steam, its wide, crashing wake. I paddle until I am exhausted and then I lie down in the dinghy, let the waves rock me to sleep.

***

I wake long before dawn and stare at the stars. It's all so big up there, so cold sometimes, so crushing. It's pure, black, and bottomless. It's too much. I look at the stars until they fade, watch the edges of the sky bleed to gray. I want to cry but then the sun is up, light pouring over everything and all I see is Ramen, curled on his side in the dawn and the golden light, spilling out from his chest.

***

The next night it rains torrentially, twice, for thirty minutes each time. I sleep like a thousand year-old log and wake in the morning to a wet sleeping bag and water coming in through the mesh of the tent. I sit up in my bag and rub my face, stare at the shrinking bag of trailmix in my lap, the few handfuls of granola. Tomorrow morning we'll reach White Pass, where there's a convenience store and I have a resupply box. But what will I eat until then?

Why am I running out of food? I say to myself. I thought that for sure I'd brought enough on this section. You'd think, too, that at this point in the trail I'd have this figured out. And maybe I have. Maybe I know exactly how much food I should bring, and I chose not to bring it. All I do every day is walk. The lighter my pack is, the faster I walk, and the more fun the walking is. Food is heavy and maybe I just don't want to carry it any more.

I think about this as I hike through the cold fog towards Goat Rocks. Today my pack is blasphemously light, but the lack of food is scary. I pose a question to myself- is risking running out of food more tolerable than carrying a heavy pack? *Yes,* I decide. *The hunger is worth it.*

Ramen is in excellent spirits; a trail angel gave him a new pair of socks.

"Does sex feel as good as these new socks?" he asks me.

"I don't know," I say.

I pull ahead of Ramen after a few miles and around midday I stop to rest on a wide, gravelly slope below a wind-blasted ridge. There are puddles

296

here and there, rock cairns, the remnants of snow piles. We'll reach Goat Rocks today; I haven't been there, but it's supposed to be more beautiful than almost anything. Right now fog clings to the face of the mountain, obscuring the views, but it seems to be burning off, so that's good. I try to turn on my phone but it just vibrates and shuts off again. Dead, and too foggy to charge it with my solar charger. So no maps, and no photographs. At least the trail is well marked.

Something red in the distance begins to climb towards me and grows larger and larger as it switchbacks up the mountain. Suddenly Instigate is there and she flops down on the spongy, rocky ground beside me as though onto the most comfortable bed.

"Twenty-seven miles," she says. "I did twenty-seven miles yesterday, and I didn't start hiking until noon."

"Daaaaaaaaaang," I say. I'm so happy to see my friend again. A bit of sun has broken through the fog and begins to warm us. Instigate takes off her shoes and massages her feet. I close my eyes and let my mind wander.

"Should we sit here for a little while, and wait for Ramen?" I say.

"Yeah," says Instigate.

When I open my eyes again Ramen is marching up the mountain, strong under the weight of his giant pack. He has all sorts of stuff in there- stacks of extraneous paper maps from sections we've already finished, a book, a steel pot, a change of clothes he doesn't wear. Although Ramen is younger than me, more muscular than me, and a dude, I still hike faster than he does, because my pack is light and because my feet don't hurt me, like his do. I think about this as I watch him work his way up the switchbacks.

"I had to stop and take a bunch of photos," says Ramen when he reaches us. His big DSLR camera is hanging around his neck on a strap.

A few weeks ago, my friend Kristi took a trip to Goat Rocks with her girlfriend. *I saw some PCT hikers,* she texted me afterward. *They were practically running.*

Now the fog is burning off and we're hiking along the ridgeline way on top of the world, 360 degrees of mountains breaking away like waves and the frozen sorcerer's castle of Mt. Rainier to the north and I am trying to live up to that text message. I am running on the downhills towards the twisted spine of the "knife edge", moving my trekking poles like ski poles scrambling over the rocks feeling like I'm flying in an airplane, the earth a convoluted thing and here I am looking down on it, great stacks of rocks reaching towards the sky, light up above and shadow down below.

We stop on the knife edge and I put trail mix into my mouth, drink the last of my water, watch the wind beat the gnarled trees. We hike on and I finally crash next to a little stream in a sun-drenched meadow, lie down face down on my sleeping pad and say-

"I just need to lie here for a few minutes." My hiking partners oblige and when at last we move on we drop down in elevation, into the shadowed forest. I'm hungry and tired and to keep up morale Instigate and I joke about putting on elk costumes and running in circles in front of the bow hunters we've been seeing on the trail, saying *oh no oh no oh no oh no!* Ramen doesn't understand why this is funny but Instigate and I can't stop laughing, from humor or weariness or both. At dusk we reach a campsite in a dull clearing, a few off-season mosquitoes bumping around in the air. I explain to Instigate that I have no food and she generously shares her chickpea dinner and stale trail mix with me, saying that she has plenty. This officially bonds us for life, as sharing your food with another thru-hiker is one of the most symbolically generous things you can possibly do, ever, in the history of everything. We heat up the chickpeas in Ramen's pot, taking off the foil lid too soon and poking at them, impatient. While I'm brushing my teeth after dinner, Ramen kneels next to me and rubs his head against me like a cat. I crawl into his tent at dark and unroll my sleeping pad next to his, fluff out my sleeping bag. I unsnap it into "quilt mode" and once we're making out I pull it over us.

"We should try and sleep tonight," says Ramen.

"I think since you can't fuck me," I say, "you try and fuck my face with your face."

"Yeah," he says.

***

I wake in the morning to the sound of the alarm on Ramen's phone- church

298

bells, like the church bells of St. Josephs, the Catholic church in the little desert town where I went to highschool. Dong, dong, dong, dong. I remember stepping from my grandmother's Oldsmobile that smelled of air conditioner, head staticky from lack of sleep, moving from the bleak sunshine into the dim interior of the church. Standing and sitting, standing and sitting. Compulsively working the pages of the songbooks. Afterward there were donuts in the basement and breakfast with my uncles at the railroad-themed greasy spoon down the street. Huge white platters of food covered in pork gravy, biscuits melting in the middle of it all.

The thought of biscuits shoots me upright in my sleeping bag. I stare at the walls of the tent. White Pass. It's only eleven miles to White Pass, where there's a convenience store. And a resupply box for me. I pick up my Gatorade bottle and take a long drink of water. I know what's in the resupply box, more trail mix and granola, but I don't even care. I'm like a hamster at this point, obediently eating my little hamster food. I suppose a part of me has died. But I ain't mad.

Ramen is awake too, eyes tired and with a wild nest of shiny black hair. Dandruff in his mustache. I can smell the heat of him as he emerges from his sleeping bag, his warm beating heart. We good-naturedly do the morning tent dance, whereby two people navigate in a tent that's built for one. As soon as I'm dressed, I toss my things out the tent door and arrange myself on my sleeping pad on the damp ground to eat my breakfast. Instigate is up as well, chewing on trail food and crinkling plastic bags. After breakfast, I shake my water bottle; empty. I went to bed thirsty. Now I'm extra thirsty, and the next water's not for eight miles. Oh well. Going without; what else is new?

Instigate and I hike together through the warm morning, and I grow thirstier and thirstier as we walk. At some point I find myself fantasizing about diet coke with lime, of all things, which I use to drink in great quantities when I was a teenager and worked in restaurants. At last we reach the flat, mucky lake, and I crouch on its edges to fill up my bottles. There are floaties in the water, and the tiny creatures with their tiny propellers, but my steripen will make short work of them. Or at least of their DNA.

I finish gathering water and Instigate and I take our leave, hiking on drowsily towards the highway. When we finally reach it, that anticlimactic ribbon of asphalt, the sky has clouded over and we walk the last mile along the shoulder in silence, each of us in our own private land of hunger and fatigue. Cars blow by, little blasts of wind from another world; people in parallel realities headed somewhere for some important reason, playing out the dramas of their lives. The gas station/convenience store looms ahead and then it is upon us, benches out front lined with dirty backpacks. We drop our packs on the ground and step inside the little store, setting the bells that hang from the doorhandle to jangling.

Ah, the convenience store. Never in my life, before the PCT, have I studied a convenience store's shelves so closely, never before have I relied on one so heavily for sustenance. The candy bars you don't want to eat, the dusty powerbars, the random selection of chips. The brisk business of cigarettes and energy drinks. A little glass case of chicken strips and stale burritos, if you're lucky.

Today we are lucky. We claim our chicken strips and sit down at the cluster of little round tables with the other hikers, some of whom we know and some new faces- even this late in the game. Egg is here, which is exciting, her resupply box exploded all over her table, fishing out the things she's tired of and offering them to other hikers. I have a fistful of mayonnaise packets and I gleefully mix them with ketchup for my chicken strips, happily doubling the number of calories. A Shakira song comes on the radio in back and Egg turns up the volume and dances around at the back of the store. I wish the other hikers would get up and dance, but I know they won't. We're walkers, not dancers. After Shakira an awful Coldplay song comes on and Egg turns down the volume again, returns to her table to sort her food.

I get a text message from Spark. He's hitched into Packwood, twenty miles away. *I'm eating pizza,* he says. *Where are y'all at?*

We're at White Pass! I text him back. *Come meet us!*

The sun has broken through the clouds, and I unpack my wet things and spread them on the picnic tables outside. There's an inn next to the gas station, and I become fixated on the idea of taking a shower, although I don't know anyone who has a room this early in the morning, and all the hikers from last night have checked out. I wander over to the inn and ask the manager if I can buy a shower, but he says no and I return to my picnic table, where I sort through my boring resupply box. Trailmix, granola, a couple of foil packets of tuna. A bar of halvah and a snickers bar. Emergen-c and caffeinated crystal light powder. I supplement this with

300

tortilla chips and salt and vinegar potato chips from inside the store, and as many mayonnaise packets as I can swipe from the deli without drawing attention. Enough food for a hundred miles? I don't know. I don't care.

I rest my head on the table. I feel tired and my morale is very low.

"Janitor just got a room," says Instigate. Janitor is section hiking southbound; I leap from the table and run to the inn.

"Can I take a shower here?" I ask him. He's just getting settled, taking off his shoes and unpacking his pack. I realize distantly that I am being very obnoxious.

"Yes, yes, sure," he says.

I shut myself in the tiny bathroom and turn the wall heater up as high as it will go. I stare at my face in the mirror- grime on top of sunburn, wild hair. I turn my head back and forth. I look tired at some angles, better at others. In two days I'll be thirty-one. Am I young or old? I don't know.

I wash my clothes while I'm in the shower, scrubbing them with cheap hotel soap, rinsing them, rolling them dry in a hotel towel before putting them back on. Afterward I feel like a new person, and I thank Janitor and walk back to the picnic tables, where some people are packing up to hike out and some are sprawled on the gravel, napping. Spark has arrived and is attempting to stuff a massive burrito into his mouth. He leaves the burrito on the table while he runs into the store and Instigate hides it, which almost leads to a fistfight. Instigate does eventually hand over the burrito and a gentle peace returns to the picnic tables. All I want to do is sleep, or at least space out for a really long time, but it's only two o'clock and napping will not bring Canada any closer. Ramen is the first to really motivate, snapping closed his pack and heaving it onto his back. I am inspired by this and I manage to get my things together and follow him towards the lake behind the store, on a trail which leads back to the PCT. Spark and Instigate are faster than me; I know they'll catch up soon enough.

We're climbing up some steep switchbacks when Ramen says-

"So if you don't believe in god, what do you believe in?"

"Um," I say vaguely, "I believe in everything?"

Somehow, I manage to walk through my fatigue and by late afternoon I'm

301

cruising, mashing up the switchbacks talking a mile a minute and watching the light fade. I try to explain my spirituality to Ramen but I don't really know how, and my efforts just make him smile, like he's laughing at me. I decide to stop talking but it's hard, and I keep trying.

"Trees," I say. "You know, trees. Also parts of Zen Buddhism? Seek the mystery and stuff."

Ramen looks amused.

"I'm not really into centralized patriarchal religions that perpetuate genocide," I say. "I'm deeply spiritual. I don't have to explain my spirituality to you."

Ramen's not even paying attention anymore. He's stopped at a vista point, taking pictures of the boring mountains with his giant DSLR.

"FUCK!" says Ramen. He's beating furiously at his leg. A wasp's nest in the trail, and one of them got him. We both start running, our packs jouncing against our backs. Nothing like a little wasp swarm to get the adrenaline going.

Dusk finds us at a flat campsite next to a little lake and we pitch our tents and crawl inside against the gathering cold. I eat my sad trailmix dinner and think of Spark and Instigate. I had hoped that they would catch us tonight but they haven't, and my heart aches for the cat pack. For their reckless, freewheeling humor, their good-natured stoicism. Tomorrow, then. Most likely I will see them tomorrow? Canada is only 350 miles away but I can't think about that right now. It starts to sprinkle as I sit in my tent and I string up the little cuben fiber "door." The sound of the rain grows louder, but it's not too cold so I don't mind. I brush my teeth and snuggle down in my sleeping quilt, letting the water lull me to sleep.

***

It rains all night and I sleep/wake sleep/wake to bursts of lightning, the water pounding the forest. I manage to stay warm and dry in my magic tent, which is made of butterfly wings. Ramen wakes me at six, with a proposition; there's a side trail that drops four thousand feet down the mountain to a place called The Grove of the Patriarchs, wherein thousand year-old redcedars and massive, monolithic doug-firs can be seen. I love

302

me some old growth, so I say *why not?* After The Grove of the Patriarchs, we'll take another trail that loops back to the PCT. Our side trip will add an extra fourteen miles. The only drawback is that Spark and Instigate will likely pass us while we're down below, and then we'll have to catch them.

I tear the top from a packet of caffeinated crystal light and dump it into my filthy Gatorade bottle. We're going to have to hike fast, and I need to get pumped. Outside the rain has stopped and the world is bathed in fog; we climb uphill through the misty trees for eight miles to the trail junction and then stand, eating snacks from the pockets of our hipbelts, looking at the trail that cuts away down the mountain.

"Should we do this?" says Ramen.

"Yeah," I say.

My stomach fills with nervous excitement. We're going to *leave the PCT.* We're about to hike on *another trail.* This feels like a really big deal to me. My feet and heart, and this point, have become attuned to the PCT; to its whims and fancies, its general shape and overall temperament, and to the subtle trail of electrons left by the hundreds of hikers just ahead of us. I've grown with the PCT, changed with the PCT. For the past four months, I've spent every waking moment nurturing and maintaining my relationship with this eighteen-inch by 2660-mile ribbon of dirt. I am not my own free agent, charging through the wilderness; I am as faithful and obedient as an ant.

But Ramen has maps, so that's cool. He pulls them from his pack; they're printouts from the internet, vague overview maps, and they don't have nearly as much data as I'm used to working with (and the mileages, I think with alarm, are probably wrong!) but we're following a clearly marked trail to a boardwalk-encircled cedar grove next to the highway, so I guess there's not a lot to worry about.

We hike down, down, down and the forest grows slowly more lush; now there is moss, now there are big nurse logs, now the standing doug-firs are larger. I run down the switchbacks, just for fun, my pack bouncing on my back. I want to run all the way to the bottom; I want to arrive among the cedars breathless. I want to drop into the old-growth like a stone into a well. When at last we reach the highway, my feet are sore and I feel the beginnings of a new blister; going downhill can be rough.

"And tomorrow we climb back up," says Ramen, ominously.

We take a lunch break next to a frothing river whose name I do not remember. The cedar grove is only two miles away but sometimes you put off eating for a long time and then your low blood sugar stops you in your tracks, forcing you to eat right where you are. I fill my bottles in the river and eat my pathetic lunch, staring morosely into my food bag. Ramen dumps his food bag into the dirt and looks at the bright packages, half of them empty.

"I'm not sure I have enough food for this section," he says.

"Yeah," I say. "Join the club. I'm, like, its president."

We glance at each other, sharing looks of concern. So we don't have enough food. What can we do?

Nothing. We can walk.

"The trail provides," I say hopefully. It's a saying you hear a lot, and so far, at least, it's proven to be true. And by that I mean there has been lots, and lots, and lots of trail magic. And plenty of highways where one can hitch to town. And then even more trail magic. But now we're in Washington, with its long stretches of roadless wilderness and remote resupply points, and the odds are not exactly in our favor.

"We'll be fine," I say again.

Ramen frowns as he eats his payday bar. I impulsively pick up one of my snickers bars and toss it into his pile. The other I'm saving for tomorrow, for my birthday.

"Are you sure?" he says, looking at the little candy bar.

"Yeah," I say. "They make me feel kind of awful, anyway." Really I just want him to stop worrying so much. Turn that frown upside down.

Ramen gives me kind of a dark look. I know it's a really big deal, giving another hiker your snickers bar. But these are hard times, in Washington, and hard times call for extreme measures. For morale. And besides, I know that everything will work out. I can't explain how I know it, but I do.

I also know that Ramen needs more calories than I do. His pack is heavy and he has more muscle mass; the more muscle mass you have, the more calories you burn just being alive. His blood sugar crashes before mine does, and he can't go as long without eating. And yet, we're carrying the same amount of food. This is one reason that I think women thrive on the PCT, while many of the men end up sort of… starving. They simply cannot eat enough to replace the calories they're burning. And the logistics of doing so would be ridiculous; we're hiking from sunup to sundown. There is very little time to eat.

Hungry or no, the cedar grove makes us ecstatic. Trees so big they play tricks on your eyes, hulking from the earth like ancient beasts. So old, so full of secrets… I circle one of them, touching its plaited bark. This tree has seen… what? So much. So many things. I lean my body against the tree and smell its non-smell. The smell of the forest, the smell of the world where I live. The ground that I sleep on, the air that I breathe. Trees! The forest! Tell me, I think, moving my fingers over its convoluted surface. I know that the outer part of the tree is dead, that only the core, deep inside, is alive. I also know that the mass of the tree below ground is roughly equal to the mass of the tree aboveground. This patient tree, just standing here through the centuries. Watching without judgment. Watching the megafauna disappear, the Europeans come with their axes, the AmeriCorps volunteers reverently building this boardwalk. This tree and its unconditional love.

We climb over a giant, mossy nurse log to a secret little spot. We take off our shirts and Ramen sits against the log and grabs me from behind, pulling my back against his chest. I turn and see a group of tourists in polar fleece standing on the boardwalk. But they're not looking; they're looking at the trees. I lean back against Ramen in the warm sun and suddenly there is that feeling, that little flash of something. I close my eyes. I can hear Ramen's heart.

"That feeling," I say.

"What?" says Ramen.

But I am still feeling it. Like being outside of my body; like being up in the sky looking down. Like being in the future, outside of time. Like seeing all of this together, complete, exactly the way it is. And knowing it for what it is, in its entirety.

"I don't know how to explain it," I say. Ramen kisses the top of my head. He picks up my hand in his warm hand and laces his fingers through mine.

I keep my eyes closed. The last time I got this feeling, I was cutting carrots for dinner in my little trailer in Portland and I cried for hours. The feeling wouldn't stop moving through me, this knowledge, this retroactive understanding. The intolerable beauty of a single moment. A gift from the universe almost too large to hold.

I hike slowly in the afternoon, feeling stoned. We walk through the forest along the river; we pass so many big, beautiful trees. We cross the river in the evening on a footbridge just as the rain begins to fall. Lightly at first, and then harder. There's no way we're night-hiking in this dark, cold rain to Chinook Pass, where the trail meets back up with the PCT. Dark comes so early now, in September! We pitch Ramen's tent in a loamy little spot next to the water and crawl inside, eat dinner in our sleeping bags listening to the rain pour down.

"I hope our stuff stays dry," I say, as the rain pounds even harder. And harder still, like a monsoon. Lightning flashes, illuminating the tent. I do a poor job of brushing my teeth, line up my water bottles and then lie down to watch the show. The tent flashes again and then thunder cracks, rending the fabric of the sky. My heart is pounding.

"I'm scared," I say to Ramen. It's true. He kisses me. I turn into him and our sleeping pads slide around, pushing my bag against the steamy tent wall. I pull the bag away; I want to maintain some semblance of dryness. If it continues to rain tomorrow, I won't have a chance to dry my bag. It's warm tonight but what if tomorrow night, at higher elevation, we are not as lucky? A wet sleeping bag in a wet tent in the cold. I shudder, and Ramen pulls me closer. I feel a patter on my legs and look down- there is water falling on me. It's begun to rain *inside* the tent.

"Fuck it," I say, and kiss him, as the drumming of the rain grows louder still.

***

All night lightning flashes, water pounds on the tent, water leaks through the tent and onto my bag. I wake, I sleep, I wake, I sleep. I cuddle against Ramen in my damp bag in a state of wake/sleep as the water continues to fall in torrents. Thunder cracks, rattling the ground.

I fall asleep towards morning when the rain becomes more gentle. I wake to Ramen's church bells. It's my birthday.

"Balkan pop music?" says Ramen. He pulls his phone from the pile of dirty clothing next to his head and pokes at it. Oh joyous sounds. We yank open the tent door, look out at the wet, cold forest and laugh. We don't want to get up. We don't want to get up today at all. Not even one little bit. I pull the gallon Ziploc of trailmix from my pack and paw through it. I've eaten almost all of the raisins and prunes, which are my favorite part. Just almonds and coconut now. I take a handful and sort it in my damp palm. Time for hamster breakfast.

I mix caffeinated crystal light into my water while lying on my stomach, my shirt off. Ramen's warm palm is on the small of my back.

"Please don't ever carry a condom," he says. "I'll fall."

"I'll get a condom just in case," I say. "But I won't tell you I have it."

Ramen frowns.

Packing up my wet tent, wet sleeping bag, wet sleeping pad and then putting on my cold, clingy wet rain jacket leaves me in a foul mood. But then as soon as I'm hiking I feel better- we're climbing and the trail is nearly overgrown with fat, ripe blueberries- I'm eating handful after handful and yet there are still infinity of them, brushing up against me as I hike. They're the best blueberries we've had so far on the trail, grown heavy and sweet on this hillside that must get a lot of sun when it's clear.

"It's my birthday!" I shout as I eat the blueberries. "It's my birthday today!" Ramen is behind me, huffing and puffing.

"How do you go so fast uphill?" he says.

"I don't know," I shout, "happiness? And my pack is lighter than yours. And caffeine!"

At last we've gained the four thousand feet we lost when we left the PCT and we reach Chinook pass, where we are unceremoniously deposited back on our home trail. It's cold up here, much colder than down in the valley where we camped, and the world is hung with wet fog. We crouch next to a glassy lake beneath the boughs of a redcedar, eating a little lunch. It has begun to rain again.

"Fuck," I say as I scrape the tuna from the bottom of a foil packet. "I'm cold." I'm shivering, and I can't seem to get warm. All I have is my running shorts, t-shirt, and wet rain jacket, and the temperature feels like it's right around forty degrees. I could put on my down jacket, but then it would get wet while I hike and I wouldn't be able to wear it when I sleep, which is when I really need it. I think of the sodden sleeping bag in my pack, and then look up at the clouds. It doesn't seem like the sun is going to break through today- we're not going to get a chance to dry our stuff. Oh fuck. Oh fuck oh fuck.

"You think we can do thirty miles today?" I ask Ramen.

"I don't know," he says.

I'm looking at the maps on my phone. At thirty miles, there's a shelter with a woodstove. So at thirty miles there is heat, a warm place to sleep, a way to dry our stuff. Salvation. And I'm certain that that's where our friends will be tonight. Spark and Instigate's stuff will have gotten just as wet as ours in the storm and I can almost feel them out there, gunning for the shelter.

And what if we don't make it? Wet sleeping bag, wet tent, wet everything. I'd shiver, if I wasn't already shivering.

I touch the birthday snickers in the pocket of my rain jacket. Not yet, I think. You have to hike so fast.

We're hiking on a ridgeline way up above everything when suddenly Ramen and I have cellphone reception, for the first time in days. We sit on the narrow, rocky trail, our backs against the slope, and poke at our phones. I have birthday voicemails and text messages from friends and it makes me feel a little less lonely, a little less sad and despairing way up on this ridgeline in the North Cascades without even my cat pack here to tell me that they love me. I poke and poke at my phone until it's time to hike again and then I push myself to walk faster, faster still. It's cold and I'm chilled and walking fast is the only way to stay warm. I don't see the forested slopes draped in fog, the little streams trickling across the trail, the bright lichen on the rocks. I want nothing more right now than to be with people that I love, somewhere warm, somewhere far away from all of this.

I eat my birthday snickers in front of a lake. A man and his son are out in the lake in waders, fishing. I give my phone to Ramen so that he can take a picture of me eating my birthday snickers.

"You make this really dumb face in photos," says Ramen, as he hands the phone back to me.

"You're supposed to direct me," I say. "I don't know what face to make."

Everything is wrong today.

I'm ahead of Ramen and it's near dusk when I realize that I can do it. I can hike the thirty miles. I can make it to the shelter. I look at the time on my phone, look at the mileage that's left, remember our late start and average out my pace. I might not get there until ten, but I know I can do it. I know I've got it in me. I look behind me at the trail. Where is Ramen? At this point, I can either haul ass and pull farther ahead or stop and wait for him. I'm pulling a scrap of paper from my little notebook to write him a note telling him I've gone ahead to the shelter when he rounds the bend, charging under his heavy pack, trekking poles sticking into the earth like spears.

"I was just thinking we should camp," he says when he reaches me. "My foot is really bothering me."

"Dang," I say, looking out into the darkening woods. The cabin slips away, and is gone.

In a mile we find what may or may not be a campsite, according to our maps, and stomp around in the dark woods, looking for a spot flat enough for Ramen's tent. There's a little trickle of a stream springing out of the mossy hillside and I gather water there, using the "leaf method" wherein one wedges a leaf into the trickle of water to make a tiny spout to fill one's bottles. As I'm waiting for the bottles to fill, I think of Spark and Instigate in the warm cabin, and maybe Egg and other hikers we've met, laughing and having a good time. I think of showing up, flinging open the wide wooden door, the soft orange light of the woodstove. *Happy birthday!* Everyone would shout, and then I would crawl into a living pile of my friends. I shiver in my wet rain jacket as the water slowly fills my bottle.

And of course, to top it all off, I have hardly any food left. I sit on my wet sleeping pad on the damp ground as Ramen pitches the tent, feeding myself handfuls of trailmix and granola. Tonight I am tired, hungry, and demoralized. I am depleted in every way. And since the sun has set, it's grown colder- the coldest night we've had so far in Washington. After

Ramen is settled I crawl into the tent, roll out my sleeping pad, and put on my down jacket, which is somewhat dry. At least I have that. I lie down and unstuff my wet sleeping quilt, pulling the limp thing over my body. The fabric is clammy and I start to shiver. I close my eyes. Lying on the cold ground under my wet sleeping quilt right at this moment when I'm so cold is one of the most uncomfortable things I've ever experienced, and it rocks some deep part of my psyche. I squeeze my eyes shut tighter. My edge. I have found my hypothermia edge. Ramen tugs up the quilt and pulls my body to his, until we're curled together on his sleeping pad. Still I'm shivering, still I can't get warm. I am lethargic and cold, delirious in a strange way, staring at the tent wall waiting for sleep to come. Sleep won't come and I lie awake, shaking. Some crucial part of me has lost its heat like opening the door on a small, warm room and that part of me just can't seem to get right again. I'm hungry, too. I've been hiking for many months and nearly every day now I am deeply, deeply hungry. I shut my eyes and finally, at some indeterminate hour, I sleep.

***

When I wake I am actually warm. During the night my body heat dried my bag a bit and now, in the morning, the bag is insulating me, holding precious warmth close to my body. This buoys my spirits like nothing else and I unzip the tent to look at the forest. There's fog outside, but no rain. Everything is right in the world again.

"Time to hike," says Ramen, groggily. He takes a swig of water and runs his hands over his face. He looks tired, and I'm sure I do too. Between everything being cold and wet and the constant need to make out, will we ever sleep again?

"Let's get to Canada," I say, "so we can tear each other's hearts out." I put my hand to his chest and make a ripping motion, pretend to heave his heart into the forest.

We reach the Ulrich Shelter just before noon. The small log cabin is empty of people but I put my hand on the woodstove and find that it's still warm. We look at the register that hangs from a string on the wall- Egg, Instigate, Spark, some other hikers. Everyone was here last night. I feel a bit of resentment as I stuff newsprint into the woodstove and criss-cross kindling on top of it. We're drawing close to Canada and every moment is precious.

Soon we'll fall off the end of the trail, out into the Nothing. I may never see these people again. How can I miss even one night with them?

We hang our stuff to dry in the dim warm cabin and sit on the wooden benches along the walls as the fire starts to roar, going through the contents of our packs. I have only a few handfuls of food left, but I try not to think about it. How much farther to Snoqualmie, the closest highway and our next resupply? Forty miles?

There's the sound of voices outside and we step onto the deck to see a group of men in Power Ranger suits, making their way across the meadow. When they reach us I see that they're dirt bikers, not power rangers, and they're carrying cans of cheap beer. They shout hello at us in that open way that people reserve for strangers they meet in the middle of nowhere.

"We're a bachelor party," says the biggest dude, his special suit folded halfway down around his waist. "We're biking from place to place and camping."

We tell them that we're walking to Canada on the PCT.

"You hear about Anish?" says a rangy-looking one with a can of miller high life. "Woman who broke the speed record this year?"

"She broke it by four days!" I say.

"You guys need anything?" says the first man. "Beer?"

"You have any extra food?" say Ramen and I simultaneously. The men look at each other.

"Yeah, we've got some stuff. We've been going into town to eat at night so we don't need a lot of it. Bars, you like bars?"

"Anything," I say. "We will eat anything." The men disappear and I jump up and down on the deck, waving my arms in the air with happiness. Inside the cabin it's finally warm, and my limp rag of a sleeping quilt is beginning to re-puff. My rain jacket is dry, my sleeping pads are dry, my down jacket is dry. Everything is going to be all right.

When the men return they have an armload of brick-sized protein bars in shiny wrappers (SuperMaxExtreme500!), a can of chili, and a foot-long sub. Also caffeinated fruit snacks and a couple of payday bars. We thank

311

them profusely, wonderful dirt-biker angels of the forest, and then spread our feast on the benches in the cabin. I have no can opener so I set the chili on the ground and hack it open with the axe, and then prop it on the woodstove until it bubbles over. I eat a king-size payday bar and one of the superlative whey protein bars, extract the chili from the mangled can with my titanium spoon, and then fall into a sort of daze. I'm warm, dry, and weirdly well fed. I suddenly want to sleep very, very much. Just then, a southbound hiker shows up and tells us that there's trail magic at Tacoma Pass. If we rush, we can get there tonight. So I eat caffeinated fruit snacks instead of napping.

I get a fifth wind in the afternoon and hike fast, chatting with Ramen about spirituality, the nature of the universe, everything. The sun sets and the stars come out- it's a clear, beautiful night, the Milky Way doing its special magic thing, and I have a warm dry sleeping bag to look forward to. I wave my hand across the sky.

"Everything is fine," I say, "forever and ever and ever." We drop down into lush old growth and stop to swing our headlamps around, looking at the monolithic doug-firs. "This forest loves us so much," I say. "can't you feel it?" We reach the gravel road and the trail magic a few hours after dark, a closed-up travel trailer parked behind a pickup, a canvas canopy with camp chairs, a table and a grill, a row of coolers. There's a couple of nice flat spots at the edge of the forest and we set up Ramen's tent in one of them and happily make our little nest, knowing that we'll wake up to hot food and soda and oranges, like Christmas morning. Sleep calls to us, the lullaby of the Milky Way overwhelms us, we are warm and dry and not hungry and finally, we are able to rest.

***

In the morning the trail angel, an older gentleman who goes by the name of Not Phil's Dad, grills us breakfast hotdogs while we sit in the camp furniture in all our layers, eating twizzlers and drinking soda. We ask Not Phil's Dad if he's seen Spark and Instigate and he says they passed through the previous afternoon with plans to camp at the abandoned weather station in seven miles. We eat our hotdogs with gusto and then head out, with a little less gusto. We reach said weather station late in the morning just as the sun busts through the clouds, shining down warm and nice on everything and finally breaking this spell of bad weather we've been having. The weather station is a boarded up house and a bunch of humming, ladder-like structures topped in rusted metal doo-dads that creak eerily in the wind. Other than this eerie creaking, there is no sound. I spread out my sleeping bag to dry in the sun and then roll out my sleeping pad.

"I just need to lie down for a few minutes," I say. I rest my cheek against the dirty foam of my pad and gaze across the gravel lot. I see a handful of butterflies alight on a pile of what looks like dogshit, but must be bear. Or human shit? Ramen sits in the shade, scraping the last of his nutella from the jar. Finally he succumbs as well, propping himself against his pack and nodding off. When I wake, it's afternoon.

"Dang," I say.

Two miles later, we reach more trail magic; a tent made of blue tarps and a grill, where a young couple is making burgers. Their names are Stumbling Norwegian and Honey Bee, and they are thru-hikers from another year. I eat my burger wrapped in lettuce, ketchup and mustard dripping down my wrists. I drink a PBR, too, for some awful reason, and Ramen eats from a giant tub of candy. By the time we leave I'm feeling loopy and strange, sort of alternately hyper and sick to my stomach. I'm stung by a wasp and I run for a little while, suddenly alarmed at the constant buzzing of the forest, and then my stomach lurches and I have to sit. The only thing I can think to do is drink an emergen-c. I mix one into my Gatorade bottle half-full of stream water and sit on a mossy log, watching the patterns of light on the ground. I catch up to Ramen at a flat, marshy lake, and we pitch his tent right next to the trail. Tonight my body feels achy and hot and I'm exhausted, even more so than usual. What's going on with me? I press my fingers to my neck- the glands there are sore and a little swollen. I think of my near-hypothermia a few nights ago. Dang. I can't get sick now.

At least we're only eight miles from Snoqualmie, where we'll catch up to Spark and Instigate. I imagine a hot shower, a warm hotel bed. And I have some long underwear bottoms waiting for me there at the Chevron, with my resupply box. After Snoqualmie I'll have something to wear besides my running shorts and I'll be a little warmer, a little more prepared for fall in the Northern Cascades.

Won't I?

***

I sleep or do not sleep, it is dark, the air is cold and Ramen is there, impossibly alive... for how many more nights? There is just this moment, this foggy night-day, these ghost-vapors and the whites of our eyes, glowing in the tent. I do not need to sleep or rest. I am too alive to rest. I need nothing. My heart is mixed up in my blood, somehow, I can't tell where parts of me end or begin. Soon there is the sound of footsteps and Rabbit Stick, a hiker in his seventies, passes by our tent.

"Time to hike, you're late!" he says.

It's morning.

For the next eight miles I walk in slow motion, putting one foot in front of the other as the sun wobbles higher in the sky. My body is not doing that thing, today, that it has become so good at doing- that converting of glucose into energy for movement. My legs are made of sand; I am propelling myself forward through sheer force of will. I Don't Want to Exercise Today, But I Have to Anyway- Adventures in Thru-Hiking. It's too hot inside my skull.

I feel peaceful about it though. Sort of dreamy. I drag myself along the warm dappled path. Through the shady forest, up and over a series of earthly contortions, and at last out into a broad mown hillside that looks out over the highway, the motel, Snoqualmie Pass.

"That was the longest eight miles of my life," I say.

It's unbearably hot down at the highway and now there is this busy gas station, the cars pulling in and out, other hikers milling around who we haven't seen before but who look a lot like the hikers we already know (extras for the unfolding drama that is our lives?) and inside the gas station racks of things that will make me feel more awful than I already do and everyone's resupply boxes piled together in a great mountain, back behind one of the walk-in coolers. I dig blearily for my box but I'm having trouble processing the long lines of script on the boxes, the sprawling sharpie marks, the identical priority mail cartons.

"I need to sit down for a few minutes," I say to Ramen. I sit at a faded yellow booth in the corner of the Chevron and text Instigate. I learn that she's out to breakfast with Egg and Spark and a friend who hiked the PCT with her father in the seventies. They'll be back shortly- do we want to get a motel room? I do, we do, but what is the order of things here? Water. I follow a series of narrow hallways to a utility sink in the back of the store and fill my Gatorade bottle, staring at the dirty mop and bucket. I drink but my throat is very sore and it's difficult to swallow. Then I tackle the stack of resupply boxes again, lifting each one in turn, moving it to a different corner of the walk-in and restacking it, but still I cannot find the box addressed to me. Where is my long underwear? I find Ramen outside, leaning against a concrete pillar in the shade, holding one of my boxes.

"I found this for you," he says. It's another momentous occasion in the history of hiker generosity, an act for which the PCTA should award a medal, post-trail. "The Priority Mail Heart, for locating another hiker's resupply box in the chaos of the Snoqualmie Chevron walk-in." It's my food box, which is good; I'll have to look again for my long underwear later.

We walk to the Summit Inn, which is right next to the Chevron, and stand in the cool carpeted lobby digging through the row of hiker boxes while the woman at the front desk checks to see if there is a room for us. There is, but first we must listen to a long lecture about room stacking. Apparently last year there were some "naughty hikers" who snuck extra people into their room through the window. But all was seen on the security cameras and the whole gang was busted. We don't want to end up like those naughty hikers, now do we?

I shake my head no but my heart is saying yes.

In the room I immediately peel off my clothes and climb into the shower. I turn on the water and wash everything away- the dirt, the heat, the sun. The fatigue and hunger of this last section and my apprehension for the next. I rinse out my outfit, roll it dry in a towel and when I step out of the shower I am new again, and ready for the next thing. What is the next thing? Food.

We eat teriyaki at the diner attached to the hotel and when we're finished our friends appear, carrying their packs and looking happy and bright. Spark will come back to the room as we're allowed to have three people but Instigate, we decide, will sneak in a bit later. We agree on an exciting series of secret signals and then I shoulder her pack and she heads out to the parking lot to hang with the other hikers at the picnic table, where a bunch of free beer has recently appeared. In the room I collapse on the bed and grill Spark about everything that has happened since I was separated from the cat pack. It turns out that during the monsoon, when Ramen and I were camped down in the grove of the patriarchs, Spark and Instigate were at Chinook Pass, way on top of the mountain. The rain was so heavy that they slept in the pit toilets, which Spark dubs the "Rainier Hostel."

"It wasn't that bad," he says. "We kept the door cracked a little."

The blinds rattle as Instigate climbs in the window. We clap and cheer.

"I had to circle the parking lot a couple times," she says. "The front desk lady came outside to smoke a cigarette."

Soon we are all hungry again and we crowd into the RV/food cart in the Chevron parking lot, where one can buy a bowl of rice and curried meat and shredded cabbage, with pineapple upside-down cake on top, for only five dollars. It is a strangely Portland-like dining experience. The woman who runs the food cart tells us that she lives in a ghost town nearby.

"The town itself is just boarded up buildings," she says. "Except for one guy and his dogs. The rest of us live on the outskirts." Afterward we return to our room, which is by this time already trashed (bottles and plastic bags strewn across the floor, dirty socks, used towels, tents strung over the furniture to dry, linens everywhichway) and collapse on the beds in awkward positions, exhausted. We flip through the TV channels, but each show is more shocking and disorienting than the last. At last there is an old silent film, soft sepia tone and no words, just bland enough for our weary palates. The film involves a train, which is apparently a Real Train, crossing a burning bridge, which is apparently a Real Burning Bridge, just as the burning bridge collapses into a river, which is also real. There is a round woman with a round face in a round dress, and she must sometimes climb into a sack. Other times she is more proactive, tying things to trees and lighting things on fire. There is a man wearing eye liner and he is ridiculously strong and alarmingly quick. His stunts- jumping from car to car on a moving train, flinging railroad ties off of a moving train, tearing up sections of track- are also real. There are heaps of men in varying civil war uniforms that I can't keep straight. We all take turns making the different characters "talk" and, as we can't keep the plot straight anyway, the movie takes on a life of its own. When the movie is over it's late, but we're not sure how late, and I feel weary and feverish but also happy from all the laughing. I lie awake in the hotel bed listening to the others sleep, like I do, and staring at the hexagons of light on the wall. I feel cold so I drag the covers over me but then I'm suddenly hot, and I fling them off. My back hurts and then my calves ache, and then I need a drink of water. I shut my eyes. I can't be sick. I just can't. I can't afford to take a zero tomorrow, in every sense of the word. No money, no food, no time. Only an overwhelming sense of urgency. There are only two more resupplies between here and the border- this is no time to rest. And anyway, what's the worst it could be? The flu?

The flu passes. Right?

***

I wake before dawn flushed with fever and decide that no matter what, I'm going to hike. I lie waiting for the first light of morning to leak around the curtains and then watch this light move across the wall, pushing the shadows around. Ramen stirs and wraps his body around mine. I turn and look at him- his clear green eyes, irises ringed in hazel.

"I feel so sick," I say.

"You're pretty when you're sick," says Ramen.

I can hear the measured breathing of the others, still asleep, tangled in the sheets. All I want to do is hike. It's what my body knows, what I've been doing for the last 2,400 miles. It's all I can remember.

And besides, I'm broke. I can't afford any more hotel rooms. I've been subsisting on trailmix and gingersnap granola since Oregon and walking as fast as I can. It's the tenth of September and Canada is so, so close.

There's a pancake house attached to the Summit Inn and we walk there in our hiking clothes, hair mussed from sleeping, cheeks sunburnt. In the pancake house they're playing Lauren Hill and I order a chili cheeseburger and French fries. Instigate gets a waffle and Spark and Ramen order chicken fried steak and eggs. The food comes out looking lost on huge white platters, lukewarm, and I swear my burger tastes like catfood. I drink a lot of coffee and pound the table with my cutlery.

"Hike, hike, hike," I say.

Our next resupply is at the Dinsmores' in Skykomish, seventy-five miles north across the wild Northern Cascades. Although it's been raining, we're in a good weather window now- it's bright and sunny and warm. Back at

317

the hotel room we repack our bags, sort through our resupply boxes. I am the last one ready to go and I clip my pack closed, lift it onto my back. Ramen stands in the doorway, watching me.

"I feel so confused," he says.

"Why?" I say.

"I really like you," he says.

"I really like you too," I say.

We hike out of Snoqualmie in the afternoon and switchback up the mountain in the heat. I can do this, I think. This is not so bad. Soon the light fades and so does our enthusiasm, and after eight miles we pitch our tents in some invasive grasses next to a lake. There is a barking dog nearby and an unseen ukulele player, strumming on the ridge. I pick ripe huckleberries among the unburied catholes and then lie laughing in the grass with the others, watching the night come on.

"What should I do with my life after the trail?" says Spark, as he scrapes the last of the food from his pot.

"I don't know," I say.

Instigate is eating her curry, Ramen has his noodles. My appetite is suspiciously absent. My throat feels hot and I press a finger to my neck; something is swollen there, some sort of gland. Isn't there something that happens, where a gland or something in your throat swells up? I don't know. I climb into Ramen's tent and burrow down into my sleeping quilt. Ramen is on his stomach beside me, digging through his ditty bag, looking for his contact solution. Ramen is always losing his things and then finally finding them, amid lots of swearing, at the very bottom of his pack. I look at his profile, the way his glossy dark hair falls across his forehead. His youth.

Ramen finds his contact solution, takes out his contacts, pulls me into his arms.

"Only 260 miles left," I say.

"I'm gonna miss you," he says. I can't tell, but I think he's crying. The warmth of his body envelopes me. Out here in the cold wilderness, it's the

318

best feeling I know. The ukulele player keeps strumming, out there in the dark.

***

Morning finds my eyes crusted over, face red and weepy, head stuffed up as though with cotton. Everything hurts everywhere. *Time to hike!* I'm at the back of the group, dragging myself up the switchbacks. The light is too bright today, the heat too hot, the cold too cold. I am alone until I bump up against the tail end of lunchtime, everyone gathered at a bridge. I sit and eat food that tastes like nothing and then watch my friends leave me, one by one. I've got to keep up, I think. There's only so much trail left. If I lose them now, I might not see them again. The thought scrolls through my brain in alarming technicolor. After lunch I stumble when I walk, can't find the right places for my feet. I trip and fall in a shallow river, sit in the hot sun waiting to dry. 2,400 miles and I haven't fallen into a river, until today. I rub my face with my hands. Hike, I think. You've just got to keep up. Then I'm climbing up through a burn, out of water, stopping every two miles to rest my body in the dappled shade. By the time I reach the lake at the top the land is draped in cold shadow, and only Ramen is there. I collapse onto my sleeping pad.

"Do you want me to fill your water bottles?" says Ramen.

"Ok," I say. I am unable to sit up. Morale is in the gutter.

"You look like death," says Ramen.

"Gee, thanks," I say.

Somehow I commit to three more miles and follow Ramen's boot tracks along the ridge to a little shelf overlooking everything where we camp in the dusk and sit, watching the stars come out. Ramen fires up his canister stove for tea and I eat a bar of halvah. The Milky Way unfurls gratuitously and morale shoots back up in a promising way. By our reckoning our friends are camped just a few miles ahead; we should be able to catch them tomorrow. And Skykomish, the next resupply, is just two days away. I press my fingers into my neck, into the weird swollen thing there. What *is* that?

***

In the morning I wake in a strange dream state. I prod my neck again with my fingers. *Tonsillitis.* I suddenly remember that there is such a thing as tonsillitis. A tonsil- that is what that swollen, painful thing is.

"Does tonsillitis go away on its own?" I ask Ramen.

"I don't think so," he says.

"Like, ever?"

"I don't know."

Ramen pulls out his maps; he has real paper maps, the PCT highlighted with green highlighter, whereas I only have an app on my phone. Ramen's maps show side trails, roads, places to bail. Ramen traces his finger along a side trail in five miles that leads to a lake- Waptus Lake. At Waptus Lake, there's a little symbol for a campground. And a road? It looks like there might even be a rudimentary road there.

Washington on the PCT is roadless wilderness area after roadless wilderness area. If I am to bail before the highway in forty miles, then it seems that Waptus Lake is my best bet.

"I guess that's what I'll do," I say, staring at the faint dotted lines on the map. "Try to get to Waptus Lake."

"Do you want to take my map?" Says Ramen.

"No," I say. "No way. Then you won't have a map! You keep it. I have GPS at least."

It's true; my app may not show any other trails besides the PCT but it does show the lake and where I am, a little red dot in a vast topography of mountains and valleys.

Ramen and I stand on the sun-warmed wooden bridge over the Waptus River and say our goodbyes. He'll charge ahead to catch our friends and I'll meet them all at the Dinsmores' in Skykomish after hiking out on this side trail, hitching to a highway somewhere and then somehow scoring some antibiotics. It's a sketchy plan at best, but it's the only one I've got.

"If I don't see you again," says Ramen, with his hand on my chest. But he doesn't say anything.

I watch Ramen walk away into the forest and then lie on my back on the bridge, trying to collect the dregs of my strength. I know I have tonsillitis and it's making me feverish but still, skipping forty miles this late in the trail feels awful. Can't I just hike out, like a regular person? I pull myself up, shoulder my pack and begin to walk. After only a few minutes I'm leaning against a tree, blinking and disoriented. *No,* says a little part of me. *You have to get out.*

I miss the trail to Waptus Lake. Being upright is difficult, walking is difficult, paying attention to my surroundings is difficult. The path is bright and dusty, the trees tangled and unrevealing, and there are no other hikers anywhere. After another mile there is a little wooden sign, nailed to a tree. *Waptus Lake,* with an arrow. A different side trail, but the same destination? After 2,400 miles of hiking I understand the arbitrary nature of trail signage, the foolishness of navigating without a map. But my weary fever delirium alternates with a flushed, high feeling in which I feel that I can do anything.

Here goes nothing, I think, as I turn down this mysterious side trail.

After a short distance the trail reaches the Waptus River, but the footbridge is washed out. A paper detour sign is stapled to a tree, pointing upriver. I walk upriver to a shallow spot and rock-hop across as best I can, but on the other side the trail goes both directions, and I'm unsure of which fork to take. I look at the GPS on my phone; there's the red dot that is me, and there is the lake. I turn left, and follow the trail away from the river and into the forest. It cuts uphill and then splits, rejoining itself a moment later. It branches once and then branches again. *Waptus Pass,* says a sign. I don't know what that means but it sounds ominous, so I choose the other trail. There's another fork and both options are going the wrong direction, away from the lake. A little while later the trail splits again, mysteriously. I feel a bit like Alice in Wonderland and I keep checking my phone, making sure the water is still nearby. At last, I break through the trees at a sandy campsite and there is the lake, long and wild and aquamarine. I am at the far edge of the water and as far as I can tell, the trail ends right here. There is no sign of a campground, a road, or any human habitation at all.

"Hello?" I call, across the lake. It is flat and still and sun-drenched and the mountains rise up around it on all sides.

Hello, hello, hello, echoes the lake back at me.

I am suddenly overcome with fatigue and I spread my sleeping pad out in the shade and curl up on my side, bag of trailmix in front of me. I want to sleep but my head feels confused. My sense of urgency is fighting with my weary body. *You've got to hike!* Says one part of me. *Get out of here! Today you can walk, but tomorrow you may not be able to!*

No, says another part of me. *Sleep. Sleep right here, as long as you need to. You've got enough food and you're near water. Just try to sleep it off.*

I look at the bag of trailmix and feel my stomach turn over. It's true, I do have enough food for a few extra days, but only because I haven't been eating any. And anyway this isn't the flu. It's tonsillitis. It's not going to go away on its own.

I stand up, roll up my sleeping pad, and try to think. There *was* a little symbol for a campground at Waptus Lake. And there *was* a dotted line for a road. I look out at the long, narrow lake. Judging from its size on my phone's topo map, I'd say it's about a mile and a half from one end to the other. There's no trail, but what if I just bushwhack around it? What if the campground and the dirt road are on the other end of the lake, hidden out of sight? Sure, I could turn around and hike back to the PCT and walk the last 40 miles to the highway over the course of several days, but what if the only thing between me and some antibiotics is a little bushwhacking? How hard could it be?

Some part of me knows that I am not making the best navigational choices, but the other part of me doesn't care.

Fuck yeah, says the manic part of my fever brain. *Bushwhacking whoooooo!*

Devil's club. Thorny salmonberry. Big fallen doug-firs. I pick my way through the sloping forest at the edge of the water, attempting to intuit a path through the madness. Everywhere is dense understory and huge, mossy blowdowns; nowhere is straightforward and flat. *Just don't break your leg,* I say aloud as I pull myself up onto a massive nurse log and walk the length of it before hopping down again into a tangle of vine maple. *Don't break your leg.* It's hard to focus with my fever-brain and I find myself stopping often and staring out at the leafy forest, momentarily confused. Where the devil's club is too dense I walk in the water at the

322

edge of the lake, stepping carefully over submerged logs and sometimes sinking deep into the mud, the water up to the crotch of my running shorts. Don't fall in, I think. Don't fall in with your pack on. Then it's back to the forest, pushing my way through the tangled plants, moving with excruciating slowness. At one point I check my GPS and see that I'm halfway around the lake. I've been bushwhacking for two hours and haven't seen a single sign of human life, save for a piece of faded microtrash on the water's edge. I sit down on a log, exhausted, and drink from my dirty Gatorade bottle. I'm weak from hunger and fatigue and my bare legs are covered in scratches. I feel suddenly, irrevocably alone and all at once I start to sob, loud and hoarse like a wounded bear. Panic percolates up through my body. *I'm lost,* I say to the silent forest. *I'm lost I'm lost I'm lost.*

But I'm not lost. If I keep bushwhacking I'll reach the other side of the lake, and from there I can climb straight up the forested hillside, back to the PCT. I will have made a big, senseless loop, but I'll be back on the PCT. I'm not lost at all.

Focus, Carrot, I say to myself, wiping the snot from my face with the back of my hand. *Let's say you're not bushwhacking. Let's say you're walking calmly around the edge of a lake. No big deal. I mean, animals do this shit all the time.*

I resume my slow progress around the lake, repeating *animals do this shit all the time, animals do this shit all the time.* I count my blessings- I'm not injured, I've got plenty of daylight, and it's not even raining. I may be deep in a tangled forest far from anyone and anything I know, burning up with fever and weak with fatigue, but at least my pack is light and I've got trailmix to keep me from starvation.

By the time I reach the other end of the lake I'm feeling stoked and just a little proud of myself, which is good because I am suddenly faced with a riparian zone so mucky and convoluted that I have to admit to myself that the local animals do not, most likely, come this way.

Wide streambeds of deep mud, crowded with fallen logs. Alder as impenetrable as a brick wall. Marsh. I pick my way forward and back, forward and back. Dead-ending at open water, turning around. Trying another way. Forcing my way through vine maple, plants slapping me in the face, thorns scratching up my legs. How do they even build trails? I think, as I work my way towards the forested slope on the other side of the

323

lake. How do they even do anything? The surface of the earth is so convoluted, so crowded with strong, willful, living things. I splash my way across a channel of the Waptus River and through some tall grass, stumbling into the flat places where the animals lie. It's quiet here, at the other end of the lake, and almost uncomfortably wild. I am certain now that there is no campground, and no road. I stop wondering how I could've read the map so wrong and focus on pushing forward, towards the slope that tilts up towards the PCT. At last, the chaotic riparian zone is behind me and I break into open forest and clamber my way up, hand over hand in the swordfern. Up, up, up, straight up to what I know waits for me. And then there is a break in the trees, a bit of flattened earth just out of reach, and then I am standing on the trail and the trail is there beneath me, that familiar ribbon of dirt, my home. That gentle dusty path, that superhighway through the tangled wilderness. My whole world, eighteen inches by 2,660 miles long.

I'm at a campsite next to a sparkling stream, five miles before the trail junction where I left the PCT. I sit on a sun-baked log next to a fire ring and stare at the afternoon light, which puddles companionably on the ground.

I have never felt so safe.

I sit for a long time, staring out at the forest and then I walk to the cold stream and take off all my clothes and dunk my body in the water, splashing away the dust and the fever sweat. I dry myself with my damp t-shirt, put on my long underwear bottoms (which I finally found at the Chevron in Snoqualmie just before leaving) and down jacket and set up my tent on the soft, loamy ground. At six p.m. I crawl into my tent and pull my sleeping quilt up to my chin, curling my body into a warm little ball inside the downy cloud. I do some housekeeping in my head. How far did I hike today? Fifteen miles, eight of them off the PCT? How much of that was bushwhacking? And I'll have to redo those five PCT miles, since I headed the opposite direction around the lake, making a giant circle. That leaves thirty-seven miles until the highway. I can hear the water tumbling gently in the stream, the warm evening wind moving in the trees. I try not to think of my friends, who are more than a day ahead of me now. Who I may never see again. I try not to dwell on the feeling of black loneliness that lies in the pit of my stomach.

***

I wake at midnight in a panic. *Hike! Hike! Hike!* screams my restless fever brain. *You have to get up and hike!* Outside my tent the forest is absolute blackness; there isn't even any moon. *Hike! Hike! Hike!* screams my brain again. I am completely drenched in sweat; my sleeping clothes are shellacked to my body. I pull them off and lie naked in the tent; I can't believe how hot I am. I feel as though I'm suffocating. *Hike!* Screams my brain. *Thirty-seven miles! If you start right now you can make it! Don't let your friends get too far ahead!* I think of Ramen, Instigate, Spark. *If you don't catch up now you'll be alone forever! No one will wait for you! You'll have to walk the rest of the way to Canada alone! Alone! Completely alone! Completely and irrevocably alone!!*

I look at the time on my phone- it's two a.m. But wasn't it just midnight? I feel so confused. I wipe at my face; my hairline is wet with sweat.

Just stay in the tent, Carrot, says a small, reasonable part of me. *Just stay. Inside. The tent.*

I listen to this small part of me and lie sprawled on my damp sleeping pad, staring out into the darkness. Demons, fears, anxieties swirl around me, moving in and out of cognitive focus, taunting me and then disappearing, like smoke. What if I never catch my friends, my dear trail family, the people I've hiked with for the last two thousand miles? What if I do have to hike the rest of the way to Canada alone? What is the black, desperate loneliness, this precipice of isolation over whose edge I'm gasping? I can't remember the last time I've felt this awful, this scared, this anxious.

I fall asleep at an indeterminate hour and when I wake the forest is light again, soft sunshine moving on the ground. I pack my things away as fast as I can, tear down the tent. I feel awful, but energized- *thirty-seven miles, thirty-seven miles.* It's seven a.m. I switch into zombie hiker mode and march, putting one foot in front of the other. I pass Giggles and Sundog, two other hikers.

"Are you ok?" they ask me.

"Yeah," I say. "I just have to get to the highway."

Giggles frowns.

"Are you sure? Are you sure you're ok?"

"Yeah," I say. "I just have to hike."

I drag myself ten miles uphill in the heat and then the bottom falls out of my center. I'm hungry and I try to eat my trailmix but it tastes awful. Low moment, I think. I am having a low moment right now. I don't want to walk. I don't want to walk right now. That's basically the sum of it. I'm not having any fun right now, out here doing this fun thing that I do. I'm not having fun and yet, there is no way to be magically whisked off the trail. There is no "stop" button. There is no "Just kidding, I don't actually want to be here in this reality right now, can I go back out the wardrobe into the other reality again. The reality that includes urgent care clinics and excludes forced exercise. The sedentary reality with an abundance of fresh foods and, oh my god can you imagine it, chairs." I close my eyes and think these thoughts but when I open my eyes all I see are my own two feet and the dusty trail. The part of me that is pissed about all my suffering just sort of gives up then. That part of me just sort of dies. Is this sad? I can't tell. What's left behind is a numb emptiness, a sound like radio static.

The only way out is thru, I think.

In the afternoon I get my period. Of course. Luckily my body recognizes that I'm basically dying so it's a barely-period, a sort of nod to the practice of having a menstrual cycle. I have nothing for it so I cut up a pair of old long underwear that Egg gave me in Snoqualmie. I'm amazed that even with the obsessively light way that I pack I can still find something to turn into menstrual pads. But the truth is that you can bleed on anything. Like you could probably bleed on moss. Or on the ground. I'm feral, I think. I need nothing.

I hike down through an eerie glacial valley, a sort of cleft in the mountains, mushrooms popping from the duff and water trickling underneath everything. Dark falls and I keep hiking, switchbacking up the mountain, feeling peaceful. At eight o'clock I've gone twenty-five miles and I reach a small campsite on top of the world, ridges rolling away in all directions, the last of the orange flame-light disappearing behind the mountains. Mt. Baker in the distance, the glint of a fire lookout. The stars come on one by one and I sit on the cold ground and look up at the sky, mesmerized. All mine, I think. Usually I get service on ridges like this but the battery in my phone is dead, so I can't check it for messages. I can't check to see if my friends have texted me, if they're waiting for me. If there's anyone else left in the world besides myself.

I wake before six and practically jump from my sleeping quilt. It's only twelve miles to the highway. I stuff my things away in the still-dark, clip my pack on as the sky transitions to morning. I am running down the switchbacks, too impatient to eat breakfast, too impatient to drink water. The sun comes out full-force but I am too impatient to put on sunscreen. Just gotta get there, just gotta get there. My stomach is wild with butterflies. I begin to see day hikers and my heart jumps in my chest, like when you're at sea and there are birds and you know you're nearing land.

"How far are we from the highway?" I ask the day hikers. My phone is dead so I can't check my maps. The day hikers answer in riddles.

"The highway is just up there," says a young man with a pitbull.

"You'll turn a corner and you'll see it," says an elderly woman gathering boletes.

Time becomes elastic and the minutes stretch into infinity. Around each corner, hope springs up and then is dashed like a wave against the rocks. By the time I reach the trailhead parkinglot I am empty. A man sees me with my pack and hails me over. He's grilling hotdogs behind his pickup truck, and introduces himself as TenSpeed.

"You want a beer?" he says.

"No thank you," I say. "Do you have any water?"

TenSpeed opens a cooler full of ice and fishes out a bottle of water. There's broccoli in the cooler too, and a sack of carrots. He's set up here for thru-hikers- he's been ferrying them to the Dinsmores'. I grab a couple of carrots and sit in one of the camp chairs, gnawing on them. I drink the water and then another. The highway is just behind us, traffic buzzing past. People are coming and going all around.

TenSpeed is telling a story about the CDT and idly poking at the hotdogs with a pronged utensil.

"Can I charge my phone in your truck?" I ask him. I smile as though I've been listening to his story. TenSpeed looks puzzled. Was that the wrong response? Maybe it was a sad story. "I'm trying to get in touch with my friends," I say. "To see if they waited for me at the Dinsmores'. I fell behind."

"Of course," he says. He's still looking at me funny. I plug my phone into the USB port in his pickup and try to turn it on but I can't; it needs to charge for a minute. I look in the truck's rearview mirror- my face is simultaneously ashen and sunburnt and very dirty. I sit in the camp chair again and drink some more water. TenSpeed is telling another story.

"Do you know if there's an urgent care around here?" I ask him. "I'd look it up on my phone but it's dead. I think I have tonsillitis? When you have tonsillitis you take antibiotics, right?"

"There's an urgent care in Everett," says TenSpeed, his brow furrowed. "I can take you there."

I don't know how far Everett is. I can't conceptualize distance right now. How far are we from anything? I check my phone again. It bursts into life and begins to bleep.

Where are you honey bun? says a text from Instigate. There's one from Spark too- *Dear Shnookums, where are thou?* There's a voicemail from Ramen; his voice is impossibly low.

"I'm hiking out," he says. "I'll, ah, see you down the trail."

That's it? I think. Just an awkward voicemail? That's all I get?

I call Instigate's phone and she picks up; she and Spark are at the library in Skykomish, checking their email on the computers. Dilly-dallying around.

"I have to go find antibiotics," I say. "I don't know how long that will take. I think I can hike out in the morning?"

"We'll stay another night and wait for you," says Instigate. "Of course we'll wait."

Relief floods into my body and I collapse backward in the truck seat, almost start to cry.

I walk back to the ring of camp chairs behind the truck and look at TenSpeed, turning his hotdogs on the grill.

"I'll give you a ride to urgent care," he says, "I just have to find someone to eat these hotdogs first. I was hoping some more hikers would show up."

"I will eat all of those hotdogs," I say.

And I do.

***

The urgent care in Everett is a grand, white, spotless place and I am ushered into a little room.

"You want an US Weekly?" says the nurse, before she leaves. I flip through the magazine, looking at pictures of Kim Kardashian. What would it be like to be Kim Kardashian? What would that even be like? Eventually the doctor appears and wraps my hand in his warm hand. I talk with him for ten minutes.

"Sounds like tonsillitis," he says, as he writes me a prescription for amoxycillin. My bill is $200.

After urgent care we drive to Rite-Aid so I can fill my prescription. In the car, I learn that Ten-Speed lives on a sailboat in Seattle and works as a plumber. He thru-hikes as many summers as he can. At Rite-Aid I grab stuff off the shelves, almost at random, to supplement my resupply. Salt and vinegar potato chips, tortilla chips, a couple of bars. I wish I had more time to buy food, but I have to get back to the Dinsmores'. There's so much to do before we hike out in the morning. So Rite-Aid resupply, plus what's in my box in Skykomish, will have to do.

At the Dinsmores' I change into loaner clothes, stuff my disgusting hiking clothes in the washer, and take a shower. Instigate and Spark are staying in town tonight at a hotel with some other hikers since they stayed at the Dinsmores' last night but Egg is here, and it is so good to finally, finally see a friend. We explode our things in the big garage-like bunkhouse and sit around, sorting our resupplies and laughing. I took my first dose of antibiotics after leaving Rite-Aid and I might be imagining it, but I think I feel a little better. My morale is up, anyway- I'm here, I'm safe, and Spark, Instigate, and Egg all waited for me. I don't have to hike the rest of the way to Canada alone. I dig through the hiker box, pulling out random bars and odds and ends, things I might want to eat. In my resupply box is the usual- a massive bag of trail mix, a massive bag of granola. A few packets of tuna and a bar of halvah. I show the bag of trailmix to Egg and make vomiting noises.

"You're bringing all that?" she says. "A whole gallon ziploc of trailmix?"

"Yeah," I say. "It's the bulk of my calories."

Egg frowns.

"You should dump half of it into another bag and leave it in the hiker box. Don't bring all that."

"But what will I eat?" I say.

"I've got extra food. I've got so much food. I just bought a whole loaf of bread. If you run out on the trail I can give you some of mine."

I hold the bag in my hands. It *is* a lot of trailmix. And I *haven't* been able to finish it the last couple of sections. In a life or death situation it would save me from starving but the truth is, it's disgusting and I would rather go hungry than eat it. Or carry it. I pull an empty gallon ziploc from my resupply box and dump half the trailmix into it. I'm free, I think.

Someone yells "Dinner!" and we stand outside around the grill, assembling burgers. Mine is a double bunless concoction smothered in barbeque sauce. The sun sets but the evening is warm and I lie in the grass next to the train tracks that run past the Dinsmores' house and text Ramen. A train blows by above me, lights slicing the dark. I'm missing Ramen something fierce, a sort of dull ache in my gut. It hurts that he didn't wait for me, and I can't say I understand it. I want to forgive him, but I just don't understand.

I miss you, I text him. *Wish you were here in the dark with me, listening to the trains.*

There's a guide to the CDT in the bunkhouse and I lie in bed after everyone has fallen asleep, reading it. I'm not even done with this trail yet but I can't wait for the next one. Finally, I put the book down and switch off my headlamp. Washington has been brutal so far, but I would still rather be here than almost anywhere. Thru-hiking feels like life, it feels like being alive.

It feels more real than anything.

***

I wake in the dark, starving. I turn on my phone, cupping my hand over the face to keep the light from waking the others, and look at the time- 2:30

a.m. I press my fingers against my neck; my tonsil is a little less painful than it was yesterday. And I am suddenly so, so hungry.

Stealthily I creep from my bed, extract the jumbo bag of Juanitas tortilla chips from my food bag, crack the big door to the bunkhouse, and ease myself out into the cold night. I sit on the grass below the train tracks, eating tortilla chips and scrolling on my phone. When I look into the bag again half the chips are gone. This bag of tortilla chips was meant to be part of my resupply, and I won't have time to get another one before I hike out tomorrow. But I guess I was hungry; apparently, now that my fever is gone my body is starting to realize how little I've been feeding it. I've literally been starving myself, and I've been hiking twenty-five mile days. I feel deeply, deeply depleted, way down in my bones. I look into the bag of tortilla chips again. Just a few more handfuls, I tell myself, and then I'll put them away.

I sneak back into bed and pull the quilt over my head, try to get myself to sleep. But I feel super awake, all systems go, ready for anything. My body is all sorts of confused. The hunger, the walking, the fever delirium, the excitement and action of being in town. What I really need is rest, but there's no way my brain will give that to me right now. *Canada, Canada, Canada,* says the rhythm of my pounding heart. My calf seizes in a charlie horse and I press my foot against the end of the bed, stretching it out again. I've been getting these cramps every night, as well as at other random times, like when I'm crawling in and out of my tent.

The last hours of the night creep by with excruciating slowness but at last it's light enough to get up and I quietly pack my things away. Soon Egg is up too, happily stuffing away her sleeping bag, and we move our packs outside into the gray dawn. For breakfast I eat a chocolate clif bar I found in the hiker box and then we're off, crossing the street to stand in front of the closed-up little store there, thumbs out trying to hitch a ride back to the trail. There's barely any traffic, just a few sleepy humans headed to their early shifts. I still feel unnaturally pumped, but I know that in a few hours I'll crash. I just hope I can put in a good day's worth of miles before then.

At last Dude in a Pickup Truck, the patron saint of hitchhikers, stops for us and takes us all the way back to the trailhead. Then begins the difficult task of actually hiking, and already my hiking boner is starting to go. I'm just so depleted; I need to rest so bad. But no. There is only time for hiking now. And we're climbing up this morning, to boot- up, up, away from the highway, back up towards the ridge of the Cascades. Egg and I stop to break at a small stream a few miles in and Spark and Instigate appear, trekking poles clacking on the trail. I am incredibly happy to be reunited and suddenly I am overwhelmed with the urgency of it all- the urgency of reaching Canada, the urgency of squeezing all that I can out of these last few days. I feel as though my heart might burst.

The day consists of many small passes and I drag myself up and over each of them, sometimes fast and sometimes slow. My system sputters and then runs smoothly, sputters and runs smoothly, but it never dies. I've walked a fair ways this summer, eaten my share of trail mix, put a lot of miles on this heart of mine. I've just got to make it to the border.

In the evening I catch up with Spark and Instigate at a crowded campsite next to a stream, tents pitched in every little crevice back in the trees. Dark comes alarmingly early now, in mid-September, and I search out a campsite by headlamp, finally finding a triangular spot of bare duff, slightly tilted, that's just big enough for my little tent. In the last few hours the sky has clouded over and just as I'm staking out the guylines it starts to rain. Well, I think, I guess our spell of good weather has officially ended. Then the wind picks up, woo woo woo, and there's a flash of lightning. I crawl into my tent just as the rain begins to really pound, but I'm sheltered by a big nurse log on one side and the boughs of a redcedar overhead, so only a gentle tapping reaches my tent. I am so grateful for this and I curl up in my sleeping bag, feeling safe and warm and good. And, with any luck, I'll even stay dry.

BOOM! goes the sky. Outside the night is impossibly black, the world a mess of dark sky, dark land, dark water, not a shred of light anywhere. I am in a ship; I am at the bottom of the sea.

***

I sleep beautifully there in the dark, stormy forest, sheltered beneath the redcedar, the storm raging all around me. I sleep deeply, I sleep soundly; it's the first good sleep I've had in what feels like weeks, ever since that fateful, hypothermic night of my birthday. Now, at last, I'm not feverish, I'm not starving, I'm not cold or wet. I'm safe on the trail with my friends, on my good hard sleeping pad on the soft loamy ground, way up in the dark mountains far from everything. Finally my body is able to let go.

I wake in the dim, gray morning and eat a little trail mix in my sleeping bag; the bag is damp on account of brushing up against the side of the tent but I figure it'll be dry enough for tonight. The night after that, though, I don't know. If it rains like this every day I won't have a chance to dry it in the sun, and each night the bag will be a little more wet. This section is a hundred miles, or four days. So two more nights in this bag and then Stehekin, our next resupply. I peer out the mesh at the dripping forest. How do people keep their sleeping bags dry in Washington in September? I just don't understand it.

Outside my tent the air is cold and it's drizzling, that light mist that gathers on your face and eyelashes and slowly works its way into every part of your clothing. I open up the trash compactor bag that serves as a pack liner, stuff my things down inside it, and then stretch my pack cover over the outside of my pack. I stock my hipbelt pockets with hamster food and fill my bottles in the stream. I'm wearing just my running shorts, my t-shirt, and my rain jacket. I'm saving my long underwear bottoms and down jacket to sleep in. I pull the hood of my rain jacket up over my head. I wish I had gloves and a hat.

The cold makes me stiff and being stiff makes me slow. I stumble along the trail, which is difficult this section, rocky and narrow as it clings to the mountainside and then up, up, up over gravelly passes draped in fog. Boulders everywhere, downed trees to climb over, slippery mud. It's especially cold on the passes and I hike as fast as I can to stay warm; the water's already wicked its way through my rain jacket and if I stop to rest I may never get warm again. It's forty degrees and I'm soaked to the skin; hypothermia's chasing me like a dog.

To make matters worse, I've already lost Spark and Instigate. Instigate doesn't have a rain jacket at all, just a long-sleeve thermal top and thermal tights; her m.o. in the rain has always been "can't stop hiking or I'll die." And when she wants to hike fast, she flies- she doesn't stop to eat or drink or rest, she just mashes miles. She'll be flying down the trail until camp, wherever that is. And Spark will be with her; he hikes four miles an hour, even in good weather. The only reason we see him at all is because he stops to wait for us, posts up in the shade to read his sci-fi books. But not today.

Today I'm on my own. I'm shaking with hunger and I stop to pull the wet bag of trail mix from my hipbelt, but my hands are too numb to work the zipper. Tears well up in my eyes but I finally get it out, palm some damp trailmix and then stuff the bag back in my pocket, not bothering with the zipper. Another factor I hadn't considered is that when it's cold like this, I need to eat almost constantly, especially in the depleted state I'm in, in order to keep my core warm. At least once every hour. I'm eating my food much faster this section than I'd expected, and yet it barely stokes the fire inside of me. I should've brought more food than usual, but instead I dumped half my trailmix into the hiker box at the Dinsmores'. Why did I do that? Now, I realize, I'll have to ration my food. I'll be hungry until Stehekin. And cold. Very, very cold.

I climb up onto another dreary pass and the wind picks up, blowing the tiny, stinging rain into my face. I haven't drank any water all morning and I stop to fill my bottles at a stream but it's a struggle to get the tops off the bottles with my numb hands, a struggle to use my steripen, a struggle to hold the bottles in order to drink. By the time I'm ready to go again I'm shivering uncontrollably and I start to cry, snot and tears mixing with the cold rain dripping down my face. I try to hike quickly to warm up but I'm stumbling, slipping on the damp rocks, mincing my way down the other side of the pass. At last I drop below treeline and the dim forest blocks the wind, the path is loamy and straight. Finally I am able to hike fast.

In the evening I happen upon a giant encampment in the woods. Tarps, tables, coleman stoves, coolers. Day hikers everywhere, milling around in their bright, new raingear.

"Hullo," says one of them to me. "You a thru-hiker?"

"Yes," I say. "Do you guys have any extra food?"

"No," he says. "We don't." He looks a little exasperated and I realize that I am most likely not the first one to ask him this.

"Have you seen two other thru-hikers?" I say. "A woman with long hair and a guy?"

"We've seen so many," he says. "But the guy had some short facial hair? I think they passed about forty minutes ago. They said they were headed to Fire Creek."

Fire Creek- that's seven more miles. No way in hell I'm camping alone tonight. I check the time on my phone. If I'm fast, I can make it there by nine.

"Thank you," I say. The man gives me a tight little smile, and I realize how I must look- the foolish thru-hiker in running shorts with bare legs, soaked to the bone, hungry and carrying no food.

Going nowhere fast.

Night falls and it's too cloudy for moonlight. I switch on my headlamp but the battery is dying, not that the thing made much light in the first place. Now there's just a dim circle that barely shows the trail. Next time, I tell myself, I'll bring a real headlamp. I list all the things I'd do differently, if I had the chance to do Washington in September again- more layers, synthetic instead of a down jacket, gloves and a hat, a double wall tent. More food. A better headlamp. I'm circling the mountain on a narrow trail, thick wet salmonberry on one side of me and a steep, crumbling dropoff on the other. I remember that I once heard someone refer to the Washington part of the PCT as "the car wash" and now, as broad, dripping salmonberry leaves slap against my torso and bare legs, I think I understand why. Now and then the trail is washed out and there are only the footsteps of other hikers to follow across the loose, sloping soil. And in almost every fold of the mountain there is a wide, shallow stream. I pick my way across these streams in the inadequate light from my headlamp, slipping and soaking my feet in the icy water. At one point I see the small, yellow point of another headlamp, far away in another fold of the mountain, and I feel hope break open inside me- Spark and Instigate! But the trail, just at that moment, becomes rocky and uneven and I am forced to hike slower, stepping carefully so as not to fall off the mountain entirely. As the hour grows late I grow colder, and more stumbly, and thirstier, and more hungry. But I can't stop, won't stop and besides, there'd be nowhere to camp if I did. There is only the black, vertical face of the mountain and beyond it the dark, uncaring night.

I am delirious with cold, thirst, and hunger when at last I reach the muddy, trampled campsite beside Fire Creek.

"Carrot?" says Instigate, from inside her tent. "Is that you? You night-hiked so late."

"I didn't want to camp alone," I say.

I wish there was a tent big enough for all of us- a big, square tent filled with pillows and blankets, a hundred thousand blankets, and a king-sized air mattress. And a dog? A big fluffy dog. A pile of dogs. But there is not and I am faced with setting up my wet tent in this wet clearing in the rain, in the last faint light of my headlamp. But first I must unclip my hip belt, and my hands are so numb that this is proving impossible to do. I start to cry a little bit, panic percolating up through me, and at last I unclip the belt by pushing the sides of my hands into it. I sling off my wet, rain-soaked pack, pull out my water bottle and take a long drink of water, gripping the bottle with two palms like a three-year-old. Then, of course, there are the myriad little manipulations of setting up my tent and I suffer through each of them, coming up with clever ways to do everything with just the palms of my hands. This, I think with sudden alarm, is what it would be like to not have any fingers. When at last my tent is up, my ground sheet and sleeping pad are spread out, I am in my tent and the zipper has been wrestled nearly, but not all the way, closed, I am faced with one last humiliation; I cannot pull up my long underwear. I sit there for a little while, bare ass on the sleeping pad, long underwear up to my knees, trying to calm my breathing. I realize, then, that I am no longer cold. I don't know why this is but I figure it probably has something to do with hypothermia, and I hook my hands under the waistband of my long underwear and lie on my back, flopping like a fish until I've finally gotten them up. Then I pull my sleeping bag from my pack and realize, with horror, that it's completely soaked.

There must've been a tear in my trash bag pack liner. I pull the liner out to examine it and discover that this is true.

Well, I think. What can you do. I lie back and pull the bag over me- at least it's not quite as wet as it was on my birthday. Still, I can't get warm enough to sleep and I simply lie there, curled in a ball on my side, shivering and miserable, waiting for whatever the next thing might be. And I've lost enough weight at this point in the trail that my hipbones ache when I lie down, even when I'm on my back.

It doesn't get much worse than this, I think. But there's nothing, nothing, nothing to be done.

***

I wake in the morning to Scrub, another hiker, standing outside my tent. He's wearing long hiking pants and a rain jacket and he's soaked from head to toe.

"Good morning," he says.

"Beautiful day for a hike," I say. It is, of course, thirty-five degrees and raining.

I sit in my bag and eat trail mix, trying to motivate to get up and hike. I feel flushed and haggard and my sleeping bag is just about as wet as when I went to bed; my body heat dried it some but then it was up against the wall of my tent, so it wicked up all that condensation. And if it rains all day again today? And stays this cold? I try not to think about tonight. Instead, I do an honest inventory of my food- a little trail mix, a little granola, a couple of bars. A packet of tuna. It's fifty miles until Stehekin and I realize with alarm that I've got maybe fifteen hundred calories in my filthy yellow food bag. I'm burning four thousand calories a day right now, hiking twenty-five mile days over steep, rocky passes in the freezing rain. And I started out this section depleted, with a hunger I could feel down in my bones. Fifty miles on fifteen hundred calories. At the beginning of the trail, maybe I could do it. But I've been hiking for almost five months and my body is done with this. Done with all of it.

Not that I have a choice.

I'm slow and stumbly again this morning, going over the high cold passes. Wet through my rain jacket, cold mist numbing my hands until they ache. Can't drink water because my fingers don't work, won't let myself eat until I'm dizzy from hunger. Trying to ration the last of my food. I break into tears again on a bleak, windswept pass, rocky trail slick with water, cold weather tumbling over the mountaintops. Dreary valleys rolling away, somber forests in the bottomlands. Winter so close I can smell it. And here I am way up high, a little mammal, so unprepared. I don't want to die of exposure, I think. I really, really don't.

Warm layers. And more food. My god, why didn't I bring those things.

What is that saying? Never a mistake, always a lesson.

I switchback down the mountain into the mossy forest where the air is a little more still and a little warmer and the boughs of the trees protect me from rain. At a trail junction I find Spark and Instigate, sitting in the duff- Spark is running out of food, too, although he does have an infinite amount of chocolate whey protein, which he mixes with creek water and instant coffee.

"Caffeine is an appetite suppressant," he says, offering me his gatorade bottle of the stuff.

I take a big swig- it is delicious.

Now, at this junction, we must make a decision. The trail to the right is the "old PCT," and the trail to the left is the "new PCT." Apparently, the "old PCT" has a washed-out bridge and that is why the "new PCT" exists. But we are curious creatures and we say, what the hell. Let's take the old PCT.

Trail not maintained! says a sign, ominously. But what does that even mean?

We switchback down, down, down the mountain and at the bottom we find ourselves in an old growth forest of magical proportions. Big standing trees, big downed trees, everything strung all over with usnea and padded with several inches of moss. The understory is a riot of ferns and tumbled logs and the trail grows narrower and more feral until we are following it the way one would follow a wild animal, or maybe a rabbit with a stopwatch who is very, very late. None of the huge trees that have fallen across the trail in the last however many years have been removed and so we follow the trail as it leads us up onto them, across their broad surfaces and down, off the other side, back onto the spongy forest floor. We cross many downed trees this way and the forest grows still lusher, and more deep, and more enchanted, until we can almost feel it there around us, a living, breathing entity.

"This is, like, the best part of the whole PCT," I say.

"I was just gonna say that," says Spark.

We decide that next year, we'll set up trail magic deep in this forest, on the "old PCT." We'll affix a packet of instant mashed potatoes to a bit of fishing line and leave it at the trail junction, and in this way we'll lure thru-hikers to our trail magic. At the trail magic we'll have mushrooms and beer, but no food. Instigate, Spark and I will be dressed as Abe Lincoln, a bear, and a race car driver, respectively, and we'll stay in character the entire time. We'll have a whistling pet marmot that acts as our oracle, a china tea set, a chest of dressup clothes, and candle lanterns strung in the trees. When evening comes, we'll invite the hikers to sleep in hollowed-out logs under piles of ratted quilts. We also decide that this forest is carnivorous, and that is the real reason the PCT was rerouted. And if one were to take mushrooms here, one would inevitably hear the forest whispering... *sleeeeeeeeep, why don't you lie down in this nice bed of moss and sleeeeeeeeeeeeep.* And then one would lie down, be overcome with weariness, and sleep for a hundred years, wherein the moss would DIGEST ONE.

I'm having so much fun, I forget how hungry I am. The company of dear hiking friends has turned tragedy into hilarity. If only I were as fast as they are, so I could walk with them all day, and they wouldn't have to wait for me. It's hard being the slowest one in the group.

By and by, we reach a wall of impenetrable alder where the trail just sort of... ends. Beyond the alder is the great, rushing Suiattle River, churning and frothing its way west. We pick our way through the alder and find ourselves on a sandy river bank, no bridge in sight. We know that the PCT is on the other side of this mess of silty water, but how to reach it? This is by far the deepest, fastest, and most roiling river we've had to ford; in fact, this being a low snow year in the Sierras, this is the first dangerous body of water we've had to cross at all. We walk up and down the sandy bank, feeling like stranded kittens, wondering what to do. I pull up the legs of my long underwear and take a few steps out into the calmest part of the river, steeling myself with my trekking poles. It feels as though the earth is about to be ripped out from under me, and I carefully wrestle my way back to the bank.

We walk up the bank a ways, now and then crossing another set of footprints. I wonder who it could be? Ramen is ahead of us, although I'm not sure how far. Someone else was here recently, wandering up and down this bank, looking for a way across.

There is a narrow log, slick and wet, that spans the water, the top end on our side and the base high up on the other bank. The log is too slippery and steeply angled to walk across but maybe, if we can grip it somehow, we can climb up it? Spark has a brilliant holding-on-with-your-legs tilted-log-scooting technique and he demonstrates, after which Instigate and I follow suit. Then we are safely on the other side, pumped about our adventure. We scramble up the forested slope, back to the PCT.

Dark falls and I am hungry and my headlamp is dying but I know that I am gonna make it. I stop to eat a bit of my food and fall behind the others and then I am hiking alone, crossing streams in the moonlight and feeling for the trail when my headlamp finally grows too dim to actually see. I am dehydrated and shaky from hunger and cold but I just have to get to the campsite, which will be next to a stream a few miles ahead, and then I can finally rest.

From a distance, the hiker tents glow like magical orbs among the narrow trunks of the trees. One, two, three, four tents- so many hikers here! I feel my way from one glowing-orb tent to the next, peering at the bright faces swathed in raingear, cooking dinner over the blue flames of pop-can stoves. Scrub, Hermes and Lotus, Instigate and Spark. Instigate is the bright point of her headlamp, bobbing around in the darkness.

"We got you a present," she says. "He's camped next to the stream."

My heart falls into my stomach. The solitude of these past few nights, the loneliness. Everything I wanted since Ramen left me on that wooden footbridge, back when I was feverish. And then, he didn't wait for me. He wasn't in Skykomish. He wasn't at the Dinsmores'. He was one of the first ones to hike out that morning; he left me nothing but a perfunctory voicemail.

I know I shouldn't go to his tent. I should set up right here, next to my friends who care about me. In the morning Ramen will be gone, and that will be that. I most likely won't see him again until the border. And by then, it will be too late.

His headlamp is glowing through the wall of his tent.

"Meow?"

He sticks his head out the vestibule.

"I've been draggin' ass," he says. "My foot's been killing me."

I sit on the ground outside his tent, drop my pack, fish around in my food bag for my dinner- a handful of granola. All of my clothing is wet but I am numb-cold, that place beyond cold.

"Yeah," I say. "I'm surprised we caught you."

My fingers don't work so I palm the granola and stuff it in my face, rinse it down with a little creek water. It's the last of my water, but I don't want to go poking around in the dark to find the stream to get more. I'm so, so cold. Better to be dehydrated.

340

"You take the old PCT?" I say.

"Yeah," says Ramen.

"It was really cool," I say.

"Yeah. You know when I hiked out of Skykomish, I was one of the first ones, and I thought everyone would catch me. But they didn't. They didn't catch me until tonight. It's been fucking lonely."

"You didn't wait for me," I say. "I was so sick. And when I got to Skykomish, you weren't there."

"I'm sorry," says Ramen. "I should've waited."

"If you would've known how sick I was, would you have waited?"

"Yes," says Ramen. "I would've waited."

I look out at the dark forest, the mist accumulating on every living thing, dripping onto the ground.

"You want to share a tent?"

"You can sleep in here if you want."

"Yeah but do you *want* to share a tent?"

"Yeah."

I unfurl my sleeping pad in Ramen's tent and crawl inside. I feel enormously weak. I unstuff my wet sleeping bag and Ramen pulls me to him, presses my body against the heat of his body.

"You're so thin." He's pushing his fingers into my spine. "You're so, so thin. But you're still my Carrot."

"This is the warmest I've been in days," I say.

"I'm so sorry I left you," he says. "Will you forgive me?"

"Yes," I say, although I'm not sure. I don't understand it; I don't understand any of it. All of this- love, humans, the world.

"You make me wish I wasn't a Catholic," he says. "I want you to know that."

341

The rain falls down outside, taps on the outside of the tent. In this moment it is everything, it is the whole universe, spinning away into forever. But still I don't understand it. What is fleeting, and what is mine to keep? Already I feel a great sorrow building inside me, a knowing feeling of loss. How did I get here, and how will I find my bearings once all of this is gone?

***

I wake at six in the dim, rainy forest but instead of getting up to hike, as I had planned to do, I drift in and out of sleep/lie in Ramen's arms listening to the rain fall. I feel weak from hunger and very, very thirsty.

It is the last day of the section, and we are twenty-three long miles from the dirt road that leads into Stehekin, our final resupply before the border. Stehekin is a tiny Washington town that can only be reached by plane, boat, or, in our case, by the shuttle that will pick us up at the PCT. I know nothing of Stehekin except that it's not really big enough to call a town, it sits on a lake, and there is a bakery there. Not just any bakery, but a bakery of legends. A bakery that Martha Stewart visited, a bakery that appeared in Sunset magazine. A bakery I've been hearing about for the last two thousand miles.

I poke around in my food bag; I've got around five hundred calories left. Five hundred calories for twenty-three miles, dear lord. Ramen is in no better shape; he's got a couple of candy bars and that's it. And a tiny, single-serving packet of instant oatmeal. I sit on the ground outside Ramen's tent, holding a handful of granola in my damp palm. My breakfast, and I can't eat again until I'm dizzy, passing-out dizzy. It's the only way I'll make it to Stehekin. I fill my bottles in the stream, squatting in the rain on the slick streambank, and make myself drink a liter. Hunger makes a person more vulnerable to hypothermia, as does dehydration. It'd be stupid not to hydrate now, at least, when I can still use my hands.

Spark and Instigate are already gone, but Scrub is just packing up.

"You guys got much food left?" he says.

"Fuck no," I say. "We're basically out."

"Me too," he says.

So we're in the same boat, this section, all of us. Racing, racing, racing to get to the bakery.

Ramen and I start the day off right by climbing up onto a cold, windy pass, where tiny rain drenches our clothing and needles us in the face. Luckily, I can wear my down jacket under my rain jacket today since it's the last day of the section and I won't need it to sleep tonight. It'll take at least a couple of hours for the thing to get soaked through. By then, hopefully, we'll be down at lower elevation in the forest, safe from the freezing, windblown rain. And in the meantime I'll be warm.

It's nice to hike over the pass in the awful, miserable rain with Ramen. It's nice to crouch with Ramen next to a frigid stream, eating my last handful of trailmix while I wait for my water purifier to work. It's nice to walk behind him while I secretly cry inside my rain jacket hood, my cold, stiff hands almost too painful to bear. It's nice to not be alone while I hike through the North Cascades in late September without the proper gear- while I attempt, for another day, to avoid death by hypothermia.

I am dizzy and so I eat a little. I am dizzy and so I eat a little. And then, my food is gone.

Dear reader, let me tell you a story about hunger. Many people in the western world never experience true hunger. I don't mean hungry-for-a-few-hours hunger but scary, bone deep, days-on-end hunger. It's a terrifying, raw ache that is completely outside the experience of almost everyone I know. We live in a world that overflows with cheap, if poisonous, food; it is not uncommon to be chronically ill on account of what you eat, but it is relatively rare to be hungry.

I grew up hungry. My mother is schizophrenic, and while welfare paid for our rent while she was raising my brother and me, she wasn't able to keep up with the paperwork for our foodstamps (most of the time she couldn't write her name, or communicate, or make coherent sentences) and so we lost our food benefits when I was very young. In winter, the free school lunch was often the only meal I had and in the summer I would go days, sometimes, without eating. Literally without eating. Searching the sidewalks for bits of food, opening the cupboards again and again, hoping food would somehow magically appear. Hunger was a ghost, hunger was my constant companion, hunger was a dog that chased me. I shoplifted, I ate from dumpsters, I stole money from my mother's purse, the little bit of cash we got each month that she used to buy cigarettes. I was weak, I couldn't focus at school, I was constantly sick. When I did eat it was fast food, cans from the food bank, those little pies that come in wax paper. But mostly, I was hungry.

I still have issues with food. There always has to *be* food, and I need to somehow be in *control* of my food. I obsess about what I'm eating, which has manifested itself in different ways throughout my life. And I eat faster than anyone I know.

But mostly, being this hungry is deeply, deeply triggering for me.

We're off the pass now and the trail is flat and loamy and winds pleasantly through a forest of doug-firs. It's a gentle downhill the rest of the way to the shuttle. There's a river alongside the trail, should I be thirsty, and my hands are thawed enough to use. There's even a little bit of sun, peaking through the clouds; it seems as though this storm has blown over; we'll have a sunny zero day in Stehekin.

I am, of course, in my own personal hell.

My food is gone. I'm dizzy with hunger and fatigue. I'm stumbling. Forward motion is difficult. And at the same time, every single one of the emergency alarms in my body is going off at full blast. Panic, fear, panic, fear, percolating up through me, washing over me and away. Ghosts, unresolved sadnesses, feelings of abandonment. I am stumbling through a fog of pure, distilled terror. The sediment at the bottom of my gas tank. My childhood.

I have not felt this hungry since I was a kid. There are triggers inside of me, which I imagine as light switches, a whole bank of them, and they are being flipped, one after the other after the other, by frantic, invisible hands. Tiny hands; the hands of tiny me. Tiny, helpless me. All alone and so, so hungry.

I sit down in the pine needles on the edge of the trail. I'm not sure if I can go on. I don't know how long I'm there and then Ramen appears.

"What happened to you?" he says. "I was waiting up ahead and you never showed up." I asked him to wait for me, today, because I was afraid I'd black out, and for morale. *I don't want to hike alone today,* I said.

"I'm sorry," I say. "I just had to sit down." Ramen plops down next to me and extracts the last bit of food from his pack, the packet of raw instant oatmeal, which he cheerfully eats. Scrub appears, and unwraps his last bar. We laugh about our food situation, and then we keep hiking; there is nothing else to do. I think about tonight, about the bakery; I try to ignore the screaming inside my body. I use the trick I used on the long, waterless descent from the San Jacintos- *This day is already over. Your whole life is already over. You're in Stehekin, you're well fed, you're done with the trail; whatever comes after that has already happened. All of the future and all of the past together, on the head of a pin. There is no such thing as time.* This makes me feel better for a moment but then the demons are back, haunting me. Sadness, abandonment, panic and the deepest, blackest despair. I'm six years old; I'm eating spoonfuls of sugar and biting into raw potatoes. Malnourishment wakes me and my brother in the night, a hollow sensation in our stomachs and aching cramps in our legs; it's dark, we're on a bare mattress on the ground and the apartment is filled with cigarette smoke, and there isn't any food. Our mother is awake in the other room, crouched over the radio, talking to herself. She smells of burned rubber and sickness. She herself subsists on mountain dew and black tea and her clothes hang on her as though they're draped on a skeleton. If we ask her for food she ignores us until she can't anymore, at which point she beats us.

I'm a little kid. No, I'm hiking in the forest. I feel strange in my head, in my stomach, in my bones. I keep falling behind, even though we're going downhill and even though I'm usually faster than Ramen. When we're only four miles from the trailhead I tell him to go on ahead.

"I'll make it," I say. "I'll see you there."

And I will make it. I know this, I really know this. But right now, on the trail, hiking is one of the hardest things I've ever done.

Oh Washington, I think. Oh Washington in September. With the wrong gear and no food!

Everything *has* already happened. I reach the dirt road in the wilderness, I walk down it; I realize I'm going the wrong way, I turn around. I reach the little cabin where the park ranger lives, flower boxes under the windows and woodsmoke puffing merrily from the stovepipe. Out front is the bench to catch the shuttle to Stehekin and Ramen and Scrub are there, tents spread out in the grass to dry. We still have a half hour until the bus comes.

I sit on the bench next to Ramen and shiver. I've been so hungry I almost forgot how cold I was. I dig around in my food bag to see if I have one last emergen-C and there, hidden beneath the crumpled trash, is an intact Luna bar.

"Look at this!" I say, holding it up in the light. The foil catches the sun and shines. It is peppermint stick flavor. I break the bar in half and give half to Ramen and we sit chewing the hunk of sugary joy, morale momentarily buoyed.

The shuttle arrives just as the sun sinks behind the mountains and I sit in my seat on the warm bus, shivering, as we bounce along the rutted road toward the lake. The road is only five miles long; it goes out to the PCT but no farther. There are cars in Stehekin, but people only use them to drive back and forth between their houses and the village. Many of the cars do not have license plates; they are not registered.

"Tell you what," says the driver. I try to focus on what he's saying, but it's difficult. "I've got to refuel this bus. The refueling station is at the landfill. You want to go to the landfill? There's an area where people dump things they don't want. You can go through it, maybe find something you like."

"Heck yes," we say in unison. That is exactly what we want to do.

At the dump there is a big aluminum bunker with an American flag, and inside the bunker are piles of discarded household goods. And a rack of clothing- I look through the clothing and there, waiting for me, is the giant wool peacoat of my dreams. I put it on and know that as long as I am in Stehekin and as long as I have this magic peacoat, I will never be cold again.

We reach the village right at dusk. There is one building which houses the hotel, restaurant, and store, and down the dirt road a few paces is the tiny post office. The bakery is, of course, closed. On the outskirts of the village we'd spied Spark and Instigate, setting up their tents in the free campsites next to the road, and we'd waved to them from the shuttle. Spark and Instigate caught the earlier bus and so had time to dry their things in the sun, while our sleeping bags and tents are still soaked. There's no way I'm camping tonight.

We inquire about a room for the three of us in the little store and while we're waiting for information I eat an icecream snickers bar, which makes my blood sugar do crazy, crazy things. I also buy a bag of salt and vinegar chips. At last the clerk tells us that there is a room available, that it is the size of a closet, and that it costs one hundred and fifty dollars. I feel numb as I hand over my debit card; I will be very, very poor after this. But the thought of a warm bed with blankets and some sort of bangin' wall heater makes me feel almost drunk.

In the restaurant we ask our server what is the very largest thing on the menu and he tells us it is the nachos. I ask him *how big* and he holds his arms out like he's gripping a tree. I order the nachos and a dish of buffalo wings. Scrub orders a plate of pasta and a quesadilla. Ramen orders chicken alfredo.

I surreptitiously eat salt and vinegar chips while we wait for our food. I feel ridiculous in my giant peacoat; the other diners are all older patrons on holiday, well groomed in expensive Pendleton, talking in low voices over glasses of wine. A hiker we don't know sits at a table in the corner, but he looks like he's been here a few days. Or maybe he's not a thru-hiker. He writes calmly in his journal, DSLR resting next to his beerglass. His Patagonia is freshly laundered. Now and then, he regales the table next to him with some tale or other from his travels.

The nachos are bigger than my wildest dreams. A platter of chips buried under melted cheddar and mounded with hot refried beans, salsa, guacamole, olives. I eat every single one of them along with my buffalo wings and then I lick the tabasco from my fingers. Ramen and Scrub finish their food and then we sit for a moment and stare, bewildered. We are finally, finally no longer hungry. We hadn't expected this moment to ever arrive and now that it has, we aren't quite sure what to do.

In our tiny hotel room we explode our packs everywhere and soon every surface is covered with trash and tiny, dirty pieces of gear that look like trash. The wall heater is busted or the pilot's not lit and I pull off the front panel and tamper with it until it kicks on. Then I turn it up all the way, transforming our room into a sauna. We take turns in the shower and when it's my turn I stand under the hot water for a long time, waiting for it to reach into my bones. It almost, but not quite, does. Scrub gets one bed and Ramen and I get the other. Then the lamps are off and everything is still, window cracked to let out some of the suffocating heat.

Ramen touches the whole length of my body, beneath the blankets, gently, quietly. He strokes my skin with his rough fingertips. I am shaking. We don't kiss; we don't want to make any sound that would wake Scrub. Desire wracks us in waves; we let it move through us and leave us shaking, we wait for the next wave to arrive. We are standing at the edge of the ocean; we are standing at the end of the world. It is just the two of us, at both the beginning and end of time. We should be sleeping, we are exhausted in so many ways, but instead we are doing this; because what else is there, anyway? At the end of time, when all is said and done, when everything is accounted for- what else even is there?

"I love you," says Ramen, quietly.

"What?" I say.

"I really, really like you," he says.

"I love you too," I say.

***

In the morning we check out and pile our bags in the sun on the warm deck. I wander down the road to the post office, which is a tiny room on the ground floor of a larger building. Inside the entryway is a shelf of battered pulp fiction and on the floor, a box of cucumbers from someone's garden. In the post office a grumpy man with an eye patch shuffles around, moving things here and there. There are packages stacked to the ceiling and Pink Floyd is playing on the stereo.

I pick up my resupply box and grab a few cucumbers on the way out. The cucumbers are knobby and delicious and I eat one as I walk back to the lodge/restaurant/store. The sun has just come up over the mountains and Lake Chelan glitters in the morning light. At the dock a group of visitors stands with their luggage, waiting for a boat.

For breakfast I buy another bag of salt and vinegar chips and sit on the deck, eating them. Ramen buys a half gallon of milk and, somewhat repulsively, drinks the entire thing. The bus pulls up and rumbles to a stop; it is the shuttle to the bakery, which is two miles down the road in the direction of the PCT. We gleefully pile on and watch the lake roll past as we edge our way out of the village. On the side of the road that is not the lake, there are farms.

"There's a farm where you can buy goat cheese, lettuce, stuff like that," says the shuttle driver. "I can drop you there if you want."

But we only want the bakery.

The Stehekin Pastry Company is a quaint little building tucked in the trees alongside the dirt road. There is a bit of lawn out front rife with children, and elderly tourists sit at a picnic table in the sun, methodically dismantling sticky buns. Inside we find Spark, Instigate, Lotus, and Hermes, drinking coffee in big wooden chairs and reading such exotic publications as The New York Times and Oprah Magazine. The inside of the bakery is warm and smells of cinnamon; the walls are made of golden wood, as are the long tables washed in morning light. Behind the glass pastry cases beautiful young people pull trays of cookies and fresh sticky buns from gleaming ovens, their cheeks flushed with heat. Other young people slice steaming pizzas on the wooden butcher block and set the pizzas on silver stands atop the pastry cases. Inside the pastry cases there is of course every imaginable baked good, overly large, piping hot and dripping with a generous amount of icing. There are also wicker baskets, piled high with loaves of bread. And everyone is smiling.

"I am going to pretend I can digest gluten," I say.

"Yeah," say Lotus, as she bites into a brownie. "I'm pretending I'm not vegan."

Ramen and I buy an entire blackberry pie, take it to a table by the big sunny windows that look out at the road, and eat it in five minutes.

"You guys PCT hikers?" says one of the bakers when we bring the silver pie pan back to the front and drop it in the bus tub.

"Yeah," I say. "How could you tell?" I then buy two slices of sausage pizza and two gluten-free chocolate cookies from the day-old shelf. I eat the pizza slowly, while staring out the window and flipping through a copy of US Weekly. So much has happened to Kim Kardashian since I've been on the trail- how will I ever catch up? When the pizza is gone, I descend into a glutenfog in which I am stupid and dull and can only sit back and watch while the hikers around me converse, laughing now and then at the funny things that they say. I ask Instigate and Spark what their plans are for the day and they say that they're staying right here, in these chairs in the bakery, for the foreseeable future. Spark is on his fifth cup of coffee.

I want to get back to the village to set up my things to dry in the sun and Ramen wants to go to a talk at the ranger station/visitor's center so we pile onto the shuttle and I watch, drowsily, as the lake goes by again. The ranger's station sits on a little hill with a view of the lake and inside there are bird books, plant books, books about every single thing. There is also a huge relief map of the area, under glass, which has the PCT on it, so that's cool. I look up a couple of kinds of lichen in the plant books, walk back out into the sun, and immediately forget their names. At the other end of the village are the free campsites, sort of carved out of the hill, tucked into the trees. Each one has a picnic table, a nice flat spot for a tent, and there is a shitter with running water. I wander amongst them, looking for the best one. I feel, almost certainly, as though I am in heaven. I pick a site that's private but still has some sun and spread out my things, and then roll out my sleeping pad and lie down for a nap. Across the road there is the gentle lapping of the lake at the lakeshore, and now and then there is the shuttle. There is no other sound.

I wake a little later and sit on my pad. I eat one of the chocolate cookies. It is afternoon. By and by Ramen, Spark, and Instigate appear and claim tent sites. Egg rolls into town with another big group of hikers; she was a day behind us this section. In the evening we all make our way over the restaurant and I order my second round of nachos. Someone has a giant bottle of whiskey and I hide it in my peacoat, surreptitiously taking swigs when the servers aren't looking. It comes out that Scrub and I both know all the words to *That Summer* by Garth Brooks, and we sing it together, serenading the long table of hikers. The group of us is in our own magical thru-hiker bubble; the rest of the restaurant is oblivious to our belligerent fun.

I went to work for her that summer
A teenage kid so far from home
She was a lonely widow woman
Hell-bent to make it on her own
We were a thousand miles from nowhere
Wheat fields as far as I could see
Both needing something from each other
Not knowing yet what that might be

'Til she came to me one evening
Hot cup of coffee and a smile
In a dress that I was certain
She hadn't worn in quite a while

350

There was a difference in her laughter
There was a softness in her eyes
And on the air there was a hunger
Even a boy could recognize

After eating we all reconvene at one of the picnic tables in the camping area. Scrub has a bunch of pop music and contemporary country on his phone and he plays DJ, picking songs that we all know the words to and we sing along, loudly, in the dark. The whiskey bottle goes round until it is empty and we laugh and sing until there is no more laughing and singing left inside of us, and we're spent. Then I crawl into Ramen's tent in the cold clear night and snuggle down in my warm, dry sleeping bag on the good hard ground. The moon is full and presently it rises, shining like a silver spotlight on the fabric of the tent.

***

In the morning I take an awful, awful shit on account of all the gluten I ate the day before and for this reason I am five minutes late for the shuttle back to the trailhead. I run down the dirt road towards the lodge where the bus is and clamber aboard; everyone else is already seated, waiting for me. There are some elderly tourists on one side of the bus and they glare at me as I add my pack to the mountain of packs on the floor behind the driver. I have made the tourists five minutes late for their breakfast at the bakery and they are very, very angry.

I look out the window at the lake as we bump along the dirt road one last time. It's a clear morning and the sunlight is working its way down the mountain towards the water. There are only eighty more trail miles to the Canadian border, plus another eight from there to the Manning Park Lodge- in four days we'll be finished. And it's not even raining! I'm still exhausted- it's a deep sort of exhaustion that I won't even begin to shake, I imagine, until the trail is over. But at least it's not raining. At least I have that.

The bakery is thick with yellow sunbeams and the smell of ginger cookies. Spark is already there, drinking coffee and reading sci-fi; he woke at six, before anyone else, and walked to the bakery in the first light. I stand in line with the other hikers and watch, alarmed, as the baked goods in the glass case disappear. We are all buying big paper sacks of stuff; we all brought too little food in the last section, and so we are supplementing our resupplies for this section with large amounts of baked goods. When I reach the counter the glass case is nearly empty and then, miraculously, it refills. The people behind me breathe a sigh of relief; the great anti-climax of PCT 2013, averted. Hallelujah. I buy a cinnamon roll the size of my face and a bacon cheddar croissant the width of my arm. I sit at a wooden table and tear the cinnamon roll limb from limb and have many, many tiny orgasms until everyone has bought everything in the bakery and it is time to go.

Although I'd planned to save the bacon cheddar croissant for lunch, I pull it from its greasy paper bag and begin to consume it on the bus; flakes of pastry and bits of bacon fall into my lap and after a time my eyes glaze over and I have to put it away. My morning glutenfog, now, is monumental, and when we reach the footbridge that leads to the PCT I stumble from the bus and sort of stand there, trying to figure out what it was that I was supposed to do.

Ah, right. Hike.

The sun is out now, and it is warm. I shed my layers and shoulder my pack, the cinnamon roll and the croissant a mass of glue in my stomach. We're climbing for fourteen miles and I am nothing, this morning, if not slow. Soon nearly everyone has passed me and I plod wearily up the switchbacks, stopping now and then to stare at the vistas and space out. I am, at this point, what Instigate calls "vista'd out-" I barely see the views. In fact, I have grown very, very weary of them. Ridgelines, bah! The convoluted surface of the earth! Light and shadow! I am over all of it. Which is, in a larger context, hilarious.

Around noon I happen upon Instigate and Spark, lying in a patch of sun next to a river. Spark has a pair of binoculars he found on the trail and he lazily glasses the granite mountaintops. I sit on the ground and eat the last of my bacon-cheddar croissant, and this time I'm hungry enough that I hope I'll burn through it before it turns to glue. My metabolism, at this point, is a woodstove with the flue and the draw wide open, burning up glucose faster than I can possibly shovel it in. Burn, burn, burn, I think as I eat the last pieces of the thick, greasy pastry.

My glutenfog breaks in the afternoon and I hike happily to Rainy Pass, where we all gather for dinner next to the pit toilets. I force-feed myself trailmix and try and convince Spark and Instigate to get jobs in some remote place with me next winter, so that we can all stick together.

"Come on," I say. "It will be so fun!"

Just then a group of day-hikers appears, dudes in their thirties with sturdy, brightly-colored clothing.

"You guys thru-hikers?" they say. "You want any beer?"

The men give us four beers, a bag of homemade beef jerky, and a bladder of wine. Ramen and I hand our beers off to Instigate and Spark, along with the wine, and the four of us split the jerky. Dusk is gathering in the forest and we've still got a ways to go before the campsite just below the pass; Ramen and I pack up and set out, leaving Instigate and Spark on the grassy knoll where they are engaged in the serious business of getting drunk.

As we climb up towards the pass, subalpine larch appears for the first time on the PCT, and Ramen grows very excited. It's a pale-green, wispy conifer that loses its needles in the fall and it is Ramen's favorite tree, besides western redcedar. We are both feeling happy and fast and we reach the campsite below the pass a little after dark and swing our headlamps around, looking for a place to camp. It seems as though everyone else who left Stehekin when we did is here, and their tents glow warmly in the little hollows beneath the trees. The sky is clouded over in a foreboding way and Ramen and I stumble around in the dark for a while, looking for a spot big enough for the both of us that won't turn into a mudhole in a storm. At last we find a cozy, slightly lumpy spot and throw up our shelter. It's cold now and I shiver as I crawl into Ramen's tent. As soon as we're both in the tent a little warmth gathers around us and I zip up the door, sealing it inside.

"No making out," I say. "We have to sleep tonight."

"Ok," says Ramen. "Maybe just a little making out."

"Just a little making out," I say. "Then sleep."

At some point in the night we hear Spark and Instigate stumble into camp and set up their tents in the rain, which has just begun to fall. I am so tired and so weary but I am also nearly insane with the desire to put Ramen's cock inside me, to fuck, to finish once and for all this thing we start, over and over and over and then abandon right at the edge of... what. Right at the edge of what.

"You're making me insane," I say when we're drifting off, pressed close together in the chasm between our sleeping pads, the inside of the tent dripping with condensation from our breath. But Ramen is already asleep.

***

I wake up early to the cold rain pattering on my tent and procrastinate getting up for a while which means that, once again, I am the last out of camp. Thankfully, Ramen is slow this morning too and we hike together up onto the freezing, windy, rain-soaked pass where I get to experience, once again, near-hypothermia and hands so numb I can't use them for anything. Just hike fast, I think. Hike fast and you won't die. I shut my brain off and do just that, let the suffering just sort of break over me in waves. I am miserable, though, and unable to take care of my basic needs like drinking water and eating snacks, and so when we finally stop for lunch in a chilly clearing in the dim forest I am very hungry and very thirsty and my morale is very low. There is a trapezoid of sun on the loamy forest floor and we chase it around but it's no use; it's too small to give us any warmth. At last we hike on at which point we discover, just around a bend, an entire grassy hillside baking in the sun. We collapse, grateful, onto the grass, and spread our wet tents and sleeping bags across it. At least my bag will be dry tonight, I think, as I lie facedown in the grass and let the magic fireball in the sky warm my tired bones. At least I have that.

"I fucking love you," says Ramen, next to me. Suddenly I feel like I'm going to cry.

It's afternoon by the time we hike on. Now that it's not raining I can wear my down jacket, and I'm toasty warm as we climb up onto another pass. The fog on this pass has been swept away and we can see the granite mountains opposite us, rising up towards the clouds like wizards' castles.

Our goal today is to make it to Hart's Pass, where we have heard word that there may or may not be bacon cheeseburgers. If there is ever a section of the PCT that needs trail magic, it is this one; my reserves are gone, as are the reserves of my friends. We are running on the dregs of the dregs of fumes; we are running on air. On stubborn promises, or because we have forgotten what it feels like to quit. We are walking out of habit; it is amazing that we are still walking at all.

The rain begins again in earnest. The trail is washed out, here and there, in small sections, and we pick our way across the steep, crumbled earth. We pass a couple leading a string of pack-llamas, on a section of trail that clings precariously to the mountainside. The llamas are drenched and smell like wool. They stick their necks out sideways to see us around the humans, who are on foot; the animals carry big saddlebags and are strapped all over with camp chairs, water jugs, things like that.

Dusk falls and then darkness and so we night-hike, following the narrow trail as it rings the mountain. Below us are the dark folds of a valley; now and then we see a little yellow light, flickering in the darkness, and our hearts jump. And then we're on the other side of the mountain and the light is gone, and so we are completely alone, in this great lonely wilderness, this expansive blackness that holds nothing and everything all at once. I feel as though I am suspended in space, out here in this timeless forest. This place that has no time.

We round a bend and hear voices and then we are stumbling into the trail magic at an indeterminate hour; there is a warm flickering fire and our friends sitting around it on stumps. Someone is playing the guitar and there is a picnic table, spread all over with an incredible amount of food. This epic, wonderful trail magic is courtesy of Slayer and Slick B, both from Bellingham. We sit around the fire with our faces half-in and half-out of the light and eat the sausages that our host cooks for us. I also eat an apple, an orange, some chocolate, and part of a sleeve of oreo cookies. Our friends are staring sleepily into the fire and then, one by one, they drift off to their tents, which are set up beneath the trees. Ramen and I find a spot and I sit on a damp log and chatter helpfully as he pitches the tent and then we climb inside of it, curl together against the damp.

Onwards, I think. To whatever the future might hold.

***

I wake in the morning to freezing rain and lie in the tent, kissing Ramen and making time disappear until it's nearly nine and we can't wait around any longer or all our friends will go away, the pancakes and trail magic will be gone, we'll never make it to Canada and we'll die here, together, in this tent, crushed by the oncoming winter.

Would that be so bad?

I grumpily pull on my wet rain jacket, tear down the tent, and walk to the trail magic to find that our friends are still here, wearing all of their rain gear, huddled around a smoky fire eating pancakes off of paper plates. I down four or five sausages, a cup of coffee, and many handfuls of chocolate covered almonds. We throw our plates in the fire and watch them burst into flames and then curl away into nothing, one by one, and then it's well into the morning and there's only one thing left to do.

It's September 21st. Winter is coming to the North Cascades, and we're only thirty-eight miles from Manning Park. This trail's not gonna walk itself.

Ramen and I are, once again, the last ones to leave camp. So we'll be holding up the rear, per usual. I remember back before the rain, when I was fast. When I was full of light and life and joy and the sunbeams puddled warmly on the loamy trail.

Not in this cold rain, not anymore.

It's another day of foggy, freezing passes in my wet rainjacket and wet t-shirt, stumbling and muscling through to some other thing, trusting. Not even trusting, not even thinking, just walking. There's no fire left inside of me, no hope, no special magic happy feeling. No endorphins. I'm just walking over this windy freezing pass, suffering, and I'll be walking here forever. Tomorrow I'll be here, in a hundred years I'll be here. Sniffling to myself, wiping my snot on the back of my cold numb fist. Me and this pass, forever and ever and ever.

And tonight we camp way up high, below another pass. And my sleeping bag is soaked from the rain last night, from the walls of the tent, from condensation.

I try not to think about it.

Just before dusk we find a flat, mossy campsite a half-mile below our last pass and Ramen pitches his tent close to a couple of twisted yellow cedars, in hopes of sheltering us from the storm. We figure that Instigate and Spark and the others are booking it just ahead of us, trying to make it to the lake in five miles. I walk back down the mountain to where a little rivulet crosses the trail and dip my bottles in the icy water. When I stand up again, the rain has turned to snow.

"Snow!" I say to Ramen, with joy. "Snow!" I say to Ramen, with trepidation.

It's our last night on the trail and I am almost too weary to eat. But I am so, so hungry and I know that if I don't eat I'll wake up in the night, stomach clawing at itself, and I won't be able to get back to sleep. I'm dehydrated too, and I make myself drink an icy half-liter of water, and I pour the rest into my peanut butter jar of instant split pea soup, which I'd been too cold to assemble an hour ago so that it would be ready to eat by now. Still, within minutes the soup has magically transformed from green dust into edible split-pea icecream, and I lie on my stomach in my sleeping bag, spooning this repulsive but calorie-containing substance into my mouth. Ramen cooks double-dinner on his canister stove in the vestibule, filling the tent with condensation. The condensation gathers into droplets and runs down the walls of the tent onto my bag, but no matter- the thing is already soaked.

After dinner I am very cold and very grumpy and I wrap myself up like a burrito in my sleeping quilt, pull it up over my face and cinch it shut with just a little hole for my nose to stick out. If I lie just so, I think, and am very, very still, I might be able to trap a little bit of heat, even though my bag is wet and I am wet and the tent is wet and outside is wet and the rain has just turned to snow. I don't know why I think this but I cling to it, convinced that if I just don't move *at all* I'll be able to get warm. Ramen is trying to talk to me, but I don't feel like talking. He touches my shoulder through the quilt.

"Carrot?" he says. "Carrot?"

"I'm really cold," I say.

Ramen holds a book up to the hole in my sleeping bag.

"Do you want me to tell you about the book I've been reading? I'm almost at the end."

"Ok," I say.

"It'll make us feel better," he says.

"Ok."

It's a book about an arctic expedition back in the eighteen-hundreds, a bunch of white men on a ship cutting their way through the pack ice, looking for whales to slaughter. Ramen proceeds to recite the entire plot to me, from the first chapter. On the trail we call this "second-hand books-" there is also "second-hand Youtube", wherein you recite and/or act out the plot of a Youtube video, and "second-hand movie," wherein you recite the entire plot of a movie. In Ramen's book, the men on the ship are stranded when the hull smashes into some pack ice and becomes stuck. The men end up dismantling the ship and burning the entire thing for fuel, after which they set out in kayaks, paddling from ice floe to ice floe. They are stranded for a very long time, eating sea mammals and barely making it, and in the end only a few members of the party survive. By the time Ramen has finished reading I've managed to accumulate a bit of small, pathetic warmth in my sleeping bag, and I *do* feel a little better.

"Hey," says Ramen. "It's our last night on the trail."

"Yeah," I say.

I know this should be an auspicious evening but I am too grumpy, probably hypothermic, and I can't think reasonably. Finally I lift the edge of the quilt, feel the cold air rush in and, shivering, envelope Ramen like an octopus.

"I'm so cold," I say. Ramen wraps his arms around me more tightly but I can feel the cold coming in, into all the little gaps. He kisses me, his mouth like garlic noodles and something else, a sort of hunger. A part of me melts and warms my blood and suddenly I am elastic again, I am liquid, I am warm. And yet I am raw, I am empty, I am at the end of everything. I pull my sleeping bag around me and turn away to try and sleep. Outside the snow continues to fall and the world has gone very still. There is nothing, anymore, to do but try and sleep.

***

I wake at first light to discover that I'm being crushed. Crushed by the sides of the tent, crushed against Ramen who is crushed against me. My legs are trapped in the low end of the tent and I kick at the sides, knocking the heavy snow onto the ground. Ramen is kicking too and then we're punching at the walls of the tent, freeing ourselves. We were both cold nearly all night, only able to sleep for a couple of hours. A couple of sweet, blissful hours where there was enough snow piled on the tent to insulate us, but not so much that the tent collapsed onto us entirely.

Snow has drifted into the vestibule of the tent and at the bottom of the snow pile there is just one little hole, letting in light and air. Snow has come into the tent; there is snow on my pack and snow in my shoes. Ramen's dinner from last night, still in its pot, is covered in snow. I unzip the vestibule and push it open to discover that gray, rainy Washington has been replaced in the night with a wonderland of soft, unblemished white. Snow is mounded beautifully on the boughs of the trees and piled a foot deep on the ground. Snow still falls, drifting from the clouds like confetti. Ramen and I exclaim. Everything is still and pure, the world gone gentle while we slept.

And I have no idea how we're going to find the trail.

"GPS," I say a few minutes later, when I'm sitting on my sleeping pad outside Ramen's tent, trying to make myself eat a little breakfast. "We can use the GPS on my phone. That will tell us where the trail is."

"Thank god for that," says Ramen, who is putting on every piece of clothing in his pack.

I return to the task of trying to eat, palming wet trailmix from a wet plastic bag while sitting on my butt in the snow. But everything feels so bad already- my clothes are wet, my shoes are wet, my feet and hands are numb. There's that last remaining flicker of warmth in my core, and I know I need to stoke it with some trailmix before I hike. But it's hard.

We decide not to use our trekking poles today, as holding wet steel in our numb hands while hiking through the snow sounds like just about the worst thing ever. My hands are already too numb to work the little button that collapses my poles and I hand them off to Ramen, feeling like a pathetic fool. He makes satisfying grunting noises and bangs at them until they become unstuck. Then we tear down the sad, wet tent, stuff everything away (me grimacing as I try to use my hands to clip the buckles on my pack), and it's time to hike.

The snow is beautiful and light, and it is our last day on the trail. We are only twelve miles from the border and twenty miles from the Manning Park Lodge, where our friends will be waiting for us and where there will be an amplitude of warm, dry heat. And yet we are numb, cold, and exhausted and it feels as though we are in the middle of nowhere, light-years from anything and everything that could comfort us. And our magic little thoroughfare, the trail that would carry us out of this wilderness, is gone beneath a foot of fresh snow. And in a couple of miles there is a pass. So now we must find our way over a pass, in the snow, with no trail.

My morale is very low.

I don't like to feel weak. I like to be the strong one, the one with the good attitude in the face of difficulty, the one who never gives up. And yet this morning I concede defeat and stumble slowly towards the pass, eyes on the ground, stepping carefully into Ramen's footprints so I don't fall off the mountain. Up ahead Ramen good-naturedly breaks the trail in the blowing snow, turns to me now and then and smiles, holds up morale for the both of us. And today I am so, so grateful for this.

We switchback up to the pass, over its white, glittering top, and down the other side. I'm sliding in the snow in my trail runners, tripping without my trekking poles, my hands up in the sleeves of my down jacket to keep them warm. Sometimes there is a faint outline in the snow where the trail is, sometimes there is not. But between Ramen's excellent navigational sense and my GPS, we are able to find the switchbacks and as we drop down in elevation the snow grows wetter and begins to fall from the trees in big clumps. And then we're passing the lake and there are our friends' footprints, slushing up the trail, and my heart leaps in my chest. We drop even further in elevation and then the ground is clear completely and the snow has turned to rain, and we stop at an icy stream to fill our bottles. I take a long drink and march on, every part of me cold, the light inside of me flickering, flickering. I am delirious with exhaustion, fatigue, my body stumbly from a chill that never ends and I really have to take a shit. But there's no way I'm stopping now.

The monument is small and dowdy in the rain, standing wooden in its trampled little clearing, flanked on either side by a long, narrow clearcut. The US-Canadian border. The northern terminus of the Pacific Crest Trail. I see the wooden post and start to sob, all the feelings coming out of me at once, and then I push my way into the trees to find a place to take a shit. I'm still sobbing, even while I'm pooping, and so I'm pooping and crying, blearily groping the ground for moss with which to wipe, pulling up my running shorts, crying as I walk back to the monument, sucking up the last of my tears just as Ramen appears, thinking *what did I just do? And why didn't it ever feel like I was doing anything at all? And how do so many small things become one great big thing?* I'm shivering as I pull my damp phone from the wet pocket of my rain jacket and wipe the humidity off the lens to take a photo. There's a note for us, scratched in the mud- *Dear Carrot and Ramen, we got cold, XOXO, meow.* Our dear, dear friends! We wrestle open the smaller, metal monument to get the trail register that's inside. Once acquired we flip through the damp pages, hungrily reading the entries from the people we know. I try to hold the pen, but my hands are numb. I pause for a moment, rub my hands together and try again. This time I can control the pen, although my handwriting is awful.

They say there's a long, narrow ribbon of space-time
that stretches from Mexico to Canada.
I hear you can live there, for a little while,
as long as you keep moving.
But be careful, it will break your heart.

***

When I wake in the morning I don't know where I am. I sit up in bed and stare out the big window at the backyard, and wait for reality to collect itself- I'm at Seamus' house in Portland. Outside the rain is coming down, hard, the wind lashing the trees. It's the same storm that, a few hundred miles north, is still dumping snow in the Northern Cascades, stopping the progress of all the hikers who were behind us.

I remember saying goodbye to Ramen in the parkinglot of the Manning Park Lodge. Standing on that wet concrete, my hand pressed to his chest, clouds rolling over the peaks above us.

"This is it," I said.

I cried in the hotel room. I stripped off my wet clothes and sat on the toilet in the bathroom and sobbed. Instigate knocked softly on the door.

"I'm sorry," I said. "I can't stop crying." I looked at my pack on the bathroom floor, my bits of gear exploded everywhere; those small specific bits that had been my life, my whole life, for so long. Chapstick with a piece of duct tape wrapped around it. Floss with a sewing needle inside. My simple life. I climbed into the shower and sat under the hot water and wrapped my arms around my knees and bawled, snot and tears mixing with the shower water and going away, down the drain.

"You need anything?" said Instigate, filling her Gatorade bottle in the bathroom sink.

"I'm so cold," I said. Instigate microwaved me a cup of tea and piled blankets on top of me in the bed. Then she laid on top of the blankets and wrapped her arms around me, turning me into a burrito.

There was a sauna in another wing of the building and we braved a short walk in the cold rain to reach it, our bare feet slapping on the concrete. I lay in the dark close room on the warm wood and finally, increment by increment, I felt the cold leave me. The cold that had been in my bones since Ramen and I left the Grove of the Patriarchs on my birthday, that had been my steadfast friend for nearly all of Washington. Soon I was warm down to my very core and instead of cold I felt an exhaustion that was too deep to even name. Back in the hotel room there wasn't much to say and we ate dinner from our food bags and Spark flipped through the channels on the TV, finally settling on an old gangster movie. Outside the world had grown dark and Instigate was asleep, curled on her side under the blankets, and then Spark was too and it was just me, awake, head full of questions, trying to make sense of it all, of anything.

I cover my face with my hands, rub my eyes, and when I open them again, something appalling has happened; life has ceased to be linear. I am sitting on Seamus' bed looking out the window at the storm and reality is spreading out from me in all directions, like water. It ripples outward with each little movement, bumping against the walls and the backs of the chairs, and then the ripples cease and there is stillness. Just the sound of the wind, and the storm. And there are no clues, anywhere, as to which direction I should go.

I stare at the wind lashing the trees. For months I have been on the trail, the trail has been my whole life. Now I feel something hulking, teetering, casting a long shadow. Cautiously I get out of bed and take a few experimental steps on the soft carpet. My calf seizes and I lean against the desk to stretch it out. The pain is alarming but is comforting, too; a reminder of a life I've grown to love. The hulking thing retreats, and then is gone. So I have a little while longer, I think.

I go running, which is painful. I run five miles, ten miles, twelve. I don't get winded. I run under the tumultuous clouds, along the paved city streets. I don't know why I'm running. I pack up my trailer and liquidate my online bookstore. I've decided to move to the country. Where I will go and what I will do when I get there, I do not yet know. I get the numbers *2660* tattooed on my knuckles- the mileage of the PCT. I hate the tattoo at first, and then I grow to love it. I love it just a little and then more each day, as my life on the trail grows more distant, more irrelevant, more disconnected from all the people and things around me. The numbers become a soothing talisman, a badge of honor, a reminder of the place I was. Of the place I'd rather be. *It existed. It was real.*

More real than anything.

***

I sell my trailer to a woman on Craigslist, put most of my possessions on the curb and drive south on I-5 in the rain, until the city falls away and then the smaller towns, and the Siskiyou Mountains rise up around me in the dark, and the rain dries up and it grows colder, and the stars are hard and bright. I turn off the highway onto a dark country road and park, after a number of miles, in front of a dilapidated house on a handful of acres, mist rising up off the ground and outbuildings melting into the earth. The house belongs to a friend of a friend; I'll stay here for the month of November, talk to people, have a look around, figure out what sort of life I might make. I stand in the yard and shiver; there are no lights anywhere and above me, I can see the Milky Way.

I sink into the springy mattress in a bright, carpeted bedroom and stare at myself in the mirror, all bundled up in wool against the cold. I live here, I think. Outside, in the woodshed, I find wood to split, carry it inside, and built a fire. A couple of cats come and go while I sit in front of the woodstove, watching the flames move over the kindling.

In the mornings, I walk through the meadows behind the house down to the stream, look up at the sky, and feel the sadness begin to lift from me like fog. Just the beginnings, a gentle rising away. New sadness is still falling, like ash from an old eruption, but there is movement now, a moving through, the beginning process of grieving. The middle part? I don't know. I don't know where I am; I realize now, with new awareness, that I have never grieved before. How long before new grief stops coming. How long before all grief is accounted for and I can begin the tedious process of sorting through the tangled barrels, picking off the useful bits, letting the wind carrying the rest away.

I don't know what my new life looks like yet, or how to build it. *Patience*, I say to myself. *You have to be patient. Nothing is ever the way you think it will be and then, suddenly, it is. But not in any way you can predict. You just have to trust.*

I talk to Instigate on the phone, almost every day; she's moved to Cleveland, where she's working as a bike messenger. Cleveland is having one of the coldest winters on record, and biking around the city in the snow and ice is epically difficult. This makes her happy. Spark is at his parents' house in Georgia, drinking beer and playing video games, hiding from the world for a little while longer. In a few months he'll move to Asheville and get a job at a wilderness therapy camp, working with at-risk youth. Ramen is in Antarctica.

I know I won't see him again.

***

I have a dream now, not every night, but often enough. I'm back on the PCT, walking on the soft trail in the evening, feeling good. The sun is beginning to sink behind the trees. I'm thinking of dinner, or my ass chafe, or of nothing at all. I round a bend and Instigate and Spark are there, sitting in the dirt, waiting for me.

"Just six more miles to camp," says Instigate. She's wearing her ninja suit and her hair is in her face, the last of the sun shining on it. Spark is picking at his mustache, which is overgrown. His shoes are so covered in dust that you can't see the red part anymore.

"Just six more miles," says Instigate, again.

"I can do it," I say. I'll walk six miles, I'll walk a hundred miles.

I'll walk forever if I have to.

Acknowledgments

They say that a book is built around a great scaffolding, and it is the author's job to make the scaffolding invisible. So I am here to tell you now: no book of worth comes into being without the support of a great number of people. Literally hundreds of people have helped make this book possible.

I am eternally indebted to Dannie Kline and Allison Carr for the editing help. Independent publishing is terrifying; if this book is less boring/less full of errors than it would have been, it is thanks to the two of you. You are both incredibly clever and your observations were invaluable. (Note: no one is editing these acknowledgments, if I misused the semi-colon just now it is no fault but my own.)

Thank you to Alejandra "Rocket Llama" Wilson for the beautiful cover. You took an abstract concept and made it into a really neat picture, which seems like magic.

So much gratitude to the trail angels who helped me in 2013: TenSpeed, the Dinsmores, Not Phil's Dad, Linda & Bob in San Diego, Barney and Sandy Mann, Stumbling Norwegian and Honey Bee, Serpent Slayer and Slick B, Shrek, Terrie and Joe Anderson (I still dream of that taco salad), Donna and Jeff Saufley. Donna Saufley, you are a saint. I hope one day you come to understand how much good you've put into the world. Thank you for so tirelessly facilitating so many peoples' hero's journeys. Your attitude towards your fellow human beings is a huge inspiration to me.

Thank you to Cooper and Mykhiel for watching my dogs, to Seamus for being a friend and giving me a place to crash even though I couldn't offer anything in return. Thanks to A.M. and Burton as well, for hosting us when we were in Portland.

Thank you to the Pacific Crest Trail Association, for providing so much important infrastructure and for everything that you do. One day I hope I can give back some of what the trail has given to me.

Much gratitude to Halfmile and Guthook for the great maps, apps and trail data that they provide.

Thank you to all of my crowdfunding backers, for believing in me, and for being patient when this book took a year longer to write than I thought it would. I'd especially like to thank M. Purdey, C. Burford, D. Andersson, C. Tomberg, S.V. Newton, A. Hedrick, W. Lindley, J. Santee, S. Jacobsson, C. Troyer, L. Vandermark, K.M. Hall, C. Jennings, J. Erwin, A. Googans, H.W. Hattley and G.K. Lott.

Thank you to everyone who has read and followed my blog over the last seven years.

C. Weiss- I wanted to thank you last, because I wanted to say something profound, but now I'm not sure how to write what I mean. Your advice, your care packages, your funny, clever emails of concern and encouragement, your physical and emotional support, helped me more than I can say. I have never had a parent; for a little while, because of you, I felt as though I did. Maybe that's weird, or maybe it's the way that art, throughout history, has always been made. Thank you.

Wait, don't go yet!

Are you interested in hiking the Pacific Crest Trail? Check out the Pacific Crest Trail Association's website for maps, resources, links and other awesome information- pcta.org

If you enjoyed this book, please consider leaving an honest review on the book's Amazon page. The more reviews this book has, the more visible it will become, according to Amazon's internal algorithms. Thank you!

Starting May 2015, I'll be thru-hiking the 2,800 mile Continental Divide Trail. If you'd like to follow along on my adventures, including photos and daily blog posts from the trail, mosey on over to my blog- carrotquinn.com.

You can also follow me on instagram- instagram.com/carrotquinn

Thanks for reading!

Made in the USA
San Bernardino, CA
26 April 2016